Communist Party
Membership in the U.S.S.R.
1917-1967

Studies of the Russian Institute
Columbia University

Communist Party
Membership in the U.S.S.R.

1917-1967

T. H. RIGBY

1968

PRINCETON UNIVERSITY PRESS

PRINCETON, NEW JERSEY

The Russian Institute of Columbia University sponsors
the *Studies of the Russian Institute* in the belief that
their publication contributes to scholarly research and
public understanding. In this way the Institute, while
not necessarily endorsing their conclusions, is pleased
to make available the results of some of the research
conducted under its auspices. A list of the *Studies of
the Russian Institute* appears at the back of the book.

This book has been composed in Times Roman type.

Printed in the United States of America
by Princeton University Press

For Norma, Nina and Ted

Contents

Tables

Acknowledgments

The personnel aspects of Soviet politics have interested me for a number of years, and this book attempts to summarize my work on one of these aspects. Its publication therefore provides me with a welcome opportunity to express my profound gratitude to all those persons and institutions that have encouraged and assisted my work over the years, and particularly to George Bolsover, Violet Conolly, Merle Fainsod, Henry Mayer, Percy Partridge, Henry Roberts, William A. Robson, Leonard Schapiro and Hugh Seton-Watson; to the University of Melbourne, the London School of Economics and Political Science and the School of Slavonic and East European Studies of the University of London, Columbia University and the Australian National University; to the libraries of these universities, as well as to the National Library of Australia, the British Museum, the U.S. Library of Congress, the New York Public Library and the Hoover Library; and to the Ford and Rockefeller Foundations.

I should also like to thank those who have read drafts of this book, or parts of it, at various stages, for their invaluable suggestions, and particularly John Armstrong, Myron Rush, Leonard Schapiro, Alexander Dallin, John Hazard and other members of the Russian Institute at Columbia. I am grateful to Paul Rosta for his painstaking checking of the manuscript, to Louise Luke, Natalie Staples and Marjorie Putney for their editorial assistance, to Renate Brauer for help with the index, and to the secretarial staff of the Political Science Departments of the Australian National University and the London School of Economics and Political Science.

My greatest debt is to the three persons to whom this book is respectfully and affectionately dedicated.

T. H. RIGBY

Canberra
September 10, 1968

xiii

So it is these [the Rulers] that may properly be called Guardians in the true sense, it being their function to see to it that friends at home shall not wish, and enemies abroad not be able, to harm the state; while the young men whom up to now we have been calling Guardians, should properly be labelled Auxiliaries, it being their function to enforce the execution of the decisions of the Rulers.—PLATO, The Republic, *Book* III, *414.*

Now there are diversities of gifts, but the same Spirit. And there are differences of administrations, but the same Lord. And there are diversities of operations, but it is the same God, who worketh all in all. But the manifestation of the Spirit is given to every man to profit withal. For to one is given by the Spirit the word of wisdom; to another the word of knowledge by the same Spirit; to another faith by the same Spirit; to another the gifts of healing by the same Spirit; to another the working of miracles; to another prophecy; to another discerning of spirits; to another divers kinds of tongues; to another the interpretation of tongues. But all these worketh that one and the self-same Spirit, dividing to every man severally as he will.—SAINT PAUL, 1 Corinthians 12.

The [Communist] Party is the mind, honor and conscience of our epoch.—LENIN.

Abbreviations Used in Footnotes and Bibliography

(Details on these publications are given in the bibliography)

B	*Bol'shevik*
BR	*Bakinskii rabochii*
BSE	*Bol'shaia Sovetskaia Entsiklopedia*, 1st edn., 2nd edn.
I	*Izvestiia*
Izv Ts K	*Izvestiia Tsentral'nogo Komiteta* . . .
K	*Kommunist* (journal)
K(A)	*Kommunist* (Armenian newspaper)
KP	*Kazakhstanskaia pravda*
KPSS v rez	*Kommunisticheskaia Partiia Sovetskogo Soiuza: v rezoliutsiiakh i resheniiakh s"ezdov, konferentsii i plenumov Ts K.*
KT	*Kommunist Tadzhikistana*
LP	*Leningradskaia pravda*
LZ	*Leninskoe znamia*
MB	*Moskovskii bol'shevik*
MP	*Moskovskaia pravda*
P	*Pravda*
PS	*Partiinoe stroitel'stvo*
PU	*Pravda Ukrainy*
PV	*Pravda vostoka*
PZh	*Partiinaia zhizn'*
SB	*Sovetskaia Belorussiia*
SE	*Sovetskaia Estoniia*
SK	*Sovetskaia Kirgiziia*
S Lat	*Sovetskaia Latviia*
S Lit	*Sovetskaia Litva*
SM	*Sovetskaia Moldaviia*
SPR	*Spravochnik partiinogo rabotnika* (The Party Worker's Handbook)
SR	*Sovetskaia Rossiia*
SU	*Sovetskaia Ukraina*
TI	*Turkmenskaia iskra*
V I KPSS	*Voprosy istorii KPSS*
WKP	The Smolensk Archive
ZV	*Zaria vostoka*

Introduction

THIS BOOK is concerned with the history of recruitment to the Soviet Communist Party and the composition of the party during the first half-century of the Soviet regime. In view of the vast and many-sided importance of the Communist Party in Soviet society, this subject has naturally attracted the attention of many students of the history, politics and government of the U.S.S.R. and much valuable information has been made available to Western readers in books and articles published over the past ten or fifteen years.[1] This, however, is the first attempt at a comprehensive, book-length treatment of the subject.

Uses and Purposes of the Study

It is the author's hope that this book will be of value to persons interested in many different aspects of Soviet society. The dominating influence of the Communist Party of the Soviet Union (CPSU) permeates all fields of political, administrative, economic, security, informational, educational, intellectual and artistic activity, largely through the medium of its members working in these fields. Consequently party membership patterns and policies are an essential element in understanding the various specialized aspects of Soviet ac-

[1] See especially Merle Fainsod, *How Russia Is Ruled* (rev. edn.), (Cambridge, Mass., 1963), Chap. 8; Vernon V. Aspaturian, "The Soviet Union," Chap. VII, in Roy C. Macridis and Robert E. Ward, eds., *Modern Political Systems: Europe* (Englewood Cliffs, N.J., 1963); Leonard Schapiro, *The Communist Party of the Soviet Union* (New York, 1960), especially Chaps. 13 and 17; Boris Meissner, *Russland im Umbruch: der Wandel in der Herrschaftsordnung und sozialen Struktur der Sowjetunion* (Frankfurt, 1951); T. H. Rigby, "The Social Composition of Recruitment and Distribution of CPSU Membership," *The American Slavic and East European Review*, No. 3, 1957.

tuality. In bringing together, predigesting and presenting in a modified chronological framework the available data about CPSU membership, the author is therefore seeking to make a contribution to Soviet studies generally.

It is for the history and operation of the Soviet political system, however, that our subject has its greatest significance, and here there are important lessons not only for the Sovietologist, but for other political scientists as well.

For the student of comparative politics, the U.S.S.R. has long served as a typical example of a now widespread modern variety of political system, which we shall call the "state-party system," otherwise known as "totalitarianism," "authoritarian single-party system," "movement regime," etc. The state-party system is one in which a centralized, disciplined voluntary organization (the "party") has won a monopoly of political power, superimposed its bureaucracy on that of the state, and seeks to deploy all institutions and associations in the society for the achievement of aims formulated by its leadership. The composition of the "state party" is a topic that calls for close comparative study, particularly in view of the diversification of communist regimes and the emergence of a number of new noncommunist state party systems in Africa and Asia in recent years. This pioneering work may hope to provide part of the data, as well as indicating a tentative conceptual framework for such a study, and meanwhile, insofar as the U.S.S.R. is accepted as representative of the state-party system, offer an interim picture of the character and determinants of party membership in this kind of system.

The significance of our topic for the comparatist does not end here, however. The CPSU performs or participates in a number of functions which occur in any complex political system, though frequently in quite different institutional set-

2

tings. The interplay between various functional demands and the CPSU's social composition and recruitment programs is therefore of considerable theoretical interest. The author does not pretend to have achieved an exhaustive or definitive theoretical treatment of his data. On the contrary, it is his earnest wish that social theorists will have the patience to consider his account of the facts and the grace to improve on his interpretations. Furthermore, too rigid a theoretical framework has been deliberately avoided, as this might defeat the other purposes of this book outlined in the preceding paragraphs. Nonetheless, certain general notions about the relationship of the party's membership policies and composition to the evolution and functioning of the system have undoubtedly guided the author in the pursuit and selection of data, and, as refined and amplified in the process of analysis, have provided a loose conceptual framework for this book.

A Note on Party Membership Doctrine

This framework has been constructed in terms of political functions, rather than of political structure or culture, although the latter naturally figure in our exposition of functional categories. Before proceeding with this exposition, however, it will be well to consider a preliminary point, namely the extent to which CPSU recruitment patterns and composition may be interpreted in terms of official political doctrine, i.e. the dominant strand in Soviet political culture.

The ideas of Marx and Lenin called the party into existence and have continued to legitimate it throughout its history. Not only have its leaders been men more or less profoundly convinced of the truth of Marxist-Leninist doctrine, but they have been constantly obliged to invoke it in justification of their major decisions. Neither Marx nor Lenin laid down any precise formula for the ideal communist party,

3

as to its size or social composition or the age, education or other possible criteria of membership. They did, however, provide two powerful orientations. The first, deriving from basic Marxist principles, is the orientation towards a special association of the party with the proletariat or manual, wage-earning class. Marxism itself is held to be both "science" and the ideology of the working class; the communist party is the party of the working class; its coming to power is the "proletarian revolution" and ushers in the "dictatorship of the proletariat," which amounts "in essence" to rule by the party.

The second orientation derives from the concept of the party as the *vanguard* of the proletariat, which was perhaps Lenin's most important contribution to Marxism. Although communists in Russia and throughout the world have subsequently maintained the universal validity of the vanguard concept, Lenin originally propounded it in relation to the heavily autocratic political conditions of tsarist Russia, and at the time the most distinguished leaders of Russian and European Marxism treated it as dangerously heretical. Lenin attacked the notion of a party that any worker could join. If the autocracy was to be overthrown and a socialist order ultimately created, the party must be a highly centralized and disciplined organization, functioning conspiratorially where necessary, and directing and coordinating the trade unions and all other "mass" organizations of the workers in a unified struggle consistently guided by Marxist theory. The party would be "the most advanced detachment of the working class." At the same time, though it should certainly aim to recruit workers, Lenin was far from insisting that it should consist entirely or even necessarily predominantly of working class members. On the contrary, much of the membership and most of the leadership of the party, in its early stages at least, would have to be drawn from the intelligentsia, to

4

which a knowledge of Marxist theory was at first virtually confined: it was their task to bring a "socialist awareness" to the workers, who by their own spontaneous efforts could not rise above a "trade union awareness" of their situation, interests and possibilities. The elitist implications of the "vanguard" concept were immediately perceived and commented on by many of Lenin's Marxist contemporaries.

There is an obvious tension between these two membership orientations embedded in Marxist-Leninist doctrine. As Merle Fainsod has put it: "The logic of elitism runs counter to the inherited symbolism of the party as a detachment of the working class. The membership policy of the party faces the constant strain of mediating between the indispensable requirements of a Party-dominated directing apparatus on the one hand, and, on the other, the desirability of enlisting support among the mass of ordinary workers and farmers."[2] Since the ideology contains no guidance on harmonizing the two orientations, a zigzagging from one to the other is as likely as pursuit of the happy mean between them. It is a situation that allows for much doctrinal manipulation to cover policies motivated by nondoctrinal considerations. As we shall see, these two orientations, originating in and sustained by the official ideology, do exert an important influence on party membership policies, setting rough boundaries to changes and fluctuations in policy, and exerting powerful pressures for policy reversal when these boundaries are approached or exceeded. However, it is clear that these doc-

---

[2] Fainsod, *op.cit.*, p. 247. Alfred G. Meyer makes the same point in somewhat different terms when he writes of the competing pull of "loyalty" and "competence" in party recruitment policy. See *The Soviet Political System: An Interpretation* (New York, 1965), pp. 138-139. Cf. also Adam B. Ulam, in Samuel H. Beer and Adam B. Ulam, eds., *Patterns of Government: The Major Political Systems of Europe* (New York, 1958), p. 687.

5

trinal imperatives are far too vague and general to serve as an overall framework for the analysis of party membership policies.

The Party's Basic Function

Has the CPSU a single overriding function that determines the character of its membership? Lenin originally saw the party as an organization of *professional* revolutionaries directing and coordinating all other working class organizations towards common objectives. At first glance the formula that the CPSU is the "leading and directing force" in Soviet society seems like a simple transposition of this original functional concept to the bolsheviks' new situation as a ruling party, leading us to expect that party membership in the U.S.S.R. should amount to a *profession*, that the membership should simply have transformed itself into a coordinating bureaucracy superimposed on the state and society, and that the process of recruitment to the party should be synonymous with appointment to full-time work in this coordinating bureaucracy, much like consecration to the priesthood in a theocracy or appointment as commissioned officer in a military regime. In fact, however, though the party certainly *includes* a coordinating bureaucracy of full-time party members, it is much more than this, and the problem of the functions of membership is accordingly far more complex.

It should first be noted that even the notion of the pre-revolutionary party as an organization of professional revolutionaries is a misleading oversimplification. Whatever reality it may have had during Lenin's first attempts to implement his organizational principles in 1902-1904, the enrollment during and immediately after the 1905 Revolution of tens of thousands of workers, students, intellectuals and others quickly made nonsense of it. It is true that the mass exodus

6

from the revolutionary parties that followed the renewal of police repression in 1907 soon reduced the bolsheviks once more to a hard core of a few thousand members, but these now included a large proportion of factory workers who were never full-time revolutionaries, who often had families to support and needed to keep working at their trades, and whose contribution to party work consisted in the carrying out of routine assignments in their spare time under the direction of local committee members. The directing corps of the underground, such as there was of it, was still mainly composed of "professionals," but meanwhile between these and the worker members there began to emerge a new stratum of bolsheviks active in legal trade union, welfare, educational and other institutions (including even the Duma) and who, despite frequent harassment by the authorities, were able to use their work in these various spheres to advance the cause of the party.[3]

The hypothesis seems worth considering that this threefold division of the prerevolutionary bolshevik organization subsequently served as a mold which helped to shape the functional evolution of the CPSU membership in the postrevolutionary period. In the immediate aftermath of the seizure of power a few score thousand bolsheviks, it is true, swallowed up the state, and in their turn, were virtually swallowed up by it. For a year or so party membership, indeed, came to have very little significance except insofar as it involved office in

[3] The author is indebted for the facts on which this analysis of the prerevolutionary membership is based to an unpublished study by Daphne Gollan, of the Australian National University, of the bolshevik underground in Russia in 1907-1912. Inside Russia the disruption caused by Lenin's "Otzovist" and "Bogdanovite" critics seems to have been partly due to the stresses and strains attending the emergence of this more complex and sophisticated membership pattern, contrasting as it did with the primitive revolutionary purity of the "What Is to Be Done?" blueprint.

7

the machinery of the Soviet state. In 1919-1921, however, with the growth of the party first to a half and then to three-quarters of a million members and the creation of a new party bureaucracy functionally paralleling the organs of the state and superordinated to them, a threefold division of the membership reemerged. The first category consisted of the full-time party officials, who might be compared with the "professional revolutionaries" of the past. The second category consisted of party members occupying leading posts in government bodies, the armed forces, trade unions and other institutions. These might be compared with the bolsheviks active in nonparty bodies before 1917. And the third category consisted of the ordinary rank-and-file members of party cells in the factories, offices, military units, villages, educational institutions, etc., who might be compared with the employed worker communists of the prerevolutionary period.

Despite the preeminence of the party apparatus in the new administrative structure of the regime, many of the most powerful and respected members of the party, including Lenin himself, remained in our second category of membership, holding no formal party offices. Such members, however, frequently had seats in the leading deliberative and executive bodies of the party—the party committees and their bureaus and presidia, culminating in the Central Committee and its Political Bureau—and it was in these bodies, rather than in the party apparatus as such, that the sovereignty of the party in the political system was vested.

Before passing to a more specific examination of political functions as they involve our main categories of party membership, there is one further dimension of the problem to be noted. The doctrine of the party as the "leading and directing force" in Soviet society immediately invites the questions:

"leading where?" and "directing to what end?" And the answer to both questions is, of course, "to communism." The CPSU of today continues the revolutionary enterprise of Lenin's original organization of bolsheviks, an enterprise that will be completed only when society operates wholly in accordance with the principle "from each according to his ability, to each according to his needs," and the state has "withered away." Viewed in this light, the basic function of the CPSU is one of *transformation*, the creation of new institutions, new techniques and a new man, with a new morality and new beliefs. Hence the "transforming" ethos of Soviet political communication—sweeping away the old, building up the new—and the constant flux of political and economic programs and administrative structures. Yet if the direction and impulse of this transformation are to be maintained, there is one thing that must remain inviolate through all this flux: the role and character of the party, including its basic doctrine, its centralized, disciplined internal structure, and its "dictatorship" over all social institutions, associations, processes and activities. If, then, seen over time the basic function of the CPSU in Soviet society is one of "leading and directing," at any particular point in time it is an *integrating* function, giving meaning to the parts and coherence to the whole. We have come close to indicating this when writing of the party's "coordinating bureaucracy." We shall see, however, that the *integration* which the CPSU provides for Soviet society is something far broader than mere administrative coordination. There is a dialectical relationship between the "leading and directing" and "integrating" aspects of the party's basic function. Although, as we have seen, they are two sides of a single coin, yet there is a tension between them, since constant innovation tends to erode or-

9

der, coherence and security, both externally and on the psychological level.[4] This "contradiction" between the dynamic and static aspects of the party's basic function should be kept in mind in studying the history of party membership policies. Let us note here, however, that the leading and directing aspect is primarily entrusted to our first category of membership, namely the full-time party officials, while our third category, the rank-and-file members of party cells (since 1934 called primary party organizations) are concerned far more with the integration aspect, and the tension between the two aspects is most acutely focused on the second category, the CPSU members occupying leading posts in nonparty bodies.

The Multiplicity of Party Functions

While the attempt to identify the party's "basic" function and to seek out its implications for CPSU membership policies opens up some valuable perspectives, it is clearly no more adequate as a general framework of analysis than is the reference to doctrinal imperatives. Indeed, writers on the CPSU usually identify a number of membership determinants, described as a rule in functional terms. Thus Merle Fainsod has related CPSU membership policies to the interplay, under ever-changing conditions, of "the Party's doctrinal predilections, the changing responsibilities which it has assumed, the need to fuse the Party into a trustworthy and efficient governing elite, and the pressure to strengthen its hold on those strata of Soviet society which were likely to yield it maximum support."[5] Maurice Duverger relates party

[4] Cf. the author's article "Security and Modernization in Tsarist and Communist Russia," *Survey: a Journal of East European Affairs*, No. 63, June 1967.

[5] Fainsod, *op.cit.*, pp. 247-248.

10

membership patterns in single-party systems to the party's social and political functions: recruitment of elites and instructing and training them, providing leadership and supervision of all government bodies and associations, channeling communication between regime and people, both upwards and downwards, and securing compliance with regime policies.[6] John Armstrong makes the additional point that the party membership serves as a reserve of manpower at the complete disposal of the regime, embracing many of the country's most energetic and talented citizens, and capable of being deployed in times of crisis in the most difficult assignments.[7] Brzezinski and Huntington relate CPSU membership to the processes of socialization and politicization, political participation and control.[8] These provide valuable pointers for constructing a functional framework for the study of the CPSU membership. Further pointers emerge when we consider the CPSU's own view of its political functions. When they seek to expound what is meant by the leading and directing role of the CPSU in Soviet society, Soviet writers usually give the following list of functions:

1. supplying leading cadres for all social organisms, governmental and otherwise;

2. giving guiding directions (*rukovodiashchie ukazaniia*), derived from basic party doctrines and current party priorities, on all important matters requiring decision in governmental and nongovernmental bodies;

---

[6] Maurice Duverger, *Political Parties* (London, 1954), pp. 257-259.

[7] John A. Armstrong, *Ideology, Politics and Government in the Soviet Union: An Introduction* (New York, 1962), pp. 49-50. Armstrong also indicates the importance of the party membership in indoctrinating the population, political elite recruitment and supervision of all social organisms. *Ibid.*, pp. 50-54.

[8] See Zbigniew Brzezinski and Samuel P. Huntington, *Political Power: USA/USSR* (New York, 1964), pp. 76-101.

11

3. systematically checking up on how these directions are carried out (*proverka ispolneniia*—literally "verification of fulfillment");

4. "mobilizing the masses" for the successful fulfillment of these directions.

This analysis of the CPSU's functions clearly has important implications for membership policies. We may note, for example, that it provides a crude explanatory framework for our three categories of party membership (see page 8): function 1 in this list demands our second category of members, function 2 demands our first category, while our third category of members makes sense in terms of functions 3 and 4.

The CPSU Rules

For a full picture of how the CPSU views the political functions inhering in its membership, however, we must turn to the party rules (*ustav*). Since this document is the most important primary source for our topic, we will quote extensively from it (in the version as amended at the Twenty-Second CPSU Congress in 1961), both to indicate the point of departure for our own analysis and to provide the reader with an independent basis of evaluation.

The rules begin with a preamble which defines the CPSU as "the militant experienced vanguard of the Soviet people, uniting on voluntary principles the advanced, most aware (*soznatel'naia*) part of the working class, kolkhoz (collective farm) peasantry and intelligentsia of the U.S.S.R." Following a review of the historical process whereby "the Communist Party, the party of the working class, has now become the party of the whole Soviet people," the preamble goes on

12

to present an expanded version of the "leading and directing force" concept:

The party exists for the people and serves the people. It is the highest form of social-political organization, the leading and directing force of Soviet society. The party guides the great creative activity of the Soviet people, and imparts an organized, planned and scientifically based character to its struggle for the attainment of the final aim—the victory of communism.

The preamble concludes with an assertion of the inviolability of the party's historic organizational and doctrinal principles.[9]

More concrete aspects of the "leading and directing force" concept, with clear implications for party membership policies, are touched on in the section of the rules which deals with the top bodies of the party. Here it is stated that the Central Committee:

exercises the selection and distribution of leading cadres, directs the work of central state and voluntary organizations of the working people *through the party groups in them* [author's emphasis], sets up various bodies, institutions and enterprises of the party, appoints the editors of central newspapers and journals, which work under its control . . .[10]

The relationship between party and nonparty bodies is further spelt out in a section concerned with the party's republican, regional and local organizations, the duties of which include: "leadership of the soviets, trade unions, komsomol (the Young Communist League), cooperative and other vol-

[9] *XII s"ezd Kommunisticheskoi Partii Sovetskogo Soiuza: stenograficheskii otchët* (Moscow, 1962), Vol. III, pp. 337-338.
[10] *Ibid.* pp. 346-347.

13

untary organizations of the working people through the party groups in them. . . ."[11] These "party groups" are later dealt with in a special section of the rules, which states that "in all questions the party groups must be strictly and undeviatingly guided by the decisions of leading party organs," which are identified as the party committees at various levels.[12] These provisions are echoed and complemented in Article 126 of the current (1936) Constitution of the U.S.S.R., which includes the passage:

> . . . the most active and aware citizens from the ranks of the working class and other strata of the working people unite in the Communist Party of the Soviet Union, which is the advanced detachment of the working people in their struggle for the strengthening and development of the socialist system and represents the guiding nucleus (*rukovodiashchee iadro*) of all organizations of the working people, both voluntary (*obshchestvennye*) and governmental (*gosudarstvennye*).

A number of further party membership functions emerge when we consider the section in the party rules dealing with primary party organizations, the basic units of the party, which are set up at all places of work employing the necessary minimum of three party members. The primary party organization:

    a.   receives new members into the CPSU;
    b.   trains communists . . .
    c.   organizes the study by communists of Marxist-Leninist theory in close connection with the practical work of constructing communism . . .
    d.   concerns itself with raising the vanguard role of com-

[11] *Ibid.*, p. 348.   [12] *Ibid.*, p. 355.

14

munists in labor, and in the social-political and economic (*khoziaistvennaia*) life of the enterprise, kolkhoz, institution, educational establishment, etc.;

e. comes out as organizer of the toilers in deciding current
    questions of constructing communism, leads socialist
    emulation for the fulfillment of state plans and the
    obligations of the working people, mobilizes the masses
    for bringing to light and making better use of internal
    reserves . . . secures the strengthening of labor
    discipline . . .

f. carries on mass-agitational and propaganda activi-
    ties . . .

g. on the basis of the broad deployment of criticism and
    self-criticism, wages a struggle with manifestations of
    bureaucratism, localism, violations of state discipline,
    puts a stop to attempts to deceive the state, takes meas-
    ures against ill-discipline, mismanagement and waste-
    fulness . . .

h. affords assistance to the okrug (circuit), city or raion
    (district) committee of the party in all the latter's
    activity, and accounts to it for its work.[13]

And finally we may consider what the rules have to say
about the obligations of party members. This draws together
much of what is said elsewhere about membership functions,
but also opens up a number of new aspects.

The party member is obliged:

a. to fight for the creation of the material-technical base
    of communism, to serve as an example of the com-
    munist attitude to work, to increase labor productivity,
    to stand forth as a pioneer (*zastrel'shchik*) of all that
    is new and progressive, to support and disseminate ad-

[13] *Ibid.*, p. 352.

vanced experience, to master technique and perfect his qualifications, to guard and increase public, socialist property, which is the foundation of the might and prosperity of our Socialist Motherland;

b. to firmly and undeviatingly carry out the decisions of the party, to explain the party's decisions to the masses, to foster the strengthening and extension of the party's links with the masses, to be sensitive and attentive to people and to respond promptly to the spiritual and material needs (*zaprosy i nuzhdy*) of the working people;

c. to participate actively in the political life of the country, in the administration of state affairs, in economic and cultural construction, to give an example of the fulfillment of public duty, and to aid the development and consolidation of communist social relationships;

d. to master Marxist-Leninist theory, to raise his ideological level, to foster the formation and training (*vospitanie*) of the man of communist society. To conduct a decisive struggle with all manifestations of bourgeois ideology, with the vestiges of private-property psychology, with religious prejudices and other carry-overs from the past, to observe the principles of communist morality, and to place social before personal interests;

e. to be an active channel to the masses of the working people for the ideas of socialist internationalism and Soviet patriotism, to carry on a struggle with the vestiges of nationalism and chauvinism, to foster both by deed and word the strengthening of friendship between the peoples of the U.S.S.R., and of fraternal links between the Soviet people and the peoples of the countries of the socialist camp and with the proletarians and working peoples of all countries;

16

f. to strengthen by all (possible) means the ideological and organizational unity of the party, to guard the party against the penetration of its ranks by people unworthy of the lofty title of communist, to be truthful and honest towards the party and the people, and to show vigilance and to preserve party and state secrets;

g. to develop criticism and self-criticism, to boldly expose shortcomings and secure their elimination, to fight against empty show (*paradnost'*), conceit, complacency, parochialism, to give a decisive rebuff to all efforts at the suppression of criticism, to come out against all actions which inflict damage on the party and the state, and to report on them to party organs, up to and including the Central Committee of the CPSU;

h. to pursue undeviatingly the party's line on the choice of cadres according to their political and practical (*delovye*) qualities. To be uncompromising in all cases where Leninist principles of the selection and training of cadres are violated;

i. to observe party and state discipline, which is equally obligatory upon all members of the party. The party has (only) one discipline and one law for all communists, irrespective of their past services or the posts they hold;

j. to foster by all (possible) means the strengthening of the defensive might of the U.S.S.R. and to wage a tireless struggle for peace and friendship between peoples.[14]

Merely to assemble these provisions of the party rules is to be convinced of the great multiplicity and complexity of party membership functions. Some of these functions inhere

14 *Ibid.*, pp. 338-339.

wholly or mainly in one or other of our three membership categories, while others are diffused throughout the membership as a whole. As it stands, this catalogue of "obligations" is too loose, specific and jargon-ridden to serve as an operative framework for rendering CPSU membership policies and composition intelligible in functional terms. To distill such a framework from it, it needs to be consolidated and dejargonized, and its provisions systematically checked against the relevant facts of Soviet political behavior. This is a considerable enterprise, and to pursue it here would require a lengthy digression from the central concerns of this study.[15] We must therefore omit this stage in our argument, proceeding straight to its results, as assimilated to a general functional framework for the analysis and comparison of political systems.

An Analytical Framework

The framework we shall employ here is a fairly radical adaptation of that proposed by Gabriel Almond in his Introduction to *The Politics of the Developing Areas*.[16] The work

[15] The most useful empirical account of party activities and functions is in Fainsod, *How Russia Is Ruled*, Chap. 7. For a stimulating analysis in functional terms, see Meyer, *op.cit.*, Chap. IV, especially pp. 109-116.

[16] Gabriel A. Almond and James S. Coleman, eds., *The Politics of Developing Areas* (Princeton, N.J., 1960). In discussing Almond's framework and outlining our own, we evade the whole debate about the logic and efficacy of functional definition and analysis in the social sciences. For criticism of "functionalism," see W. G. Runciman, *Social Science and Political Theory* (Cambridge, 1965), p. 40, and T. B. Bottomore, *Sociology: A Guide to Problems and Literature* (London, 1962), pp. 38-40. In employing a functional approach, we claim no more than that it is heuristically more useful than other approaches open to us. Cf. Dorothy Emmet, *Rules, Roles and Relations* (St. Martin's Press, 1966), p. 130. See also W. J. M. Mackenzie,

of Almond and his co-authors represents a major step forward in the comparative study of political systems. Several of their concepts and insights are of considerable value in the study of Soviet political processes. At the same time, Almond's analytical framework is not devoid of gaps and difficulties. It would clearly be inappropriate to attempt here an extended critique of his approach or a detailed exposition of our proposed adaptations. Nonetheless some preliminary evaluation and exposition is necessary in order to explain and justify the use of functional categories in our analysis.

Almond distinguishes four input functions (also referred to as "political" functions), namely (1) political socialization and recruitment, (2) interest articulation, (3) interest aggregation, and (4) political communication; and three output functions (also referred to as "governmental" functions), namely (5) rule-making, (6) rule application, and (7) rule adjudication. The output functions, as Almond points out, approximate the traditional categories of legislative, administrative and judicial functions, "except that an effort has been made to free them of their structural overtones."[17] Political socialization is defined as "the process of induction into the political culture. Its end product is a set of attitudes—cognitions, value standards, and feelings—toward

Politics and Social Science (London, 1967), pp. 90-91, 319-321. Almond's own approach has developed considerably since 1960. See his "Political Systems and Political Change," *The American Behavioral Scientist*, Vol. 5, No. 7 (June 1963), "A Developmental Approach to Political Systems," *World Politics*, 17 (1965), and G. Bingham Powell, Jr., *Comparative Politics: A Developmental Approach* (Boston, 1966). Powell was unavailable when this book was being formulated; it contains new ideas aimed at meeting some of the problems raised in my discussion: it gives more attention to governmental functions, supplements the political-function category with political capability, and discusses the Soviet political system.

[17] *Ibid.,* p. 17.

the political system, its various roles, and role incumbents."[18] Political recruitment takes the political socialization function a step further by inducting selected persons into the specialized roles of the political system.[19] Interest articulation occurs on the boundary between society and polity, where the interests of social groups are voiced in such a way as to constitute a demand for political action.[20] Interest aggregation, which overlaps with interest articulation, "may be accomplished by means of the formulation of general policies in which interests are combined, accommodated, etc., or by means of the recruitment of political personnel, more or less committed to a particular pattern of policy."[21] Political communication is of course the medium of all the other functions.

The student of Soviet politics cannot fail to be impressed by the culture bias of the schema. Almond, indeed, states that his functional categories were derived from "the distinctive political activities existing in Western complex systems." While disclaiming that his categorization is necessarily the best for all analytical purposes, he suggests that it has particular value for comparing modern Western systems with transitional and traditional ones.[22] One would like to qualify this by saying that while it helps the student who has learnt his politics through the study of Western polities to make sense of more exotic systems, it does so at the cost of treating the Western political process as the norm (albeit less blatantly so than in some earlier attempts at classification of political systems). This does not appear to have been the intention of Almond, and it calls for further exploration.

Governmental action resulting from articulated and aggregated demands originating in particular sectors of society is certainly typical of the political process in the modern

---

[18] *Ibid.*, p. 28.   [20] *Ibid.*, pp. 8, 33.   [22] *Ibid.*, p. 16.
[19] *Ibid.*, p. 31.   [21] *Ibid.*, p. 39.

"Western" countries that the present author has elsewhere described as market societies, where social coordination is largely effected by the competitive interaction and mutual accommodation of more or less autonomous groups. It is not typical, however, of the political process either in traditional societies, or in that other type of modern society, the organizational society, of which our state-party systems are the characteristic form of polity.[23] It is not surprising, therefore, that Western systems have developed political structures particularly well-adapted to performing the articulating and aggregating functions, and that other systems fail to measure up when comparison centers on these functions.

Turning to the Soviet Union, we find that the very principle of competitive political processes is doctrinally unacceptable, and that political structures are designed to *prevent* claims based on special interests from being articulated at all, but rather to function exclusively as downward channels for the decisions of those at the top who are held to know best what the "true" interests of all groups are. As Almond rightly observes, they are not wholly successful in this, but such polities nonetheless show a striking imbalance between political input and governmental output, if analysis is confined to his categorization of functions. Almond acknowledges this when he indicates that in totalitarian systems "the output of authoritative policy is not paralleled by, but only somewhat mitigated by, the input of demands and alternative policies," and in a penetrating remark, he points to the prevalence in such systems, alongside the interest-articulation and aggregation function, of "a high rate of coercive social mobilization."[24]

[23] See T. H. Rigby, "Traditional, Market and Organizational Societies and the U.S.S.R.," *World Politics*, Vol. xvi, No. 4 (July 1964), 539-557.
[24] Almond and Coleman, *op.cit.*, p. 41.

21

The incompleteness of Almond's schema for analysis of the Soviet system is partly accounted for by a defect to which he himself modestly draws attention, namely the sketchy treatment of the "governmental" functions. His categorization of functions provides a sharp instrument for analysis of those political phases in which the demands of particular interests are processed for governmental action, but a blunt one for analyzing what goes on in the government itself. This creates problems for the student of highly centralized systems, not least because many of the inputs in such systems emerge *within* the government itself, often from its leading personnel. Everyone knows that in a dictatorship or absolute monarchy governmental outputs are often inexplicable without reference to such inputs as the top man's personal psychology, digestion or marital relations. This, however, is not a point that requires much attention for our present purposes, and the problem, as we have indicated, is considerably wider than this.

Almond defines the political system as "that system of interactions to be found in all independent societies which performs the functions of integration and adaptation (both internally and vis-à-vis other societies) by means of the employment, or threat of employment, of more or less legitimate physical compulsion. The political system is the legitimate, order-maintaining or transforming system in the society."[25] This is an excellent definition (at least for *our present purposes*), but when compared with Almond's list of political functions, it raises the question whether the latter meets one of the essential requirements of a "system," namely comprehensiveness. For what it does is to concentrate on the "adaptive" aspect of the political system (and the internal adaptive aspect at that), at the expense of the "integrative"

[25] *Ibid.*, p. 7.

aspect, on the "transforming" aspect at the expense of the "order-maintaining" (we prefer here "system-maintaining") aspect, while at the same time identifying the transforming aspect with the competitive processes prominent in Western market societies, while the mobilizational processes prominent in organizational societies are mentioned incidentally, as an anomalous case.

On the system-maintaining and integrating side we would include two of Almond's functions, namely political socialization and recruitment, and rule-application, though for reasons to be explained below, we would amend the latter to "rule *and policy* application"; and then we would add three more, all of them implicit in his definition of the political system. The first of these is political legitimation and identification. This is the function of maintaining the political culture. From the point of view of the individual it might be seen as a continuation through life of the processes of political socialization, but it would be less misleading to think of it rather as the processes whereby the individual, once inducted through political socialization into the political culture of his society, thereafter participates in that culture. It would be hard to think of a polity in which the individual, having undergone the experience of political socialization, is thereby fully "programmed" for ever more to produce the responses required by his political system, without requiring any further injections of its political culture through his adult life. On the contrary, through a stream of communications issuing from structures which may or may not be specialized to the culture-maintenance function, and through the symbolism of special roles and rituals (in which the individual may be an active or passive, direct or vicarious participant), the political system operates constantly to dispose him to accept the legitimacy of its structures, processes, roles and role-

23

incumbents, and to identify his personality and interests with them. In the case of traditional polities, the importance and autonomy of the legitimating and identification function is obvious to all. The student of modern Western polities, however, might be forgiven for tending to underplay this function, for it often suffers there from a relative poverty of specialized structure and process, and its performance largely occurs parasitically on the performance of other functions. But who could doubt, for instance, that elections, say, in Britain or the United States, are concerned not only with the articulation and aggregation of interests, but also, among other things, with the function of legitimation and identification? In state-party polities this function also has its characteristic modes, some of which will soon emerge.

The other two system-maintaining and integrating functions we would add are external and internal order-maintenance. These are the basic, central functions of the *political* system in any society. They consist in the employment or threat of physical compulsion to counter external or internal attacks or threats against the society as a whole, its polity, its political structures, processes or legitimating beliefs, roles or rituals, or against particular legitimate interests of the society as a whole or its constituent groups or individuals. In complex societies the structures characteristically associated with the exercise of these functions are, of course, armies and foreign services on the one hand, and police forces and law courts on the other (for rule adjudication is part of the internal order-maintenance function).

At this point we may note in passing that the distinction between "input" and "output" functions, between "political" and "governmental" functions, has already broken down. We would hold that any conceptual scheme that rests heavily on these dichotomies is culture-bound to "Western," market society.

Turning now to the transforming and adaptive aspect of the political system, we will begin by expanding Almond's function of interest-articulation, defined as demands and suggestions for government action, into a larger one of initiation. The asymmetry between (political) input and (governmental) output which seems often to appear when we seek to apply Almond's model is due largely to its implication that the raw material out of which proposals for government action are processed consist entirely of "demands" or "claims" expressing the "interests" of particular groups. This is far from being the case, even in the highly interest-group-responsive politics of Western market societies. Government action is frequently initiated by the proposals of specialist advisers or bureaucrats seeking to further their view of the "national interest." A more or less *disinterested* concern for the national interest is often also an important ingredient in the public discussion of policy alternatives on current issues. To accommodate such facts to the interest-articulation concept one would either have to envisage cases of highly indirect and unconscious "virtual representation" of particular interests, or treat the "national interest" as one particular interest among many; both these alternatives are arguable, but both also are obvious candidates for Occam's razor. Without going along with the romantic assumption that altruism has no part in politics, we may readily acknowledge that the kind of political initiative of which we are speaking is frequently motivated by a desire for personal honor or advancement. We may even add that once he has proposed a line of action, a man acquires thereby an interest in its success, for "in a bureaucracy ideas do not stand on their merits alone.

It is not only an opinion or an idea that wins, but also a man."[26] And we may further concede that once he has succeeded in mustering associational, institutional or informal-group support for his initiative, group interests have become involved. But this is a very different thing from attributing all political initiatives to a preexisting group interest. Nor would we agree with those who might acknowledge the existence of "disinterested" initiative, but would reduce its role in the political process to that of a catalyst unleashing group interests.

All this applies equally to the aggregation function. It is not only group demands, claims and interests that are aggregated, but also "disinterested" proposals and the support they have engendered; and "disinterested" professionalism, bureaucratic experience and political judgment also enter into the aggregating process itself. It would therefore be more accurately labeled "initiative-aggregation," rather than "interest-aggregation."

In practice, both disinterested and interest-based impulses are probably involved in most cases of political initiative and initiative-aggregation. Frequently one kind of impulse is unacknowledged or underplayed, being attached as it were parasitically to the other. It is not unknown for political leaders seeking support for policies motivated by broad national interests to canvass it among particular associations or institutions on the grounds of their alleged group interest. The opposite, however, is far commoner. How often in the experience of all polities do we find broader social or national interests being invoked in support of proposals actually motivated by particular interests! But the thing to note here is that the appeal to national interest is far from always mere

[26] Victor A. Thompson, "Hierarchy, Specialization and Organizational Conflict," *Administrative Science Quarterly*, V (1960-61), p. 503.

rhetoric; its presence often reflects the fact that spokesmen for special interests, in framing their proposals, have taken account of the need to reach accommodation not only with the advocates of other special interests, but also with those of the national interest.

The objective of the political initiative and aggregation processes is the making of desired new rules or policies by bodies properly empowered to command government action at the appropriate level—presidents, cabinets, representative assemblies, etc., or at lower levels, provincial governors, city and county councils, mayors, etc. This is the central and most dramatic act in the transforming and adaptive aspect of the political system. We decline here to draw an analytical line between rules and more specific measures adopted by governments, on the grounds that the dichotomy assumed thereby collapses under examination into a specificity-generality continuum,[27] and that, even when translated from structural into functional terms, this distinction remains a gracious but misleading concession to the eighteenth-century division of powers theory. The "executive branch of government" is heavily involved both in the "adaptive" function of making new rules and policies and the "maintenance" function of applying existing rules and policies. Nonetheless, so long as no rigid dichotomy is implied, we see some advantage in speaking of rules *and* policies, the latter term being chosen for its vagueness as to specificity (thus a government may adopt a deflation policy or a containment policy, no less than a policy to nationalize the steel industry or to raise pensions by 15 percent).

Our final transformation and adaptation function is po-

[27] Cf. T. H. Rigby, "Max Weber's Typology of Authority: A Difficulty and Some Suggestions," *Australian and New Zealand Journal of Sociology*, Vol. II, No. 1 (1966), 11.

litical mobilization. By this we mean the explanation of new rules and policies to those who will be affected by them and the effort to secure their willing, informed and active cooperation in implementing them. Well-publicized processes of interest-articulation and interest-aggregation ideally provide resultant government measures with an adequate level of public understanding and support in advance. Nevertheless, even in the highly interest-responsive polities of modern market societies mobilization plays a greater part than is commonly acknowledged. Examples may be seen in various phases of the political process: the efforts of interest associations and party executives to rally support behind new programs, leaders or candidates; the use made of representative assemblies to explain and justify government policies; the "public relations" activities of government agencies. Since, however, well-publicized interest-articulation and interest-aggregation are in part functionally interchangeable with political mobilization, the latter really comes into its own in authoritarian systems which abhor politicking and are bent on programs of transformation: like the U.S.S.R. From one point of view, political mobilization may be regarded as an extension of the political socialization function: it seeks to socialize the citizen specifically to the beliefs, attitudes and responses implicit in new rules and policies. But it also overlaps with the legitimation and identification function, for mobilization campaigns operate to reinforce the legitimacy of the political system and its culture at the same time as deploying these for specific purposes, and they may serve as one of the main devices for citizen participation in the political culture.[28]

[28] For an important pioneering study of the political mobilization function, see J. P. Nettl, *Political Mobilization: A Sociological Analysis of Methods and Conflicts* (London, 1967).

Political communication is a *transmission* function, equally essential to the exercise of both the system-maintenance and transformation functions of the political system. There is a second transmission function which is no less essential, namely the realization, appropriation and deployment of power. Power is the sanction-backed capacity to influence the activity of others.[29] Every political system has an infrastructure of power as well as an infrastructure of communication. These may be compared metaphorically with the circulatory and nervous systems of a living organism; and just as a bodily part will atrophy if cut off from either of these systems, so may a political or governmental organ become functionally inoperative if isolated from the flow of either communication or power. Access to communication and access to power are among the main determinants of the effectiveness of a political actor. This is not to claim that they are the *sole* determinants. There are circumstances in which a proposal for action badly communicated from a weak power position may win a large response, and the opposite

[29] Cf. Rigby, "Max Weber's Typology of Authority." The concept of political power is, of course, variously understood and employed, and it is sufficient to define our own use here without discussing the alternatives. For different perspectives, see Max Weber, *The Theory of Social and Economic Organization* (New York, 1947), Sections III and IV; Herbert Goldhamer and Edward A. Shils, "Types of Power and Status," *American Journal of Sociology*, Vol. XLV (1939), 171-182; Bertrand Russell, *Power: A New Social Analysis* (New York, 1938); Harold D. Lasswell and Abraham Kaplan, *Power and Society: A Framework for Political Inquiry* (New Haven, 1950); Richard A. Schermerhorn, *Society and Power* (New York, 1961); Karl W. Deutsch, *The Nerves of Government* (New York, 1966), Chap. 7. It is difficult for the Sovietologist to share the diffidence manifested by some contemporary Western political scientists with respect to the concept of power. Nor is he likely to be tempted by obvious difficulties of measurement to define it away as simply the untutored layman's romantic abstraction from more quantifiable behavioral variables.

29

also occurs. Our point is simply that communication and power are important independent variables in the operation of politics and government.

All political structures and roles are invested with certain opportunities of access to communications media and channels. Opportunity of access, however, is not the same thing as use, and the political impact of particular structures and status-incumbents will largely depend on their success in developing effective patterns of use of these opportunities. Similarly political systems, through constitutions, conventions, rules of parties and associations, laws and governmental regulations, prescribe the *powers* attaching to particular statuses and collectivities and structures, and lay down procedural rules for the derivation and delegation of powers. Again, however, legitimate *powers* are only potential *power*. Moreover, no polity is so well articulated that the totality of power is neatly parceled out among its constituent units: this would require a level of changelessness, consensus and objective self-knowledge that no society enjoys. For these two reasons, effective participation in the political process depends on the success of efforts to realize the potential power made available by the formal distribution of powers, to appropriate part of the "free power" floating in the interstices of the formal structure, and to deploy this power in pursuit of given objectives.[30] To illustrate these points we need look no further than the differences in extent, character and use of power by incumbents of the United States presidency over the last forty years.

Societies vary enormously in their patterns of distribution

[30] Cf. our account of power as a transmission function with Deutsch's metaphor of power as currency (*op.cit.*, pp. 120-122). See also Peter M. Blau, *Exchange and Power in Social Life* (New York, 1964), and E. C. Banfield, *Political Influence* (Glencoe, Free Press, 1961).

of power. Modern market societies are characterized by a relatively large measure of "free power" (i.e. potential access to power unassigned as "powers"), competition for which is more or less institutionalized and functionally linked with the processes of initiative-aggregation. It is only an apparent paradox that this is combined with limitations on the power available to the most powerful statuses, collectivities and structures—for the market could not survive a power monopoly. By contrast, both traditional and organizational societies abhor "free power," because it is potentially disruptive of their more or less rigid structures, and they seek a maximum identification of power with powers, while at the same time tending to an overwhelming concentration of "free power" at the apex of the power structure. One consequence of this is relative instability and variability of power at the top, combined with relative stability and consistency at lower levels, changes in the latter tending to be consequential on changes in the former.

This discussion of the functions of the political system may be summarized by listing them as follows:

A. System-maintenance and integration

1. Internal order-maintenance
2. External order-maintenance
3. Political socialization and recruitment
4. Legitimation and identification (political culture-maintenance)
5. Rule and policy application

B. Transformation and adaptation

6. Political initiation
7. Initiative-aggregation
8. Rule and policy making
9. Political mobilization

31

C. Transmission

10. Communication
11. Power realization, appropriation and deployment

Political Functions of CPSU Membership

The Communist Party is heavily involved in all political functions in the U.S.S.R. A systematic discussion of the political functions of the CPSU would therefore amount to a general account of the Soviet political system. This would far transcend our present needs and objectives. What is required here is a brief consideration of those special features of the exercise of political functions in the U.S.S.R. that one might expect to have some bearing on the recruitment policies and composition of the party, in order to identify the most promising questions to have in mind in the course of our investigation.

Despite its ubiquitous involvement, the party does not exercise a monopoly of any political function. A number of functions are entrusted to specialized structures. This applies to: internal order-maintenance (the militia, political police, internal troops, courts, procuracy, prisons, corrective labor camps, various government inspectorates, and in recent years the "comradely courts" and *druzhiny* or voluntary auxiliary police); external order-maintenance (armed services, foreign ministry, intelligence and counterintelligence agencies); rule and policy application (the state administration, industrial administration, trade unions, cooperatives and certain other "voluntary" associations); and communication (the mass media). Here the party is primarily concerned to exercise overall guidance and supervision over these specialized structures through its own apparatus and through the "guiding nucleus" of its own members in them. Clearly the question of what constitutes an adequate "guiding nucleus" is going to be an important one for party membership policies.

At the same time, the party participates in certain special ways in each of these functions. CPSU contacts with foreign communist parties form an important auxiliary channel of Soviet foreign policy (cf. item e of the obligations of party members). In the armed forces, in addition to the network of primary party organizations, the party maintains a special hierarchy of political officers, and in times of war there have been special mobilizations of party members for military service (cf. item j of the obligations).

All complex bureaucratic structures include special instrumentalities (auditors, inspectors, etc.) for verifying that officials perform their tasks efficiently and honestly, and in the spirit as well as the letter of the law. This checking-up job straddles the two functions of internal order-maintenance and rule and policy application. In Russia it is known as "control" (*kontrol'*, cf. French *contrôle*, German *Kontrolle*). In tsarist times the job was mainly entrusted to a Ministry of State Control, which has been continued under various guises and titles through the Soviet period. However, the party has always had a major responsibility for "control" as well. As we have seen, "verification of fulfillment" is one of the four major aspects of the party's "leading and directing" role distinguished by Soviet scholars. Item g of the tasks of primary party organizations (p. 15) and items f through j of the obligations of party members (p. 17) spell out various aspects of the party's control program. These make it clear that the job involves not only party apparatus officials and party members in key agency positions, but also groups of party members spread through the various sectors and levels of the agencies "controlled."

The party's special responsibilities for communication are

33

very diverse and important. Many of them spring from the dominant position of the party in the performance of other political functions, which we shall consider in a moment. But the party also acts as a kind of gearbox controlling the whole communication network throughout the country. Its apparatus provides the top leadership with a channel of communication linking it with all hierarchical levels of each and every agency and institution, and ultimately with the rank-and-file party members and through them with the basic units of all organizations and with the "masses." At the same time unauthorized communication is closely restricted through the severe sanctions attaching to a whole battery of offenses: divulging of state secrets, rumor-mongering, "counterrevolutionary propaganda," "counterrevolutionary organization," etc. (See also item f of the obligations of party members.) These two things in conjunction enable the leadership to exercise a remarkable degree of control over who communicates what to whom, and over what information and ideas are available to particular categories of the population. Absolute communication control would, of course, be both humanly and technologically impossible, and its effectiveness will obviously be affected by the general level and character of repression in the country, which has varied greatly over the Soviet period. Nonetheless, a high degree of communication control is one of the distinguishing features of the Soviet and other state-party systems, and one that might be expected to exert an influence over the way party members are distributed through various institutions, hierarchical levels, work groups and local communities.

We now move to a group of political functions in which the party not only exerts overall control and supervision, but figures as the most active direct participant. The first of these is political socialization and recruitment. The groundwork of political socialization is laid in kindergarten and school, reinforced by participation successively in the Little Octobrists, Young Pioneers and Young Communist League (komsomol). In all these phases it is very closely directed by the party.[31] Political socialization reaches its most crucial phase, however, when the Soviet adolescent or youth enters employment. Confronting for the first time many of the most important realities of Soviet life, he is meanwhile exposed to a constant barrage of measures—meetings, "agitational" sessions in small groups, wall newspapers, etc.—aimed at producing a "correct" understanding of these realities and a "correct" attitude towards them. At the same time he is inducted into the responses expected of him as a worker and citizen: into his effective rights and responsibilities vis-à-vis those performing various authority roles, into how he should behave at a meeting and in discussion, and into what kind of initiatives, suggestions, questions and criticism are acceptable, couched in what terms and exercised in what milieus and through what channels. All this is the job of the primary party organization in his workplace, acting directly and through the medium of the workplace trade union, komsomol, club and other units. The party member, moreover, is expected to contribute to the socialization of his younger workmates not only through institutionalized organizational and propaganda activities, but also through setting an example of right behavior and thinking, both as worker and citizen, and by advising and correcting his nonparty comrades.

Political recruitment is well characterized by Almond as

[31] It is also likely that, as suggested by Geoffrey Gorer, Margaret Mead and others, infant and childhood experiences in the family and in peer-groups tend to socialize Russian youngsters to certain deep-lying strands in Russian political culture to which the Soviet system has adapted itself. The cultural elements and mechanisms involved have not yet, however, been adequately elucidated.

35

induction into the specialized roles of the political system.[32] Party membership itself is such a specialized role, and it is the responsibility of primary party organizations to pick out suitable candidates and, through a graded program of study and practical assignments, to induct them into this role. At the same time, in view of the concept of the party as "guiding nucleus" in all organizations, and the stress on *political* qualities in personnel selection (see obligations of party members, item h), it is obvious that performance as a party member is at least potentially an important factor in recruitment to other specialized political roles.[33]

A scrutiny of the tasks of primary party organizations and the responsibilities of party members (see pp. 14-17) reveals the importance attached to the functions of political socialization and mobilization at this level. Political mobilization, as we have noted, may be regarded as the socialization of citizens to new rules and policies. It is one of the four functions of the party specifically noted by Soviet scholars. To a large extent the party exercises this function through the mass media, the soviets, the trade unions and other "mass organizations," and the demands of dynamic and properly oriented mobilization constitute a further reason for the party to maintain an adequate leavening of its members in these organizations. At the same time, much of the burden of mobilization, particularly in the face-to-face situations on which the party

[32] Almond and Coleman, *op.cit.*, p. 31.

[33] See Frederick C. Barghoorn, *Politics in the USSR* (Boston, 1966), Chaps. iii-vi, and Brzezinski and Huntington, *op.cit.*, Chap. ii. These are the most valuable attempts to date to present a functional account of the Soviet political system, Barghoorn actually basing his approach on the Almond-Powell model. See also Frederick C. Barghoorn, "Soviet Russia: Orthodoxy and Adaptiveness," in Lucian W. Pye and Sidney Verba, eds., *Political Culture and Political Development* (Princeton, N.J., 1965).

lays great stress, again falls on the primary party organizations, and typically involves the mass of party members.

Political legitimation and identification in the U.S.S.R. is in part a by-product of the function of mobilization. In addition, however, much of the party's propaganda effort, especially via the mass media, books, special articles and the arts, is specifically designed to demonstrate or celebrate the legitimacy of the Soviet political and social system and to foster the citizen's identification with it. It therefore creates a number of specialized roles for party members. In both institutionalized and informal face-to-face encounters with "the masses" at workshop and residential levels, party members are also expected to be constantly on the watch for opportunities to extol the legitimacy of the system and its political culture and to defend them against erroneous views and attitudes (see obligations of party members, items d and e). Here the legitimation function frequently shades into the internal order-maintenance function. But perhaps the most important aspect of the legitimation and identification function resides in the symbolism and rituals attaching to the soviets and to the party itself. Elections, sessions of soviets, and party congresses, conferences and even the plenary sessions of party committees, like the cognate activities in modern Western polities, dramatize the legitimacy of the system and involve citizens in it through their direct or vicarious participation. This draws attention to the symbolic implications of party membership patterns. Since the legitimacy of the system resides largely in the soviets, which are supposed to be representative of the best elements in Soviet society, the party's claim to leadership generates symbolic as well as manipulative imperatives for it to maintain a substantial representation in the soviets. Clearly, moreover, the implications of the manipulative and symbolic imperatives are not necessarily always identical, nor is the optimum balance between them necessarily the same for all levels at any one time. The other great legitimating structure in the U.S.S.R. is the CPSU itself. The party's claim to rule is embedded in its doctrine, which, as we have already seen, requires a membership which is *both* drawn from the people (with pride of place to the working class) *and* composed of the "best, most advanced" members of society. Actual membership policies must therefore seek to vindicate this claim and thereby the legitimacy of the system. Since elite groups will also tend to recruit the "best, most advanced" citizens, it is perfectly acceptable for such groups to be relatively overrepresented in the party membership; this must not reach the point, however, where the *popular* basis of the membership becomes too narrow. This popular basis is symbolically functional not only in this broad legitimating context, but also as a source of popular identification with the regime through the "virtual representation" which different occupational, ethnic, sex, age, residential and educational categories enjoy by having some of their number in the party.[34] The conflicting pull between the elitist and popular orientations of party membership doctrine has already been discussed. The demands of "virtual representation" of different social categories defined in terms of overlapping variables are also, quite obviously, not necessarily in harmony; it may not always be possible, for example, simultaneously to achieve the optimum ratio both of occupational and ethnic groups. The current balance between these various conflicting demands will clearly be sensitive to shifts in the political, social and ideological preoccupations of the party leadership.

Although rule and policy making in the U.S.S.R. is

[34] The applicability in this context of the concept of "virtual representation" was suggested to the author by John A. Armstrong.

jealously monopolized by the CPSU, it is so closely concentrated in the inner circles of the leadership that ensuring the proper exercise of this function could scarcely figure as a consideration influencing membership policies. Of course new rules and policies relating to many fields of government may well have implications for party membership policies, but it is not the rule- and policy-making function itself that determines these implications. This, then, is one political function that is unlikely to throw much light on the history of CPSU recruitment and composition.

What of the political initiative and initiative-aggregation functions? This is one of the most complex aspects of the political system, and it is particularly difficult to outline in a few paragraphs. In the West we tend to identify responsible government with *responsive* government; that is, the adaptive and transforming activity of the political system is seen as occurring by way of *responses* to developments within society as articulated by the social groups affected. To the Leninist such an approach would amount to "bowing down to spontaneity," and would therefore be grossly *irresponsible*. For him the adaptive and transforming aspect of government involves the *conscious direction* of social developments by the party leadership in the light of the existing objective realities and of Marxist-Leninist theory. This is the rationale behind the relatively limited role of the political initiative and initiative-aggregation functions in the Soviet system, which we have already noted. It is not that suggestions and criticism from below are in themselves objectionable; it is rather that these are not supposed to touch the substance of party-government policies, but only the implementation of these policies by specialized agencies and subordinate officials and groups. The actual discussion of policy alternatives is typically concentrated in the upper levels of the party and

39

other bureaucratic hierarchies. Though the party aims to dominate the aggregation process, through the role of its Politburo and Central Committee apparatus and through the maintenance of high party membership levels in the upper echelons of the various bureaucracies, both the Council of Ministers and to a minor extent the Presidium of the Supreme Soviet also participate in this function.

At the same time, it would be a serious oversimplification to conclude that Soviet policy making is totally uninfluenced by pressures from below. To start with, the party rules provide for selected current issues to be thrown open to general discussion in the party when the leadership is insufficiently unanimous about them, and several such discussions, albeit constrained within a narrow range of choices, have in fact taken place (largely in the late 1950's when Khrushchev was still consolidating his position). Secondly, the constant discussion among specialists in the general and specialized press, at meetings and conferences, and in the course of their day-to-day work—discussion ostensibly confined to broadly theoretical or narrowly factual aspects of their specialities— often carries implications for policy making, though these are rarely made explicit. And finally, since ends and means cannot be kept entirely in watertight compartments, suggestions and criticism about the *implementation* of current policies inevitably throw light on the appropriateness of these policies or the need for others. In these various ways, new ideas and facts are brought to the attention of the policy makers, and they learn something about group preferences.

In theory, this upward pressure of opinion is supposed to be wholly disinterested, and participants invariably invoke the principles of communism or the higher interests of the Soviet state. In practice, any policy change will affect interests, and the furtherance of particular interests is undoubtedly often an unacknowledged concern in much ostensibly disinterested discussion. And here we should add that it is not only, and perhaps not primarily, via this upward pressure of opinion that particular interests are furthered in the Soviet Union. More important is the twist that particular interests are able to give to policies in the course of implementing them: thus ministries or local economic councils give preference to "their" enterprises in distributing materials or products in short supply; factory managements contrive to secure "easy" plans; educators see to it that the best students get straight to college without meeting the requirement of two years production work; peasants exchange their new-born calves with better-bred ones belonging to the collective; local authorities in Georgia remove only *some* of their statues of Stalin—the examples, from different times, places, and areas of policy are innumerable. The process whereby occupational, ethnic, local and other groups advance their interests in the course of carrying out assigned tasks is analogous to, and shades into, the practice of *blat* (pull) in the conduct of day-to-day personal affairs. Both arise from the essential role of informal practices in greasing the works of any highly bureaucratized structure. To attempt wholly to eliminate such practices would have the same disastrous effect on the functioning of the system as does "working to rule" by a labor union in the West. Yet if not controlled and circumscribed, these practices would get out of hand and negate the purposes of leadership policies. And this is where the party membership comes in, for only with the aid of individuals directly involved can the mechanism of informal practices be understood and manipulated. A glance at the obligations of party members (pp. 15-17, see especially items d, e, g and h) will reveal the importance attached to the membership in containing the furtherance of special interests. The spread

41

of party members through all social groups is thus of advantage to the leadership in identifying, delimiting, canalizing and, where possible, using for its own purposes, both "parasitic" interest-articulation at the policy-discussion stage and the deflection of national policies to serve special interests at the policy-implementation stage.

This leaves us with the political transmission function of power realization, appropriation and deployment. The multifaceted participation of CPSU members in Soviet political life makes it obvious that joining the party will enhance any individual's access to power. At the same time, since participation in a number of political functions is limited to party members employed in positions of authority or in particular fields (e.g. trade union work, management, armed forces), *how much* it enhances his access to power will largely depend on the nature and hierarchical level of his official employment (cf. our earlier discussion of the three categories of party membership, p. 8). One political consequence of these facts about the power access attaching to party membership is that the representation of a particular group in the party may be taken as an indication (though not necessarily conclusive) of the political importance of this group. We should point out, however, that political importance is not necessarily convertible into the promotion of group interests, for the reasons already discussed.

It is when we look from the top down, rather than from the bottom up, that the power implications of party membership patterns stand out. The number and distribution of the party members under his direction is obviously an important factor in the power position of any party official. It will affect, for instance, the position of the secretary of the party organization in an industrial plant vis-à-vis the plant director. The strength of the party organizations in the industrial plants of

42

a given region will affect the power position of the regional party secretary in his dealings with the industrial ministries concerned. The officials responsible for the fine arts in the central party apparatus of one of the republics will find it easier to control literary developments in the republic if there is a strong party organization in the writers' union. Or to put the matter in its widest context, the number and distribution of party members will affect the power position of the CPSU apparatus in relation to that of other political structures in the U.S.S.R. There is one additional factor involved. The size of delegations to party conferences and congresses is proportional to the membership of the party organizations concerned, and therefore affects the voting power at the disposal of the leaders of these organizations.

Here, however, two important qualifications are needed. Firstly, from what has been said one might suppose the interest of party officials in maximizing party membership to be so great that it is a wonder the whole adult population has not been drawn into the party. The reason it has not, of course, is that many of the party's functions depend on the minority, "advanced detachment" position of its members, possessing special prestige and advantages, but also special burdens and responsibilities. In other words, if the party came to embrace all or most of the population, it would be necessary to invent an "inner party." Nonetheless, we do appear to be faced with the question whether the party's political functions do not invest it with powerful and fundamental growth tendencies which are likely to reassert themselves through the various zigzags of policy. The second qualification is that we have been speaking, so far, only of *potential* power. Whether or not the power potentially available to a party official by virtue of having a large, well-deployed party organization under his command will actually

43

be realized and used by him in a given power relationship will depend on a number of factors, including the availability of other channels of power and the will of his superiors. Thus a factory party secretary will hesitate to mobilize his members against the management unless he is assured of the support of the city or district party committee, and the crucial consideration for a regional party secretary in tackling an industrial ministry is the goodwill of the Central Committee apparatus. If, then, one suspects some party membership policy or practice to have been influenced by power considerations, it is not sufficient to refer to the power aspects of the party membership in the abstract; the matter must be studied in its total power context. And finally, we should recall a point mentioned in our earlier discussion of the power function. A disproportionate amount of "free power" in the Soviet system is concentrated at the top, and those at the top tend to be very jealous of unauthorized power uses at lower levels. For this reason, the scope for local officials to manipulate party membership policies for their own purposes is likely to be narrow; such manipulation is far more likely to be part of a general pattern initiated by power moves at the top of the hierarchy.

Nonfunctional Determinants

The assumption behind what has been written so far is that we can explain CPSU recruitment policies and both the continuities and discontinuities in party membership patterns in terms of the functions performed by the party membership in the Soviet political system. Alfred G. Meyer writes that "entry into the Party is essentially a process of co-option, in which the Party rather than the prospective member takes the initiative. Application for membership is usually made at the suggestion of the primary organization."[35] If this were the whole truth, our assumption would be correct, since it would mean that the party leadership was able to choose just the "mix" of members it thought necessary for its purposes. We will see evidence in the following chapters, however, that it is not the whole truth. In his book *A Difficult Spring*, Valentin Ovechkin recounts a conversation between a raikom (district party committee) secretary and a worthy kolkhoz blacksmith with whom he has become acquainted in the hospital. The party secretary asks the other why he has never joined the party. After attempting to fob him off with *pro forma* answers, the kolkhoznik eventually confesses that the main reason is that his handwriting is too poor to hold down an official job, for which, in any case, he has no great ambition.

> I like my own trade, and all I want is to see the kolkhoz run properly and to get a decent return for your work. I do have some feeling I'd like to be in the party, but I don't want to be put in an official job. And the trouble as I see it is that things have got fixed that way. If I join, they can tell me as a matter of party discipline, "chuck your smithy, grab this briefcase." But I'm not interested in a briefcase. I'm not dead set on becoming a boss.[36]

Two implications of this exchange should be noted. The first is the reason given by the blacksmith why one might, or might not, wish to join the party: that it is almost certain to lead to an assignment to administrative or white-collar work. This opens up a many-faceted problem to which we

[35] Meyer, *op.cit.*, p. 139.
[36] Valentin Ovechkin, *Trudnaia vesna* (A Difficult Spring), (Moscow, 1956).

45

recur more than once in this book. The second implication is that the wishes and motives of the individual concerned *are* relevant to whether or not he becomes a CPSU member, and this is the point we are concerned with here. Though there are situations in which an individual has no real choice when asked to join the party, more often than not he can refuse without seriously unpleasant consequences—apart, of course, from denying himself the advantages of party membership. Furthermore, if one wishes strongly enough to be in the party, it is often possible to arrange to be "co-opted." The situation has analogies in many clubs and associations in Western countries where members are constitutionally recruited by invitation. The balance between co-option and individual choice has varied over time, place and sphere of employment, but there is always an element of both whenever a new member is recruited.

This means that personal reasons for and against joining the CPSU have an influence on what sort of members the party gets. These reasons are far more complex than the fictitious conversation reported by Ovechkin indicates. Being a party member involves considerable extra demands on your time and energies. It places you under an additional discipline to which ordinary citizens are not subject, one which may involve onerous, difficult or dangerous assignments. Your life and conversation, both public and private, are far more "on show" than those of your nonparty associates, and you are constantly required to acknowledge and affirm your belief in the values, aims and policies of the regime. It makes you more vulnerable politically, particularly in periods of arbitrary and repressive government. It may erect barriers between you and your colleagues, friends and relatives. On the other hand, it opens up possibilities of promotion and career-making which may be of crucial importance if you aspire to certain fields and levels of employment. It gives you contacts and channels helpful not only in making your career, but in securing many other advantages in daily life— both for yourself, and for your family and friends. It gives the loyal, devoted, public-spirited or altruistic citizen special opportunities of service to the state or the community. You are told far more both about your own country and the outside world, and the power of the desire to know should not be underestimated in a society starved of information.[37]

The importance of this for our purposes is that the balance between the advantages and disadvantages of party membership may not seem the same to people of different occupational, ethnic, educational and age groups, to townsmen and villagers, to men and to women. The element of personal choice in joining the party may therefore distort the results of official recruitment policies and produce a "mix" of members that does not entirely correspond to the functional requirements we have been discussing. Of course, the party may attempt to correct these distortions by special recruitment or expulsion campaigns, but as we shall see, these efforts tend to produce secondary distortions. The Soviet leadership cannot necessarily get just the combination of members it wants.

This means that in our concern to relate membership policies and patterns in the CPSU to functional aspects of the Soviet political system, we should not ignore the possible importance of functionally neutral or dysfunctional factors. These factors are rooted in sociological or social-psychological facts which obtrude on the political system only because the political leadership does not properly understand them or cannot properly control them. They are ex-

[37] For a useful discussion of the advantages and burdens of party membership, see Meyer, *op.cit.*, pp. 140-142.

amples of what Almond calls "poor boundary maintenance" between the society and the polity.[38] It is not our task to study these classes of facts here, but we should seek to identify and, where possible, to measure their impact on party membership trends.

Limits of the Study

The body of this study is presented in two parts. In the first, the main lines of CPSU recruitment policies and trends in membership, particularly social and occupational trends, are discussed in historical sequence. In Part Two a number of special aspects are isolated for separate treatment. This device has been dictated by the complexity of our data, which creates serious problems of exposition in convenient and assimilable form.

It should be clear from what has already been said that there is scarcely an aspect of the Soviet political (and indeed social) system which does not impinge on our subject. Obviously, we cannot attempt more than a cursory discussion of many of these topics here, and for a fuller examination the reader should refer to those general works on Soviet politics and government mentioned in the footnotes and Bibliography. By the same token, while we have attempted in Part One to sketch in as much of the general political history of the Soviet Union as is necessary to render meaningful the changes in official policies and the realization of these policies in practice, it has not been our aim to include in this book a complete and carefully documented Soviet political history.

Our study is severely limited by the selectivity of Soviet published data. We should like to know about the occupation, education, etc. of members' parents; whether or not their parents, spouses or other relatives are in the party; their

[38] Almond and Coleman, *op.cit.*, pp. 8, 35.

income, residential circumstances, private interests and hob-
bies, marital status and number of children; their military
service. Religion is obviously not a variable of party membership, but it would be interesting to know about the religious affiliation and involvement of parents. The exclusion
of these and other topics from our analysis does not mean
that they have been judged politically or sociologically irrele-
vant, but simply that significant data are not available. A
further problem is that the amount and quality of information
on different aspects of our topic vary greatly over time; this
causes a degree of inconsistency in our treatment of different periods, and leaves gaps in some places. The period on
which the best information is available corresponds roughly
with the 1920's, and the war years and the post-Stalin period
vie for the second best.

Our study is also limited in time. We have selected the first
fifty years of the Soviet regime as a significant and manage-
able period for a specialized study of this kind. We have
excluded the prerevolutionary years, since our concern has
been with the party membership as an aspect of a functioning political system. This does not mean that earlier membership traditions or the number of prerevolutionary members
remaining in the CPSU at later periods are not significant,
but we mention these facts only in relation to developments
in the Soviet period.

A further self-imposed limitation should also be mentioned. As we have seen, different categories of the CPSU
membership participate unequally in the political functions
of the party. Special interest attaches to those inner circles of the party who share in its decision-making processes. John A. Armstrong has furnished a pioneer study of
these circles in his *The Soviet Bureaucratic Elite*: *A Case
Study of the Ukrainian Apparatus*, and other scholars are

49

currently working on special aspects of the "party elite." A comparative analysis of the characteristics of this elite in relation to those of the mass membership of the party would clearly possess considerable theoretical and practical interest. This, however, we have not attempted here, since it would add immoderately to the length and complexity of an already large book, and we consider, for reasons we have already attempted to show, that the general membership of the party is a topic of sufficient importance to warrant a specialized study of its own.

In this Introduction we have attempted to outline the analytical framework which has guided the collection and interpretation of data for this study. This framework is implicit in the body of the book, but we have avoided rigid pigeonholing of data in terms of abstract concepts or constant explicit reference back to our analytical framework, since this would overload the text with jargon and exasperate readers who did not happen to be students of comparative politics or political sociology. In the Conclusion we attempt to summarize our findings in terms of this framework, and draw attention to some additional facets and problems that emerge in the study.

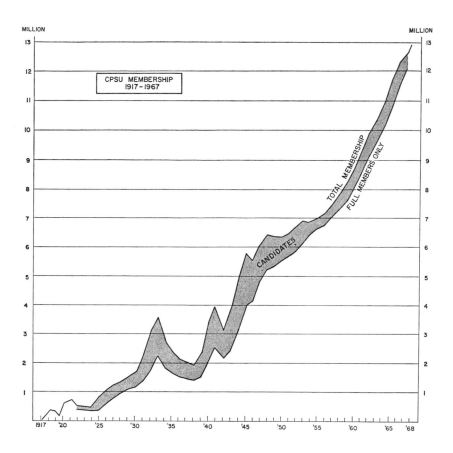

MILLION

MILLION

CPSU MEMBERSHIP
1917-1967

TOTAL MEMBERSHIP

FULL MEMBERS ONLY

CANDIDATES

51

CPSU MEMBERSHIP, 1917-1967

Year	Full Members	Candidates	Total
1917	24,000	None	24,000
1918 (March)	390,000	None	390,000
1919 (March)	350,000		350,000
1920 (March)	611,978		611,978
1921 (March)	732,521		732,521
1922	410,430	117,924	528,354
1923	381,400	117,700	499,100
1924	350,000	122,000	472,000
1925	440,365	361,439	801,804
1926	639,652	440,162	1,079,814
1927	786,288	426,217	1,212,505
1928	914,307	391,547	1,305,854
1929	1,090,508	444,854	1,535,362
1930	1,184,651	493,259	1,677,910
1931	1,369,406	842,819	2,212,225
1932	1,769,773	1,347,477	3,117,250
1933	2,203,951	1,351,387	3,555,338
1934	1,826,756	874,252	2,701,008
1935	1,659,104	699,610	2,358,714
1936	1,489,907	586,935	2,076,842
1937	1,453,828	527,869	1,981,697
1938	1,405,879	514,123	1,920,002
1939	1,514,181	792,792	2,306,973
1940	1,982,743	1,417,232	3,399,975
1941	2,490,479	1,381,986	3,872,465
1942	2,155,336	908,540	3,063,876
1943	2,451,511	1,403,190	3,854,701
1944	3,126,627	1,791,934	4,918,561
1945	3,965,530	1,794,839	5,760,369
1946	4,127,689	1,383,173	5,510,862
1947	4,774,886	1,277,015	6,051,901
1948	5,181,199	1,209,082	6,390,281
1949	5,334,811	1,017,761	6,352,572
1950	5,510,787	829,396	6,340,183
1951	5,658,577	804,398	6,462,975
1952	5,853,200	854,339	6,707,539
1953	6,067,027	830,197	6,897,224

Year	Full Members	Candidates	Total
1954	6,402,284	462,579	6,864,863
1955	6,610,238	346,867	6,957,105
1956	6,767,644	405,877	7,173,521
1957	7,001,114	493,459	7,494,573
1958	7,296,559	546,637	7,843,196
1959	7,622,356	616,775	8,239,131
1960	8,017,249	691,418	8,708,667
1961	8,472,396	803,430	9,275,826
1962	9,051,934	839,134	9,891,068
1963	9,581,149	806,047	10,387,196
1964	10,182,916	839,453	11,022,369
1965	10,811,443	946,726	11,758,169
1966	11,548,287	809,021	12,357,308
1967	12,135,103	549,030	12,684,133
1967 (July)			12,947,926

1 Figures as at January 1 unless otherwise indicated.

2 SOURCE: *Partiinaia zhizn'*, No. 19, October 1967, pp. 8-10. The source explains that the figures for 1918 were worked out by the Institute of Marxism-Leninism of the CPSU Central Committee on the basis of reports of local party conferences held in the preceding months; that those for 1919, based on the organizational report of the Central Committee to the Eighth Congress, were exclusive of party members located in areas under White control; and that those for 1920 and 1921 were based on data presented to the Ninth and Tenth Congresses. In general, figures for the Civil War years must be regarded as approximations only. For details of conflicting estimates for this period, see pp. 68-69.

3 There were already candidates (probationary members) in 1919, but this status was not regularized till December of that year. Separate figures for full members and candidates are not available before 1922. The source on which our table is based implies that candidates were not included in the totals shown for the years 1920 and 1921, these figures representing full members only. There would appear some reason for doubting this. According to A. S. Bubnov, in *Bol'shaia sovetskaia entsiklopediia*, 1st edn., Vol. XI, col. 531, *full* members numbered 431,400 in January 1920 and 576,000 in January 1921. If, however, there were in fact 732,521 full members in March 1921 and total party membership was therefore well above this figure, the scale of the subsequent expulsions and withdrawals from the party was considerably greater than is usually supposed.

4 The figures shown here for 1927, which were evidently based on the party census of January 10 of that year, are significantly lower than those derived from current statistical returns supplied by subordinate party organizations to the Central Committee (see pp. 161-162).

5 Discrepancies in official data on party membership, though less marked

than for the Civil War period, persist for the years up to 1932. To illustrate this, we set out in the table below the figures given for 1924-1932 by three sources: A. S. Bubnov, in *Bol'shaia sovetskaia entsiklopediia*, 1st edn., Vol. XI, col. 531, Table 1, "Dinamika chislennogo sostava VKP(b)"; E. Iaroslavskii, *Za bol'shevistskuiu proverku i chistku riadov partii* (Moscow, 1933), pp. 47-48; and *Partiinaia zhizn'*, No. 19, October 1967, p. 9 (also No. 20, October 1947, pp. 77-80). While many of the discrepancies revealed here are slight, in four cases they range from 6 to 9 percent.

Total party membership January	*Bubnov*	*Iaroslavskii*	*Partiinaia zhizn'*
1924	472,000	446,089	472,000
1925	798,804	731,117	801,804
1926	1,078,185	1,002,489	1,079,814
1927	1,147,074	1,131,256	1,212,805
1928	1,304,471	1,302,854	1,305,854
1929	1,532,362	1,532,347	1,535,362
1930	1,674,910	1,674,910	1,677,910
1931		2,057,400	2,212,225
1932		3,078,282	3,117,250

Bubnov further complicates the picture by giving significantly different figures in his Table 2, "Sootnoshenie chlenov partii i kandidatov v VKP(b)," appearing in the same column as the table reproduced above: these figures are closer to those given by *Partiinaia zhizn'*, but not identical. In most cases no ready explanations for these discrepancies are forthcoming. The *Partiinaia zhizn'* figure for 1927 is based on the Central Committee's current statistics, and Bubnov's figure on the party census. Iaroslavskii's consistently lower figures may possibly be due to the exclusion from his totals of persons who had ceased to participate in party activities by the relevant dates and who were subsequently removed from the party records for "passivity" and nonpayment of dues; but this is conjectural. Since other figures given by Iaroslavskii in this source also conflict with figures given by *prima facie* more "official" sources, his figures may be the least authoritative. Recent Soviet writers follow either the Bubnov or the *Partiinaia zhizn'* figures, but not always consistently. For instance, I. Glazyrin, in his *Regulirovanie sostava KPSS v period stroitel'stva sotsializma* (Moscow, 1957), gives the Bubnov figures for January 1926 (p. 26) and the *Partiinaia zhizn'* figures for January 1930 (p. 67). It would appear that party membership records still left something to be desired during this period, as was, indeed, declared to be the case when the Central Committee launched its "verification of party documents" in 1935 (see p. 206). Subsequent to this, however, there appear to be no contradictions in the data, although the complete accuracy of published figures for the war years may be open to some doubt (see pp. 260, 279).

Part One

CPSU Membership History

Chapter 1

From Revolutionary Underground to State Party

THE COLLAPSE of the tsarist regime in February 1917 fulfilled the dreams of generations of the Russian radical intelligentsia. The opposition parties, however, could claim little direct credit for it. The February Revolution was a spontaneous mutiny of the urban masses and soldiers, which took most of the "professional revolutionaries," including the bolsheviks, by surprise. Pending the convening of a Constituent Assembly a Provisional Government was formed, consisting of representatives of major parties opposed to the autocracy but excluding the bolsheviks. At the same time soviets (councils) chosen by the rebellious workers and soldiers acquired a large share of power, notably in the capital, where the Petrograd Soviet exercised an effective veto over the decisions of the Provisional Government. The soviets became the major focus of competition between the various left-wing parties.

As confusion and disintegration spread in the months following the Revolution, the political skill and will-power of one man assumed decisive importance. Lenin, the founder and unchallenged leader of the Bolshevik Party, set out to inspire, nag and maneuver his followers into seizing power. At first he envisaged this as taking place through a transfer of plenary powers to bolshevik-controlled soviets; later, as the prospects of dominating the soviets seemed to recede, he called on the Bolshevik Party to take power directly, employing armed detachments of workers formed for the purpose. In October 1917 this second tactic was successfully implemented, but the happy coincidence of acquiring a majority in the Second Congress of Soviets permitted the bolshevik government to clothe itself in the authority of the soviets and to govern through them.

The success of the bolsheviks in the scramble for power following the downfall of tsarism was largely due to their superior organization and discipline, to the mass appeal of their policies of peace (in effect, at any price) and of immediate seizure of the gentry's land and its distribution among the peasants, policies over which circumstances and the scruples of their rivals gave them a virtual monopoly.[1]

The bolshevik seizure of power accelerated the polarization of political forces in Russia and in the following months the country drifted into a bitter and fearfully destructive civil war, in which the bolsheviks did not achieve final victory until the beginning of 1921. Had it not been for the intense and prolonged crisis of these early years, who can say what kind of polity would have evolved from the mixture of autocratic and democratic elements which coexisted in the structure and tradition of bolshevism? As it was, in encouraging the *de facto* proscription of other parties and the concentration of initiative and decision making inside the party in the hands of its centralized hierarchy of officials, the Civil War fostered that dictatorship of the central party leadership which has been the keystone of the Soviet political order ever since.[2]

During the first months of bolshevik rule, a strain of utopianism colored Lenin's approach to economic and administrative problems, contrasting curiously with the ruthless realism he invariably displayed where the question of power was per-

[1] See Leonard Schapiro, *The Communist Party of the Soviet Union* (New York, 1960), Chap. 9 (cited hereafter as *The CPSU*).
[2] *Ibid.*, Chaps. 10-13.

ceived to be involved. As he then saw it, the skills of management amounted merely to routine bookkeeping operations which any literate person could master, technical specialists could and would deploy their expertise under the control of the workers as effectively as under the capitalists, the workers and peasants could take a wide measure of responsibility for running production and local services, without the danger of their challenging bolshevik leadership on important questions, and effective campaigns of education and persuasion would leave only a minor role for coercion.[3]

The Civil War introduced a harsh corrective. Strict discipline, "one-man management," the omnipresence of coercion, and privileges for military and civilian specialists, became the order of the day. They found institutional expression in the smothering of "workers' control" under a centralized industrial bureaucracy, the armed requisitioning of foodstuffs from the peasants, the great power acquired by the political police (the Cheka), and the bureaucratization of the soviets and the party.

Party Growth in 1917

Official sources estimate bolshevik membership at the beginning of 1917 at 23,600.[4] The February Revolution produced a flood of new members for the now legalized parties of the Left, and the bolsheviks' tradition of highly selective admission did not prevent them from sharing actively in this expansion. Indeed, while there is no record of any decision

[3] See, in particular, Lenin's article "Uderzhat li bol'sheviki gosudarstvennuiu vlast'?" (Will the Bolsheviks Retain State Power?), *Sochineniia*, Vol. xxxiv, pp. 287-339. A useful summary is contained in Fainsod, *How Russia Is Ruled*, pp. 88-89.

[4] See A. S. Bubnov, in *BSE* (1st edn.), Vol. xi, col. 531. While the state of party records at this period does not encourage confidence in the precision of this estimate, no alternative figure seems ever to have been proposed.

being taken by the leadership, or even of their having discussed the question, it seems to have been treated as axiomatic that the carefully selective membership policies of the past, designed for the conditions of the conspiratorial underground, had now lost their validity, and that the drive to maximize the party's influence in sharp competition with other parties necessarily involved recruitment of new members on a mass scale.

On March 19 the Moscow Oblast (Regional) Bureau, which coordinated party work in thirteen guberniyas (provinces) of central Russia, issued a statement containing the following passage: "Now, after nineteen years of illegal activity, our party is coming out into the open. All the chains with which the police regime of the autocracy bound our work have been removed. No one any longer prevents us from building up our organizations, no one prevents them from growing numerically and extending their influence to all phases of the workers' movement."[5] The same approach was evident in statements on membership growth made by representatives of local committees at the April 1917 Conference and the Sixth Congress in August 1917,[6] and it seems at no stage to have been questioned by the central leadership of the party, either on these occasions or in discussions in the Central Committee itself.[7] The result was a headlong growth in party membership throughout 1917.

[5] Quoted in S. Kukushkin, *Moskovskie bol'sheviki v gody pervoi mirovoi voiny i Fevral'skoi revoliutsii* (Moscow, 1963), p. 169.

[6] See *Sed'maia (aprel'skaia) konferentsiia RSDRP (bol'shevikov): Protokoly* (Moscow, 1958), pp. 123-128 (cited hereafter as *VII konf.*); *Shestoi s"ezd RSDRP (bol'shevikov): Protokoly* (Moscow, 1958), pp. 44-96 (cited hereafter as *VI s"ezd*).

[7] See *Protokoly Tsentral'nogo Komiteta RSDRP(b). Avgust 1917 g.—fevral' 1918 g.* (Moscow, 1958). The fact that this record of Central Committee proceedings over a six-month period contains not a single mention of party membership and recruitment problems

The exact dimensions of this expansion cannot be traced with precision. The Central Committee received little statistical information from local organizations, which had neither the motivation nor the resources to maintain careful records. The inadequacies in our data may be indicated by comparing estimates of party membership at the time of the April 1917 Conference given by different official sources. In the report of the Conference's Credentials Commission, membership was put at 79,000.[8] However, calculations made by the Statistical Department of the Central Committee during the early 1920's put the party's size in April 1917 at 46,000.[9] The larger contemporary figure, which fits in better with party claims as to the extent of mass support in 1917, continues to be reproduced in Soviet propaganda material, and a 1958 study asserted that it was confirmed by analysis of the records of local committees held in the Central Party Archives.[10]

Similar confusion exists as to membership at the time of the bolshevik seizure of power in October 1917. A week before the event Sverdlov told the Central Committee that the party had grown to about 400,000.[11] Four months later, however, in a report to the Seventh Congress in which he emphasized that the party had continued its rapid growth, he put its

suggests that existing practices were not seen by the leadership as involving any serious issues of policy or tactics.

[8] *VII konf.*, p. 149.

[9] See *Vserossiiskaia perepis' chlenov RKP 1922 goda* (Moscow, 1925), p. 89. A. S. Bubnov, in *BSE* (1st edn.), Vol. xi, col. 531, further reduces the estimate to 40,000, while specifically noting that the contemporary estimate was 79,000.

[10] V. V. Anikeev, "Svedeniia o bol'shevistskikh organizatsiakh s marta po dekabr' 1917 goda" (Information on Bolshevik Organizations from March to December 1917), *V I KPSS*, No. 2, 1958, p. 127.

[11] *Protokoly Tsentral'nogo Komiteta RSDRP(b). Avgust 1917— fevral' 1918*, p. 94.

membership at only 300,000.[12] Subsequent recalculations by the Statistical Department yielded a membership figure in January 1918 as low as 115,000.[13] Sverdlov had given the figure of 400,000 in the course of an optimistic survey of the party's organizational position offered in support of Lenin's plan for an immediate coup, and, in the light of the contradictory evidence mentioned, its accuracy may reasonably be doubted. Yet the 1958 Soviet study cited above declared that this figure, too, was consistent with data held in the Central Party Archives.[14]

Apart from the patchiness of contemporary records, two other factors probably contributed to these conflicting estimates. First, the organizational dismemberment of the Russian Social Democratic movement into separate Bolshevik and Menshevik parties was far from complete at the local level. Throughout 1917 many local party organizations continued to identify themselves simply as "Social Democratic," and, even when their leadership accepted the bolshevik program and the authority of the bolshevik Central Committee, there could often be room for doubt as to how consciously or solidly bolshevik their followers were. Secondly, not all who enrolled in the various left-wing parties in the atmosphere of excitement and confusion reigning in 1917 followed this up with any real participation in party activities. While contemporary bolshevik estimates of party growth could probably do no more than total up enrollment figures reported by the cells, the far lower estimates made subsequently by the Statis-

[12] Ia. M. Sverdlov, *Izbrannye proizvedeniia* (Moscow, 1959), Vol. II, p. 133.

[13] Bubnov, in *BSE*, Vol. XI, col. 531.

[14] Anikeev, in *V I KPSS*, No. 2, 1958, p. 131. The most recent Soviet estimate of membership in October 1917 is 350,000. See *K*, No. 15, October 1967, p. 87.

tical Department suggest a more rigorous test of what constituted a party member than the mere act of enrollment.

Despite these inadequacies in our data and difficulties of interpretation, the essential picture seems clear enough. In the months following the downfall of the tsarist regime, the party expanded at a hectic rate. By the time of the seizure of power, the 20,000 or so men of the bolshevik underground had been reduced to a small fraction of the party membership; whether this fraction was a tenth or only a fifteenth is a question of secondary interest (in March 1918 it is said to have been 8 percent).[15]

According to calculations made during the 1920's, about 60 percent of the bolshevik underground were workers, 8 percent were peasants, and a third were drawn from middle class groups (professional and white-collar workers, intelligentsia, students, etc.).[16] But what of those who joined after the downfall of the monarchy? Given the contemporary state of party records, any detailed breakdown of their social composition is obviously out of the question. It is possible, however, to arrive at some conclusions as to overall trends. A resolution of the Sixth Party Congress (August 1917) contains the following passage: "The withdrawal of the intelligentsia from the ranks of the proletarian party, which began in 1905, became a mass phenomenon after the February Revolution, when the class content of our party's activity inescapably defined the attitude of nonproletarian elements towards it."[17]

Although we might well entertain doubts as to the *explanation* offered us here, the *fact* of "the withdrawal of the in-

[15] A. A. Timofeevskii et al., eds. *V. I. Lenin i stroitel'stvo partii v pervye gody sovetskoi vlasti* (Moscow, 1965), p. 64.

[16] See Bubnov, in *BSE*, Vol. XI, col. 533.

[17] *VI s"ezd*, p. 268.

telligentsia" is well attested. A questionnaire issued to delegates to the Sixth Congress on the organizational activities of local committees included a question as to which social groups they had succeeded in drawing into active party work. The following are typical answers: "The work is conducted entirely by local working class members. No intelligentsia."[18] "The work is carried on by local forces, thrown up by the Revolution; there are no intellectuals, teachers or students."[19] "Party workers coming from the local working class—there are hardly any intellectuals."[20] There were a few replies indicating that intellectuals still played a major part in certain local organizations, while some others mentioned them as a secondary factor. But the great majority of local organizations reported that they were relying wholly or mainly on working class activists, most of them newcomers to party activity.[21]

Further evidence pointing in the same direction was contained in floor reports made at the Congress by spokesmen for the regional and local committees. For example, the Volga oblast representative reported:

> The intelligentsia, as everywhere else, has broken away not only from us Bolsheviks, whom it regards as traitors, but also from the Mensheviks and Socialist Revolutionaries as well, who have far fewer intellectual followers than one might have expected. The majority of the intelligentsia have shifted over to the Cadets. In large towns there are [no more than] five or six party workers of long standing drawn from the intelligentsia. Of course this

[18] *Ibid.*, p. 340.   [19] *Ibid.*, p. 328.   [20] *Ibid.*, p. 348.
[21] For the complete results of this enquiry, see *ibid.*, pp. 319-390. Cf. *Bol'shevistskie organizatsii Ukrainy (noiabr' 1917—aprel' 1918 gg.)*, (Kiev, 1962), pp. 236-240.

obliges working class members to participate more actively in party life.[22]

According to the Grozny uezd (county) spokesman:

Before the Revolution we had a small organization, consisting mainly of students. . . . After the Revolution work went at a feverish pace. Although we had only two or three party workers, they succeeded in moving about in all the factories organizing cells and quickly electing committees. They began to organize meetings and lectures. The intelligentsia did not join us, despite invitations. It is typical that among our speakers there was not a single intellectual. The workers were obliged to make do entirely with their own resources.[23]

Such accounts of the "withdrawal of the intelligentsia" indicate that the intellectuals were not only failing to join the bolsheviks in significant numbers, they were also becoming an ever smaller minority in the burgeoning hierarchy of party committees and organizers. The process appears to have been neither engineered nor wished for by the party leadership, but rather to have reflected political factors lying beyond their control.

Another source of information about the social composition of these 1917 recruits, to which we shall now turn, appears at first glance to contradict the evidence just discussed. Some years after the Revolution, the Statistical Department of the Central Committee attempted to estimate the social composition of the party membership at different stages of its history. The figures arrived at show no rise during 1917 in the proportion of party members drawn from the work-

[22] *VI S''ezd*, p. 89. [23] *Ibid.*, p. 93.

ing class. Indeed there is a slight fall (from 60 to 57 percent between January 1917 and January 1918).[24] This is accounted for in part by a sharp increase in peasant members (from 8 to 15 percent), who appear in the vast majority of cases to have joined the party in the army rather than in their villages.[25] But the interesting figure was that for *sluzhashchie* (salaried staff or white-collar workers) and others, i.e. those engaged in nonmanual occupations. This category declined by only 3 percent (from 32 percent to 29 percent) of the party membership in the course of 1917. This implies that some tens of thousands of persons employed in nonmanual occupations entered the party during the year of revolution, which at first glance conflicts with contemporary evidence of a "flight of the intelligentsia."

There are several possible explanations. First, there is evidence of an increase in the enlistment of nonmanual workers as the Bolshevik regime became established (see p. 75), and it is possible that this began on a sufficient scale as early as November and December 1917 to affect recruitment figures for the year. If we are right in suggesting that the Statistical Department arrived at its conservative estimate of party membership during this period by eliminating those who enrolled in the party, and then promptly dropped out of sight, the apparent contradiction in the evidence regarding the recruitment of nonmanual workers might be resolved by the hypothesis that while these did indeed constitute a small proportion of those enlisted in 1917, they tended to take their party membership more seriously and therefore more of them than of the manual workers stayed in the party long enough to be included in the Statistical De-

[24] Bubnov, in *BSE*, Vol. xi, col. 533.

[25] See answers to question 8 in the questionnaire issued to Sixth Congress delegates, *VI s"ezd*, pp. 319-390.

partment's count. This is pure speculation, but it is pertinent to note that in the 1920's white-collar recruits were acknowledged to be far more tenacious in preserving their party membership than any other social group (see pp. 108, 158).

The most likely explanation, however, is that the contemporary spokesmen and the party statisticians of the 1920's were simply talking about different groups. Although in the Soviet period the words *intelligentsia* and *sluzhashchie* converged in meaning, until they were used virtually interchangeably to denote nonmanual (white-collar) employment groups, their prerevolutionary meanings were quite different. The *sluzhashchie* were those engaged in service (*sluzhba*). Originally focused on government service, the term was extended to cover service in banking, transport, trading and other hierarchically structured organizations, and carried overtones of commitment to the established order. The *intelligentsia*, by contrast, consisted of those men and women of education, whatever their occupation or social status, who were oriented more or less *critically* towards the established order. Despite some ambiguity, contemporary references to a "flight of the intelligentsia" seem to refer by and large to this second group. On the other hand, in sections, at least, of the *sluzhashchie*, for example, sales assistants and junior office workers the party appears to have made some impact during 1917,[26] and it may well be that they provided a greater proportion of recruits than local leaders realized or were prepared to advertise.

We may say then that persons drawn from the prerevolutionary intelligentsia were a declining element in the Bolshevik Party during 1917, while greater prominence was as-

[26] For evidence from Moscow and Cheliabinsk, see *ibid.*, pp. 325, 382.

sumed by manual worker members and to a lesser extent by members drawn from the peasantry and the humbler levels of the white-collar class.

Civil War Expansion: Phase One

For the first year and a half after the bolshevik seizure of power, defective records continue to frustrate any precise account of changes in the party's composition. At the Seventh Congress in March 1918, the Credentials Commission contested the right of one delegate to attend, on the grounds that the organization he represented contained not 3,500 members, as was claimed, but more like 1,000, or even 500; whereupon one speaker commented that, if the membership attributed by other delegates to their organizations were to be systematically checked, a large proportion of them might find themselves excluded from the Congress.[27] A year later, on the eve of the Eighth Congress, the Central Committee Secretary Sverdlov estimated the total membership at about 700,000 whereas calculations made at the Congress itself on the basis of the reports of delegates suggested that it was more like 350,000.[28] This haziness about even such a basic fact as the crude size of the party is hardly surprising if one considers that, up to March 1919, the Central Committee

[27] *Sed'moi ekstrennyi s"ezd RKP(b): stenograficheskii otchët* (Moscow, 1962) pp. 115-116 (cited hereafter as *VII s"ezd*). The figure 390,000 bolsheviks at the time of the Seventh Congress shown in our table on p. 52 is derived from a recent calculation by the Institute of Marxism-Leninism attached to the CPSU Central Committee on the basis of local conference reports in the months preceding the Congress. (See *PZh*, No. 19, October 1967, p. 10.) It is clear, however, that these local figures were often far from accurate. As already noted, it was calculated by the Central Committee Statistical Department in the 1920's that membership in January 1918 was only 115,000 (see footnote 13).

[28] *Vos'moi s"ezd RKP(b): Protokoly* (Moscow, 1959), p. 280 (cited hereafter as *VIII s"ezd*).

was receiving regular reports from the party committees of only 3 out of the 36 guberniyas and 52 out of the 219 uezds, while with respect to 103 uezds the Central Committee did not even know whether or not party organizations were in existence.[29] It is further worth noting that even the most conservative of contemporary estimates appear grossly inflated if compared with those subsequently arrived at by the Statistical Department. The latter put membership in January 1919 at only 251,000.[30]

Whichever set of figures one employs, however, it appears that the party membership approximately doubled in the year and a half following the October Revolution. Bearing in mind that the communists[31] now constituted the ruling party, this growth is not very impressive. If the contemporary figures are accepted, it was numerically smaller than in the eight months *before* the seizure of power. It is true that a considerable amount of territory passed out of communist control during this period; some thousands of communists found themselves cut off in areas occupied by the Germans, and later by the White armies, and in such areas recruitment to the party was of course very limited. Many others lost their lives in the mounting Civil War (see p. 242). It is doubtful, however, if these facts fully account for the relatively modest growth during this period. More restrictive recruitment policies also appear to have played a part.

Despite the weakness of contemporary party records, there can be little doubt as to the massive enlistment of new members in the immediate aftermath of the October Revolution. Information given at the Seventh Congress in March 1918

[29] *Ibid.*, p. 496.
[30] Cited by Bubnov in *BSE*, Vol. xi, col. 531.
[31] The official title of the party was changed at the Seventh Congress (March 1918) from "Russian Social Democratic Workers' Party (bolsheviks)" to "Russian Communist Party (bolsheviks)."

indicates that those organizations whose membership was known with reasonable accuracy had been expanding rapidly, while dozens of new organizations had been formed.[32] This growth, moreover, was still highly spontaneous and subject to very little central guidance.[33] Membership trends were in fact just one of the many aspects of the party's internal affairs which the leadership had no time to give their attention to in the heat of establishing the new regime.

During the short breathing-space between the conclusion of the Brest-Litovsk Treaty and the outbreak of full-scale Civil War, however, the party began to take stock of itself. Internal party organization and discipline were discussed at a meeting of the Central Committee held on May 18, 1918.[34] The result was a resolution stating that "the harmony and discipline of our organizations have been seriously disturbed," and including among the reasons for this "the influx of broad masses into our party."[35] Local organizations were enjoined to take remedial measures. While the main stress was placed on party indoctrination and training and the proper functioning of local committees, the need was also indicated for ridding the party of "undesirable hangers-on" and for restricting entry, on the grounds that "the party may well suffer numerical losses, but it will gain in quality. It will also gain in strength."[36]

Among the devices employed by the Moscow, Petrograd and several local committees in pursuance of these objectives, perhaps the most important was the "membership reregistration," in which all persons wishing to remain in the party were, in effect, obliged to reapply, and their record and background were then supposed to be critically scrutinized to

[32] See *VII s"ezd*, pp. 3-4. [33] *Ibid.*, pp. 238-239.
[34] See Timofeevskii, *op.cit.*, p. 64.
[35] *P*, May 22, 1918. [36] *P*, May 19, 1918.

determine whether they were worthy of reenrollment. While the direct effect of these local reregistrations was later stated to have been rather limited,[37] there can be little doubt that they helped to tighten up party discipline and there were some areas, at least, where they brought a sharp drop in membership.[38]

At the Sixth Congress in August 1917 a clause had been inserted into the party rules stating that "new members are accepted by local party organizations upon recommendation by two party members and endorsement by the next general meeting of the members of the organization."[39] During the early months of 1918, however, this procedure was widely ignored and applicants were simply enrolled as members without any recommendation or scrutiny.[40] Following the May 18 resolution, not only was this rule more strictly applied, but many local committees reinforced it with additional requirements of their own, demanding more than two recommendations, laying down that those making recommendations must have been members themselves for some given period, publicly displaying the names of applicants and asking citizens to report anything against them, and finally, by establishing various kinds and degrees of associate or provisional membership.[41]

This last point deserves some elaboration. So-called sympathizers' groups, first recorded as early as January 1918,[42] had assumed considerable prominence by the summer of that year. Lenin himself took up the idea of sympathizers' groups

[37] See *Izv Ts K*, No. 8, December 2, 1919.
[38] Timofeevskii, *op.cit.*, p. 66. For reports of local reregistrations, see *P*, June 5, 8 and 23 and July 14, 1918.
[39] See *KPSS v rez*, Vol. I, p. 384.
[40] Timofeevskii, *op.cit.*, p. 105.
[41] *Ibid.*, pp. 66-67.   [42] See *P*, February 22, 1918.

at a meeting of the Moscow Committee on August 16,[43] and his suggestions underlay the rules for the groups subsequently adopted by the Committee.[44] The character of the groups varied considerably in different areas. Some were amorphous collections of hangers-on, others tight-knit bodies functioning under close supervision according to formal rules. While most were attached to party cells, others existed independently and were controlled directly by the local committees. In some places they were seen primarily as a form of association with the party for individuals supporting the bolshevik regime but with reservations about some aspect of its rules or objectives. More often they were envisaged rather as training-grounds for likely recruits to the party. Elsewhere their main function was to be what was later called a "driving-belt" between the local party committee and the masses.

The heyday of the sympathizers' groups, however, proved to be short-lived. During 1919 many of them came into disrepute either because joining them had become an empty formality obligatory upon certain categories of citizens, or because they were serving as an avenue for "careerists" of dubious antecedents to worm their way into the party. Some party committees reacted by tightening up requirements for admission to the groups, but many simply disbanded them.[45] Another factor contributing to the decline of their importance was the increasing use the party was able to make of such organizations as trade unions, poor peasants' organizations and women's and youth organizations as "driving-belts" to the masses. And finally, as a training-ground for party members the sympathizers' groups were soon being supplanted by the institution of periods of provisional or probationary mem-

[43] See Lenin, *Sochineniia*, Vol. xxxvii, pp. 46, 567.
[44] See *P*, August 22, 1918.
[45] See, e.g. *P*, July 23 and September 7, 1919.

bership (*kandidatskii stazh*). The status of "sympathizer" as a form of associate or novitiate membership was abolished in December 1919,[46] although it was destined to be revived for a time in the later 1920's and the 1930's (see pp. 202, 232).

The *kandidatskii stazh* also took a variety of forms. The period involved varied from one to nine months, and some organizations laid down different periods for different social groups. Everywhere, however, *kandidaty* (candidates or probationers) differed from "sympathizers" in that they were persons who had actually applied for party membership, who had met all formal requirements with respect to recommendations, etc., but whose acceptance as full members was made conditional upon their performance during the probationary period.[47] In December 1919 uniform provisions for candidates were approved by the Eighth Conference of the party and the following clauses inserted into the party rules.

5. All persons wishing to become members of the party undergo a period of probation, which is aimed at providing basic familiarity with the program and tactics of the party and checking the personal qualities of the candidates.

6. New members are accepted as candidates on the recommendation of two members of the party of six months standing, upon verification of their recommendations by the local party committee.

7. Workers and peasants are obliged to remain as candidates for no less than two months, and others for no less than six.

8. Candidates are entitled to attend open general meetings of the party organizations with a consultative voice.

[46] See *Vos'maia konferentsiia RKP(b): Protokoly* (Moscow, 1961), p. 140 (cited hereafter as *VIII konf.*).

[47] See Timofeevskii, *op.cit.*, pp. 66-67, 105-109.

9. Candidates pay the usual membership dues to the treasury of the local party committee.[48]

Unlike the "sympathizers," candidates have remained a permanent element in the CPSU although the rules governing them changed a number of times before assuming their present form in 1939.

Civil War Expansion: Phase Two

It would appear, then, that the relatively slow growth of the party between the October Revolution and the Eighth Congress in March 1919 was substantially due to the "reregistrations" and to the various measures introduced during the period to make entry more difficult. This was, in fact, implied at the Congress by Zinoviev, the official *rapporteur* on organizational matters. In pointing out that membership was only 350,000, and not the 700,000 estimated by Sverdlov, Zinoviev remarked that "we have been too cautious here. We have erected too many obstacles."[49]

These "obstacles" had been designed to preserve the proletarian character of the party and prevent its being swamped by "careerist elements." In the opinion of a number of Eighth Congress delegates, however, they were having the opposite effect. One local party representative had this to say: "We get directives from the center, telling us to be on our guard against too many workers getting into the party. Workers are not allowed into the party, but officials of the soviets, and all sorts of young ladies employed as typists can get in without delay."[50] One does not have to seek far for the reason. With the seizure of power, the majority of leading bolsheviks at all levels had moved into the key positions in the executive committees of the soviets, which now took over direct control of

[48] *KPSS v rez*, Vol. I, pp. 461-462.
[49] *VIII s"ezd*, p. 280.   [50] *Ibid.*, p. 173.

74

the remnants of the tsarist administration. The hierarchy of party committees was quickly displaced by the hierarchy of soviet executive committees as the main arm of the bolshevik leadership.[51] A measure of this is the fact that only a sixth of the delegates to the Eighth Congress were engaged full time in party work, while two-thirds of them held posts in the soviets.[52] But what of the junior staff of the soviet administration? In the struggle to establish an effective administration, men and women with administrative and office experience were precious and could not be replaced overnight by working class bolsheviks. At the same time, if they were willing to take out party membership, the regime could not but welcome this. By compromising them in the eyes of the "counterrevolutionaries," placing them under party discipline and exposing them to more intensive indoctrination, joining the party would surely enhance their reliability.

But this was not without its dangers. A number of speakers referred to the tendency for local communists to merge with soviet officialdom in a new privileged stratum, using their party membership to secure for themselves and their friends and relatives such advantages as extra rations, preference in housing and job promotion.[53] The extent to which party membership had already been reduced to a weapon in the scramble for jobs is illustrated by the following passage in Zinoviev's report: "There have been cases in Moscow where a man turns up at the raikom [district committee] at 8 p.m. to take out party membership, and when he is told to come back the next day, he replies: 'Do me a good turn, I'm going for a job tomorrow and I need a party card right away.' "[54]

[51] See Schapiro, *The CPSU*, p. 242.
[52] *VIII s"ezd*, p. 454.
[53] *Ibid.*, pp. 168-169, 177, 181-182.
[54] *Ibid.*, p. 294.

It was clear that the leadership had now decided that existing arrangements were inadequate to halt these tendencies, and a new approach was needed if the party was not to alienate the sympathies of the masses and cease to be an instrument adapted to the revolutionary transformation of society. The Eighth Congress decided on three measures to meet this situation: the doors of the party would be thrown "wide open" to workers and to working class and peasant youth; a highly selective policy would be pursued in the recruitment of persons who were neither workers nor peasants; and a general "reregistration" of all party members would be undertaken with a view to sifting out unsuitable people, special attention being paid to those who joined after October 1917.[55]

The general reregistration of mid-1919 developed into the first major purge of the party membership.[56] Its aim, as defined in a Central Committee instruction, was "the cleansing of the party of noncommunist elements, particularly people who have attached themselves to it because of its ruling position and who are using the title of party member in their personal interests." The operation was carried out by the local party committees, and the committee members themselves were not obliged to reregister. Communists wishing to retain their party membership were obliged to fill in a personal questionnaire, pay any arrears of dues, and present recommendations by two other members of at least six months' standing and known to the committee as reliable communists. The committee was instructed to refuse new party cards to the following groups: (1) persons convicted of "acts unworthy of a communist" (drunkenness, abuse of official posi-

[55] *Ibid.*, p. 423.
[56] It is recognized as such by official party historians. See Lenin, *Sochineniia*, Vol. xxxix, p. 506, footnote 89.

tion etc.); (2) deserters from the Red Army; (3) persons who had violated party instructions; (4) those failing to attend party meetings without proper cause; (5) nonpayers of membership dues. The "reregistration" was to be completed by July 1, 1919 and while it was on, no new members were to be admitted.[57]

A contemporary estimate put the number of withdrawals and expulsions occasioned by the "reregistration" at 10 to 15 percent in the cities, and "much higher" in the rural areas. The exact number, however, cannot be determined, because the "reregistration" was quickly overtaken by developments which applied even more potent surgery to the party membership. In the middle months of 1919, the Civil War entered a critical phase, the regime's chances of survival appeared to deteriorate rapidly, and, in an atmosphere of siege and semi-panic, all party members were declared subject to mobilization for service at the front. Scores of thousands thereupon withdrew from the party. All in all, as a result of the "reregistration," the mobilizations, loss of life and the contraction of Soviet-controlled territory, the party shrank between March and August 1919 from 350,000 to about 150,000.[58] Lenin commented: "The mobilization of communists for the war has helped us. The cowards and good-for-nothings have run away from the party. Good riddance. This reduction in the party's membership represents an enormous increase in its weight and strength."[59] This was all very well, but the evaporation of the party now clearly represented as serious a threat to the regime as had formerly its corruption.

[57] See *P*, April 24, 1919. The instruction may also be found in *Izv Ts K*, No. 1, May 28, 1919.

[58] *Izv Ts K*, No. 8, December 2, 1919.

[59] Lenin, *Sochineniia*, Vol. xxxix, p. 27.

So far nothing positive had been done in furtherance of the Eighth Congress decision to "throw the doors of the party wide open" to "healthy proletarian and peasant elements." On September 26, however, the Central Committee decided on a crash program to implement this decision. A few weeks earlier the Petrograd Committee had held a "party week," during which the formalities attaching to enlistment in the party were reduced to a minimum and an active campaign was conducted to induce workers to join. The Central Committee now decided to launch such a "party week" on a national scale. Recruitment meetings were to be held in factories and barracks, at which a general invitation would be issued to enlist on the spot, the usual requirement of two recommendations in writing being waived (although subsequent endorsement by the existing members of the cell was still required). Communist officials were expected to go out to their former places of work and each recruit at least one new member. At the same time committees were cautioned to limit recruitment strictly to workers, peasants and Red Army men, and to emphasize at recruitment meetings the strains and responsibilities of party membership rather than its privileges.

In numerical terms, "party week" was a striking success. New recruits numbered at least 160,000.[60] This expansion continued in the following months. Party membership rose from 430,000 at the beginning of 1920, to over 600,000 by the Ninth Congress in March 1920, and to almost three-quarters of a million by the Tenth Congress in March 1921.[61]

[60] An early estimate put the figure at 160,000 to 180,000; see *Izv Ts K*, No. 8, December 2, 1919. Later a figure "over 200,000" was suggested (*ibid.*, No. 15, March 24, 1920).

[61] Bubnov in *BSE*, Vol. XI, col. 531. Cf. *PZh*, No. 19, October 1967, pp. 9-10.

The influx of new members led to a large extension of the network of party cells in industrial plants, especially in the major centers. Some organizations sought to help this process along by concentrating special recruitment efforts on those plants and factories lacking a party cell, while others set about systematically redistributing party members in the factories so as to achieve the necessary minimum number of members to form a party cell in as many factories as possible.[62]

It was also at this period that the party first began to establish itself on any scale in the rural areas. The Ninth Congress resolved to give special priority to expanding party organizational and propaganda activities among the peasantry,[63] and to this end the Central Committee dispatched 135 party workers to the various guberniyas (provinces). By September 1920 these had gathered around them a corps of 307 organizers stationed in guberniya and uezd (county) headquarters, and 1,564 working in the volosts (rural cantons) themselves.[64] These organizers had the task of selecting and training agitators to be sent to the villages to form the nucleus of village cells. As a result of these efforts in urban and rural areas alike, the number of party cells doubled during 1920.[65]

As we have seen, however, Lenin and the other bolshevik leaders constantly stressed that numerical growth did not necessarily mean a "healthy" party membership, and once one looks beyond the question of numbers, the success of this second phase of mass recruitment appears more equivocal.

[62] See Timofeevskii, op.cit., pp. 142-143.
[63] KPSS v rez, Vol. I, p. 500.
[64] Izv Ts K, No. 22, September 18, 1920.
[65] See Timofeevskii, op.cit., pp. 143-145.

The ostensible aim of the "reregistration" purge and the mass intake initiated by "party week" was to replace "corrupt and careerist elements" by "healthy proletarian elements of town and country," and so to counter the drift towards "bureaucratization" of the party. And yet the first thing that happened to the majority of these "healthy elements" was that they were absorbed into the bureaucracy. The party leaders made no bones about this. At the Eighth Congress, Zinoviev explicitly linked the need for large-scale recruitment with the demand for party members to staff the burgeoning state apparatus.[66] Nor was there any attempt to play this down when addressing the potential recruits themselves. Lenin, for example, issued the following appeal at the launching of "party week."

Join the party, comrades, nonparty workers and laboring peasants! We are not handing you any privileges, we are calling on you for hard work, for the job of building the state. If you are a sincere supporter of communism, set to this job more boldly, do not be afraid of the novelty and difficulty of the job, do not be put off by the prejudice that only people with administrative training can do this work. Rank-and-file workers and laboring peasants in ever greater number can and must lead the work of building socialism.[67]

Furthermore, the potential recruit had only to look at how the current membership was employed to see what effect enlistment was likely to have on his position. Analysis of a large representative sample of party members in October

[66] *VIII s"ezd*, p. 281.
[67] Lenin, *Sochineniia*, Vol. XXXIX, p. 226. For similar statements, see *ibid.*, pp. 225 and 234-235. The appeal was printed in *Pravda* and *Izvestiia* on October 12, 1919.

1919 showed that only 11 percent of them were now working in factories. Over 60 percent were employees of the state or party administration. A quarter were in the Red Army, but of these a large part undoubtedly occupied positions of military or political authority. Thus, the proportion of communists remaining in rank-and-file positions can scarcely have been more than one in five, and may have been far less.[68]

It is clear, then, that the factory worker or peasant entering the party at this time had every reason to expect fairly early transfer to a position of greater responsibility. Nor, on the whole, would his expectations have been disappointed. Summing up the results of "party week" towards the end of October 1919, Lenin wrote that "it is necessary *boldly* to give them [the recruits] the most varied state work, in order to try them out in practice."[69] In many cases, where they were not ready for immediate posting to responsible jobs, they should be assigned to "control" ex-tsarist officials and specialists, while at the same time learning to take over from them.[70] At the Eighth Party Conference in December 1919, in an official report on the training and employment of new recruits, Bukharin described the harnessing of them to work of administrative and social (*obshchestvennyi*) responsibility as "our central task."[71]

From the vantage point of the historian, it now seems obvious that the party leadership was proceeding to expose the new crop of communists to precisely those influences

[68] See *Izv Ts K*, No. 15, March 24, 1920. The sample covered 17,312 members. Though treated by the Central Committee as representative, it is doubtful whether very sophisticated methods were employed to ensure this.

[69] Lenin, *Sochineniia*, Vol. xxxix, p. 235.

[70] *Ibid.*, p. 236.

[71] *VIII konf.*, p. 161. For the official "theses" on the employment of new party members, see *ibid.*, pp. 200-202.

81

which had led to the "corruption" and "careerism" of so many of their predecessors. If, however, they showed little awareness of this problem, this was due neither to hypocrisy nor stupidity, but rather to their acceptance of the following three propositions which seemed not unreasonable in the light of their outlook and circumstances:

1. Genuine proletarians and "exploited" peasants were far less likely to succumb to the temptations of office than persons drawn from the white-collar, intellectual and well-to-do strata generally.

2. Although some danger of "bureaucratization" of working class communists nevertheless existed, this could be countered provided certain precautionary measures were taken. Thus the Eighth Congress resolved that communists who were members of soviets should give fortnightly reports to their electors and those former workers who were now on full-time administrative work should return to their factory for at least one month in four.[72] Much faith was invested in the efficacy of the probationary period (*kandidatskii stazh*) which was made general in the party, as we have seen, at the Eighth Conference in December 1919.

3. Persons assuming the risks and strains of party membership when the regime had its back to the wall must certainly be convinced supporters of communism, rather than hangers-on with selfish motives. As the written report of the Central Committee to the Eighth Conference put it, "a party membership ticket under these circumstances meant something approaching a candidature for Denikin's gallows."[73]

Plausible as these propositions may have seemed at the time, the external observer may well see cause for skepticism.

[72] *VIII s"ezd*, pp. 423-424.
[73] *Izv Ts K*, No. 8, December 2, 1919.

The belief in the relative incorruptibility of the proletarian appeared to rest partly on a highly questionable assumption of perceived solidarity of interests with the regime, and partly on a Marxian equivalent of the myth of the "noble savage." In any case, there is little in the subsequent history of the CPSU to add to its credibility. The provisions for ex-worker communists to maintain contact with their old milieu and for putting new members through their paces as probationers were, perhaps, useful in themselves, but their value was impaired far more than was realized by the practical difficulties involved, especially under Civil War conditions, and the tendency of such devices in any human association to be applied formalistically. The confidence placed in "Denikin's gallows" and the lack of immediate material reward as deterrents to "careerism" and "bureaucratization" betrayed a simplistic understanding of the mechanisms whereby men may be corrupted by power and office.

When we turn to the empirical evidence, we find ample justification for these doubts. Firstly, it seems highly unlikely that the losses of membership due to the "reregistration" purge and the withdrawal of "cowards" in mid-1919 were confined mainly to people who had joined the party for careerist reasons *after* its attainment of power. The October 1919 analysis of party membership referred to earlier showed that 12 percent of the sample had joined the party between the February and October Revolutions and 20 percent between the October Revolution and December 1918. Since there was probably about the same number of recruits during these two periods, this indicates that the attrition of members who joined in the months before the seizure of power was considerably higher than that of members who joined in the months following it.[74]

[74] *Ibid.*, No. 15, March 24, 1920.

Secondly, we must consider the results of the second general "reregistration" of party members, which took place between August and October 1920. The initial purpose of this reregistration was the issuing of new uniform membership cards approved and distributed by the Central Committee, which put an end to the confused diversity of cards previously issued by local organizations on their own authority. At the same time, however, local organizations were instructed to make it the occasion for "cleansing the party of noncommunist elements, and chiefly of persons who have attached themselves to the party because of its ruling position and employing the title of party member in their personal interests."[75] No figures were published on the numbers excluded from the party as a whole during the second general reregistration. In Petrograd the proportion was 10 percent, in the Sokolniki raion of Moscow 9 percent, while in Ufa it was 34 percent. In general the percentage of expulsions was lower in major industrial centers, and higher in smaller towns and rural districts. Apart from expulsions, many members simply did not present themselves for reregistration, but took advantage of the occasion to quietly drop out of the party. In Kronstadt this applied to fully a quarter of all communists, a fact which assumes considerable interest in view of the rising against the party leadership there six months later.[76] The scale of expulsions and withdrawals from the party during the second reregistration would appear to call in question the adequacy of the factors relied on in the latter part of the Civil War to keep "unworthy" people out of the party. Even more telling in this regard, perhaps, were the results of the 1921 purge of "bureaucratized and corrupt elements," which, as we shall see, cost the party a quarter of its membership.

[75] See *ibid.*, No. 20, August 18, 1920.
[76] See Timofeevskii, *op.cit.*, pp. 151-154.

And finally, we may consider the changes in the social composition of the party in this period. If we were to judge by the official statements reported above, we would expect some increase in the nonproletarian element in the first eighteen months following the seizure of power, and rapid proletarianization of membership thereafter. There is a little contemporary evidence which supports this. One analysis claimed that most of those lost to the party as a result of the "reregistration" and mobilization of communists in mid-1919 were drawn from the intelligentsia and lower middle classes.[77] A breakdown of the recruits brought in during "party week" estimated that in the towns 47 percent of them were workers and 53 percent Red Army men, while in the rural districts 69 percent were workers, 10 percent Red Army men and 20 percent peasants.[78] However, the subsequent calculations of the changing social composition of the party undertaken by the Statistical Department, reproduced in Table 1,[79] give an entirely different picture.

TABLE 1: OFFICIAL CLASS ANALYSIS OF THE PARTY, 1917-1921

Year	Workers Percent	Peasants Percent	White-collar workers and others Percent
1917	60.2	7.5	32.2
1918	56.9	14.5	28.6
1919	47.8	21.8	30.4
1920	43.8	25.1	31.1
1921	41.0	28.2	30.8

[77] *Izv Ts K*, No. 8, December 2, 1919.
[78] *Ibid.*, No. 15, March 24, 1920.
[79] SOURCE: Bubnov in *BSE*, Vol. XI, col. 534.

Two comments are in order on this table. Firstly, the figures purport to represent neither current occupation, nor the occupation of one's father ("social origin") but basic occupation *on the eve of the Revolution*.[80] Secondly, their precision should not be exaggerated. On the one hand, imperfect records would make them at best an approximation, particularly during the first half of the period. On the other hand, the advantages of proletarian status and suspicion of "class alien elements" prompted many recruits to conceal or distort their prerevolutionary background. This was a point that was later made much of by the "Workers' Opposition,"[81] while "concealment of class origin" was a formula frequently used to justify expulsions from the party during the 1920's and 1930's (e.g. this applied to 13 percent of those expelled from the Leningrad Party Organization during the 1933 purge).[82] As against this, there were apparently cases where local committees registered members not in terms of their basic prerevolutionary occupation, but in terms of their current employment.[83] While no adjustment of the official breakdown to allow for these factors is possible on the available information, on balance there was probably some inflation of the percentage of communists recorded as "working class."

Notwithstanding these difficulties in the official figures, the trends they indicate seem marked enough to draw some general conclusions. What is most striking is that the proportion of working class communists, far from increasing, declined steadily throughout the years of revolution and Civil War. From three in five at the time of the fall of tsarism, it had

[80] Later a different basis was employed. See p. 159.

[81] See, e.g. *X s"ezd RKP(b): stenograficheskii otchët* (Moscow, 1963), p. 75 (cited hereafter as *X s"ezd*).

[82] See *PZh*, No. 20, October 1947, p. 78.

[83] See Timofeevskii, *op.cit.*, p. 149.

sunk to two in five by the final victory of the communist regime. The beneficiaries were the peasants, who increased
from a negligible element in 1917 to over a quarter of the
membership at the end of the Civil War. But it is interesting
to observe that this increase of peasant membership was
achieved at the expense of the workers, and *not* of the intelligentsia and white-collar strata. The latter remained remarkably stable at a little under one-third of the membership
throughout the period. It is particularly worthy of note that,
contrary to contemporary expectations, the convulsions of
1919 actually produced a slight *increase* in the proportion of
white-collar people in the party, while this group must have
provided nearly 200,000 of the recruits entering the party in
the mass intake initiated by "party week."

Certain important conclusions emerge from this account
of party membership changes during the Civil War.

1. Although the leadership attempted to regulate the composition of the party, actual changes tended to diverge radically from those intended.

2. There was an evident tension between the need to associate communists with the administration of the country
and the concern to maintain vital links with the laboring
masses. In practice it was the second motive that tended to
give way, owing to pressing practical necessities and probably
also to the outlook and motives of the members themselves.

3. People drawn from the white-collar and educated strata
continued to be very strongly overrepresented in the party in
proportion to population, despite active measures to proletarianize the membership.

These matters deserve special emphasis, since they persisted in subsequent periods and their varied manifestations,
in fact, provide much of the subject matter of this book.

Chapter 2

Victory—and a Purge

ALTHOUGH THE bolsheviks termed their seizure of power a socialist revolution, they had decided in advance neither on a concrete program of social changes nor on the institutional mechanisms through which their revolution would be implemented. Partly this was a matter of ideology: as Marxists, they were not inclined either to consider details of policy abstracted from the actual circumstances (the "balance of class forces") at the moment of their implementation, or to give much thought to the structure of institutions—what mattered was not the mechanism itself, but who (what class) operated the mechanism, and in whose interests. These were facets of Marxist thinking on which Lenin laid particular emphasis. More than this, however, the bolshevik lack of blueprints for revolutionary policies and institutions was due to their expectation that the revolution would quickly spread to the major industrial countries of Western Europe, and in particular to Germany, which, being more advanced economically, would take the lead in "building socialism." An argument over the possibility of building "socialism in one country" would have seemed absurd at this early period, when no one seriously envisaged the survival of the "proletarian revolution" in isolation in backward Russia. Survive it did, however, and since the basic questions of ends and means had not been settled in advance, it is not surprising that they made themselves felt with growing insistency as the communist regime consolidated itself.

The social and political order with which Russia emerged from the Civil War was the result of improvised solutions to

multifarious urgent problems where the one constant preoccupation was survival. The raw material on which the bolshevik leaders worked, moreover, was not just the old tsarist
society, but that society as modified by the forces which their
own Revolution had set in motion: the peasants seizing the
land, the workers seizing the factories, artists asserting absolute freedom of creation, libertarians proclaiming the demise
of "bourgeois" morality and so on. The resultant amalgam,
"war communism," although to some it seemed the embryo
of the future communist millennium, was neither a coherent
whole nor a logically necessary projection of Marxist theory.
As we have seen, "war communism" in its political and administrative aspects involved a swing from persuasion to
coercion, from spontaneity to discipline, from the proletarian
amateur to the bourgeois expert, from workers' control and
participation to centralized bureaucratic management and
administration.

These processes evoked sharp resentment in various sections of the population. Peasant hostility over the armed
requisitions was restrained only by fear of the greater evil of
restoration of the landlords. The workers had to suffer not
only intense material deprivation, but the thwarting of their
syndicalist impulses: what sort of a proletarian revolution
was it when the worker had to jump to the orders of a privileged stratum of communist officials and bourgeois experts?

A sense of frustration was scarcely less marked within the
party itself. Here bureaucratization had taken the form first
of the absorption of the leading party strata into the government and soviet administration, and then, beginning in 1919,
of the creation of a full-time party apparatus, superimposed
on that of the soviets, which increasingly reduced the life of
local party organizations to an appendage of its essentially
administrative activities. As improved records and communi-

89

cations permitted effective centralized direction of party cadres, the precarious balance which had existed between the elective and appointive principles in the choice of party committees was destroyed, and the latter, increasingly dominated by their secretaries, were converted into a hierarchy of agents of the Center, no longer answerable to the generality of party members in any real sense. These trends could not fail to arouse misgivings among many communists and to provoke moves to preserve features of the party which many felt to be essential: the internal democracy which had tempered its centralized structure, and its identification with the working class. In 1919 and 1920 factions which became known as the Democratic Centralists and the Workers' Opposition emerged to articulate these attitudes.

So long as the cause of the Revolution was in danger, these various resentments and criticisms were held in check. As the Civil War drew to a close, however, they erupted in a series of direct challenges to the authority of the party leadership. There was a crop of local peasant revolts. Serious strikes occurred, even in Petrograd itself, at which communists were sometimes removed from mass strike meetings. At the Kronstadt naval base, one of the strongholds of the Revolution, a mutiny broke out aimed at replacing the communist dictatorship with newly elected soviets representative of all "worker and peasant parties." The mutiny was supported by a substantial proportion of Kronstadt communists, and sympathy strikes occurred in other centers. Within the party itself, the opposition passed from general charges of bureaucratization to rejection of specific Central Committee policies and nominees. The Central Committee themselves unwittingly reinforced this development. Finding themselves divided on the proper role of the trade unions, they allowed the election of delegates to the Tenth Congress (March 1921) to be con-

90

tested by the supporters of different "platforms" on the trade union question, thereby permitting the Workers' Opposition and Democratic Centralists to challenge Central Committee adherents electorally on an issue providing an ideal focus for their resentments.

The Tenth Congress Decisions

The party leadership met this multiple challenge, which came to a head at the time of the Tenth Congress, by a combination of repression and appeasement. On the one hand the Kronstadt rising and local peasant violence were put down with the utmost severity, and noncommunist groups, particularly the Mensheviks and Socialist Revolutionaries, were deprived of the last vestiges of political freedom. On the other hand a series of measures was launched to relieve the major economic grievances of the rural and urban masses: the grain requisitions were replaced by a graduated tax in kind, and private enterprise was revived in trade and cautiously extended to industry, especially the consumer branches. Within a year or two this "New Economic Policy" (NEP) had substantially revived production, and moderated the hardships of the Civil War era.[1]

The stick and the carrot were likewise employed to deal with intraparty opposition. The Tenth Congress decision "On the Syndicalist and Anarchist Deviation in Our Party" outlawed the ideas of the Workers' Opposition,[2] while that "On Party Unity" condemned all factionalism and provided for expulsion from the party of communists convicted of joining together to promote "platforms" at variance with official

---

[1] On the early stages of NEP, see E. H. Carr, *The Bolshevik Revolution 1917-1923* (London, 1952), Vol. 11, Chap. xix.

[2] *X s"ezd*, pp. 574-576.

policies.[3] At the same time the leadership promised measures which appeared to go a long way towards meeting opposition criticism. There was to be regular discussion of public issues at all levels of the party, the Eighth Congress decision about giving ex-worker communists a "spell" back on the factory floor was to be implemented, the precise employment of communists posted by the Center was to be left as far as possible to the local committees, and there was to be a "cleansing" of the party of "noncommunist elements" (elsewhere identified as "petty-bourgeois-intellectual and semi-intellectual elements") and their replacement by workers.[4] This program was labeled "workers' democracy"—a title which clearly betrays a concern to undercut the opposition.

It has been necessary for two reasons to depart at some length from our central theme to outline the developments which culminated in the decisions of the Tenth Congress: firstly because the general political background has rarely been so directly relevant to party membership policies, and secondly because these developments and these decisions proved decisive for the whole future history of the party. There is no need, however, to follow up their consequences in detail. The positive achievements of "workers' democracy" appear to have been negligible, and, indeed, could scarcely have been otherwise with the ban on "factionalism" hamstringing all independent thinking and initiative. The authority of the established leadership, by now institutionalized in the Political Bureau (Politburo) of the Central Committee, became further entrenched, and was enforced with growing single-mindedness and efficiency by the hierarchy of party

---

[3] *Ibid.*, pp. 571-573. Point 7 of this decision, containing the punitive provisions, was not made public till the Thirteenth Party Conference in 1924.

[4] *Ibid.*, pp. 564-566.

secretaries, headed, beginning in 1922, by General Secretary Stalin.[5]

We may now look more closely at the impact of the 1921 crisis on party membership policies. The Tenth Congress, as we have seen, resolved on a purge of "noncommunist elements," directed particularly at white-collar groups, and a reorientation of recruitment to focus closely on the workers. This is exactly what the Workers' Opposition had been advocating for months. Right up to the eve of the congress, however, opposition spokesmen expressing such views had been labeled "Makhaevites," "Makhaevism" being a heresy which consisted of treating the intelligentsia as a parasitic class exploiting the workers through their monopoly of specialized knowledge.[6]

What caused this partial convergence of official and opposition views? The cause undoubtedly lay in the alarming signs of the isolation of the regime which were thrust on the party leadership at the time of the congress. Bukharin, in his organizational report to the congress, referred to the policy of cleansing the party and increasing the percentage of workers as one on which a very wide measure of agreement could be attained within the party, and mentioned that similar provisions had been included in a number of rival "platforms," including that of the Workers' Opposition. The context of these remarks was a discussion of the need to rally

[5] See Leonard Schapiro, *The Origin of the Communist Autocracy* (London, 1955), Chap. XVII.

[6] See *X s"ezd*, p. 269. For the ideas of Waclaw Machajski (A. Vol'skii), the originator of the "Makhaevite" heresy, and the storm caused by this heresy within the prerevolutionary Russian socialist movement, see Max Nomad, *Rebels and Renegades* (New York, 1932), Chap. v, and L. Martov et al., *Obshchestvennoe dvizhenie v Rossii v nachale XX veka* (St. Petersburg, 1909-1914), Vol. III, pp. 523-533.

the party ideologically in the face of external threat.[7] This suggests that this turn of policy may be regarded in part as a Central Committee concession to its critics for the sake of unity. And certainly, although differences of emphasis remained (Bukharin claimed that the Workers' Opposition wanted to push otherwise sensible party membership policies to the point of absurdity),[8] the Tenth Congress did achieve something approaching a consensus on this issue.

But the need to moderate internal party differences was only one aspect. More important, perhaps, was the mounting evidence—in the form of strikes, withdrawal of worker communists from the party,[9] the removal of communists from workers' meetings and finally the Kronstadt mutiny—that the Workers' Opposition were, after all, perfectly right in asserting that the isolation of the party from the industrial proletariat had assumed dangerous proportions. Now that the end of the Civil War had left the party face to face with a hostile peasantry, the need to assure its rear by rebuilding bridges to the urban working class was particularly urgent.

There is, finally, a third aspect. However much the various factions disagreed in their diagnosis of the party's internal difficulties, they were unanimous that "petty bourgeois" influences were in some way involved. The switch from War Communism to the New Economic Policy now threatened a vast intensification of such influences. The revival of capitalist relationships, first in the countryside, and then increas-

---

[7] *X s"ezd*, pp. 230-231.   [8] *Ibid.*, pp. 330-331.

[9] Some observers believed that the withdrawal of proletarians from the party had now assumed a mass scale; e.g. *ibid.*, pp. 236-237. Bukharin attempted to contest this by pointing to the big numerical growth of the party since the previous congress (*ibid.*, p. 326), without, however, offering any class breakdown of the new members. As we saw in Table 1, the proportion of working class communists fell by 3 percent between January 1920 and January 1921.

ingly in the towns as well, created a social environment which rendered it ever more difficult for party members to maintain their identification with the working class and their Marxist outlook, particularly if they were working in the state or economic administration. As Zinoviev was later to put it, the party member was now required "on the one hand to be a model of communism, on the other a model businessman."[10] No Marxist could fail to discern here a most serious threat to the integrity of the regime and the revolutionary cause. Although these implications were but dimly perceived at the time of the Tenth Congress, when only the first steps were being taken towards NEP, they were subsequently invoked as the chief reason for maintaining the Tenth Congress membership policies, with their strong proletarian orientation. A year later, for example, the Eleventh Congress was to resolve as follows:

. . . the party, in view of the inescapability of a partial revival of capitalism, has to take an active part in regulating the relationships resulting from this fact. It is now required of the party member that he learn how to trade profitably in the interests of the state while at the same time avoiding cutting himself off from the masses. On the one hand, the most active section of the party membership has to dive head first into economic and commercial activities, which are now associated with capitalist relationships. On the other hand, these same active party members have to fight in the most energetic manner against capitalist relationships and show the masses the true path to socialism while setting an example of self-sacrificing work for its realization.

[10] *Odinnadtsatyi s"ezd RKP(b): stenograficheskii otchët* (Moscow, 1961), p. 395 (cited hereafter as *XI s"ezd*).

95

The circumstances of the transition period undoubtedly conceal a potential deterioration of the party's composition and its infection with petty bourgeois influences. The basic proletarian cadre of the party must at all times be aware of this danger and take all the measures against it which follow from this concatenation of conditions.[11]

We may conclude, then, that the membership policies pursued by the party leadership in the early 1920's, which consisted of seeking to raise working class membership, restricting entry of white-collar groups, and ridding the party of "petty bourgeois elements," flowed naturally from the critical conditions facing the party at this juncture and the leadership's reaction to these conditions: its concern to find common ground, wherever possible, with the party opposition; its realization that the isolation of the party from the urban workers had reached a dangerous level; and its concern to counter bourgeois influences anticipated from the NEP.

The 1921 Purge

Moves to implement the decision to undertake a general purge of the party began three months after the Tenth Congress. On June 21, 1921 Lenin submitted to the Politburo his proposals on the objectives and organization of the purge, and these formed the basis of a Politburo decision issued four days later.[12] The following month was taken up with creating machinery for the purge and instructing local organizations. A hierarchy of purge commissions was set up, formally independent of local party committees, and staffed, as far as possible, by members of prerevolutionary standing. These

[11] *Ibid.*, pp. 546-547.
[12] Lenin, *Sochineniia*, Vol. XLIII, pp. 361, 460, footnote 120; *P*, June 30, 1921.

commissions were to check the credentials, record and reputation of every communist, paying special attention, however, to those of bourgeois, white-collar or intelligentsia origin and to those in government service. Particular vigilance was enjoined with respect to former members of other political parties and former tsarist officials. So far as workers were concerned, the formalities were to be cut to a minimum. Care and discrimination were required in checking peasant members. "Kulak elements" should be rooted out, but genuine "poor peasants" were not to be antagonized but should be kept in the party "at all costs."[13]

The purge itself began in August 1921; it was completed in most areas by the end of the year but in some places dragged on through 1922. The number expelled or withdrawing voluntarily in the course of the purge amounted to nearly a quarter of the total membership. The main charges were passivity, careerism, failing to carry out party instructions, drunkenness, corruption, practicing religion and joining the party with counterrevolutionary aims. Of those party members registered as workers, only one in six was expelled, compared with over a third of the "white-collar workers and others" and two-fifths of the peasants.[14]

[13] *SPR*, No. 2, pp. 74-78; *P*, July 27, 1921.

[14] *Sotsial'nyi i natsional'nyi sostav VKP(b): Itogi vsesoiuznoi partiinoi perepisi 1927 goda* (Moscow, 1927), p. 16; *Izv Ts K*, No. 41, April 1922. One by-product of the purge was to highlight the continued inadequacies of party records. Thus, the Don Oblast Committee reported that "it was revealed during the purge that records had been maintained in the Don Committee fearfully chaotically and so inaccurately that instead of the 5,000 members shown on the records, there were actually 9,000 in the organization." See P. V. Barchukov, *Vosstanovitel'nyi period na Donu (1921-1925 gg.): sbornik dokumentov* (The Reconstruction Period on the Don [1921-1925]: Collection of Documents), (Rostov, 1962), p. 131. This presumably resulted from the failure of local committees to record

To what extent was the 1921 purge used by the leadership to punish or discipline the opposition? In launching the purge, Lenin had said that "all members of the Russian Communist Party who are in the slightest degree suspicious or unreliable or have not demonstrated their steadiness should be got rid of."[15] It is hard to believe that this and similar statements[16] were not intended to include the various groupings which had recently been a thorn in the side of the Central Committee, especially when we recall that the Tenth Congress decision on the "Syndicalist and Anarchist Deviation" (i.e. the Workers' Opposition) had alleged that this deviation was partly occasioned by the penetration of the party by noncommunist elements with a petty bourgeois back-

---

many communists returning from the Red Army, and is most unlikely to have been confined to this one area. If it was at all widespread, party membership must have been considerably higher on the eve of the purge than contemporary records revealed, and party losses during the purge may therefore have been far greater than indicated by the official figures.

[15] Lenin, *Sochineniia*, Vol. XLIII, p. 361.

[16] See, e.g. *ibid.*, Vol. XLIV, p. 124. That the purge was intended to combat "wrong" political thinking as well as careerism and moral corruption becomes even clearer in the statements of regional party authorities. A resolution on the implementation of the Tenth Congress decisions passed by a regional party conference in June 1921 referred as follows to the forthcoming purge: "The Tenth Congress categorically proclaimed the necessity of unity in the party at the present time. In order to strengthen the party and prepare it for its new tasks, in order for this party to remain organized and authoritative in the eyes of the proletariat and the peasantry, it is necessary immediately to undertake a purge of the party of all elements who have attached themselves to it or found their way into it by chance, and to begin an immediate struggle with the wavering and ideological deviation of members of the Russian Communist Party." V. Osipov et al., eds., *Saratovskaia partiinaia organizatsiia v gody vosstanovleniia narodnogo khoziaistva* (Saratov, 1960), p. 37.

ground,[17] which was one of the categories against which the purge was specifically directed. At the same time the leadership was most insistent that this was not intended. "Deviations" were not among the reasons given for expulsion, and the Central Committee circular on the purge specifically warned that "repressions aimed at people with other ideas in the party (against members of the former 'Workers' Opposition,' for example) are in no case permissible."[18] There is a certain amount of negative evidence which might be taken as suggesting that the spirit of this injunction was observed. No *prominent* oppositionist appears to have been expelled during the purge. Complaints by "former" oppositionists of victimization by local purge commissions are conspicuous by their absence, despite the fact that disaffected communists were still quite vocal in alleging other forms of discrimination, and at the Eleventh Congress, for instance, the Central Committee was accused of employing its powers of appointment to demote and "exile" its critics.[19] At the same time it must have been a rare purge commission member who was not more apt to discern signs of unreliability in the critically outspoken communist than in his more docile comrades, while certain of the purge criteria, especially "refusal to carry out party directives" (which accounted for 11 percent of all expulsions),[20] were almost made to order for opposi-

[17] *X s"ezd*, p. 574.   [18] *P*, July 27, 1921.

[19] See, e.g. *XI s"ezd*, p. 127.

[20] *Izv Ts K*, No. 40, March 1922. Local committees were not always as circumspect as Moscow in avoiding formulations which could be regarded as incitement to the victimization of oppositionists. A letter from the Vladimir gubkom and guberniya purge commission to ukoms on the tasks of party cells in connection with the purge, included the following passage: "All noncommunist people and those who do not submit easily to communist reprocessing (*obrabotka*) and manifest nonproletarian moods, since they are garbage from the party's point of view, should be decisively chucked

tionists. Nor can it be doubted that oppositionists were included among the many communists who withdrew voluntarily from the party at this period. In the Samara guberniya, 35 percent of the party membership resigned when the Central Committee dismissed the oppositionist leadership of the guberniya committee.[21]

Recruitment Policy: 1921-1923

As we have noted, the Tenth Congress resolved not only on a purge of the existing membership, but on a definite policy towards the admission of new members. This had both a negative aspect—admission should be more strictly selective—and a positive one—there should be an effort to build up the proletarian element. In practice, to quote one of the delegates to the Eleventh Congress, "the whole second, positive part—the drawing in of new masses of workers throughout the length and breadth of Russia—came to nothing. No work whatsoever was undertaken to this end."[22]

The Tenth Congress itself introduced the first of a series of restrictive measures which became the central feature of party recruitment policy during the next three years. The names of persons wishing to join the party were to be announced in advance, so that fellow-workers would have the opportunity of giving any information they might possess suggesting their unsuitability; those recommending recruits had to be members of at least one year's standing (it had

---

out (*vykinuty*)." See V. G. Mochalov, *Vladimirskaia partiinaia organizatsiia v gody vosstanovleniia narodnogo khoziaistva (1921-1925 gody): sbornik dokumentov* (The Vladimir Party Organization in the Years of Reconstruction of the Economy [1921-25]: Collection of Documents), (Vladimir, 1963), p. 63.

[21] See Timofeevskii, *op.cit.*, pp. 229-230.

[22] *XI s"ezd*, p. 463.

formerly been six months), and should the recruit violate party discipline the recommending persons were themselves made subject to punishment (including expulsion from the party if the mistake were repeated); the probationary period was extended from six months to a year for recruits who were "neither workers nor peasants" (i.e. mainly white-collar groups).[23]

The rate of recruitment appears to have slowed down immediately, and during the purge it was stopped altogether, with the exception of a trickle described as workers and peasants "who had demonstrated their devotion to the revolution during the Civil War and manifested a conscious attitude towards communism." The Eleventh Congress in November 1921 resolved to retain this arrangement until the next Congress.[24]

The Eleventh Congress, which met in March 1922, established three recruitment categories: (1) workers and Red Army men of worker or peasant origin; (2) peasants and handicraftsmen (other than those serving in the Army); (3) others (white-collar workers, etc.). Existing admission rules were amended to increase discrimination between these categories, with respect to the number of recommendations required and the minimum length of membership of those making recommendations, the administrative level on which final approval was necessary, and, in particular, the length of the probationary period. Category one were now required to spend six months as candidates, category two, a full year and category three, two years. These provisions were intended to remain in force at least until the next party congress.[25]

A year later the Twelfth Congress reduced the number of recommendations required for worker recruits and resolved

[23] *KPSS v rez*, Vol. I, pp. 520-521.
[24] *Ibid.*, p. 597.   [25] *Ibid.*, pp. 623-624.

to put a moratorium on the transfer of nonworkers from candidate to full-member status—to last until the Thirteenth Congress.[26]

The edge of these restrictive measures was quite clearly set against nonworkers, and especially against white-collar groups. The results, however, were very disappointing. The proportion of working class communists (this was still measured in terms of prerevolutionary occupation) rose by 3 percent during the purge year of 1921, and then remained unchanged at 44 percent for the next two years.[27] It was clear that discrimination against nonworkers in considering applications for admission was insufficient to ensure a substantial increase in worker representation, unless matched by active measures to encourage workers to join. The reasons for this will be considered below, but we must first note that the consequences of this negative approach, although evidently unintended, were nevertheless fully apparent to contemporaries and, indeed, became a matter of dispute between the Central Committee and its critics.

The point at issue was not whether it would be desirable to recruit more proletarians to the party, but whether genuine proletarians were available to be recruited. It was Lenin who took the most pessimistic view on this. In two letters addressed to Central Committee Secretary Molotov on the eve of the Eleventh Congress he pointed out that, "starting with the War, the factory workers of Russia have become far less proletarian in composition than before, because the people who entered the factories during the War were those who wanted to escape from military service," while "for quite a large number of intellectual and quasi-intellectual elements, becoming workers presents absolutely no difficulty whatso-

[26] *Ibid.*, p. 727.
[27] Bubnov, in *BSE*, Vol. XI, col. 533.

ever under our conditions." Since, therefore, the "workers" were no longer necessarily "proletarians," much the same degree of caution was needed in admitting them to the party as with other social strata. Specifically, Lenin recommended that the preferential six-month probationary period should apply only to those workers who had been employed in large-scale undertakings for at least ten years, while for other workers it should be fixed at eighteen months. Lenin was aware that his approach might lead to a further reduction in party membership, but was not dismayed at this prospect. "If there are three or four hundred thousand members in our party, then even this is too many, since all available data point definitely to the inadequate level of training of the existing membership."[28]

Although the Central Committee rejected Lenin's proposals on the probationary period for workers,[29] the leadership evidently felt constrained to cleave fairly close to Lenin's approach in the public position they adopted on this question, whatever private reservations they might have had. This is apparent, for example, in Zinoviev's organizational report to the Eleventh Congress. The old working class, said Zinoviev, had become *déclassé* by the cataclysms of war and revolution; its best elements had either perished, been absorbed into the bureaucracy, or had left for the villages, while those that remained were the old, the war-wounded, the least enterprising, and they were substantially diluted by petty bourgeois elements.[30] Consequently there was little scope for improving the proletarian character of the party by increasing the size of the factory cells. The main effort should therefore be concentrated on training the existing membership. "We should not be chasing after quantity, but after quality.

[28] *XI s"ezd*, pp. 735-736. [29] *Ibid.*, p. 737.
[30] *Ibid.*, pp. 387-388.

103

. . . Let us close the doors and grant access only to those comrades who will bring a genuinely healthy spirit into the party. Let us shut the others out. The workers will understand this."[31]

Although these principles were duly incorporated into the congress decisions,[32] they were strongly contested by a number of delegates. Moscow Party Secretary, I. A. Zelensky, pointing out that the Tenth Congress decision on transferring ex-worker communists from offices to the factory floor had proved abortive, argued that active recruitment of workers was the *only* way to arrest the further de-proletarianization of the party and that the prospects for such recruitment were far better than Zinoviev had suggested.[33] The last point was taken up by another delegate, R. V. Pikel'. If one accepted Zinoviev's view that 90 percent of the workers were now *déclassé*, he argued, one had also to note that only 1 percent of them were in the party. "Where are the other 9 percent of conscious workers? Answer me this, comrade Zinoviev: if a conscious, developed worker remains outside the ranks of the party, is this a misunderstanding or is it as it should be?"[34]

To the outside observer, there seems to have been an element of truth on both sides in this dispute. The leadership's skepticism as to the availability of genuine proletarians to recruit was probably well founded. On the other hand, their critics were undoubtedly correct in predicting a continued de-proletarianization of the party if substantial numbers of proletarian recruits could not be found.

[31] *Ibid.*, p. 404. See also the Central Committee "Theses" on recruitment, pp. 680-685.

[32] *Ibid.*, pp. 545-554.   [33] *Ibid.*, pp. 444-445.

[34] *Ibid.*, p. 455. For similar remarks by other delegates, see *ibid.*, pp. 438, 463, 466.

There were several reasons for this. The first was the persistence of large-scale withdrawals from the party throughout this period. Such withdrawals, a natural result of the cooling of revolutionary enthusiasm and of disillusionment over the leadership's methods and policies, were already causing concern at the time of the Tenth Congress.[35] Although Opposition charges of a "mass exodus of the worker element"[36] are not borne out by the official figures, the numbers involved were certainly substantial[37] and the workers provided their full share of them.[38]

Persistence of Nonworker Recruitment

Secondly, despite the formal obstacles, a surprisingly large proportion of the new recruits continued to be nonworkers. The history of peasant membership in the Russian Communist Party during this period is a complicated one which can only be summarized here. Although scores of thousands of peasants joined the party during the Civil War, the great

[35] SPR, No. 2, pp. 78-79.

[36] See, e.g. XI s"ezd, pp. 119, 466. The view that it was the "oldest" and "best" workers that were leaving the party was not, however, confined to members of the opposition. See, e.g. Manuilsky's speech, ibid., p. 438.

[37] In 1923 there were 15,000 voluntary withdrawals from the party, compared with 25,000 expulsions. The number of full members withdrawing was only 2,000 less than the number of probationers transferred to full membership. See Izv Ts K, No. 5, May 1924.

[38] The social composition of those joining and leaving the party in 1922 was officially given as follows:

	Percentages	
	Joined	Left
Workers	43	37
Peasants	22	30
White-collar workers and others	35	22
Data unavailable		11

(SOURCE: Izv Ts K, No. 10, October 1922)

105

majority of these were in the Red Army, and village cells remained small. At the end of 1919 the total membership of the latter did not exceed 60,000.[39] Subsequent recruitment and the beginnings of demobilization took the number in rural organizations up to nearly 200,000 by September 1920, over a third of the total party membership.[40] However, once back in their villages, many peasant communists began to loosen their ties with the party, and this process became more marked after the introduction of NEP. Molotov put it as follows: "That part of the peasantry left the party which in the framework of the Communist Party could not arrange its life under the conditions of NEP. They sought freer conditions for their economic initiative as small-scale entrepreneurs in the rural or urban setting, and for this reason they left the ranks of the party."[41]

The peasants were also the class most heavily hit in the purge, and, with both expulsions and withdrawals continuing at a brisk pace, the rural cells, which had swelled to impressive proportions in 1920, now shrank rapidly. A 1922 analysis of rural membership in fifteen guberniyas showed a drop from 89,000 to 24,000 in two years, and of those that remained only 11,000 were peasants.[42] Between January and August 1922, *working* peasants made up 14 percent of those who left the party compared with 5 percent of those who joined.[43] The Central Committee now began to be alarmed, for it was clear that the peasant exodus was by no means confined to kulaks, and the party's base in the villages seemed on the point of evaporating. A Central Committee spokesman commented as follows:

[39] *Izv Ts K*, No. 8, December 2, 1919.
[40] *Ibid.*, No. 22, September 18, 1920.
[41] *XI s"ezd*, p. 48.
[42] *Izv Ts K*, No. 9, September 1922.
[43] *Ibid.*, No. 10, October 1922.

The reduction in the number of rural communists and the falling apart and decay of rural cells is mistakenly regarded as a one-sided process of the withdrawal from the party of alien peasant elements. What we have to deal with here is a different phenomenon and a dangerous one for the party—the decay and narrowing down of the party's main support in the countryside—the proletarian and semi-proletarian poor.[44]

This situation prompted intensified efforts to enroll peasants in the party during 1923, which appear to have met with a degree of success. Little data on this point is available, but the official breakdowns of the social composition of the party, while they distort the picture by reflecting prerevolutionary occupation rather than current occupation, give some indication of membership trends. These show a 2.5 percent reduction in the proportion of "peasant" membership during 1921 and 1922, and a rise of 3.1 percent in 1923.[45]

When we turn to the other main nonproletarian category, the white-collar workers and intelligentsia, the story is more straightforward. Despite the strong discrimination against these groups in both admission and expulsion policies, their share of the total party membership fell by only 3.6 percent between 1921 and 1924.[46] The explanation is by now a familiar one. Such people often had an incentive to acquire party membership which the ordinary worker or peasant lacked. One of the delegates to the Eleventh Congress, who had acquired direct experience with this problem while managing a large industrial plant, made the following comment:

Comrade Zinoviev says the workers have to present three recommendations and can be accepted after six

[44] *Ibid.*, No. 9, September 1922.
[45] *BSE*, Vol. XI, col. 533.
[46] *Ibid.*, cf. Timofeevskii, *op.cit.*, p. 237.

months probation. Workers don't particularly like going around collecting signatures. It's a different matter with your petty bourgeois fellow-travelers, who will have pleasure in collecting not only five, as Comrade Zinoviev recommends, but even ten, because their objective is to get into the party. They know how to give a bow and say, "What is your wish, I am at your service," and thereby get a higher and more honored position.[47]

If the white-collar worker tended to be much more persistent than others in his efforts to join the party, he was also far less likely to resign. In January-August 1922, for instance, white-collar workers and intelligentsia made up 35 percent of those admitted to the party and only about 24 percent of those who left.[48]

The inadequacy of negative, restrictive measures to halt the de-proletarianization of the party becomes even more apparent when one looks beyond the formal class composition of the membership to its actual occupational distribution. New people were constantly being absorbed into the ever-growing bureaucracy, and existing employees promoted. The 1921 purge accelerated this process by causing numerous vacancies from top to bottom in the various bureaucratic hierarchies. A large proportion of these posts were filled on principle or by preference with party members. There were only two possible sources of such new communist officials: admitting subordinate office personnel to party membership, thus permitting their promotion to responsible positions; and the transfer of communists from manual occupations.

An official analysis published in 1923 indicated that nearly two-thirds of the full members and half the candidate mem-

[47] *XI s'ezd*, p. 466.
[48] *Izv Ts K*, No. 10, October 1922.

bers were employed in nonmanual jobs (the differing proportions should be noted: they offer further evidence of the
tendency to shift from manual to white-collar work after
admission to the party). Of the full members, 15 percent
were shown as workers and 22 percent as peasants "engaged
in physical labor."[49] But these figures, particularly those for
the peasants, were almost certainly inflated by including communists who performed some manual work but were also
charged with administrative or supervisory responsibilities.
At the Eleventh Congress, the Secretary of the Moscow Committee stated that while 22 percent of the communists in the
capital were members of factory cells, "a good half" of these
were employed in administrative posts, and he asserted that
in other industrial centers the proportion of workers "at the
bench" was even less.[50] An analysis of the party membership in rural districts of the Riazan guberniya in 1922 showed
that 78 percent held posts in the local soviet, party or cooperative network. The situation was stated to be similar in
other guberniyas.[51] Subsequent recruitment can have had little effect on this position. Only 12 percent of those joining
the party in 1922 were workers *by actual employment*, and
only 5 percent were working peasants. A mere seventh of the
Red Army men joining were rank-and-filers.[52] These facts
make it clear that, despite the most varied and determined
countermeasures, the tendency of the party to become the
preserve of the more powerful and privileged strata of the
emergent postrevolutionary society, a tendency which was
somewhat moderated in the later stages of the Civil War, became more marked than ever during the first years of NEP.

[49] *Ibid.*, No. 5, June 1923.   [50] *XI s"ezd*, p. 443.
[51] *Izv Ts K*, No. 1, January 1922.
[52] *Ibid.*, No. 9, September 1922 and No. 10, October 1922.

Chapter 3

The Lenin Enrollment

WHILE LENIN'S death in January 1924 marked a major watershed in the history of the CPSU, the great political and social consequences which were destined to flow from it could scarcely have been apparent to contemporaries. Despite Lenin's unmatched personal authority, Soviet Russia in the early 1920's was not so much a personal dictatorship as a collective dictatorship or oligarchy, institutionalized in the Politburo, and in the course of his prolonged illness Lenin had already been supplanted as the dominant force in day-to-day decision making by a triumvirate consisting of Zinoviev, Kamenev and Stalin. Moreover, the central and territorial party bureaucracy, created in 1919-1921, and strengthened by the Tenth Congress decisions banning "factionalism" and "anarcho-syndicalism," was already the key instrument of the Politburo in maintaining its dominance. The focus of supreme power, then, and the manner of its exercise, underwent little change in the immediate aftermath of Lenin's death. This was also true of social policy; most importantly, the NEP was allowed to continue its work of rehabilitation and reconciliation. Eventually the political and social forms established in Lenin's last years were supplanted by the dictatorship of one of his heirs and by "a social revolution from above," but the transition was to take five or six years.

The dominance which Stalin came to exercise in the Soviet leadership in the late 1920's differed radically in nature from that previously enjoyed by Lenin, and this fact is of vital importance in understanding Stalin's success. Stalin's dominance rested on his mastery of the party's bureaucratic machinery, while Lenin, though not averse to using the cruder political arts to defeat any serious challenge or opposition, could usually rely on getting his own way by virtue of his enormous authority as founder of the party and its leader in Revolution and Civil War, and on the force of his oratory, personality and ideas. During Lenin's illness, and especially after his death, the other Politburo members were extremely jealous of their "collective leadership" and quick to block any attempt by individual members to assert the kind of personal dominance that had been enjoyed by Lenin. Such a threat appeared to many to be posed by Trotsky in 1923-1924 and later by Zinoviev. The supreme political importance attributed to this kind of personal prestige and authority is illustrated by Kamenev's remark to Trotsky in 1926: "it will be enough for you and Zinoviev to appear together on the platform in order to reconquer the whole party."[1]

Stalin's colleagues were, of course, aware of the power he was meanwhile accumulating in the party machine, particularly after his appointment as General Secretary in 1922. They were aware, too, that this bureaucratic power could be converted into political power pure and simple through the stacking of party conferences and the building of majorities in the higher committees and other executive bodies of the party. By the middle 1920's party bureaucrats owing their advancement to Stalin and looking to him for leadership formed a majority both in the Central Committee and at party congresses. Nevertheless, while neither the Central Committee nor the Congress had yet been reduced to a cypher, their subservience to the Politburo was now so clear for all to see that Stalin's unique influence in them did not appear as dangerous to his colleagues as it proved to be in

[1] Quoted by Isaac Deutscher, *Stalin: A Political Biography* (New York-London, 1949), p. 308.

fact. The real locus of power was the Politburo, there was not a single protégé of Stalin among its voting members prior to 1926, and Stalin gave no indication of the intention or capacity to employ his voting strength in the Congress and Central Committee in order to effect changes in the Politburo—in fact he was a firm advocate of stability of Politburo membership in the early part of this period, resisting, for example, Zinoviev's pressure to have Trotsky expelled.

Ironically, Stalin's power over the party bureaucracy and through it over the Congress and Central Committee was not only acceptable to the majority of his Politburo colleagues, but essential to them. Without it the collective dictatorship of the Politburo over the party and hence over the country at large could not be maintained, or the challenge of the pseudo-Lenins, Trotsky and Zinoviev, defeated. Stalin's retention of the General Secretaryship throughout the succession struggle was due to his identification with the shifting majority in the Politburo, his efficiency in providing that majority with a firm organizational base and votes in the Congress and Central Committee, and adroitness in avoiding a premature display of the power this potentially afforded him to dominate the Politburo.

There was a further irony. Stalin's opportunity to convert his bureaucratic power into dominance over the Politburo was provided by institutional changes which Lenin had proposed with the object of halting the trend towards bureaucratization. Shortly before his death, Lenin advocated that the tendency of the Central Committee to grow in size and meet less frequently should be continued, that it should be converted, in fact, into a sort of "superior party conference," meeting jointly with an enlarged Central Control Commission to exercise close control on behalf of the party at large over the work of the central party apparatus and particularly

112

of the Politburo. The new recruits to the Central Committee and Central Control Commission should be lower party workers drawn from the working class and peasantry.[2] The leverage which this afforded Stalin is obvious. His colleagues could scarcely oppose expansion of the membership of these bodies from the ranks of "lower party workers" most of whom were now Stalin's protégés, nor could they resist his pressure to employ the Central Committee-*cum*-Control Commission as a court of appeal from the Politburo and an organ of discipline over its members. As we noted, these arrangements were, in fact, useful to the Politburo majority in maintaining their dominance. When, however, Stalin began to use them to enhance his personal power in the Politburo, any move to change these arrangements was automatically blocked by the aura of Lenin's authority which was associated with them. Meanwhile Stalin's influence over the mass of Central Committee and Control Commission members ensured that matters referred to them for decision would be settled in his interests, and changes effected by them in the Politburo would bring in men acceptable to him. It was in this way that Stalin's supporters became a substantial minority in the Politburo in 1926, and by December 1927 an absolute majority. From being the soul of caution and moderation, Stalin now became intransigence itself. Leaders who were not personally committed to him were increasingly excluded from policy-making and by 1930 the last of them were removed from the Politburo. The foundations of Stalin's dictatorship were now laid.[3]

[2] See Lenin's articles "Kak nam reorganizovat' Rabkrin" (How We Should Reorganize Rabkrin) and "Luchshe men'she, da luchshe" (Better Less, but Better), *Sochineniia*, Vol. XLV, pp. 383-406, and his "Pis'mo k s"ezdu" (Letter to the Congress), *ibid.*, pp. 346-348.

[3] For an admirable brief account of Stalin's struggle for the suc-

Publicly the struggles between the Soviet leaders during the 1920's were, of course, articulated in terms of policy orientations rather than of naked personal power, and for most of the participants as well as for the party at large these policy disputes probably appeared to be the "real" issues. A whole series of disputes stemmed from differing interpretations of the objectives and limitations of NEP. Overlapping with this were disputes over whether a socialist society could be constructed in the Soviet Union while the rest of the world was still dominated by capitalism, and if so, how. Another range of issues centered around the Communist International (e.g. communist tactics in Germany and China, relations with the Social Democratic parties). Stalin's attitude towards these issues was highly manipulative: he used them to cement his temporary alliances and to isolate and crush his rivals, and was always ready to change his line when this became expedient for such purposes.

By about 1926 the healing work of NEP had restored rural and industrial production to prewar levels, and henceforth, in keeping with the triumphant doctrine of "socialism in one country," the emphasis moved from rehabilitation to industrialization. The demand for industrial labor and for managerial and technical personnel accelerated sharply, reaching enormous proportions during the first Five Year Plan. The problem of providing the capital for industrialization, rendered critical by the Plan's heavy concentration on the producer-goods industries, was the subject of acute theoretical debate in the late 1920's. Stalin cut across the theoretical

cession to Lenin, see Fainsod, *How Russia Is Ruled*, pp. 148-158. The best extended accounts are those by Schapiro, *The CPSU*, Chaps. 15, 16 and 20, Robert V. Daniels, *The Conscience of the Revolution: Communist Opposition in Soviet Russia* (Cambridge, Mass., 1960), Chaps. 10-13, and E. H. Carr, *The Interregnum: 1923-1924*, "Socialism in One Country" (London, 1959), Vol. II, Part III.

dispute by providing a coercive administrative solution to the problem: by forcing the peasants into so-called collective farms (kolkhozes), which were run by party appointees and obliged to restrict peasant consumption to the surplus left after "compulsory deliveries" to the state were met. In the years 1929-1933, the first Five Year Plan and collectivization laid the foundations of the Soviet industrial society of today, at the cost, however, of vast suffering and deprivation, the alienation of the bulk of the peasantry from the system, and a crippling of the moral conscience of the party.

In the decade following the death of Lenin, changing recruitment and membership policies pursued in the CPSU reflected in considerable measure the political and social developments summarized in the preceding pages, and it is part of our purpose to elucidate these connections. At the same time, we shall see ample evidence that forces little understood and imperfectly controlled by the party apparatus continued to act as important determinants of the party's composition.

Proletarianization

As a glance at the chart on page 51 will show, the period 1924-1933 was one of intensive numerical expansion, which took party membership from under half a million to over three and a half millions. The basic principle of official recruitment doctrine was consistent throughout this period—it was to build up the "proletarian core" of the party—although the extent to which actual recruitment policies can be interpreted in terms of this principle varied considerably at different stages.

Table 2[4] gives some idea of the extent of the party's pro-

[4] SOURCES: *BSE*, Vol. XI, col. 534; *PS*, No. 17, September 1931, p. 35, No. 9, 1932, pp. 50-51, and No. 21, 1932, pp. 46-48. The *BSE*

TABLE 2: CLASS COMPOSITION AND OCCUPATION OF PARTY MEMBERSHIP, 1922-1932

Date	Class composition			Current occupation		
Jan. 1	Workers	Peasants	White-collar workers	Workers	Individual and collective farmers	White-collar workers and others
	Percent	Percent	Percent	Percent	Percent	Percent
1922	44.4	26.7	28.9			
1923	44.9	25.7	29.4			
1924	44.0	28.8	27.2	18.8		
1925	56.7	26.5	16.8	41.3	9.5	49.2
1926	56.8	25.9	17.3	42.0	13.4	44.6
1927	55.1	27.3	17.6	39.4	13.7	46.9
1928	56.8	22.9	20.3	40.8	12.3	46.9
1929	61.4	21.7	16.9	44.0	13.0	43.0
1930	65.3	20.2	14.5	46.3	12.0	41.7
1931				44.1	16.3	39.5
1932	65.2	26.9	7.9	43.8	18.5	37.6

letarianization in the years 1924-1932. While the precision of these percentages should not be exaggerated, being distorted not only by error and misinformation, but also by changes of classification, as we shall see below, they appear to be accurate enough to give a reliable impression of general trends.

The first phase of proletarianization, 1924-1925, opened dramatically with the Lenin enrollment (*leninskii prizyv*), which in three months expanded the party by 40 percent through the recruitment of some 200,000 "bench-workers" (i.e. wage-laborers in industry, transport etc. actually work-

figures for 1927 have been amended by substituting the current statistics figures for the party census figures (Cf. Table 5, p. 162). This enhances comparability.

ing with their hands). The background and motivation of the Lenin enrollment deserve close consideration, as they throw considerable light on the whole proletarianization policy.

As we saw in the previous chapter, discriminatory enlistment regulations had by 1923 revealed their complete inadequacy as a cure for the drift towards deproletarianization of the party membership. Without a substantial *recruitment* of workers, the drift was clearly irreversible. Furthermore, economic recovery was bringing renewed growth of the industrial labor force—it rose from 1.1 million in 1922 to 1.6 million in 1924[5]—thus further attenuating the influence in the factories of the dwindling band of worker communists. A conference of the Ukrainian party organization in March 1923 noted that efforts to guide and influence nonparty workers were being frustrated by "the paucity of party cadres working at the bench," and advocated a shift towards the more active recruitment of industrial workers.[6]

Accumulating evidence of the physical and moral exhaustion of the existing membership further highlighted the need for new blood. A sample investigation of the health and personal situation of a thousand Smolensk communists showed that over a third had tuberculosis or were "on the verge of it," while another third were suffering from "shattered nervous systems." Only 10 percent were considered reasonably fit.[7] Alcoholism was an "evil corroding the whole organization." Of 289 communists removed from the party in Smolensk guberniya during 1923, 117 were expelled for alcoholism,

[5] Alexander Baykov, *The Development of the Soviet Economic System* (Cambridge, 1950), p. 147.
[6] See *Partiia v bor'be za vosstanovlenie narodnogo khoziaistva (1921-1925), Dokumenty i materialy* (Moscow, 1961), p. 498. For a similar move in Bashkiria, see Kh. S. Bairanov et al. eds., *Rezoliutsii oblastnykh konferintsii Bashkirskoi partiinoi organizatsii i plenumov obkoma KPSS* (Ufa, 1959), pp. 177-178.
[7] *WKP* 275, p. 25.

and 57 for criminal or administrative offences.[8] In another local study of the state of health of party members, covering 809 communists in the Nizhny-Novgorod guberniya, only 4 percent of the sample were declared fit; more than half suffered from respiratory ailments or anaemia, while the proportion found to be "nervously ill" was 16 percent in the case of communists employed "at the bench," 30 percent of those employed as party or soviet officials, and two-thirds of the GPU (political police) officials.[9]

Meanwhile the demand for party cadres did not decline, but continued to grow. The restoration of industry highlighted and aggravated the shortage of communists in management and the economic administration. Meanwhile, the return to peaceful conditions was accompanied by a resurgence of spontaneous cultural and social activity which the party lacked the personnel to keep track of and control.[10] The party was clearly falling down on one of its vital functions—that of political socialization and recruitment, and to correct this, it was to be expected that it would turn first, as its ideology demanded, to the industrial workers.

Leadership Politics and the Lenin Enrollment

Meanwhile, power considerations were beginning to point

[8] *Ibid.*, p. 20.

[9] *Izv Ts K*, Nos. 11-12, March 23, 1925.

[10] Thus a June 1924 report of the Bureau of the Don obkom on the progress of the Lenin enrollment referred to the proliferation of cultural, philanthropic and other societies of all kinds which, though making an exceptionally valuable contribution of voluntary social effort, had previously caused local committees a great deal of anxiety, due to their inability to control them. The Lenin enrollment, the report stated, would now enable the party "to give a correct and organized course to their work and to inject into them members of our party." See P. V. Barchukov, *Vosstanovitel'nyi period na Donu (1921-1925gg.): sbornik dokumentov* (Rostov, 1962), p. 343.

in the same direction. After two years of campaigning against the residual influence of the Workers' Opposition, the industrial cells no longer represented a focus of opposition to the Politburo majority. By 1923 the main threat to the dominance of Zinoviev, Kamenev and Stalin came from Trotsky, who had little appeal to the workers but possessed a considerable following among student youth and sections of government officialdom. In the jargon of a party historian discussing the motives for the Lenin enrollment, "the struggle against Trotskyism showed that it was the nonworker section of the party membership which was most subject to petty bourgeois influence."[11] The principal weapon of the triumvirate in the developing struggle with Trotsky was the power of the apparatus to contrive majorities for their resolutions in party organizations throughout the country, to have their candidates elected to higher conferences and leading committees, and to effect changes in party and government appointments. The advantages for these purposes of having a mass of inexperienced and malleable new members are obvious.

In view of these compelling practical and political considerations, what seems at first surprising is that the change in party recruitment policy was so long delayed. Despite some localized moves to step up worker recruitment,[12] both

[11] A. A. Murashev, *V leninskuiu partiiu* (Moscow, 1960), p. 13.

[12] Apart from the March 1923 decision in the Ukraine (see footnote 6), the Thirteenth Conference decision "On Party Structure" referred to "the initiative of certain organizations which have already carried out work" in the direction of enrolling bench-workers. See *KPSS v rez*, Vol. I, p. 772. See also *Izv Ts K*, Nos. 9-10, September-October 1923, p. 19. For an example of intensified recruitment of workers by a regional party organization in April-September 1923, see V. G. Mochalov, ed., *Vladimirskaia partiinaia organizatsiia v gody vosstanovleniia narodnogo khoziaistva—1921-1925 gody: sbornik dokumentov* (Vladimir, 1963), p. 173.

the overall size of the party and the ratio in it of "bench-workers" continued to decline during 1923. There is reason to suppose that the main obstacle to change was Lenin. As we noted in the previous chapter, at the time of the Eleventh Congress (1922) Lenin took an extreme position on the restriction of party recruitment. Not only did he consider the party already too big, under existing social conditions, but he specifically opposed the idea of making substantial recruitment efforts in the factories, on the ground that genuine proletarians, their attitudes tempered by years of continuous experience on the factory floor, were simply lacking. There is no reason to suppose that he changed his views on this question in the course of 1922 or 1923. Although he was not actively participating in affairs at this period, neither could the leadership easily act in contradiction to his known or assumed views, and this may well have inhibited any ideas of the triumvirate to launch a large-scale recruitment of workers, at least till their position was secured by a decisive defeat of Trotsky.

In October 1923 the triumvirate's struggle with the Opposition came to a head with a letter from Trotsky to the Central Committee attacking the "dictatorship of the Secretariat" and the triumvirate's economic policies, and a statement independently issued by 46 leading communists (largely old oppositionists working in the economic administration) making similar charges to Trotsky's and demanding a party conference representing all points of view.[13] In the weeks that followed, the dispute became increasingly public and involved ever-wider circles of the party, culminating in the Thirteenth Party Conference, January 16 to 18, which marked the complete victory of the triumvirate.

[13] See Schapiro, *The CPSU*, pp. 278-279, and Carr, *The Interregnum: 1923-1924*, Chaps. xii and xiii and Note A.

Party membership questions received very little direct attention in the dispute. They figured neither in the "platform of the 46"[14] nor, apparently, in Trotsky's letter to the Central Committee.[15] The first phase of the dispute ended with a joint meeting of the Politburo and the Presidium of the Central Control Commission held on December 5, 1923, which approved a resolution "On Party Construction," drafted by Stalin, Trotsky and Kamenev,[16] and apparently constituting a compromise settlement of the main points at issue. The resolution contained a passage on party membership which noted that "active worker communists, who should naturally constitute the link between the party and the nonparty masses, are almost entirely absorbed in administrative and managerial work," and went on to state that "the basic task in the field in question is the recruitment of new party members from among workers at the bench. . . . In the next few months work on increasing the proletarian core of the party is one of the main tasks of party organizations. . . . The party should facilitate the inflow of new cadres of production workers into party organizations and the transfer of candidates to full membership."[17]

While there was nothing in these phrases to suggest a resumption of mass recruitment, they nonetheless signaled a sharp break with the official position on party membership espoused by Lenin and current for over two years. Since this was one of the few issues where Trotsky's opposition to the triumvirate could have been unequivocally clothed in Lenin's authority, are we to regard his agreement to the inclusion of this passage as an instance of that political ineptness which

[14] The translation of the "platform of the 46" is reprinted in Carr, *The Interregnum: 1923-1924*, pp. 367-373.

[15] Although the full text of Trotsky's letter seems never to have been published. See *ibid.*, pp. 106, footnote 1, 295-297.

[16] See *ibid.*, p. 307.   [17] *P*, December 7, 1923.

121

so characterized his conduct of the leadership struggle? Or could Trotsky have reasonably regarded it as an acceptable *quid pro quo* for the addition, immediately following, of the sentence "It is likewise necessary to pay increased attention to work among the rising generation of proletarian youth."

For Trotsky was directing his main appeal to the youth: to younger party members, the komsomol, and especially the students. This was a dominant theme in a series of articles with which he now reopened the dispute.[18] The "Old Guard" of prerevolutionary bolsheviks staffing the party apparatus, he argued, had become bogged down in the bureaucratic ways engendered by the Civil War and salvation lay with the young, who must be given a greater say in affairs by democratizing party processes and advancing them to leading positions. He did not specifically argue, however, for an intensified recruitment of young people to the party. His references to recruitment were rather of a negative kind. Only one-sixth of the existing membership were workers from the bench, he stated, and while "everything must of course be done to draw into the party the greatest possible number of workers at the bench," the scale on which this could be done depended strictly on the rate of economic advance, and consequently "the membership of the party can be seriously altered (so that, for example, the factory cells make up two-thirds of its ranks) only very slowly."[19] While this remark did not escape misinterpretation as a "demagogic" appeal for the recruit-

[18] Originally published in *P*, December 11, 28 and 29, 1923, they were issued in book form the following year, under the title of *Novyi Kurs* (The New Course). The articles are most conveniently available in English in *The New Course*, by Leon Trotsky, and *The Struggle for the New Course*, with a new introduction by Max Shachtman (Ann Arbor, Mich., 1965).

[19] *P*, December 29, 1923.

ment of hundreds of thousands of workers,[20] it was clearly intended to convey that there was no use counting on a rapid increase in the proletarian element in the party as a check to bureaucratization, and thereby to strengthen his argument that everything depended on the young. It is interesting to note that Trotsky's opponents on the whole avoided taking him up directly on the assertion that the recruitment of more proletarian communists would necessarily proceed very slowly.[21] Did this reflect the still inhibiting presence of the dying Lenin?[22]

While the focus of this dispute was the debate in the pages of *Pravda*, it was also being fought out in thousands of local meetings and at the provincial conferences held to elect delegates to the Thirteenth Congress. In this, perhaps more crucial battleground, the main weapon of the triumvirate

[20] This is noted by Max Shachtman in (Trotsky) *The Struggle for the New Course* (1965 edn.), p. 252, footnote 6.

[21] For an exception, see Ryndin's article in *P*, January 22, 1924. Ryndin quoted figures on recent recruitment of factory workers in the Urals to show that "the opposition" was wrong in underestimating the potentialities of worker recruitment and in orienting themselves too much on the students.

[22] In this connection, it is worth noting a contribution of Lenin's wife, Nadezhda Krupskaia, to the debate, since at this time she was the only prominent party member who was Lenin's daily companion and under the circumstances it seems safe to assume that she would not have adopted a public position on an important issue which she believed to conflict with his views. Krupskaia accepted Trotsky's statement that only one-sixth of the party membership were benchworkers, but argued that he drew the wrong conclusion from this fact. Instead of concluding that the party must therefore place its main reliance upon the youth, he should have concluded that better use should be made of that one-sixth, so that it could effectively perform its key role of linking the party with the working class. She pointedly did *not* mention the possibility of increasing the number of worker communists so that they amounted to more than a sixth. See *P*, January 3, 1924.

was the opportunities which control of the apparatus gave them to manipulate rank-and-file opinion and voting behavior, and the desirability of strengthening this weapon by the large-scale admission of political innocents must therefore have impressed itself with particular urgency in the course of this crisis. Moreover, their conviction that the factory cells were their main area of grass-roots strength must have been deepened by the results of voting for conference delegates. In Moscow, for instance, whereas the opposition won a majority in student cells, the triumvirate won in 279 out of 346 industrial cells.[23]

This is the background to the proletarianization policy launched in January 1924. The triumvirate were already armed with an authorization of this policy in the form of the resolution of the December 5 meeting of the Politburo and the Presidium of the Central Control Commission, and this resolution was now duly solemnized by reissue with minor omissions, as a decision of the Thirteenth Conference.[24] At the same time, evidently feeling that the stakes were sufficiently high and that there was no longer much danger of Lenin's recovering to rebuke them for it, they moved immediately to implement this policy on a massive scale. They had the Conference adopt a resolution "On the Results of the Discussion and the Petty Bourgeois Deviation in the Party," the first of whose "practical conclusions" read as follows:

The proletarian core of the party must be numerically increased at all costs, along with its relative weight in the whole policy of the party. In the course of the next year

[23] See Carr, *The Interregnum: 1923-1924*, p. 327. The opposition claimed that they won control of a third of all party cells in the Red Army (*ibid.*, p. 325).

[24] See *KPSS v rez*, Vol. I, pp. 771-778. The section on party recruitment appears on p. 772.

it is necessary to intensify recruitment of workers from the bench as party members, with the object of drawing into the ranks of the Russian Communist Party no less than 100,000 new members who are genuine (*korennye*) proletarians. For this purpose it is necessary to facilitate the entry of workers into the party in every way. At the same time entry into the party should be decisively closed for this period to all nonproletarian elements.[25]

If the triumvirate still felt any lingering misgivings about possible future reactions on the part of Lenin, these were soon allayed by the great man's death three days after the conference.[26] Their first political step was to proceed with the recruitment of worker communists on a far vaster scale even than that approved at the conference. This was expressed in a decision, issued a mere ten days after Lenin's death, to launch a three months' campaign to recruit 200,000 manual workers. This decision was justified by the claim that Lenin's

[25] *Ibid.*, p. 783.

[26] It is difficult to judge how far Lenin was aware of the developments which culminated in the Thirteenth Conference. Although he spent the last months of his life at a rest-home some twenty miles out of Moscow and took no active part in affairs, he continued to receive occasional visitors and his wife N. K. Krupskaia regularly read to him from the newspapers. In this way, he may have become aware of the resolution "On Party Structure" when it was originally published on December 7, 1923. Be this as it may, Krupskaia reports his agitation when she read all the Thirteenth Conference resolutions to him on January 19 and 20. He asked many questions, and she was forced to reassure him by saying that the resolutions were passed unanimously (see Lenin, *Sochineniia*, Vol. XLV, p. 717). Did his agitation over the conference resolutions precipitate his death the next day? There were certainly plenty of points in these documents to strengthen his heartache about the way his party and his revolution were tending. Was one of these points the departure from his views on the composition of the party which he had founded and led to power?

death had provoked a great wave of sympathy towards his party among the industrial proletariat, and the campaign was correspondingly labeled "the Lenin enrollment."[27] The irony of this will be abundantly apparent from the foregoing.

The Lenin enrollment was pushed through with great vigor. The Secretariat sent out some 300 propagandists to assist local organizations in the campaign.[28] Each guberniya and oblast committee was allotted a target based on 10 percent of the industrial workers in the area, and they in turn fixed quotas for subordinate committees.[29] Intensive agitation was conducted at the workplace level under the slogans: "Workers from the bench, staunch supporters of the proletarian revolution—join the Russian Communist Party! Proletarians! Send into the party's ranks your best, foremost, most honest and bold warriors!" Although the credentials of each applicant were supposed to be individually checked before admission was granted, group applications were now authorized (a striking departure from traditional Leninist principles). Wherever possible, candidates were expected to supply the statutory number of recommendations by established party members, but local officials were empowered to waive this requirement "provided the party organization has adequately checked the candidates with the help of general meetings of workers."[30]

[27] See *KPSS v rez*, Vol. I, pp. 807-811.

[28] See *Partiia v bor'be za vosstanovlenie narodnogo khoziaistva (1921-1925)*, p. 394.

[29] Thus the Smolensk gubkom, allotted a target of 2,000 recruits, issued a decision in February 1924 fixing quotas of from 250 to 500 for the five industrial organizations in the guberniya. See Report of Smolensk gubkom to the Thirteenth Guberniya Conference, *WKP* 275.

[30] *KPSS v rez*, Vol. I, p. 810. For an example of how these rules were applied by a typical regional organization, see Mochalov, *op.cit.*, pp. 200-201.

Despite some inconsistency in published statistics,[31] there is no doubt that the targets set for the Lenin enrollment were approximately achieved. High-pressure recruitment did not stop there, however, but became a constant feature of the party scene for many years. A second "Lenin enrollment" was launched on the first anniversary of Lenin's death, bringing in a further 300,000 candidates.[32] In the two years 1924-1925, the CPSU more than doubled its membership. While recruitment slackened considerably in 1926-1927, a further quarter million were added during these years, taking total membership to 1.3 million.

Expulsions and Promotions

Closely linked with the mass recruitment of the mid-1920's were two other processes: the purging of the existing membership and the advancement of rank-and-file recruits to responsible positions. Following the 1921 purge, local control commissions kept up a brisk rate of expulsion of "corrupted elements." This accelerated markedly after the death of Lenin. According to official figures, 16,000 were expelled in 1924, 20,000 in 1925, and 25,000 in 1926.[33] In the majority of cases these expulsions resulted from the day-to-day inves-

[31] A figure of "240,000 workers" has become traditional in Soviet references to the Lenin enrollment. See, e.g. Ponomarev, *Istoriia KPSS*, p. 360; *Trinadtsatyi s"ezd RKP (b): stenograficheskii otchët*, p. 819, footnote 1 (cited hereafter as *XIII s"ezd*). However, according to contemporary sources, the total number of candidates admitted in the first half of 1924 was 212,330, of whom 180,000, admitted between February and May, constituted the Lenin enrollment (*Izv Ts K*, No. 12, October 13, 1924). The higher figure may result from the inclusion of those who applied for entry during the Lenin enrollment period but whose admission was not formally approved till June or July 1924.

[32] See Murashev, *op.cit.*, p. 47.

[33] See E. Iaroslavskii, *Za bolshevistskuiu proverku i chistku riadov partii* (Moscow, 1933), p. 47.

tigation of alleged offences, but 6,000 of those expelled in 1924-1925 were victims of a "verification" of party cells in government offices and higher education establishments,[34] which coincided with a purge of government personnel carried out by the Commissariat of Workers' and Peasants' Inspection.[35] This verification was focused on those sections of the party in which most of the supporters of Trotsky were concentrated, and, although "opposition" did not officially constitute grounds for expulsion, prominent oppositionists were adamant that voting for opposition-sponsored resolutions was the real reason for a substantial proportion of expulsions officially attributed to other offences (drunkenness, noncommunist manner of living, etc.).[36] There is also good reason to suppose that the control commissions in their day-to-day activities showed increasing discrimination against opposition supporters in these years.[37]

[34] This "verification" (*proverka*) was begun very quietly at the time of the Lenin enrollment, and was officially justified by reference to the Twelfth Congress decision declaring it "expedient in necessary cases to carry out a verification and purge of party members of particular organizations" (*KPSS v rez*, Vol. I, p. 728). The cells "verified" embraced 230,000 full and candidate members, 6 percent of whom were recommended for expulsion by the three-man verification tribunals (*partprovertroiki*). After appeals, almost half of these recommendations were put into effect by the guberniya control commissions (*XIII s"ezd*, pp. 840-841, footnote 113).

[35] This purge resulted in the sacking or deprivation of permanent status of a substantial proportion of government officials, e.g. in the various uyezds of Smolensk guberniya from 10 to 37 percent of all officials. See *WKP* 22, p. 321.

[36] See, e.g. Preobrazhensky's speech at the Thirteenth Congress, *XIII s"ezd*, pp. 192-193. Cf. Yaroslavsky's defense against this charge, *ibid.*, p. 223. See also Carr, *The Interregnum: 1923-1924*, pp. 356-357.

[37] Cf. Schapiro, *The CPSU*, p. 320. By the end of 1927, at the latest, "opposition" had become one of the formal grounds of expulsion. In a report of the Smolensk Control Commission covering the six weeks November 29, 1927 to January 10, 1928, 24 expulsions were

These expulsions opened up many avenues of promotion in the government, managerial and, to a lesser extent, the party apparatuses, and there was an immediate move to advance the new recruits of the Lenin enrollment to responsible jobs. As early as the Thirteenth Congress (May 1924) a resolution was passed stating that "the chief task standing before the party in connection with the incorporation of over 200,000 new members consists of arranging to draw them into state work. . . . This should not be hampered by the lack of training of the new members, and in particular, by their noncompletion of a party propaganda course."[38] There is no need to point out the efficacy of the rank-and-file promotion program in binding new recruits to the Stalin machine, which now controlled virtually all appointments. Even if the new recruit did not gain immediate preferment, the power of the machine to offer or withhold promotion exerted constant pressure on him to behave "reliably." Another kind of patronage in the hands of the apparatus was assignment to general educational or technical study courses, which were becoming a common stepping-stone from the factory floor to white-collar employment. During the middle 1920's an average of 6 percent of the party's manual worker members were assigned to full-time study each year.[39] A further factor was unemployment, which was widespread at this period. Unemployment was not unknown among party members. In January 1925 one party member in a hundred was out of work,[40] and by January 1927 the proportion had risen to

---

recorded, with reasons, one of which was formulated "active oppositionist, engaging covertly in opposition activity." See *WKP* 33.

[38] *KPSS v rez*, Vol. I, p. 824.

[39] See *SPR*, No. 6, Vol. I, pp. 517-518.

[40] *Izv Ts K*, Nos. 15-16, April 21, 1925.

one in twenty-five.[41] Nevertheless, being in the party undoubtedly helped in the competition to gain and retain jobs.
Although not given official approval by the Central Committee, there was a widespread practice of removing low-level
nonparty officials from government, trade union and cooperative jobs to make room for unemployed communists.[42] The
potency of these various forms of patronage in molding the
mass of new recruits into docile supporters of the party machine was subtly reinforced by the atmosphere of NEP,
which placed idealism at a discount and encouraged the calculated scramble for a share in the rising living standards.

The triumvirate was not slow in exploiting this asset. Although contrary to party rules, candidates recruited in the
Lenin enrollment were allowed to vote in the local conferences leading up to the Thirteenth Congress,[43] and this, in
conjunction with the inhibiting effect of the current "verification,"[44] helps to account for the overwhelming votes for
officially favored resolutions and congress delegates. At the
Congress itself, Stalin and his supporters sponsored what to
the initiated was a clear declaration of intention to employ
the mass recruitment of workers against emergent opposition
groups, invariably labeled "petty bourgeois": ("The greater
[social] homogeneity of the party, the raising of the percent-

[41] *Sotsial'nyi i natsional'nyi sostav VKP(b)*, p. 42.

[42] *Izv Ts K*, Nos. 15-16, April 21, 1925.

[43] See *SPR*, No. 5, p. 251. The speed with which Lenin enrollment candidates were drawn into the political life of the party is illustrated by data from the Saratov guberniya, which shows that as
early as June 1924 some 25 percent of them had been placed on
local or factory trade union committees or on the boards of clubs
or other voluntary organizations. See V. Osipov et al., eds., *Saratovskaia partiinaia organizatsiia v gody vosstanovleniia narodnogo
khoziaistva* (Saratov, 1960), p. 267.

[44] On this, again see Preobrazhensky's speech at the Thirteenth
Congress, *XIII s"ezd*, p. 192.

130

age of proletarians in its composition, can be one of the best guarantees against the penetration of the party by petty bourgeois influences and at the same time the most reliable guarantee of the unshakeable unity of the party on the basis of Leninism."[45]

At the time of the Lenin enrollment Stalin was able to turn the edge of this weapon against the Trotskyite opposition on behalf of the triumvirate. But it was not long before he was using it against the other triumvirs, Zinoviev and Kamenev. Throughout the middle and later 1920's, each time Stalin broke with his former allies and maneuvered them into opposition, he proceeded to swamp their supporters with a mass of raw recruits whose political attitudes and behavior could be freely molded by a party bureaucracy totally controlled by Stalin. Or to translate it into the gobbledygook of the late Stalin era, such mass recruitment campaigns as the Lenin enrollment proved "a firm support of the Central Committee of the Communist Party in its struggle against the Trotskyite-Zinovievite and other traitors."[46]

[45] *KPSS v rez*, Vol. I, p. 822.
[46] See *BSE* (2nd edn.), Vol. XXIV, p. 555. Cf. Isaac Deutscher, *The Prophet Unarmed* (London, 1959), p. 136.

Chapter 4

Proletarianization Slackens

THROUGHOUT THE mid-1920's, official discussions of party recruitment continued to stress the enrollment of manual workers, and workers continued to receive favored treatment in the sifting of applications. In January-February 1925, for instance, they constituted 55 to 60 percent of applicants but 74 percent of those admitted, while white-collar groups contributed 22 percent of the applicants but only 11 percent of admissions.[1] In 1926, 47 percent of the workers applying for admission were said to have been admitted, compared with 33 percent of white-collar applicants.[2] Working class candidates were officially estimated at over half a million out of the 800,000 recruits to the CPSU in 1924-1926.[3]

Nevertheless, as the reader will see from a glance at Table 2 (p. 116), the proportion of workers in the party—whether classified in terms of "social position" or of current occupation—after rising dramatically in 1924, leveled out in 1925, and then fell off in 1926. This reflected a declining ratio of workers among new recruits: the proportion fell from 92 percent of admissions in the first half of 1924, to 65 percent in the second half, to 55 percent in 1925, and to 48 percent in 1926.[4]

---

[1] *Izv Ts K,* Nos. 19-20, May 30, 1925. See also No. 35, September 14, 1925.

[2] *Ibid.,* Nos. 24-25, June 30, 1927, pp. 4-7. For a higher figure for the overall rate of admission of applicants in 1926, see E. Iaroslavskii, *Za bol'shevistskuiu proverku i chistku riadov partii* (Moscow, 1933), p. 47.

[3] *SPR,* No. 6, Vol. I, pp. 517-518.

[4] Bubnov, in *BSE,* Vol. XI, col. 534.

132

What were the reasons for this? Firstly, the party appears to have encountered difficulty in maintaining the proportion of production worker recruits at the 1924 level. Apparently the Lenin enrollment largely saturated such potential demand as existed among the workers for admission to the party, while banking up demand among other social groups. To compensate for this, many party committees in the later months of 1924 and in early 1925 had recourse to such artificial methods of sustaining the worker intake as the allocation to subordinate organizations of numerical admission quotas for the various recruitment categories.[5]

The reduced recruitment of workers was due, however, not only to the flagging relative demand for admission among the workers, but to deliberate efforts of the party leadership to increase the intake from other social groups, of which the peasantry was by far the largest and most important.

The need for substantial efforts to replenish the rural party organizations becomes apparent when one considers the sorry state to which they were reduced in the first years of NEP. The peasants had been easily the hardest-hit class in the 1921 purge and its aftermath (see above p. 106). Village cells showed a general tendency to contract, and it was to counter this, as we have seen, that the party intensified its rural re-

[5] *SPR*, No. 5, p. 269. It is indicative of current pressures that local committees sometimes found it impossible to observe the quotas they imposed on themselves. The Smolensk gubkom, for instance, was embarrassed to find that it recruited substantially more white-collar worker recruits than provided for in its quota, while there was a shortage of 15 percent in meeting the manual worker quota. See *WKP* 278, p. 35. A conference of the Kazakh party as early as May 1924 called for a "firm percentage quota" to maintain worker recruitment. See S. B. Beisembaev and P. M. Pakhmurnyi, eds., *Kommunisticheskaia Partiia Kazakhstana v dokumentakh i tsifrakh* (The Communist Party of Kazakhstan in Documents and Figures), (Alma-Ata, 1960), p. 58.

cruitment in 1923. During 1922 and 1923 village cells admitted hardly any of their candidate members to full member status.[6] The great majority of candidates in the party overdue for advancement to full membership were peasants or farm laborers. The contraction of village cells continued during the Lenin enrollment period in the first half of 1924, when peasants provided only 6 percent of new enrollments. In 1923 and 1924 about a quarter of the peasant communists actually engaged in farming left the party.[7] Those who remained, since they were the most committed supporters of the regime in the countryside, tended to be drawn into administrative work.[8] The converse also applied: it was largely those "peasants" who had obtained administrative or office jobs who sought and were granted party membership. Less than a third of the "peasants" enrolled in 1924 were still farming at the time of enlistment.[9] Consequently working peasants rarely constituted more than 20 to 30 percent of the members of rural cells, some of which, especially in the Ukraine, consisted *entirely* of men and women holding administrative or other nonmanual jobs. A large proportion of these were not natives of the locality, but were people sent in from the outside by their ukoms as part of a deliberate policy of switching rural communists around to prevent them "fall-

[6] *Izv Ts K*, Nos. 19-20, May 30, 1925.

[7] *Ibid.* See also *Izv Ts K*, No. 28, July 27, 1925.

[8] In the course of 1924 the total membership of rural cells increased from 136,996 to 154,731. However, peasants actually engaged in farming fell from 89,100 to 59,442, while the white-collar workers in these cells grew from 47,896 to 95,289. These changes were due mainly to changes of employment of the existing membership, rather than to a turnover of membership. See *Partiia v tsifrovom osveshchenii: materialy po statistike lichnogo sostava partii* (The Party Shown in Figures: Materials on the Statistics of the Personal Composition of the Party), (Moscow-Leningrad, 1925), p. 59.

[9] *Izv Ts K*, Nos. 15-16, April 21, 1925.

ing under the influence of the surrounding milieu."[10] At the beginning of 1925 less than 10 percent of the communists in the U.S.S.R. were classified as working peasants. Moreover, since the majority even of these were actually occupants of official positions who farmed in their spare time, the proportion *wholly* engaged in agriculture was probably as little as 2 to 3 percent,[11] representing not more than one person in three or four thousand of the adult peasant population. At this time most village cells, with an average size of eleven members and candidates, had to cover something like five or six village soviets, each of which might administer up to twenty separate settlements.[12]

There were, then, obvious practical reasons for attempting to increase peasant intake. These reasons, however, scarcely account for the *scale* of this increase: the proportion of newly enrolled candidates classed as peasants rose from 11 percent in 1924 to 30 percent in 1925, and to 39 percent in 1926— an all time record in the history of the CPSU.[13] There is, indeed, abundant evidence that these developments were also greatly influenced by the current struggle for power in the party leadership.

By the autumn of 1924 Stalin's links with Zinoviev and Kamenev were wearing thin. In 1925 they finally broke, and the triumvirate was replaced by an alliance between Stalin and his protégés on the one hand and Bukharin and his fellow "rightists" on the other, with Zinoviev and Kamenev criticizing from a position increasingly close to Trotsky on

[10] M. Khatasevich, "O sostave i rabote partiacheiki na sele" (On the Composition and Work of the Party Cell in the Countryside), *B*, Nos. 3-4, 1925, pp. 74-75.

[11] See *B*, No. 12, June 1926, p. 69.

[12] Khatasevich, in *B*, Nos. 3-4, 1925, p. 74.

[13] Bubnov in *BSE* (1st edn.), Vol. xi, col. 534.

the "left."[14] The main policy issue in terms of which Stalin mounted his campaign to crush his former allies was the proper attitude towards the peasantry. While the "left" represented the NEP concessions to the peasants as a short-term retreat, and advocated restrictions to prevent private-enterprise farming from becoming too prosperous, Bukharin was declaring to the peasants: "Enrich yourselves, develop your farms, do not fear that you will be subjected to restrictions."[15] The implications for party admission policy are obvious: if you are contemplating a tougher line towards the peasantry, you must guard against people from a peasant milieu assuming too much weight in the party membership, but you will have no such inhibitions about recruiting peasants if you are thinking in terms of a long-term alliance with the peasantry and seeking to consolidate this alliance. The mass intake of peasants in 1925-1926 was therefore a logical consequence of Stalin's realignment with the "right" at this period. Nor is it surprising that it should have come in for bitter criticism from Stalin's critics on the "left." In the latter part of 1925, recruitment policy became a public issue as one of the questions dividing the Politburo majority from the "Leningrad Opposition" (the supporters of Zinoviev, so-called because most of them were concentrated in the Leningrad party organization, which Zinoviev had dominated since the Revolution). Since this is the only occasion in the history of the Soviet regime on which leadership struggles have provoked sharp public debate on party membership, the development of this controversy deserves careful consideration.

The Politics of Recruiting Peasants

At the Thirteenth Congress in May 1924, when Stalin's

[14] See Schapiro, *The CPSU*, Chap. 16.
[15] *P*, April 14, 1925.

alliance with Zinoviev and Kamenev was still in force and the drive to swamp Trotsky's supporters with a flood of new recruits from the factories was at its height, certain statements were made which were destined to prove acutely embarrassing to Stalin and his supporters. The congress resolution "On Immediate Tasks of Party Construction" proclaimed the slogan of building up the proportion of workers from the bench to 50 percent of the total party membership within a twelve-month period.[16] This objective was not only not achieved within a year, it was never achieved, although it remained official policy for some six or seven years, and was pursued with varying degrees of intensity. The resolution "On the Report of the Central Committee," however, set an even more ambitious target. "The time is drawing close," it read, "when the whole basic mass of the proletariat of our Union will enter the party. The Congress obliges the Central Committee to conduct all its work in this direction, so that the vast majority of the members of the party in the near future should consist of workers directly engaged in production."[17] And Molotov added the startling gloss that the party was currently aiming at bringing the proportion of workers in its membership up to 90 percent.[18]

The short-term political advantages of this strongly worker-oriented recruitment program have already been noted. Taking a longer view, however, commitment to such a program held certain obvious disadvantages for Stalin. One was that it left him less room to maneuver than he customarily contrived to preserve for himself: by allowing his supporters to identify the rapid proletarianization of the party membership with the sacrosanct doctrine of "workers' democracy,"[19]

[16] *XIII s"ezd*, p. 606.
[17] *Ibid.*, p. 601.
[18] *Ibid.*, p. 505.
[19] See *ibid.*, pp. 499-506.

he made it difficult to retreat from this policy without inviting charges of denying "workers' democracy." It was a policy, moreover, on which he could be easily outbid, for he would be bound to oppose mass recruitment beyond the point where expansion of the rank-and-file membership of local organizations outran the power of the party bureaucracy to discipline and control them. Otherwise what had been a device to swamp the Trotskyite opposition could easily become a sorcerer's apprentice swamping the bureaucracy itself and thereby threatening the very basis of Stalin's power. In the latter part of 1925, after the triumvirate had split up, the Leningrad Opposition was to exploit these factors in its attacks on Stalin, as we shall see.

The intake of peasants began to build up very soon after the Lenin enrollment. At the Thirteenth Congress in May 1924, along with his emphasis on proletarianizing the party membership, Molotov also spoke of the need to make it easier for peasants to join.[20] In the weeks that followed local committees began to assume a more encouraging attitude towards peasants wishing to enter the party,[21] and in the second half of the year, 23,000 peasants became candidates for party membership, compared with 12,000 in the first

[20] See *XIII s"ezd*, p. 505. It is worth noting that the relevant Congress resolution (*ibid.*, pp. 604-617) does not appear to have contained the specific provisions on peasant admissions foreshadowed by Molotov.

[21] See V. Osipov et al., eds., *Saratovskaia partiinaia organizatsiia v gody vosstanovleniia narodnogo khoziaistva*, p. 304. This shift of policy was particularly welcome to party officials in rural areas, who in the course of the Lenin enrollment had been faced with the task of allaying peasant suspicions that the restriction of recruitment to workers signified a move by the party to a more hostile position towards the peasantry. The Saratov gubkom had been so disturbed by this problem that they had petitioned the Central Committee in February 1924 for some relaxation of the Lenin enrollment restrictions so far as the peasant were concerned (*ibid.*, pp. 244-245).

138

half.[22] A plenum of the Central Committee held in October 1924 issued a resolution calling for an intensification of party work in the rural areas,[23] and shortly after this a circular was sent to local committees requiring them to shift from a policy of easing the obstacles to peasant admission to the party to one of active recruitment of peasants.[24] Whatever impact this decision may have had, however, was obscured in the early part of 1925 by the launching of a "second Lenin enrollment," which again focused recruitment efforts on the industrial workers, who accounted for 74 percent of all recruits in February 1925.[25] At the same time, there seems to have been some ambivalence in official statements on recruitment during the second Lenin enrollment, which may have reflected divergent policies within the triumvirate.[26]

[22] Based on Bubnov's figures in *BSE*, Vol. XI, col. 533, Table 7.

[23] See *KPSS v rez*, Vol. I, pp. 906-911.

[24] See *SPR*, No. 5, pp. 242-243. For an example of a gubkom instruction on the implementation of these measures by the local apparatus, see V. Osipov et al., eds., *Saratovskaia partiinaia organizatsiia v gody vosstanovleniia narodnogo khoziaistva*, pp. 304-305.

[25] *Izv Ts K*, Nos. 19-20, May 30, 1925.

[26] The initiative on launching a new drive to enroll "bench-workers" in the party in honor of the anniversary of Lenin's death was taken by the Moscow Committee which, although now led by Stalin's nominee Uglanov, may still have been considerably influenced by Kamenev, who remained Chairman of the Moscow Soviet. A spokesman for the Central Committee apparatus, while acknowledging the appropriateness of this drive, warned that it should not be allowed to assume anything like the scale of the original Lenin enrollment. He also indicated that special efforts should be directed towards enlisting komsomol members and women, who had been neglected in previous mass recruitment drives. (See *P*, January 4, 1925.) Throughout the period the Central Committee continued to hold before local committees the high priority of recruiting peasants. (See, for instance, CC instruction to Voronezh gubkom, *P*, January 9, 1925.) Molotov, in an article on party recruitment on the occasion of Lenin's death, did not once mention the "second Lenin enrollment," and stressed

The real turning point was the Fourteenth Party Conference, at the end of April 1925. By this time Stalin's alliance with Zinoviev and Kamenev was at an end and his behind-the-scenes moves to undermine their influence had already begun. As yet, however, they had not come out into open opposition, and efforts were being made on both sides to convey an impression of solidarity. The conference decision on party policy towards the peasantry, though it later served as a basis for Stalin's new alliance with the Right, was greeted by Zinoviev as a fruitful compromise.[27]

The delicate stage which had been reached in relationships within the leadership was also reflected in the handling of the party membership question at the conference. Molotov's report on internal party matters, although it was concerned primarily with the stimulation of party work in the villages, made no mention of recruitment policy, and the topic was likewise avoided in the draft resolution distributed to the conference delegates. Central Committee secretary Kaganovich, in a brief reference to the composition of the party, spoke vaguely of the need to "improve" the membership in rural areas, but again avoided discussion of specific measures.[28] In his closing remarks, Molotov acknowledged the criticism of his fellow-Stalinist Yaroslavsky that the question of peasant recruitment had been neglected in his report and the draft resolution, and stated that this defect would be made good by the editorial commission entrusted with putting the resolution in its final shape after its approval by the conference.[29]

---

that "there now stands before us the task of improving and strengthening party organizations in the countryside" (*P*, January 21, 1925).

[27] See Schapiro, *The CPSU*, p. 292.

[28] *P*, April 28, 1925.

[29] *Ibid.*, April 29, 1925.

When the final version of the resolution was published, it contained a substantial passage on "Improving the Composition of the Party and Regulating Its Growth." While reaffirming the Thirteenth Congress objective of raising the proportion of bench-workers in the party to 50 percent, it forbade the imposition of recruitment quotas for different social categories—the main device employed by local organizations to raise the percentage of workers among those enrolled. Without referring specifically to the second Lenin enrollment, which had now been running for three months, it stated that "mass recruitment campaigns" were to be "unconditionally terminated." The main emphasis was placed upon the necessity "of expanding rural party organizations with the best, reliably revolutionary and politically prepared village toilers and farm laborers, poor peasants, and that part of the middle peasantry which is closest to the party." Measures to facilitate this included the reduction of the number of recommendations required by peasant applicants, exemption from the obligation to secure recommendations at all where there were no local communists who knew the applicant (subject to his producing a satisfactory impression upon interview by a party emissary), allowing ukoms to approve the admission of peasants without reference to the gubkom, as was previously required, and requiring all concerned to avoid red tape in considering peasant applications for admission to the party and for transfer from candidate to full membership.[30] To stimulate peasant support, it was also resolved to dispatch 1,000 party instructors and 3,000 propagandists to rural areas.[31]

This amounted to a radical revision of existing recruitment policies, and the tactics employed by Stalin's supporters

[30] See *KPSS v rez*, Vol. II, pp. 22-23.
[31] *Ibid.*, p. 21.

to get it enacted obviously reflected a desire to clothe this policy revision with the authority of a party conference, but without exposing it to open discussion, which would only have put weapons into the hands of the emergent Zinoviev faction.

The effects of this reorientation of party recruitment were felt almost immediately. Within weeks of the Fourteenth Conference the proportion of workers among new recruits fell by almost 20 percent.[32] According to Zinoviev, by the autumn of 1925 local committees were working toward a recruitment target of 40 percent peasants,[33] which was approximately double the intake in the first quarter of the year. The stimulation of peasant recruitment was certainly a major preoccupation of the party apparatus during this period. A conference of provincial officials on party work in rural areas, convened by the Central Committee in September, devoted much of its attention to the expansion of rural party cells.[34] In the ensuing weeks a number of local committees

[32] *Izv Ts K*, No. 41, October 26, 1925.

[33] See *XIV s"ezd Vsesoiuznoi Kommunisticheskoi Partii(b): stenograficheskii otchët* (Moscow-Leningrad, 1926), p. 126 (cited hereafter as *XIV s"ezd*), where Zinoviev quotes the Tula party newspaper *Kommunar* for October 12, 1925. Although no official instruction confirming this allegation has been discovered, it was not officially denied, and the *actual* proportion of peasants among new recruits must have been about 40 percent during this period; as already noted, the official figure for 1926 was 39 percent. The Stalinists certainly appear to have had some idea of the limits beyond which the expansion of peasant recruitment should not go. In Kirgizia, where the proportion of "middle peasants" in the party rose to 66 percent, local committees were instructed in November 1925 to modify their recruitment policy so as to bring the proportion of poor peasants, farm laborers and workers up to 50 percent. See *Rost i regulirovanie sostava Kommunisticheskoi Partii Kirgizii (1918-1962 gg.)*, (Frunze, 1962), p. 44 (cited hereafter as *KP Kirgizii*).

[34] See article by E. Kviring, *P*, October 1, 1925.

were rebuked for not recruiting enough peasants.[35] Various devices were employed to help spot suitable peasant candidates: through the activities of the komsomol cell, through careful study and sounding out of possible candidates by individual communists, by holding village meetings at which the rank-and-file peasants were encouraged to express their views on current issues affecting them, and so on; once spotted the prospective candidate was frequently tried out in some minor assignment before being enrolled. As we have noted, the Fourteenth Conference resolution had eased the statutory requirements for recommendations so far as peasant candidates were concerned. A common practice when a peasant applicant was unknown to the members of the local cell was for one of the latter to act as guarantor for the newcomer, but with the whole cell accepting responsibility for their recruit before the ukom. Predictably, the pressure on local committees encouraged artificial stimuli to peasant enlistment. In many places peasants were induced to join by promises of jobs in the local administration.[36]

Meanwhile there was one area which was virtually untouched by this campaign: that part of Northwest Russia which was controlled by Zinoviev's Leningraders. In the Leningrad guberniya, farming peasants contributed under 2 percent of the 30,000 membership increase between January and September 1925.[37] In the same period, only nine peas-

[35] See *P*, October 25, October 26 and November 6, 1925, and Mochalov, *op.cit.*, p. 307. At a party conference in the Kazakh (then known as Kirgiz) krai in December 1925, a number of local committees were rebuked for attempting to hold back peasant recruitment when it threatened to far outrun the recruitment of workers. See Beisembaev and Pakhmurnyi, *op.cit.*, p. 85.

[36] On the problems involved in recruiting peasants in the second half of 1925 and details of techniques employed, see I. Mivinskii, "On Enrolling Peasants in the Party," *P*, September 25, 1925.

[37] See report by A. Guski, *P*, November 21, 1925.

ants succeeded in gaining transfer from candidate to full membership in this area.[38] Meanwhile large-scale recruitment of workers continued in Leningrad, and typical of the measures adopted to this end was a local conference decision to enlist a further 27,000 metal-workers, with the object of making every second metal-worker in the city a party member.[39]

The position adopted by the Leningrad opposition on recruitment was a logical corollary of their opposition to "conciliatory" policies towards the peasantry. At the same time, it possessed certain tactical advantages which will be apparent from what has gone before. In the previous year the Stalin machine had committed the party to a recruitment program very strongly oriented towards the workers, and linked this to the sacrosanct principle of "workers' democracy." Stalin's effective abandonment of this policy gave Zinoviev and his followers a heaven-sent opportunity to represent themselves as the guardians of the true party line on this question, and to expose the inconsistency and hypocrisy of the Stalinists, thus lending weight to their general contention that the latter could not be relied on to prevent concessions to the peasants from degenerating into a sellout to the kulak. By outbidding the Stalinists on the policy of proletarianizing the party, they might also hope to appeal over the heads of Stalinist officials in industrial areas for the sympathies of the rank-and-file communists and nonparty workers. Molotov's complaint that the Leningrad opposition was attempting to employ the party recruitment issue so as to engage in demagoguery and flattery of the workers[40] suggests that the Stalinists, at least, expected this appeal to have some political effect. Finally, since Leningrad still contained by far the largest concentration of industrial workers in the country, a

[38] *XIV s"ezd*, p. 77.   [39] *Ibid.*, p. 448.   [40] *Ibid.*, p. 79.

worker-oriented recruitment policy was bound to favor the Leningrad opposition by raising their percentage of the total party membership and thereby the number of their delegates to party conferences and congresses.[41]

The Fourteenth Party Congress

The tactical disadvantage at which the Stalinists found themselves on this issue was reflected in their manifest concern to postpone a confrontation with the Leningrad Committee over recruitment policy. Late in September Zinoviev's protégé Zalutsky was called to Moscow to report to the Orgburo on the work of the Leningrad Committee and the Northwest Bureau of the Party. The resultant Orgburo decision, although it criticized the Leningraders sharply on a number of issues, large and small, confined its remarks on recruitment to a mild rebuke for enlisting too many white-collar workers.[42] Since some easing of the obstacles to white-collar enrollment enjoyed tacit Central Committee approval at this period,[43] and the only social category towards which Leningrad recruitment policy was strikingly at variance with that of the central party apparatus was the peasantry, a measure of hypocrisy evidently went into the framing of this decision.[44]

[41] In 1924-1925 the Leningrad party organization trebled its membership, while the rest of the party merely doubled (see V. M. Ivanov, *Iz istorii bor'by partii protiv "levogo" opportunizma* (Leningrad, 1965), p. 42. As well as forcing the intake of new candidates, the Leningrad leadership also issued an instruction to local organizations to speed up the transfer of candidates to full members, allegedly with the object of maximizing its voting delegates at the Fourteenth Congress (*ibid.*, p. 71).

[42] See *P*, October 13, 1925.

[43] See article by Smitten in *P*, December 8, 1925.

[44] During November the komsomol became a major arena of Stalinist attacks on the Leningrad Opposition, and afforded op-

Stalin's campaign against his old ally Zinoviev came to a head at the Fourteenth Party Congress, held in December 1925. In the course of the precongress discussion in the party press and at local and regional conferences, Stalin's tactics were to force the Leningraders into taking clear minority positions on issues on which differences had long existed but on which a public posture of moderation and conciliation had previously been maintained. Zinoviev and his supporters fell easily into this trap, and there was no issue on which they were readier to adopt an intransigent position than party recruitment policy, owing perhaps to the strong tactical position in which they found themselves on this issue.

The cautious position which the Stalinists intended to adopt on the recruitment issue became apparent in an article by Central Committee official Smitten published in the precongress discussion section of *Pravda* on December 8. The great intake of workers since Lenin's death, he argued, had so improved the class composition of the party that it was now possible to ease slightly the obstacles to nonproletarian enrollments which had been erected in 1921-1923. Increasing the percentage of workers in the party—particularly workers still in manual jobs—remained the first objective of recruitment policy; but the need to cement the alliance with the peasantry had now given the party a second objective: to expand the number of peasant communists. Progress towards the first objective was, broadly speaking, satisfactory,

---

portunities for indirect indictment of a number of internal party policies in Leningrad. The pro-Zinoviev Northwestern Conference of the komsomol was condemned by the komsomol Central Committee for its allegedly incorrect attitude towards the middle peasants, which expressed itself in forming peasants into so-called delegates' groups instead of allowing them to join the komsomol itself. This obviously also reflected on party recruitment policies in Leningrad. (See *P*, November 21, 1925.)

but not so the second. Although new recruits in recent months had included a considerable number officially classed as peasants, the majority of these were now employed in routine office duties, and peasants "at the plough" had constituted only 12 percent of the candidates admitted in the first half of 1925. Thus, while the prospects for recruiting more bench-workers would automatically improve with the expansion of industry, expanding party membership among the peasant farmers would require a special effort.[45]

Meanwhile Stalin's supporters and allies had commenced a diversionary move aimed at catching the Leningraders off balance and forcing them on to the defensive. On November 20[46] D. A. Sarkis, an Armenian party official employed in the Leningrad organization, sent an article to *Pravda* entitled "On Incorporating the Majority of the Industrial Proletariat into the Ranks of the Russian Communist Party," in which he made two main proposals: (a) "In its further work on regulating the growth and social composition of its organization, the party should strive in the next few years to incorporate 50-60 percent of all industrial workers into our communist ranks . . .;" and (b) "the congress should set itself the task of drawing the maximum number of workers into the party, with the object of bringing the percentage of workers (from the bench) in the party up to 90 percent by the Fifteenth Congress."[47] These proposals were completely in line with the general policy of the Leningrad organization[48] and

[45] *P*, December 8, 1925.

[46] For the date of the original document, see *XIV s"ezd*, p. 346.

[47] Details of Sarkis's original article are taken from his letter in *P*, December 9, 1925.

[48] The Leningrad Guberniya Conference resolved that "work for the further drawing of industrial workers into the party should remain at the center of the attention of party organizations. Our slogan should be to bring the proportion of party members who are

could fairly be regarded as following closely the resolutions of the previous congress and Molotov's statements on that occasion. However Bukharin, as editor of *Pravda*, refused to print the article as it stood, and handed it to Zinoviev to return. Sarkis immediately made some minor amendments and additions, but the second version of his article was also refused publication in Moscow, whereupon it appeared in *Leningradskaia Pravda.*[49]

At this point *Pravda* resorted to a subterfuge. In an unsigned article it referred to "the fantasy of certain comrades" as expressed in the proposals of Sarkis *to enlist 90 percent of the workers in the party,* and the second of Sarkis's proposals was quoted in proof of this allegation. Now the wording of this proposal was ambiguous in the Russian original as it is in our English translation, and while the meaning attributed to it by *Pravda* was obviously excluded by Sarkis's *first* proposal (which spoke of enlisting *50 to 60 percent of the workers* in the party in the next few years), the editors took good care to conceal this fact from their readers. Sarkis promptly sent a well-argued protest, which *Pravda* was constrained to publish, albeit in superfine print and with a scathing and question-begging editorial comment.[50] But the smear stuck, and throughout the precongress discussion any sign of sympathy with Leningrad recruitment policies immediately invited accusations of Sarkisovism, which was equated with the ideas of Lenin's Menshevik opponent Axelrod, who had advocated a mass workers' party.[51]

---

workers from the bench up to 80 to 90 percent in the course of the next year." This was not reported in Moscow at the time, but was quoted by Sarkis in his letter, *P*, December 9, 1925.

[49] *LP*, December 3, 1925. The article was also distributed in Leningrad in pamphlet form (see *XIV s"ezd*, p. 346).

[50] *P*, December 9, 1925.

[51] At the Ukrainian Congress, for instance, Kaganovich warned

This effectively spiked the guns of the Leningrad opposition on the recruitment issue, for all but the most sophisticated and best-informed communists must have received the impression that the Leningraders were themselves guilty of a wild deviation on this question. For the minority who might have remained unconvinced, *Pravda* also carried more reasoned arguments. Data from the 12,000 strong Krasnoe Sormovo plant in Nizhny-Novgorod was adduced to show that the party simply could not absorb a further massive intake of workers at this stage.[52] An article on Sarkis's views

the party against being led astray by the Sarkisovist-Axelrodist proposals to enlist the majority of the workers in the party immediately (*P*, December 10, 1925). See also the Ukrainian Congress resolution in *P*, December 12, 1925. For similar statements at party conferences at Tula and in the Urals, see *P*, December 11, 1925. The Moscow Guberniya Conference became an important arena for well-publicized attacks of this kind. See, for instance, reports of speeches by Bauman and Opasov in *P*, December 13, 1925. The resolution of the Moscow Guberniya Conference included the following passage: "The Conference rejects the hairbrained efforts to *immediately* draw 50 or more percent of all workers into the party. This policy, which has nothing to do with Leninism, would turn our party into an Axelrodist 'broad workers' party' and would render communist leadership of the working class impossible" (*P*, December 8, 1925). For a recent Soviet evaluation of Sarkis's proposals, see V. M. Ivanov, *op.cit.*, p. 65. Though critical, Ivanov does not repeat the contemporary Stalinist misrepresentation of the Leningrad position. However, this misrepresentation is still sometimes encountered in Soviet publications, e.g. D. I. Tiurin, *Chlenstvo v KPSS* (Moscow, 1966), p. 20.

[52] See G. Bakhaev, "Why Should the Enlistment of Workers in the Party Not Be Forced?" (*P*, December 11, 1925). Bakhaev stated that while the great majority of worker recruits during the first Lenin enrollment were young but mature adults performing creditably both in their jobs and in social activities, the second Lenin enrollment brought in a disproportionate number of totally unskilled and uneducated, socially passive candidates, many of them too old or far too young. The watering down of the political level of the party organization in the plant was indicated by widespread non-payment of dues and nonattendance at party meetings. Membership

argued that these remained quite unacceptable even if his ambiguous proposal were interpreted to mean, as he averred, that 90 percent of the party should consist of bench-workers (rather than that 90 percent of the bench-workers in the country should be taken into the party). Since 400,000 of the current membership were nonworkers, and it was neither justified nor practicable to reduce this number significantly, Sarkis's proposals would mean recruiting about three million workers in the next year, but there were in fact only two million workers in the country.[53] The Leningraders were given no opportunity to clarify their true position or to defend it: the section of Zinoviev's speech to the Leningrad Conference in which he dealt with recruitment policy was not made public in Moscow till December 17, the day before the Congress opened, although the speech was delivered on December 3.[54]

---

had outrun the capacity of the organization to mobilize and train it effectively: over half the candidates in the Krasnoe Sormovo plant had never been given any party assignments and in another district of Nizhny-Novgorod the proportion of candidates without party assignments now stood at two-thirds.

[53] See article by E. Lande, *P*, December 15, 1925.

[54] See *P*, December 17, 1925. Less controversial sections of the speech had been published by *Pravda* some days previously. Zinoviev supported Sarkis's general approach, but presented an entirely different picture of the Leningrad position on this question than the garbled version of Sarkis's proposals which had been circulated by Moscow, and one which the Stalinists would have found it far harder to counter. The party, he argued, must work towards the target of a membership consisting of 90 percent workers. This was certainly not an immediate possibility, but the time was not far off when the expansion of industry would bring the working class up to five or ten millions. It was a mistake to oppose the criteria of quantity and quality: the quality depended on the efficiency of local organizations in training the recruits once they had joined. Even the need to strengthen the party in rural areas argued for energetic recruitment of workers, for where better to get reliable cadres for party work in the villages than from reliable proletarian communists?

The Fourteenth Congress was of major importance in Stalin's campaign against Zinoviev and his supporters. Having forced them out into the open, Stalin was able to command overwhelming votes against them on major current issues, and then to employ their opposition stand at the Congress as a pretext for a purge of the Leningrad party and government apparatus, thus depriving Zinoviev of his main organizational base.

The handling of the recruitment issue was predictable from the pre-congress discussion. Stalin first broached the issue in his "Political Report," focusing his remarks on the "miserable" representation of the party in rural areas. The increase in peasant membership since the previous congress had brought only a marginal improvement: the proportion of communists among the peasantry had risen from 0.26 percent to 0.37 percent. "I do not want to suggest that it should be progressing in seven-league strides," he added, "but all the same the percentage of peasants in our party is quite insignificant. Ours is a working class party. Workers should predominate in it. This is a reflection of the fact that we have a dictatorship of the proletariat. But it is also clear that, without a union with the peasantry, a dictatorship of the proletariat is impossible, and that a given percentage of the best people from the peasantry in the membership of our party is an essential anchor for the party in the countryside. Things are still not so good on this point."[55] Neither he nor Molotov in his "organizational report" took issue with the actual views of the Leningraders on recruitment, but both of them made much play with the now familiar caricature of Sarkis's proposals. Stalin stated that, in spite of large-scale worker recruitment, the proportion of workers who were communists had risen only from 7 to 8 percent since the Thirteenth Con-

[55] *XIV s"ezd*, p. 53.

gress, and that this showed the absurdity of incorporating 90 percent of the workers in the party in the next year or two.[56] Molotov employed the official distortion of Sarkis's proposals in order to counter allegations that he had changed his own tune since the Thirteenth Congress.[57] It was in vain that Zinoviev[58] and Sarkis[59] sought to provoke a genuine debate on the points which were really at issue between them and the Stalinists: they may have had most of the arguments, but the Stalinists had their red herring—and the votes.[60] The relevant passage in the Congress resolution read as follows:

Reinforcing the party and strengthening its leading role in all fields of our construction work is more than ever necessary in the present complex situation, and this presupposes correctly regulating the party's composition. In this area the Congress considers it necessary to pursue a policy aimed at raising the quality of the membership of party organizations, at drawing ever more workers into the party and constantly raising the relative weight of the proletarian core of the party. At the same time, while re-affirming the necessity of strictly observing the established measures for limiting the entry of nonproletarian elements into the party, the Congress rejects the policy which leads to an excessive inflation of the party's ranks and to filling it with

[56] *Ibid.*, p. 52. On current definitions of who were "workers," these percentages seem to have been grossly understated by Stalin.

[57] *Ibid.*, p. 78.

[58] See *ibid.*, pp. 126-127 and 448-449.

[59] *Ibid.*, pp. 346-348.

[60] Yaroslavsky made a typical intervention on this issue, taunting the opposition with figures illustrating the heavy concentration of working class members in organizations controlled by the Stalinists. "So don't think you can say that you in Leningrad have real class antennae, while all the rest of us are infected with a petty bourgeois deviation. No one will believe you" (*ibid.*, p. 197).

semi-proletarian elements who have not been schooled in the trade unions and in proletarian organizations in general. The Congress condemns such endeavors, on the grounds that they have nothing in common with Leninism and deny the correct relationship between party (the vanguard of the class) and class, and that they would render communist leadership impossible.[61]

This closed the argument, and before long it was buried under the debris of the shattered Leningrad Opposition.

Recruitment in 1926

As we have noted, in 1926 the trend towards reduced worker recruitment and increased peasant recruitment became even more marked than in 1925. The extent to which membership policies had now moved away from the proletarian ideal is brought out most clearly if we examine the actual employment of new recruits as distinct from their social classification.

As we see in Table 3,[62] less than half of those enlisted in the CPSU in 1926 were wage earners in manual occupations, and little more than a quarter came from the "industrial proletariat," which was supposed to be the "core" of the party. Nearly half the recruits were either peasant farmers or office workers.

An interesting footnote to the question of worker recruitment during the 1920's was the much higher rate of recruitment in small enterprises than in large ones. In 1926 the proportion of communist employees ran from over a quarter in factories with less than 200 workers, to under 10 percent in factories with more than 2,000 workers. One current explanation was that (a) it was mainly skilled workers who sought

61 *KPSS v rez*, Vol. II, p. 81.
62 SOURCE: *Izv Ts K*, Nos. 22-23, June 17, 1927.

TABLE 3: CURRENT OCCUPATION OF CANDIDATES ADMITTED IN 1926

Occupation	Percent of all admitted
Factory workers	27.2
Transport workers	7.4
Other hired workers	7.8
Agricultural laborers	3.1
Peasants working exclusively on their own holdings	25.0
Peasants also doing paid administrative work	4.9
Peasants also engaged in handicrafts	0.3
Officials of party, soviets, trade unions, etc.	15.2
Artisans	0.6
Army	2.4
Students	3.4
Other employment	2.0
Unemployed	0.7

to join the party, and these were less common in larger enterprises, while (b) in larger enterprises it was harder for the party cells to extend their influence to all workers.[63] Georgii Malenkov, at that time a junior Central Committee official, had a different explanation. He suggested that the main reason was that smaller undertakings were staffed largely by "older workers," whereas the larger enterprises had taken on numbers of new, raw workers in recent years. Malenkov also contested the accepted view that the factory party organizations drew most of their recruits from skilled workers. On the contrary, it was the semiskilled workers who provided most of the recruits, in his view. Few unskilled workers joined the party, and "insufficient" highly skilled. The latter, according to Malenkov, included a "stratum of liberal workers" whose influence on the working class as a whole would have to be

[63] See E. Smitten, "O regulirovanii rosta Partii" (On Regulation of the Party's Growth), PS, No. 12, June 1926, p. 62.

countered.[64] On the main question of fact here, Malenkov's views seem to conflict with the official figures (Table 4),[65]

TABLE 4: COMMUNISTS EMPLOYED AS INDUSTRIAL WORKERS, JANUARY 1927

	Skilled Percent	Semiskilled Percent	Unskilled Percent
Members	62.8	24.3	12.9
Candidates	52.6	26.7	20.7
All communists	60.0	25.0	15.0

suggesting either some major discrepancy of definition or a marked tendency for workers to be promoted from the semi-skilled to the skilled categories soon after joining the party.

Secondary Causes of Deproletarianization

While the main force for deproletarianization of the rank-and-file membership at this time was undoubtedly the increased recruitment of peasants, other factors also operated in this direction. Firstly, in the middle 1920's decisions were taken allotting several other segments of the population temporary priority in party recruitment, and in some cases actually setting substantial admission targets. These included such diverse and overlapping groups as village teachers, trade

[64] G. Malenkov, "Vovlechenie rabochikh v Partiiu" (Drawing Workers into the Party), *B*, Nos. 21-22, November 1926, pp. 41-53.

[65] SOURCE: *Sotsial'nyi i natsional'nyi sostav VKP(b)*, p. 65. In transport the proportion of worker communists classed as skilled was even higher—68.3 percent (*ibid.*, p. 67). *Izv Ts K*, Nos. 24-25, June 28, 1926, noting that the skilled category had dropped to 42 percent of worker recruits in one guberniya, described this as highly unsatisfactory.

and consumer-cooperative employees, women, komsomol members, Cossacks and various minority nationalites.[66]

The pattern of party recruitment in the armed forces also played its part. The army, with its exceptionally favorable conditions for control and indoctrination, has always been an important source of recruits to the CPSU. In 1926, for example, there were 22,261 communists among the men demobilized on the completion of their service, and five-sixths of these had joined the party while in army service.[67] Since it was a predominantly peasant army, workers always formed a minority of those becoming party members in the course of their service; for instance, only one-third in 1926 and the first half of 1927.[68] Moreover, the great majority of servicemen joining the party seem to have been men promoted or about to be promoted to noncommissioned or commissioned rank. In February 1926 the Army Political Directorate issued a decision "On Regulating the Growth of Party Organizations in the Red Army," which stressed the need to raise both proletarian and rank-and-file representation in army party organizations.[69] While this evidently met with a measure of success, rank-and-file Red Army men remained a very small proportion of the military communists during this period.[70] (See further, Chapter 7.)

At the same time, recruitment was not the only determinant of changes in the party's composition. The varying fortunes of the existing membership also played a part. An important factor here, as we have noted, was the transfer of manual workers (and this applied to peasants too) to white-collar jobs, either by direct promotion or by way of assign-

[66] See SPR, No. 5, pp. 243, 256, 270-271.
[67] Izv Ts K, No. 13, April 8, 1927.
[68] Ibid., also Nos. 34-35, September 17, 1927.
[69] SPR, No. 6, Vol. II, pp. 189-191.
[70] See Izv Ts K, Nos. 47-48, December 2, 1926.

ment to study courses. Another factor of considerable intrinsic interest (though statistically of less significance) was the varying incidence of expulsions and of voluntary withdrawals from the party among different social groups.

While we have seen reason to suspect that a proportion of the expulsions during this period were politically motivated, most of them were probably genuine cases of violation of the law or "communist ethics" and alcoholism. Be this as it may, expulsion did not affect the main social groups in proportion to their representation in the party: peasants were by far the most frequently involved; much the same proportions of manual and white-collar workers were expelled, except among candidate members, where white-collar categories were more numerous.[71]

The pattern was very different so far as voluntary withdrawals were concerned. This category included communists either resigning formally or dropping out of party activities and failing to pay their dues, who were simply removed from the books automatically. One percent of the party membership "withdrew voluntarily" in each of the years 1924 and 1925, and 2 percent in 1926.[72] The great majority of these were workers, and what is more, the proportion of workers was increasing. Sixty percent of those withdrawing voluntarily in the first half of 1925 were employed in manual jobs, 70 percent in the second half, and 77 percent in 1926.[73] A special group of members automatically excluded comprised those who failed to register in the party census in the early months of 1927. Nearly 3 percent of the party lost their membership for this reason. Almost two-thirds of them were

[71] *Ibid.*, No. 34, September 7, 1925.
[72] *Ibid.*, Nos. 37-38, September 20, 1926 and Nos. 24-25, June 30, 1927.
[73] *Ibid.*, and also No. 34, September 7, 1925.

workers, a third were peasants, and the number of white-collar workers was negligible (although the latter made up nearly half the total party membership at this time).[74]

The reasons worker communists tended to drop out of the party, while those in administrative or office jobs did not, are by now familiar, and they were sometimes acknowledged with remarkable frankness by contemporary analysts. For example, one contributor to a Central Committee journal, reporting the reasons given for resignation during 1925 ("family reasons," "religious reasons," "inability to master political study assignments," etc.) commented as follows: "Many of these reasons are merely formal, frequently concealing such motives as heaviness of membership dues, dissatisfaction with reduction in work status, no desire to undertake elective party work, disappointment at their failure to receive additional material benefits from the party, etc. . . ."[75] Another observer commented even more revealingly: "Certain groups of white-collar elements in the party hold to it more strongly [than workers and peasants] due to the advantages in their employment which to a greater or lesser extent are bound up with their membership of the party, as the ruling party." And he went on: "From this there arises the fact that when, for example, a white-collar worker is expelled, he seeks out every possibility of remaining in the party, taking it right up to the Central Control Commission, whereas a worker rarely contests a decision on his expulsion even at the level of the Uezd Control Commission."[76]

The Party Census

The party census of 1927, more comprehensive, better organized and better reported than the first party census in

[74] *Ibid.*, Nos. 24-25, June 30, 1927, and Nos. 32-33, August 31, 1927.
[75] *Ibid.*, Nos. 37-38, September 20, 1926.
[76] *Ibid.*, Nos. 32-33, August 31, 1927.

1922, yielded a greater wealth of information about the composition of the CPSU than has ever been available before or since. Originally planned to begin on December 10, 1926 and to be completed by the end of that month, the census actually ran throughout January and dragged on in places till the middle of 1927. Analyses of census returns were given as for January 10, 1927. New party cards were issued in conjunction with the census; members not completing census returns were refused new cards and as we have noted were automatically regarded as having left the party.[77]

In considering the census data on the social composition of the party, close attention must be paid to certain problems of definition. During the 1920's, the early practice of defining "social situation" in terms of prerevolutionary occupation was dropped, without any definite new criteria being substituted. This resulted in considerable confusion in official statistical analyses. In August 1925, the Central Committee, noting that this confusion "rendered it impossible to correctly regulate the social composition of the party" issued a circular signed by Central Committee Secretary Molotov, which laid down the main principles observed by party statisticians and analysts for some years to come.

The 1925 formula retained the basic threefold division into workers, peasants and white-collar workers and others. "Workers" (*rabochie*) were defined as persons whose basic occupation was as hired physical labor in production and transport (subsequent applications of the formula indicated that hired laborers in all other fields—including agriculture —were also included with the "workers"); "peasants" (*krest'iane*) consisted of persons whose basic occupation was agriculture, stockraising, hunting or fishing, provided this was carried on as an independent undertaking or in a

[77] See *SPR*, No. 6, Vol. I, pp. 547-553 and 603-605.

collective enterprise or an enterprise belonging to parents or relatives (i.e. on any basis other than for wages); the category of "white-collar workers" (*sluzhashchie*) comprised communists whose basic occupation was administrative, managerial, cultural or educational, judicial, medical or other intellectual work, or who were employed as office staff in production enterprises or administrative or cultural institutions; the "others" included individual artisans, students, housewives, and some additional numerically insignificant categories. This breakdown was held to be based on the two considerations of "situation in production," i.e. whether self-employed or employed for wages, and "basic occupation," which was defined—and this was the most important innovation—as the occupation pursued *before joining the party*, and "which has served over a more or less prolonged period as the chief source of livelihood." It was stressed that changes of occupation once in the party did not affect "social situation."[78]

This formula was employed by the Central Committee in maintaining its current statistical records compiled from the returns submitted regularly by local committees. The 1927 census analysts, however, made some significant departures from it, in order to assimilate their classification to that employed by the government's Central Statistical Administration in its analyses of the population at large. The main departures were these: (1) the census added a number of occupations to the white-collar category, notably junior technical personnel, foremen and factory brigade leaders, storemen, firemen, office attendants and nurses; (2) where a member had held a number of jobs prior to joining the party, his "social situation" was determined by his last job (rather

[78] See *Izv Ts K*, No. 34, September 7, 1925.

than by the job he had been in longest, as was prescribed in current party statistics); (3) peasants who had worked for wages prior to recruitment were classified as either workers or white-collar workers, depending on the nature of the work.

These discrepancies in the criteria employed resulted in considerable differences between social analyses based on the census and those based on current party statistics, not only with respect to "social situation," but also in the classification of current occupation. Table 5[79] summarizes the census results relating to "social situation" and occupation, and compares them with the Central Committee Statistical Department's breakdowns of current statistical data.

While our attention is directed towards the substantial divergencies in official class and occupational analyses which inconsistencies in the classification of certain marginal groups were capable of producing, it is worth considering the effects of some further juggling with the basic categories which took place in the year or so following the party census. In March 1927, the Central Committee's Statistical Department issued a circular containing a number of "clarifications" of the classifications employed in current party statistics. The overall effect of these appeared to be to widen the worker and white-collar categories and substantially narrow the peasant category.[80] One is tempted to speculate here whether

[79] SOURCES: *Sotsial'nyi i natsional'nyi sostav VKP(b)*, pp. 26, 6-9; *Izv Ts K*, No. 40, October 31, 1927. Supporters of Zinoviev employed the census figures to argue that by relaxing the preference for manual workers in party recruitment, Stalin had permitted an alarming drop in worker representation in the party, and an official spokesman at the Fifteenth Congress was obliged to give a painstaking explanation of the statistical errors on which this criticism rested. See *Piatnadtsatyi s"ezd VKP(b): stenograficheskii otchёt* (Moscow, 1962), Vol. II, p. 405 (cited hereafter as *XV s"ezd*).

[80] The instruction will be found in *WKP* 213, pp. 115-116. In the

TABLE 5: CLASS COMPOSITION AND OCCUPATION—COMPARISON OF
CENSUS AND CURRENT STATISTICAL ANALYSES

	Current Central Committee statistics for Jan. 1, 1927	Party Census statistics for Jan. 10, 1927
	Percent	Percent
"Social situation"		
Workers	55.1	55.7
Peasants	27.3	19.0
White-collar workers and others	17.6	25.3
Occupation		
Factory and transport workers	36.8	30.0
Hired farm laborers	1.3	1.5
Peasants working own farms	10.9	8.4
Employees in offices of government and voluntary organizations	35.2	42.8
Others	17.1	18.8

such changes were in part motivated by a concern to weaken the case for "left" opposition charges of a capitulation to the peasantry. Further "clarifications," promulgated in a Central Committee decision in March 1928, included the important innovation that "communists whose basic occupation *after* joining the party is hired physical labor in indus-

---

Smolensk guberniya in the year October 1926—September 1927 the proportion of communists registered as peasants fell by 7 percent, while the proportion registered as workers rose by 3 percent and as white-collar workers by 4 percent; these changes were said to have been largely the result of reclassifications consequent upon this instruction. See *Rost i dinamika sostava gubernskoi partorganizatsii za period 1/X-1926 g.—1/X-1927 g.* (Growth and Dynamics of the Composition of the Guberniya Party Organization over the Period October 1, 1926—Ocober 1, 1927), *WKP* 33, *Protokol* No. 13.

try, transport or agriculture are to be classified as *workers*, even if they were recorded as belonging to some other social group at the time of joining the party."[81] This meant in effect reassigning a further substantial group of "peasants" to the worker category. These shifting criteria of classification compel us to treat with some reserve the official figures for "class composition" or "social situation" relating to this period.

[81] "Ob opredelenii sotsial'nogo polozheniia kommunistov, prinimaemykh v partiiu. Postanovlenie Ts K ot 13-go marta 1928 g." (On Defining the Social Situation of Communists Admitted to the Party. CC Decision of March 13, 1928), *WKP* 213. This and the attached Instruction also redefined a number of other points. For example, the vexed question of how to classify *mladshii obsluzhivaiushchii personal* (miscellaneous subordinate service staff, such as cleaners, watchmen, tearoom attendants, etc.) was finally settled by classifying them as workers if they were employed in production enterprises and as white-collar workers if employed in public offices and institutions. The decision also ordered discussions between party and government statisticians to reach agreement on the classification of factory foremen, brigade leaders, firemen and certain other groups who, as was noted above, were variously classified in the 1927 party census and the current party statistics. Unfortunately, no trace has been found of the final decision on this important group, if such a decision was in fact taken in this period. A report in the Smolensk archive of a guberniya conference of party statistical officers held in May 1928 to discuss problems of reclassifying the existing membership according to the Central Committee's revised criteria, reveals abundant evidence of confusion and incompetence, and thus raises serious doubts as to the accuracy with which this reclassification was implemented. See *WKP* 33. Details are available on the effects of these reclassifications on the official class analysis of CPSU members in the Kaluga guberniya. Here the social classification of all members was checked in the light of current criteria in December 1927 and again in June 1928. In the first check the proportion classified as peasants was reduced by 3.3 percent, while the proportion classified as workers was increased by .1 percent and as white-collar workers by 2.9 percent. In the second there was a further 1.2 percent reduction in those classified as peasants, and increases in those classified as workers and white-collar workers of .9 percent and .5 percent respectively. See *WKP* 44, p. 49.

Looking more closely at the findings of the 1927 party census as to how the membership was currently employed, we learn that nearly half a million people employed in the offices of government, party, trade union and other organizations held party cards. The party also included 343,000 factory and transport employees and just over a hundred thousand working peasants.[82] Among factory employees, the ratio of party members was one in ten for manual workers, compared with one in five for managerial and office workers.

The census also provided the first detailed information on how members registered as workers by "social situation" were currently employed. Under half were still in manual jobs, 29 percent were now officials of the government, party, trade unions, etc., 2.5 percent held junior office jobs, 7 percent were in the Red Army and nearly 5 percent were currently students. The distribution of "peasant" communists was very similar. By contrast, six-sevenths of those listed as "intelligentsia and white-collar workers" were still employed as such, although a few of these were currently in the Red Army or on study courses.[83]

[82] *Sotsial'nyi i natsional'nyi sostav VKP(b)*, p. 42.

[83] *Ibid.*, p. 47. For a detailed analysis of current employment of white-collar communists in 1927, see *Kommunisty v sostave apparata gosuchrezhdenii i obshchestvennykh organizatsii: itogi vsesoiuznoi perepisi 1927 goda* (Moscow, 1929), pp. 18ff.

Chapter 5

Proletarianization Renewed—and Ended

Every Second Communist a Bench-Worker!

The 1927 census showed that the objective of raising the proportion of bench-workers to at least 50 percent of the party membership, first proclaimed at the Thirteenth Congress in May 1924, was as far from achievement as ever, while the contraction of the "proletarian nucleus" of the party, which had been denounced at the Fourteenth Congress by Zinoviev and his supporters, was still continuing.

Even before the census, however, the first steps had been taken in a campaign which was destined in the next three years to effect a radical change in this situation. Addressing the Orgburo in October 1926, Molotov stated that the decline in working class recruitment, which had been inevitable following the Lenin enrollment, must now be arrested. Referring to the continued growth of industry, he argued that this rendered the achievement of the 50 percent bench-worker objective both feasible and essential. Molotov's views were embodied in a Central Committee decision ordering a concerted drive to recruit bench-workers with the aim of reaching this objective within the near future.[1]

Subsequently, the census results were quoted in statistical justification of this drive, and the census analysts were given the task of working out its implications in terms of recruitment ratios and schedules. They calculated that it would mean enrolling in the party some 435,000 of the country's four million manual workers within a two-year period,

[1] *Izv Ts K*, Nos. 47-48, December 2, 1926.

while simultaneously limiting recruitment from all other social groups to a maximum of 110,000.[2]

A special study and pilot project carried out in 1926-1927 to test the feasibility of drawing back into the party working class members who had dropped out in recent years was indicative of the seriousness with which the proletarianization objective was now to be pursued.[3] The immediate result of the drive was a rise in the recruitment of bench-workers from 42 percent in 1926 to 64 percent in 1927. Large though it was, this increase still fell considerably short of the census analysts' suggested goals, and it was clearly insufficient to achieve the 50 percent objective in the near future. A review of progress, coinciding with the tenth anniversary of the Bolshevik Revolution, in October 1927, initiated an intensified phase of the drive which became known as the "October enrollment," and indicated the lines along which further effort should be concentrated. The drive should be focused at the workshop level in large plants, and directed first and foremost at worker "activists"—i.e. those already active in party-directed social, welfare or other programs in the factories—only 30 percent of whom were yet in the party. The komsomol and women's organizers should be more energetic in preparing suitable candidates for admission to the party, and the obstacles to the enrollment of white-collar workers should be more stringently enforced.[4] The October enrollment, which ran till February 1928,

[2] *Sotsial'nyi i natsional'nyi sostav VKP(b)*, pp. 77-78.
[3] See *SPR*, No. 6, Vol. II, pp. 371-374. The preliminary study in Ivanovo-Voznesensk was sufficiently encouraging to inspire a CC instruction "On the Readmission of Workers from the Bench Who Have Left the Party," but no figures are available as to the concrete results of these efforts.
[4] *Izv Ts K*, No. 39, October 22, 1927.

brought in some 108,000 recruits, of whom over 80 percent were production workers. Meanwhile the Organization and Assignment Department of the Central Committee had sent out agents to regional organizations to supervise the worker-recruitment drive. As a result of these efforts, and despite a decline in the proportion of production workers recruited after the October enrollment, it averaged 68 percent for the first nine months of 1928.[5]

A further review by Malenkov in August 1928, however, stated that this was still not good enough. Bench or production workers still made up only 41 percent of total membership, and Malenkov stated that their share of recruitment would have to be raised to 80 percent and kept there for a significant period if the party's goals were to be reached.[6] Three months later this evaluation gained authoritative endorsement in a resolution of the Central Committee, which now set a firm date for the 50 percent bench-worker objective, namely December 1930.[7] The implications of this were spelled out in a directive dated January 7, 1929, which laid down that manual workers must constitute 90 percent of recruits in industrial areas, 70 percent in agricultural areas and 60 percent in the non-Russian republics. It was later claimed that these quotas were actually met in 1929. The proportion of communists who were bench-workers was now rising rapidly, from 41 percent in January 1928 to 44 percent in January 1929 and to 47 percent in December 1929. In April 1930, eighteen months after the two-year drive was launched, the ratio of production workers had reached 48.6 percent,

[5] F. M. Vaganov, "O regulirovanii sostava partii v 1928-29 gg." (On Regulation of the Party Membership in 1928-29), *V I KPSS*, No. 6, 1964, pp. 66-67.
[6] *Izv Ts K*, No. 24, August 10, 1928.
[7] *KPSS v rez*, Vol. II, pp. 420-428.

and achievement of the target now seemed certain.[8] In the Ukraine, manual workers were said to have reached 50.6 percent of the party membership by January 1, 1930.[9]

What were the reasons for the proletarianization drive of 1927-1930? The continued expansion of the industrial work force called for at least a proportional increase in the number of worker communists if the party presence on the factory floor was to be maintained. This was a powerful motive for intensified worker recruitment, especially after the sharp acceleration of industrialization in 1928. However, it was scarcely the only motive. The party showed considerable concern in 1927-1929 not only to increase the workers but also to *reduce* the strength of peasant communists in the total membership. To understand the reasons for this it will be necessary to consider certain characteristics of the rural party membership during the 1920's and relate them to changing power relationships in the leadership.

Problems of Peasant Recruitment

The recruitment of peasants during the NEP period presented the CPSU with a dilemma: the party needed a firm base among the peasantry, who made up the bulk of the Soviet population; yet village society, and especially the cultivation of a family farm, represented a "petty bourgeois" mode of life which was fundamentally out of tune with com-

[8] See *PS*. Nos. 11-12, June 1930, pp. 14-19. An example of an obkom decision detailing the local implications of Central Committee objectives in terms of precise ratios and schedules can be found in Kh. S. Sairanov et al., eds., *Rezoliutsii oblastnykh konferentsii Bashkirskoi partiinoi organizatsii i plenumov obkoma KPSS* (Resolutions of Oblast Conferences of the Bashkir Party Organization and of Plenums of the Obkom), (Ufa, 1959), pp. 419-422.

[9] F. E. Sherstiuk, "Ukreplenie rabochego iadra v period industrializatsii," (Strengthening of the Worker Nucleus in the Period of Industrialization), *V I KPSS*, No. 5, 1960, p. 123.

munism. Hence the party had to insist on evidence of active support for communism from peasant applicants, but, given the demand for loyal administrative cadres in country areas, "active support" usually soon led to promotion *out of* the peasantry. This dilemma is illustrated by the fact that, although the November 1924 decision authorizing renewed peasant recruitment specifically enjoined great caution in the enlistment of "peasants" occupying nonmanual jobs, the latter actually formed a much higher proportion of the "peasants" admitted in 1925 than of all "peasants" *applying* for admission, i.e. in practice they found it *easier* to gain admission than did peasants still engaged in farming.[10]

In the early 1920's, there were many areas where a substantial proportion of rural communists were members of communes or other collective or cooperative enterprises, and they tended to occupy the leading positions in such associations. Because of the shortage of rural party cadres, however, communist leaders of collectives and cooperatives were constantly being detached by the local party leadership and sent on assignments of various kinds, causing considerable resentment among rank-and-file members of the collectives, who labeled their communist comrades "honorary members." It also led to a good deal of disorganization of the cooperatives themselves which may have contributed to their decline in the middle 1920's, and at the height of NEP cooperative members formed a very small proportion of the rural party membership.[11]

The position of the individual peasant who joined the CPSU was a particularly ambiguous one. The distractions of party work frequently led to the serious neglect of his farm, and indeed any hesitancy in accepting party tasks be-

[10] See *Izv Ts K*, Nos. 19-20, May 30, 1925.
[11] *Ibid.*, Nos. 43-44, November 16, 1925.

cause of the urgent demands of current farming operations tended to arouse the suspicions and condemnation of his comrades in the local party organization. Small wonder that if he were a "poor peasant" he tended to be worse off economically than noncommunists possessing comparable land and facilities. The frustrations stemming from this situation undoubtedly reinforced the pressures either to leave the party or to go over to full-time administrative work.

At the same time there was always a stratum of relatively well-to-do peasant communists. This was revealed by studies of local organizations in Siberia and the Ukraine as early as 1925. The Ukrainian study also showed that a substantially higher proportion of communists than noncommunists were classified as "well-to-do" or "middle peasants."[12] These communist peasants often employed hired labor; the investigators reported that their success was usually due, however, not to "exploitation," but rather to the use of more up-to-date techniques and more intensive farming. Although they participated willingly in cooperative arrangements which did not infringe their independence, they were notoriously ingenious at finding excuses for not joining collective farms. The party, it would seem, was succeeding in attracting into its ranks a proportion of the more enterprising and independent peasants, impatient of traditional ways and eager for modernization, peasants of the character and mentality which had also given rise to the kulak group: and it is not surprising that the two categories—peasant communists and kulaks—showed some tendency to overlap.

[12] *Ibid.*, Nos. 45-46, November 30, 1925. The Siberian study is reported in *ibid.*, No. 40, October 19, 1925. See also *P*, October 1, 1925 and October 17, 1925 for data on the economic position and participation in political activity of peasants joining the party in the Tver guberniya and Kiev okrug respectively.

An ambitious study of rural communists undertaken in 1929 showed that, whereas less than one peasant household in six in the RSFSR had property worth over 800 roubles, the proportion among *communist* peasants was one in four. A far higher proportion of communist peasants than noncommunists employed hired labor—in the Ukraine the ratio was two to one. The same picture emerges with respect to farm improvements, ownership of livestock, etc.[13]

These trends were hard to square with official doctrine, which had always shown preference for the poorer farmers and farm laborers, on the grounds that as victims of exploitation these were more akin in outlook to the proletariat and more sympathetic towards "socialist" measures in agriculture. In actuality, peasants joining the party tended to be polarized into those who gave up their farms and were absorbed into the administration and those who farmed efficiently or intensively enough (if necessary employing hired labor) to spare time for their party duties without becoming impoverished. This made for the emergence of a new communist elite in the villages consisting of local officials and relatively well-to-do farmers.

The Political Factor

These were precisely the consequences which the Leningrad opposition had predicted in 1925 would flow from simultaneously encouraging peasant enterprise and energetically recruiting peasants to the party. To Stalin's allies on the Right, who thought in terms of prolonged encouragement of individual peasant farming, there was little cause for alarm in such developments. Stalin's own position, however, was

[13] A. Gaister and A. Levin, "O sostave sel'skikh partorganizatsii" (On the Composition of Rural Party Organizations), *B*, Nos. 9-10, May 1929, pp. 75-90. For a valuable discussion of party cells in rural areas in the middle and later 1920's, see M. Lewin, *Russian Peasants and Soviet Power: A Study of Collectivization* (London, 1968), pp. 119-126.

a more complicated one. His pro-peasant policies in 1925-1926 were primarily aimed at isolating Zinoviev and Kamenev and destroying their power. The destruction of this Left opposition, however, left Stalin face-to-face with the Right, the last obstacle to his achievement of dictatorial power. His tactic was now to force the Right into a posture of opposition and to this end he progressively broke with those pro-peasant policies which had previously constituted his common ground with the Right.

Among these policies was the large-scale enlistment of individual peasants in the party, which was the salient feature of party recruitment in 1925-1926. Continuation of this policy now became not only tactically undesirable, but organizationally dangerous. By the end of 1926 almost a third of the members of village cells had been in the party for less than a year, and over two-thirds of them for less than three years.[14] In other words, the rural organizations, which now contained a substantial minority of the total party membership, were composed largely of peasants for whom the CPSU was the party of encouragement for private peasant enterprise. Most of these rural members had received very little Marxist-Leninist indoctrination. The organizational obstacles which this situation could present to breaking with the pro-peasant policies of the Right are obvious.

The party machine took somewhat tentative steps to remedy this situation, or at least to contain it, even while the alliance with the Right was at its height. A *proverka* (verification) of village cells ordered at the end of 1925 pursued its desultory course until April 1927, but took in only a fraction of the rural membership and resulted in few expulsions.[15]

[14] See *Sotsial'nyi i natsional'nyi sostav VKP(b)*, p. 85.

[15] See I. Maslov, *KPSS v bor'be za ukreplenie edinstva svoikh riadov i osushchestvlenie politiki sotsialisticheskoi industrializatsii strany (1925-1927 gg.)*, (Moscow, 1955), pp. 126-127.

Of greater importance was the CC instruction to local committees to make "stricter demands" on peasant applicants for admission to the party, which was inserted in the October 1926 decision announcing the drive to achieve the 50 percent bench-worker objective. This more restrictive attitude was to apply particularly to "middle peasants" and "those bordering on middle peasant status," i.e. to anyone who was making a relative success of farming under NEP conditions. Acceptance of such applicants should now depend on "whether or not they are playing a really active part in social life in support of the Soviet regime."[16]

This decision appears to have led to a reduction in peasant recruitment during 1927. At the same time, however, with the mass of 1926 recruits completing their probationary period, the numerical strength of the peasantry among the full voting members of the CPSU was increasing sharply in the less industrialized areas of the country. In the Smolensk guberniya, for instance, peasants grew from 17 to 35 percent of full members of the CPSU between January and October 1927, while bench-workers contracted from 30 to 21 percent. Although farm laborers still constituted little more than 1 percent of the full members in the guberniya, peasants working their own farms jumped from 7 to 22 percent, and they were now the most numerous occupational group apart from officials. Furthermore, despite a slight reduction in the percentage of peasants accepted as candidates in Smolensk guberniya over the same period, the proportion of peasant recruits *farming their own land* actually increased by a further 5 percent, substantially exceeding the proportion of bench-workers recruited.[17] These trends indicate a sharp in-

[16] *Izv Ts K*, Nos. 47-48, December 2, 1926.
[17] See *WKP* 33, *Protokol* No. 13, p. 62. A recent Soviet account of this period states that "rural party cells consisted mainly of

173

crease in potential support for the policies of the Right, at precisely the period when Stalin was moving towards a break with the right-wing leaders.[18]

This is the political context of the intensified concentration on recruiting bench-workers, which began with the October enrollment at the end of 1927. The following passage from a resolution passed by a guberniya party conference in Kaluga is illustrative of the doctrinal terms in which this second drive to proletarianize the party mass membership was linked with the struggle against the Right.

> Given the cultural backwardness of the working class and the predominance of small to very small peasant production, the period of socialist reconstruction involves special difficulties in our country.
>
> . . . This demands of the party that it should strengthen in every way its links with the masses of the working class and struggle with determination against deviations from the Leninist line, both against the remnants of counter-revolutionary Trotskyism and particularly with the danger of a right deviation, which is the chief danger. . . .
>
> . . . In accordance with the general tasks of the party, under the conditions of the Kaluga guberniya, where petty bourgeois influence is especially strong, it is necessary to

---

white-collar workers and of peasants owning their own farms, while the percentage of workers, farm laborers and collective farmers in them was insignificant." See K. V. Nekrasov, *Bor'ba kommunisticheskoi partii za edinstvo svoikh riadov v period mezhdu XV i XVI s"ezdami VKP(b)*, (Struggle of the Communist Party for Unity of Its Ranks in the Period between the 15th and 16th Congresses of the CPSU), (Vologda, 1959), p. 33.

[18] Schapiro considers that Stalin had already decided to break with NEP by the time of the Fifteenth Party Congress in December 1927 (see *The CPSU*, p. 362); his moves in this direction in the first half of 1928 led to a collapse of his alliance with the Right and their going into opposition.

recruit to the party really progressive elements of the working class, capable of acting as vanguard of the laboring masses in overcoming the practical difficulties of socialist construction, repelling petty bourgeois ideological wavering, and increasing in every way the trust of the whole mass of workers and rural working people towards the party.[19]

The intensification of worker-oriented recruitment, which began with the October enrollment, quickly reduced the weight of "petty bourgeois elements" in the party. In the Kaluga guberniya peasants working their own farms constituted only 6 percent of the candidates accepted in January-June 1928 compared with 25 percent in January-June 1927. By the beginning of 1929 the proportion of peasants among the communists of Kaluga guberniya was scarcely half what it had been two years earlier.[20] As noted earlier, a January 1929 decision stipulated that even in rural areas production workers were to constitute at least 70 percent of all recruits. As a consequence, only 16 percent of the workers applying for admission to the CPSU in 1929 were rejected, compared with 55 percent of the individual peasants and 75 percent of the white-collar workers.[21] The declining ratio of peasant farmers in the party membership was reflected not only in the changed balance of urban and rural cells, but also in a degree of "proletarianization" within the rural cells themselves. Between January 1928 and April 1930 there was a fourfold increase in the number of farm laborers (classified as "work-

[19] *Materialy k XIX kaluzhskoi gubernskoi partiinoi konferentsii* (Materials for the 19th Kaluga Guberniya Party Conference), *WKP* 44, p. 12.

[20] *WKP* 44, pp. 48-49.

[21] F. Risel', "Rost partii za dva goda" (Growth of the Party over Two Years), *PS*, No. 10, May 1930, p. 10.

ers") in the party, and by the latter date they constituted 22 percent of the rural party membership.[22]

The Purge of 1929–1930

In previous chapters we observed how the revamping of the party membership was exploited by the Stalin machine in its struggle with the Trotsky and Zinoviev oppositions. The formula was a comparatively simple one: purges of those sections of the party and the bureaucracy where the opposition was strongest, accompanied by mass recruitment to provide both overwhelming votes for the machine's nominees and resolutions and malleable cadres to replace the purged oppositionists.

In 1928 Stalin began to use the same formula against the Right. The decision of the November 1928 plenum of the Central Committee ordering intensified recruitment of workers also contained the following passages: "Verification and purging of organizations of alien elements and of corrupt and bureaucratized people, etc., must be carried out far more determinedly and more systematically. . . . A bold impetus must be given to the promotion of new party cadres drawn from the workers, to all branches of the work of the state . . ."[23]

Widespread screenings had taken place even before this. In the course of 1928 seven oblast and guberniya organizations were screened, and an average of 13 percent of their

[22] S. F. Markov, "Ukreplenie sel'skikh partiinykh organizatsii v period podgotovki massovogo kolkhoznogo dvizheniia" (Strengthening of Rural Party Organizations in the Period of Preparing the Mass Kolkhoz Movement), *V I KPSS*, No. 3, 1962, p. 119. See also S. V. Neznanov, ed., *Partiia—organizator kolkhoznogo stroia* (Moscow, 1958), pp. 58-59.

[23] *KPSS v rez*, Vol. II, pp. 427-428.

party members expelled.[24] While the "Right danger" was not an overt motive for these operations, they afforded ample scope for the Stalin machine to consolidate its hold in these areas.[25] Meanwhile a little-publicized purge of administrative and managerial personnel in government and industrial agencies was also under way. No overall data on the results of this purge are available, but in the Kaluga guberniya over a quarter of the 1,169 officials checked were recommended for dismissal or reduction in status.[26] Directly linked with the struggle against the Right was the purge of party organizations in the Moscow oblast which ran from October to December 1928.[27] Finally, the implementation by rural party cadres of Stalin's first round of restrictive measures against the peasantry had served as a touchstone of loyalty to the party line, leading to many expulsions. This was referred to by Stalin in October 1928 in the following terms: "We came across representatives of the Right danger in our lower party organizations during the grain-purchasing crisis last year, when a number of communists in the volosts and villages opposed the party's policy and pursued a policy of forming a bond with kulak elements. As you know, such people were cleaned out of the party last spring. . . ." And he added ominously: "But it would be wrong to say that no such people have been left in the party. If we go higher up, to the uezd and guberniya party organizations, or if we dig deeper into

[24] See *Shestnadtsataia konferentsiia VKP(b): stenograficheskii otchët* (Moscow, 1962), p. 592 (cited hereafter as *XVI konf.*).

[25] The Smolensk archive affords a detailed picture of one of these 1928 screenings. See Merle Fainsod, *Smolensk under Soviet Rule* (London, 1958), pp. 48-52 (cited hereafter as Fainsod, *Smolensk*).

[26] See *WKP* 44, *Prilozhenie No. 1 k protokolu VI Plenuma GK ot 11-18/XII 1928 goda* (Attachment No. 1 to the Protocols of the 6th Plenum of the Gubkom Held on December 11-18, 1928).

[27] See Schapiro, *The CPSU*, pp. 368-371.

our soviet and cooperative organizations, we shall without difficulty find representatives of the Right danger and of the conciliationist tendency."[28]

Preparations for the "more determined and more systematic purging of alien elements" foreshadowed in the November 1928 plenum decision were soon under way, under the direction of E. M. Yaroslavsky, Secretary of the Party Collegium of the Central Control Commission (the supreme disciplinary authority in the CPSU), and one of Stalin's closest supporters since the early 1920's. In a statement ("theses") published in March 1929, Yaroslavsky called for a careful reexamination of the party's ranks, in order to counter petty bourgeois influences hampering the advance to socialism.[29] On the basis of this statement local party committees and control commissions began to set up their own purge machinery, even before the Sixteenth CPSU Conference, which is usually credited with initiating the purge.[30] Yaroslavsky's "theses" were endorsed by a combined plenum of the Central Committee and Central Control Commission held on the eve of the Sixteenth Conference in April 1929, and formed the basis of a conference resolution "On the Purging and Verification of Members and Candidates of the CPSU."[31] At the conference itself Yaroslavsky spoke at length to his proposals, but there was no debate.[32]

The purge ran from May 1929 to May 1930, and resulted in some 170,000 expulsions, about 11 percent of the current

[28] Stalin, *Problems of Leninism* (Moscow, 1945), p. 235. See also *P*, April 18, 1928.

[29] See *P*, March 31, 1929.

[30] For data on preparations in the Kaluga guberniya, see *WKP* 44, p. 250.

[31] See *KPSS v rez*, Vol. II, pp. 485-494.

[32] For Yaroslavsky's report, see *XVI konf.*, pp. 589-611.

membership (subsequent rehabilitations reduced these figures to 133,000 and 8 percent respectively).[33] Ostensibly it was mainly directed, like all previous purges, against "corrupt, bureaucratized and careerist elements," but among those to be "mercilessly ejected from the party," the Sixteenth Conference resolution explicitly mentioned "concealed Trotskyites, Miasnikovites [i.e. supporters of the former "Workers' Opposition"], Democratic Centralists and protagonists of other anti-party groups."[34] Indeed, Yaroslavsky had gone out of his way to ridicule those local organizations which began their preparations for the purge by examining the personal morality of their members instead of their "class" orientation,[35] i.e. whether they supported Stalin's "proletarian" line or the "petty bourgeois" line of the opposition. A frank indication of the connection between the purge and the campaign against the Right was contained in the resolution of the April 1929 plenum of the Central Committee "On Intra-Party Affairs," which affirmed the need for a general purge of the party in the context of analyzing the alleged

[33] The figure of 170,000 is quoted in S. P. Trapeznikov, *Kommunisticheskaia partiia v period nastupleniia sotsializma po vsemu frontu. Pobeda kolkhoznogo stroia v derevne* (*1929-1932 gg.*), (Moscow, 1961), pp. 38-39. Most Soviet and foreign discussions of the 1929-1930 purge quote the incomplete figure of 130,500 given at the Sixteenth Congress. Neither of these figures, nor the available breakdowns of them, take account of rehabilitations. Nearly a third of those removed appealed against their expulsion, and 36,600 were rehabilitated (*P*, April 23, 1931). Vaganov (in *V I KPSS*, No. 6, 1964, p. 70) attempts to recalculate the net expulsion rate by taking rehabilitations into account, but he appears to err in subtracting the total number of rehabilitations from the incomplete Sixteenth Congress figure for expulsions.

[34] *KPSS v rez*, Vol. II, p. 491.

[35] See *XVI konf.*, pp. 594ff.

right-opportunist fractional activity of Bukharin, Rykov and Tomsky.[36]

At the Sixteenth Congress in July 1930, when data was available on about 130,000 of the 170,000 members and candidates expelled in the purge, Yaroslavsky gave the following breakdown of the reasons for expulsion:

percent

Alien elements or connection with alien elements	17
Passivity	17
Violation of party discipline	10
Defects in personal life and conduct	22
Criminal offences	12
Other reasons	22

He added that the 10 percent purged for violation of party discipline included those guilty of "fractional activity."[37] Thus only a small proportion of expulsions was openly linked with the suppression of opposition groupings. At the same time, when there was uncertainty as to whether a man's other defects warranted his expulsion from the party, the deciding factor was whether or not he showed any hesitancy in working for the Stalinist line or any signs of sympathy with the ideas of the Right.[38] This means that actual or suspected opposition to Stalin and his policies of collectivization and industrialization accounted for a far larger proportion of the expulsions than was admitted, although in the nature of

[36] *KPSS v rez*, Vol. II, p. 433.

[37] *XVI s"ezd Vsesoiuznoi Kommunisticheskoi Partii(b)*, (Moscow-Leningrad, 1930), p. 340 (cited hereafter as *XVI s"ezd*). While no complete analysis of the official reasons for expulsion of 1929-1930 purgees seems to have been published, the Smolensk archive contains a complete breakdown of those purged in the Western oblast (see Fainsod, *Smolensk*, p. 218).

[38] See *XVI s"ezd*, pp. 339-340.

things the actual number is impossible to estimate.[39] In many cases the GPU was involved in the "unmasking" of party members guilty of opposition attitudes.[40]

The purge fell more heavily on certain classes of party members than on others. Some 8 percent of party members in industrial plants were removed, as compared with almost 10 percent in "nonproductive cells." The latter included cells in administrative bodies, which suffered relatively heavily, whereas in educational establishments the impact was slight. But the hardest hit were the rural cells, which lost some 16 percent of their membership, mostly, it was reported, individual farmers and white-collar workers.[41]

The impact of the 1929-1930 purge as a factor in Stalin's campaign to destroy his political rivals and effect his "revolution from above" cannot, however, be assessed solely in terms of those actually expelled. Perhaps its main function was prophylactic: it paralyzed criticism and prevented the right-wing leaders from gaining a hearing among the rank-and-file.

The political connection between the purge and the current campaign for the mass recruitment of workers to the party has already been remarked on. One important expression of this connection was the calling of work-place meetings of both party and nonparty employees, at which the

[39] G. K. Ordzhonikidze, the Chairman of the Central Control Commission, stated that 7,300 supporters of Trotsky had been expelled from the party between January 1928 and February 1930, of whom some 3,000 were subsequently reinstated (*XVI s"ezd*, p. 323). Yaroslavsky also mentioned various minor opposition groupings whose adherents were ejected from the party in the 1929-1930 purge (*ibid.*, p. 337). But the overwhelming majority of those expelled, explicitly or otherwise, for opposition attitudes were undoubtedly influenced by the ideas of the Right. Cf. Fainsod, *Smolensk*, pp. 211-212.

[40] *XVI s"ezd*, p. 337.

[41] F. M. Vaganov, in *V I KPSS*, No. 6, 1964, pp. 69-70.

181

purge commissions invoked "mass" opinion on local communists. Nonparty workers whose remarks and conduct at these meetings indicated their support for the official party line were marked down for recruitment.[42] The purge thus served as a sieve, ensuring that those who entered the party at this period would reinforce Stalin's majority in the party at large.

The party purge of 1929-1930 was accompanied by a purge of government employees. Rykov, Chairman of the Council of People's Commissars since Lenin's death, was not finally removed until December 1930. Not surprisingly, therefore, the government service, and particularly the central commissariats, were regarded as one of the main strongholds of the Right opposition. The government purge, directed by Stalin's supporter Ordzhonikidze, had already resulted in 51,000 dismissals by the time of the Sixteenth Congress, when it was barely a quarter completed.[43] The purge of government agencies (including the industrial administration) served not only to replace committed supporters of the Right by Stalinists, but to neutralize the influence of Rykov and other government leaders and bludgeon officials into the vigorous and uncritical implementation of Stalin's industrial and agricultural revolution. A menacing edge was given to this process by Stalin's first series of show-trials of alleged economic saboteurs.[44] Meanwhile a purge of the trade union apparatus, which had been led for several years by another right-wing leader, Tomsky, was also under way. In 1929-1930 three-quarters of the trade union officials in Mos-

[42] See, e.g. S. F. Markov, in *V I KPSS*, No. 3, 1962, p. 120; I. Glazyrin, *Regulirovanie sostava KPSS v period stroitel'stva sotsializma* (Moscow, 1957), pp. 73-78; Trapeznikov, *op.cit.*, pp. 38-39.

[43] *XVI s"ezd*, p. 316.

[44] See Zbigniew K. Brzezinski, *The Permanent Purge* (Cambridge, Mass., 1956), pp. 52-53 (cited hereafter as Brzezinski, *Purge*).

cow and Leningrad were changed, and six-sevenths of those in the Urals and the Ukraine.[45]

The ejection of actual or suspected oppositionists from party, administrative, managerial and trade union jobs opened up wide avenues of promotion for the party's new working class recruits. In 1929 alone 12 percent of the manual workers in the party were either posted directly to managerial or office jobs or sent on training courses in anticipation of such postings.[46] The 1929-1930 purge was a decisive stage in the Stalinization of the Soviet bureaucratic elite.

Building Socialism and the Deproletarianization of the Party

It is an ironical fact that the transition from NEP to a fully socialized economy rendered unattainable the official aim of a predominantly proletarian party. On the one hand, control over collectivized agriculture required a richer leavening of party members among the peasantry, while on the other, socialist industrialization gave birth to a burgeoning army of managerial, technical and administrative personnel, who for disciplinary and indoctrinational purposes had to be drawn into the party in ever-increasing numbers. In 1930-1932 this fact began to assert itself vigorously in party recruitment practice, and tentatively, in theory as well.

Throughout 1930 and 1931 the mass recruitment of workers proceeded unabated. In fact, there has probably been no period in the history of the party when the pressure on workers to join, and the ease with which they could join, has been greater. Recruitment meetings were held at which bloc applications were received from whole workshops, or even whole factories.[47] Although a critical, individual approach

---

[45] Trapeznikov, op.cit., p. 41.
[46] F. Risel', in PS, No. 10, May 1930, pp. 8-13.
[47] See Glazyrin, op.cit., pp. 80-81.

was enjoined in the checking of applicants,[48] there can be little doubt that local committees frequently lowered their sights in order to keep up their recruitment figures. Altogether over a million production and transport workers were admitted in these two years.[49]

Nevertheless, the objective of having every second communist a manual worker was never achieved, although it was officially reaffirmed in February 1930[50] and again in March 1931.[51] After reaching a maximum of 48.6 percent in April 1930, the percentage of manual workers fell to 44.1 by January 1931 and to 43.5 by January 1932.[52] This was partly due to the voluntary withdrawal of workers from the party (see below, p. 195), and partly to the continued transfer of worker communists to nonmanual occupations. In 1931 a further 152,000 communists were shifted from manual to white-collar jobs or sent on study courses.[53] But the main reason was increased recruitment from other social groups, which resulted in a declining *proportional* recruitment of workers. Workers "from the bench" fell from 86 percent of all recruits in the first quarter of 1930 to 73 percent in the second quarter.[54] The ratio continued to decline, and in 1931 it averaged only 63 percent.[55]

The green light for increased nonworker recruitment was provided by a Central Committee directive issued in Febru-

[48] See, for instance, *P*, February 11, 1930.
[49] Glazyrin, *op.cit.*, p. 84.
[50] *P*, February 11, 1930.
[51] Glazyrin, *op.cit.*, p. 84.
[52] *PS*, Nos. 11-12, June 1930, p. 19; No. 17, September 1931, p. 35; No. 21, November 1932, p. 48.
[53] See Glazyrin, *op.cit.*, p. 86.
[54] V. Vlasov, "Protiv samoteka—za ukreplenie proletarskogo iadra" (Against Letting Things Slide—for a Strengthening of the Proletarian Nucleus), *PS*, No. 17, September 1930, p. 29.
[55] *PS*, Nos. 7-8, April 1932, p. 54.

ary 1930, entitled, "On Further Work in Regulating the Growth of the Party." While emphasizing the need to recruit more workers, the directive added the following:

At the same time, taking into account the increased attraction of the party for the foremost part of the Soviet intelligentsia (the technicians, engineers, scientists, etc.) it is considered expedient to accept its best elements into the party, those who have shown their devotion to the proletarian revolution and who have been proven in active social work under the guidance of the party.

The widespread mass collectivization and implementation of the policy of liquidating the kulaks as a class, on the one hand, and the small size of rural party organizations on the other, require an expansion of the ranks of rural organizations with more agricultural laborers and state farm workers, and a more determined drawing of the foremost kolkhozniks, especially the poor ones, into the party. There is to be a vigorous recruitment of those who have shown initiative in the organization and strengthening of kolkhozes, who have been active and resolute in the struggle with the kulak, petty bourgeois property owners and survivals of petty bourgeois property attitudes, and who have been proven in active work for the implementation of current politico-economic campaigns and the fulfillment of kolkhoz obligations towards the Soviet state.[56]

The effects of this decision were felt immediately. Between the first and second quarters of 1930 peasants rose from 10 to 20 percent of the party intake, and the share of the intelligentsia rose from 4 to 7 percent.[57]

The collectivization drive, like other crises in the history

[56] *P*, February 11, 1930.
[57] V. Vlasov, in *PS*, No. 17, September 1930, p. 30.

of the regime, such as the Civil War, the struggle against Trotskyism and the Second World War, left little room for neutrality. It enabled the apparatus to identify its most active supporters, and gave it the incentive to incorporate them into the party, so as to convert them into fully committed agents. But collectivization not only led to a renewed expansion of rural party organizations; it also transformed their character. Four separate processes were involved: (a) individual peasant communists joining collectives; (b) purging of peasant communists opposed to collectivization; (c) recruitment of nonparty activists in the formative phase of the collectives; (d) shifting of the party's rural base from the village to the kolkhoz.

In 1928, on the eve of collectivization, 87 percent of the members of rural party organizations were individual peasant farmers or white-collar workers, 10 percent were farm laborers and only 3 percent collective farmers.[58] As the pressure to collectivize mounted, however, communists were prominent amongst those entering kolkhozes. As early as October 1929, when only one peasant in twenty was collectivized, the proportion among communist peasants exceeded one in three.[59] By January 1930, 20 percent of peasant households were collectivized, but this included over half the peasant communists. Three months later the proportion of peasant communists who had joined the collectives reached three-quarters,[60] and throughout the whole period of collectivization it substantially exceeded the proportion of nonparty peasants collectivized.

Nevertheless, not all peasant communists willingly gave up their independence, and as late as January 1931 there were

[58] S. F. Markov, in *V I KPSS*, No. 3, 1962, p. 114.

[59] See Trapeznikov, *op.cit.*, p. 52.

[60] See "Perestroika partiinoi raboty" (Reconstruction of Party Work), *PS*, Nos. 11-12, June 1930, pp. 36-37.

still about 40,000 individual peasants in the party.[61] We have already noted the overrepresentation of relatively well-to-do peasants in rural party organizations during the middle and later 1920's. Many of these, having for years held out resolutely against all suggestions of joining collectives, now no doubt reconciled themselves to the inevitable. Others, however, rather than sacrifice their independence without a fight, hastened to hand in their party cards.[62] Alternatively they were expelled. Some rural party officials, in fact, thought that the 1929-1930 purge was a straightforward "purge of well-to-do elements."[63] Refusal to join a kolkhoz or concealment of surplus grain was the official reason given for 4 percent of the expulsions from rural cells in the 1929-1930 purge. But dislike of collectivization was undoubtedly a crucial ingredient in a much higher proportion of expulsions, and such attitudes were certainly not confined to the more well-to-do members of village cells. The impact of collectivization is reflected in the fact that the purge removed 15 percent of the peasant communists, compared with 7 percent of the workers and 11 percent of the white-collar workers.[64] (See also p. 181.)

The recruitment of party members in the newly formed kolkhozes, which began in earnest in the second quarter of 1930, continued to accelerate. There was also a drive to provide a nucleus of party members in the burgeoning network of state farms and MTS (machine and tractor stations, which

[61] See *PS*, Nos. 11-12, June 1932, p. 47. A curious footnote on this period is that individual peasants were even allowed to join the party at the height of collectivization; 5,000 of them joined in the first quarter of 1931. See A. Mil'chakov, "Rost partii i zadachi perestroiki partiinoi raboty" (Growth of the Party and Tasks of Reconstructing Party Work), *PS*, No. 13, July 1931, p. 5.

[62] Cf. *XVI s"ezd*, p. 376.

[63] *Ibid.*, p. 339.

[64] *Ibid.*, p. 340.

owned and operated the farm machinery allocated for use in the kolkhozes). Since these were both classed as state enterprises (unlike the kolkhozes, which were legally cooperatives), their employees were listed not as peasants, but as workers and white-collar workers. Table 6[65] shows how the rural party cells expanded and changed in composition during the collectivization period. This pattern of expansion continued for the rest of 1931 and in the early months of 1932. By July 1932 there were 570,000 communists in kolkhoz cells and 160,000 in state farm and MTS cells, amounting altogether to almost a quarter of the whole party membership.[66]

Alongside this change in the predominant employment of rural communists went a change in the institutional basis of rural party organizations. Prior to mass collectivization, the great majority of rural communists were members of village cells which included both individual and collectivized peasants, local officials, teachers and other nonmanual workers. As the institutions of "socialist agriculture"—the kolkhozes, state farms and MTS—established themselves in the early 1930's, the center of gravity of rural party organizations shifted to them, and particularly to the kolkhozes. This process is clearly revealed in Table 7.[67]

Despite the sharp increase in the number of peasant communists in the collectivization era, the party remained extremely weak in rural areas. In mid-1932 only one kolkhoz in five had a party cell or organized group of candidates. Moreover, three-fifths of all kolkhoz communists were still

---

[65] SOURCE: G. Peskarev, "Dinamika rosta i problema regulirovaniia sostava partii" (Dynamics of Growth and the Problem of Regulating the Composition of the Party), *PS*, No. 17, September 1931, p. 39.

[66] See *PS*, No. 21, November 1932, p. 46. See also S. V. Neznanov, ed., *Partiia-organizator kolkhoznogo stroia*, pp. 126-128.

[67] SOURCE: *PS*, Nos. 11-12, June 1932, p. 46.

188

TABLE 6: Composition of Rural Cells, 1928-1931

Employment of members	July 1, 1928	Oct. 1, 1929	Jan. 1, 1930	Jan. 1, 1931	April 1, 1931
	Number of members and candidates on				
Workers (including agricultural)	24,119	46,892	64,669	77,330	86,601
Individual farmers	145,148	134,178	78,474	44,256	33,605
Kolkhozniks (collective farmers)	16,915	61,148	85,335	291,498	354,283

TABLE 7: Changing Balance of Rural Cells, 1929-1932

Date	Number of cells and candidates' groups	(a) state farms	(b) MTS	(c) kolkhozes	(d) villages
		Percent of cells based on			
July 1, 1929	27,039	4.7	—	5.6	89.7
April 1, 1930	29,204	5.6	0.2	31.7	62.5
Oct. 1, 1930	31,874	6.9	0.7	41.2	51.2
Jan. 1, 1931	33,325	7.4	0.9	44.9	46.8
July 1, 1931	42,113	9.3	2.7	60.7	27.3
Jan. 1, 1932	45,165	11.5	4.2	66.4	17.9

candidates, while in many areas candidate groups made up one-third to one-half of all kolkhoz party organizations, and were often led by young communists of one to three years standing.[68]

Since the communist crust in the countryside was still so wafer-thin and in view of the desperate need for reliable party cadres, it is not surprising that the promotion of peasant communists out of active participation in farming was still

[68] See PS, Nos. 17-18, September 1932, p. 26 and No. 21, November 1932, p. 46; cf. ibid., No. 1, January 1934, p. 54 and No. 2, January 1934, p. 33.

proceeding apace at this period. Although in 1932 only one-fifth of kolkhoz communists were *officially* registered as "managerial and other nonmanual workers," a careful study showed that the actual proportion was in most cases 70 to 80 percent. A party journalist commented that "certain leaders of kolkhoz cells think for some reason or other that all non-productive jobs in the village and in the kolkhoz must necessarily be filled in the first instance by party members."[69] So widespread was this tendency that the Central Committee saw fit to issue a special decision condemning it and enjoining local organizations to retain as many communists as possible in active farming jobs.[70] In the nature of the situation, however, it is doubtful whether the publication of such a decision could have had any great effect, and repeated subsequent criticism of the same phenomenon tends to confirm this. Such considerations need to be borne in mind in evaluating the evidence of official party statistics that the proportion of nonmanual workers in the party, whether measured in terms of "social situation" or of current occupation, continued to decline in the collectivization period (see Table 2, p. 116).

Scrapping the Proletarian Ideal

We have already noted the more positive attitude towards the recruitment of "the best representatives of the intelligentsia" initiated by the February 1930 decision of the Central Committee. This reflected a sharp break with traditional attitudes towards the position in the CPSU and in Soviet

[69] I. Marianskii, "Ostrye voprosy raboty kolkhoznoi iacheiki" (Difficult Questions in the Work of the Kolkhoz Cell), *PS*, No. 10, May 1932, p. 37.

[70] See *SPR*, No. 8, p. 607.

society of professional, managerial and administrative groups. In the course of 1930-1931 the regime turned its face against "petty bourgeois egalitarianism," progressively widened wage margins for skill and responsibility, and began to transform the intelligentsia-white-collar stratum from the position of second-class citizens to that of a privileged class and the main bearer of the regime's values. Stalin provided the theoretical gloss in a speech delivered in June 1931.

> . . . our country has entered a phase of development in which the working class must create its own industrial and technical intelligentsia, one that is capable of upholding the interests of the working class in production as the interests of the ruling class.
>
> No ruling class has managed without its own intelligentsia. . . .
>
> The Soviet government has taken this fact into account and has opened wide the doors of all the higher educational institutions in every branch of the national economy to members of the working class. . . .
>
> But that is only one side of the matter. The other side is that the industrial and technical intelligentsia of the working class will be recruited not only from among those who have passed through the institutions of higher learning, but also from among the practical workers in our factories. . . . [This] is the new stratum of the working class that, together with comrades who have passed through institutions of higher learning, must form the core of the intelligentsia of the working class, the core of the commanding personnel of our industry. The task is not to discourage these comrades who show initiative, but boldly to promote them to commanding positions . . . to create

suitable conditions for them to work in, not stinting money for this purpose.[71]

This conception of the "working class intelligentsia" and its relationship to the working class as a whole distinctly echoes Lenin's concept of the party as the vanguard of the proletariat. While Stalin explicitly provided for a section of the intelligentsia remaining outside the party, he clearly implied that these two elites of the working class—party and intelligentsia—should now increasingly overlap. This view, if it were to be vigorously applied, would obviously entail a rejection of the whole rationale of party recruitment over the past decade, which had aimed at a preponderance of members working on the factory floor and discriminated against those who "showed initiative" and moved out of manual jobs, by requiring more sponsors, insisting that their sponsors be members of longer standing, etc.

It was to be some years before this moral was explicitly drawn, and embodied in formal recruitment rules. Nonetheless, signs of a doctrinal reappraisal of the party's social composition and recruitment policies were not slow in appearing. An article by G. Peskarev, entitled, "The Dynamics of Growth and the Problem of Regulating the Party's Composition," which appeared in the Central Committee's organizational journal *Partiinoe stroitel'stvo* in September 1931, marks a transition in official thinking about these questions. In what appears to have been the last official reaffirmation of the 50 percent bench-worker objective, Peskarev stated that the achievement of this objective would require rigid adherence to the instruction that 80 percent of all recruits should be workers (although he explicitly included "agricultural workers"—i.e. state farm and MTS employees, who

[71] Stalin, "New Conditions, New Tasks in Economic Construction," *Problems of Leninism*, pp. 369-370.

were mainly of peasant origin—in this quota). At the same time he offered what amounted to an excuse for the declining percentage of production workers in the party over the past eighteen months, stressing that this was not due to any lack of effort in recruiting workers, but to the promotion of worker communists and to the necessary admission of large numbers of kolkhozniks during collectivization. By the same token, his remedy was not to step up the rate of worker recruitment even further, but to be more cautious in the enrollment of kolkhozniks, and to concentrate rural recruitment on "agricultural workers." He explicitly warned against "putting quantity before quality" and the indiscriminate admission of workers in order to meet formal recruitment quotas, and he reminded his readers that a large part of the labor force brought into the factories in recent years lacked any deep roots in the working class. Ostensibly Peskarev was offering a review of trends in the social composition of the party from the standpoint of accepted recruitment objectives. He made no attempt to bring these objectives into line either with actual recruitment practices since early 1930 or with the changing official evaluation of the intelligentsia. But his reassertion of old-established objectives merely provided the thread on which to string a mass of data and argumentation, whose main burden was the need for a far more cautious and restrictive recruitment policy all-around. The implications of this would not have been lost on the local party secretaries who provided the main readership of *Partiinoe stroitel'stvo*.

Perhaps the most significant passage in Peskarev's article was a review of the various "deviationist" views on the social composition of the party which had been put forward by opposition groups since the Revolution. According to his evaluation some of these had erred by ignoring the proletarian character of the party; this applied, for instance, to the Trotskyites, who advocated the unrestricted admission of students, and to the Right, who allegedly aimed at removing all discriminatory recruitment and turning the party into a "single mass party of toilers." There were others, however, who had erred by overemphasis on proletarianizing the party membership. Peskarev recalled that it was the Workers' Opposition that had first demanded closing the doors of the party to all nonworkers. He invoked Lenin's authority to label as "Makhaevites" (see p. 93) those opposed to recruiting members of the intelligentsia. He also recalled the alleged error of the Leningrad Opposition in aiming at a vast recruitment of workers and at bringing the proportion of workers in the party up to 90 percent—this would change the CPSU from a bolshevik to a menshevik party. While deviations in both directions were equally condemned, there can be little doubt that Peskarev's readers would be most impressed by his attack on those which *over*-stressed proletarian recruitment, since proletarianization had been the constant theme of official recruitment policy for so many years and local committees were currently engaged in a massive intake of workers in a desperate bid to arrest the decline in the proportion of bench-workers in the party. In the circumstances, this analysis came as a sobering reminder that, while the party should continue to place special value on the enlistment of workers, obsession with this objective could easily lead to the adoption of mistaken or even antiparty positions.[72]

While the doctrinal issues broached by Peskarev's article were taken no further at this stage, one of the points he referred to achieved considerable prominence in the second half of 1931: the danger of the declining quality of recruitment. The most authoritative discussion of this issue was given by the Ukrainian Party Secretary, P. Postyshev. In an

[72] G. Peskarev, in *PS*, No. 17, September 1931, pp. 29-44.

article on ideological training, Postyshev drew a distinction between the three main phases of mass recruitment since the 1921 purge, pointing out that whereas the first two (the Lenin and October enrollments) had brought in mostly workers possessing firm roots in the working class, the last (i.e. since 1929) had involved the enlistment of masses of young workers often recently recruited from the peasantry or the urban petty bourgeoisie. He laid stress on the difficulties of inculcating in these people genuine proletarian class attitudes.[73]

Justification for such misgivings was certainly not lacking. Since 1928, the rate of recruitment had accelerated to an unprecedented level: 300,000 candidates were accepted in 1929, twice as many in 1930, and almost a million in 1931.[74] The party was experiencing great difficulty in digesting this flood of recruits. Scores of thousands of communists (mostly, it was said, "unstable" elements among recent recruits) drifted out of the party or were excluded for "passivity" in 1930, 1931 and the first half of 1932.[75] In addition, over

[73] P. Postyshev, "Tekushchie zadachi marksistsko-leninskogo vospitaniia" (Current Tasks of Marxist-Leninist Training), *PS*, Nos. 15-16, August 1931, pp. 1-11.

[74] See *BSE*, Vol. xi, col. 534; *SPR*, No. 8, pp. 303-304; *PS*, Nos. 7-8, April 1932, p. 54.

[75] A. Frenkel, "O predstoiashchei chistke partii" (On the Forthcoming Purge of the Party), *PS*, Nos. 23-24, December 1932, p. 5. Frenkel estimated that 350,000 members and candidates "drifted away from or fell out of the party" between 1930 and mid-1932. By contrast, Yaroslavsky, in *Za bol'shevistskuiu proverku i chistku riadov partii* (For Bolshevik Verification and Checking of the Party's Ranks), (Moscow, 1933), p. 48, put the total number of expulsions and dropouts between 1930 and 1932 at only 223,000. Comparison of recruitment and membership figures suggests that Frenkel's estimate was closer to the truth. In the five years 1928-1932 the number joining the party exceeded the increase in party membership by approximately three-quarters of a million. (See *PZh*, No. 19, October 1967, pp. 9, 11).

half a million (or fully 44 percent) of those registered as candidates at the beginning of 1932 had actually completed their probationary period but were not considered adequately prepared for transfer to full membership.[76]

A pause in recruitment seemed to be called for, and by 1932 circumstances were becoming more propitious for such a pause. Mass recruitment to the party has been a feature of every period of crisis in the history of the Soviet regime, and the crisis of collectivization and industrialization in 1929-1931 was no exception. At such periods the regime has been concerned to maximize its links with the masses and to involve as closely as possible in its current purposes all those actively responding to its slogans and campaigns. From 1929 to 1931 mass recruitment was also designed to play a part in defeating the Right and eliminating its influence. But by 1932 the crisis was passing: the Five-Year Plan was on the way to completion, the "class war" in the villages was won, and the Right was routed and silenced. In the course of 1932 the recruitment rate was progressively reduced, and enrollments for the year totaled less than half the figure for 1931. This tendency culminated in the decision to halt recruitment entirely beginning in January 1933 and to undertake a further mass purge.[77]

[76] *PS*, No. 6, March 1932, p. 31.
[77] See *KPSS v rez*, Vol. II, p. 741.

Chapter 6

Enter the New Elite

IN THE years of NEP the CPSU was progressively transformed into Stalin's personal following, by means of which he eliminated all alternative leadership and laid the foundations of his personal dictatorship. In the era of collectivization and the first Five Year Plan it became a hammer with which Stalin relentlessly beat Soviet society into a completely new shape.

During the 1930's, society exacted from the party a terrible revenge. "Socialism," far from completing the triumph of the working class, begot a new class of technically trained administrators. The Revolution passed from the destruction of old bonds to the creation of new ones. Nationalism, the family and "the classics," disdained in the 1920's, were now put to use to cement the new bonds of society. The party which Stalin had shaped and wielded against all and sundry in his earlier struggles, a party run by Civil War veterans and made up of workers and peasants with at best a thin veneer of training and experience, became in these circumstances an anachronism and ceased to be appropriate to the new purposes of the dictator. The violence which the party had used against society was now turned against the party itself. Between 1933 and 1938 it was purged from top to bottom, and restocked by 1941 with new members drawn predominantly from the new "intelligentsia."

Some figures published in the latter part of 1932 give a pretty clear picture of the distribution and composition of the CPSU membership on the eve of the cataclysms of the mid-1930's. These figures have the added interest of presenting the last official breakdown of the party membership for nearly thirty years. They show that on July 1, 1932 some 11 percent of members and candidates were employed in government offices, 3 percent in the cooperative trading network, and 9 percent in educational establishments. Almost all of the remainder were working in production enterprises. This was a big change since the party census of 1927, when less than half the membership were employed in production enterprises. The extent to which recruitment in the recent past had been concentrated in the "material production" sphere is indicated by the fact that candidates made up approximately 40 percent of the membership of factory and transport cells and 60 percent of kolkhoz cells, but only 20 percent of the membership of party cells in government offices and educational establishments.[1] The social and occupational distribution of the party at this point is summarized in Table 8.[2]

These figures indicate that the policy of proletarianization, which ostensibly (though not always in fact) had guided party membership policies for nearly a decade, had met with qualified success. Comparison with data from the early and middle 1920's (see pp. 109, 162) enables us to draw up the following balance-sheet for the proletarianization era:

1. party members of working class origin had substantially increased their predominance;

[1] See *PS*, No. 21, November 1932, p. 46.

[2] SOURCES: *Ibid.*, p. 48. Another source gives very similar figures for 1933. The figures for "social position" were: workers—63.9 percent, peasants—28.3 percent, white-collar workers—7.8 percent. The figures for occupation were: workers—40.9 percent, peasants—18.4 percent, white-collar workers—31.6 percent. See N. Barsukov and I. Iudin, "Rasshirenie sotsial'noi bazy KPSS" (Broadening the Social Base of the CPSU), *Politicheskoe samoobrazovanie*, No. 6, June 1965, pp. 27-29.

TABLE 8: SOCIAL AND OCCUPATIONAL COMPOSITION OF THE PARTY
ON JULY 1, 1932

	Percent
Social position	
Workers	65.2
Peasants	26.9
White-collar workers and others	7.9
Occupation	
Workers	43.5
Collective farmers	17.9
Individual peasants	0.4
White-collar workers	28.4
Students	7.5
Artisans, etc.	0.4
Others	1.9

2. workers "from the bench," though also showing some proportional increase, ended the period well under half the total membership;

3. the biggest gainers over the period were the (now collectivized) peasants, but these nonetheless remained much worse represented than before the 1921 purge;

4. the ratio of white-collar workers had declined somewhat, but they remained the second most numerous category; together with the students they made up over a third of the total membership, and in absolute terms the number of white-collar workers in the party had greatly increased over the period.

In 1932, the CPSU in its membership was more a party of workers than of any other class. It was far more a party of workers than during Lenin's lifetime. However, as we saw in the previous chapter, the decline from a state of proletarian grace had already begun. From 1930 the proportion of re-

199

cruits to the party drawn from the "intelligentsia" began to increase, this term now being used more or less euphemistically to cover professionally or technically trained personnel, managerial, administrative and practically all other white-collar groups. At the same time the transfer of worker communists to new white-collar posts and to those vacated by purged oppositionists was proceeding apace. These two processes led to a sharp rise in the party "saturation" of key white-collar groups in the early 1930's. Between May 1930 and October 1933 the proportion of communists among directors, assistant directors and deputy directors of industrial undertakings rose from 29 percent to 70 percent.[3] In May 1930, 15 percent of the 3,295 senior agricultural executives and administrators were in the party; in November 1933 the proportion was 83 percent out of 10,086.[4] Turning to the government administration, between October 1929 and November 1933 the proportion of party members among medium and higher grade officers increased from 48 to 61 percent in the Republic Councils of People's Commissars and Central Executive Committees, from 48 to 63 percent in departments of republic commissariats and the krai and oblast executive committees, and from 63 to 93 percent in the raion executive committees.[5]

The Purges

The phenomena often referred to collectively as "the purges of the 1930's" consisted of several distinct operations which, however, flowed one into the other in a seemingly relentless series, in an atmosphere that moved from appre-

[3] *Sostav rukovodiashchikh rabotnikov i spetsialistov Soiuza SSR* (Moscow, 1936), p. 32.
[4] *Ibid.*, p. 272.
[5] *Ibid.*, pp. 286-287.

hension to fear, and from fear to hysteria, reaching a crescendo in the *Ezhovshchina* of 1937-1938.

Only the first of these operations was officially described as a "purge" (*chistka*). It was ordered by a joint resolution of the Central Committee and Central Control Commission adopted on January 12, 1933, which also halted recruitment until the purge was over. The stated aim was "to ensure iron proletarian discipline in the party and to cleanse the party's ranks of all unreliable, unstable and hanger-on elements."[6] A further decree issued three months later detailed the categories marked for expulsion:

1. Class-alien and enemy elements who have wormed their way into the party by way of deception and have remained there with the object of splitting the ranks of the party;
2. Double-dealers who thrive on deception of the party, concealing from it their real aspirations, and who, under cover of false declarations of "loyalty" to the party, actually seek to obstruct the policy of the party;
3. Open and concealed violators of the iron discipline of the party and the government, who cast doubts upon and discredit the decisions and plans laid down by the party by babbling about their "unreality" and the fact that they are "incapable of realization";
4. Degenerates who have their origin in bourgeois elements, who do not genuinely wish to fight against class enemies, who do not genuinely fight against kulak elements, self-seekers, idlers, thieves, and embezzlers of public property;
5. Careerists, self-seekers and bureaucratic elements, who make use of their being in the party and their service

[6] *KPSS v rez*, Vol. II, p. 741.

to the Soviet state for their own personal, self-seeking
ends, who are isolated from the masses and who ignore
the needs and demands of the workers and peasants;
6. Moral degenerates, who by their improper behavior
   damage the dignity of the party and stain the banner of
   the party.

In addition, attention was to be given to "honest" but
"politically illiterate" or weak-willed communists, who were
to be reduced to the status of candidates, for the purpose of
retraining directed towards their subsequent readmission
as full members. Rudzutak, Chairman of the Central Control
Commission, was put in charge of the purge, which was entrusted, however, not to the Control Commission apparatus,
but to a special hierarchy of "purge commissions" organized
from the top down. The local purge commissions conducted
their proceedings at meetings of the party cells open to their
nonparty workmates, at which each party member and candidate in turn was obliged to give an account of his background, career and performance in his job and party activities, and could be questioned, criticized or "unmasked" by
anyone present.[7]

The *chistka* was in full swing in the latter months of 1933,
but evidently less than half the membership was processed
by the scheduled completion date of November 30, and it
dragged on for some two years, remaining unfinished in some
areas when it was overtaken by the "verification of party
documents" in 1935. It resulted in the unqualified expulsion
of 16 percent of the party membership, the reduction of 6
percent from full to candidate membership and the removal
of a further 6 percent to the status of "sympathizers,"[8] a

[7] *P*, April 29, 1933. Cf. Fainsod, *Smolensk*, pp. 221-222; Glazyrin,
op.cit., pp. 92-93; Brzezinski, *Purge*, pp. 54-56.

[8] *PZh*, No. 20, October 1947, p. 79. The figures given by this

category regularized at the Seventeenth Congress in January 1934 primarily as a staging ground for would-be recruits unable to be admitted as candidates because of the ban on recruitment during the purge.[9] The *chistka* took its main toll among workers and peasants who entered the party during the mass recruitment drive of the collectivization and first Five Year Plan era and scarcely touched those older party members from which most of the party's cadres were drawn.[10] Rural communists suffered more heavily than urban, a fact which reflected itself in a slight increase in the proportion of party members classified as workers.[11]

No official breakdown is available of the grounds on which expulsions were made in the 1933-1934 purge. However, there is a sample analysis covering the rural districts of Leningrad oblast (a total of 8,582 expulsions), and since this appeared in the main organizational journal of the Central Committee, it seems reasonable to assume that the ratios it

---

source are evidently based on more complete data than the slightly different figures made public by Yaroslavsky in 1934, which summarized results from ten oblasts comprising about a million communists. See *B*, No. 15, August 1934, p. 9. Cf. Glazyrin, *op.cit.*, p. 93.

[9] See *KPSS v rez*, Vol. II, p. 769.

[10] See *B*, No. 15, August 1934, p. 9; *XVII s"ezd Vsesoiuznoi Kommunisticheskoi Partii (b): stenograficheskii otchët*, p. 287 (cited hereafter as *XVII s"ezd*). Cf. John A. Armstrong, *The Politics of Totalitarianism* (New York, 1961), pp. 9-10 (cited hereafter as Armstrong, *Totalitarianism*).

[11] *XVII s"ezd*, p. 299. I am indebted to Dr. T. P. Bernstein for pointing out that many rural areas had already suffered a sharp purge in 1932. These were areas which had suffered from particularly harsh enforcement of the grain delivery program, including the rich wheat-growing region of the Kuban, where 45 percent of the party membership were expelled. See *Ocherki istorii kollektivizatsii sel'skogo khoziaistva v soiuznykh respublikakh* (Outlines of the History of Collectivization in the Union Republics), (Moscow, 1963), p. 55.

shows between the various categories were not too far from typical. The categories broke down as follows:

	percent
Class-alien and hostile elements	13
Double-dealers	5
Degenerates who have merged with class enemies	11
Violators of party or state discipline	17
Careerists, self-seekers, bureaucratized elements	8
Morally corrupt elements	18
Passivity	27[12]

It is worth comparing these figures with the classification of those marked for expulsion under the April 1933 decree (see above, pp. 201-202). There one notes a strong emphasis on "enemies" of the party, employing their membership to damage its interests and obstruct its policies. Such political considerations play a relatively small part in this sample of expulsions, however, and the great majority were removed either because they made unscrupulous use of their party membership to secure personal benefits, were immoral or undisciplined in their personal lives or at their job, or simply failed to participate in party activities.

While 22 percent of the CPSU were expelled during the 1933-1934 purge (including those reduced to "sympathizers"), the party membership actually fell in these two years by 33 percent, or 1.2 millions. There is little reason to believe that this discrepancy was due to falsification or major errors in purge or membership figures. It almost certainly reflected a continuation of large-scale voluntary withdrawals from the party, mainly by recent recruits, which we have noted as a feature of the party scene in 1930-1932. The

[12] *PS*, No. 1, January 1934, p. 22.

purge must have given a sharp impulse to such voluntary withdrawals. These, however, were the last years when voluntary withdrawal was a significant feature of party membership trends; from 1935 on the likelihood of being identified as an "enemy" provided a sufficient disincentive both to formal resignation and to simple discontinuation of party activities.

On December 1, 1934, Sergei Kirov, the "darling of the party," secretary of the Central Committee and leader of the Leningrad party organization since the removal of Zinoviev in 1926, was assassinated. After initially implying that the murder was the work of "white guardists," party sources were soon connecting the assassin with the former "Leningrad Opposition," and the arrest of Zinoviev, Kamenev and their principal supporters quickly followed. However, statements by Khrushchev[13] and by L. S. Shaumyan, a delegate to the Seventeenth Congress,[14] imply that Stalin himself connived at the murder, in order to rid himself of a powerful subject whose growing popularity and influence were making him a serious rival for the leadership, and to justify measures of summary justice which could be used to dispose of all categories of the party and the population regarded by Stalin as dangerous or inconvenient. These substantially confirm the contemporary interpretations of the émigré historian Boris Nikolaevsky, on the basis of his conversations with Bukharin.[15]

Immediately after the Kirov murder, the Central Com-

[13] See *The Anti-Stalin Campaign and International Communism* (New York, 1956), pp. 24-26; *XXII S"ezd Kommunisticheskoi Partii Sovetskogo Soiuza* (Moscow, 1962), Vol. II, pp. 583-584 (cited hereafter as *XXII S"ezd*).

[14] See *P*, February 7, 1964.

[15] See *Letter of an Old Bolshevik* (New York, 1937). Cf. Schapiro, *The CPSU*, pp. 400-401, and Armstrong, *Totalitarianism*, pp. 20-23.

mittee wrote to all party organizations ordering the prompt "unmasking" and expulsion of former members of the Trotsky and Zinoviev oppositions. A flood of exposures followed. Meanwhile another theme was coming to the fore: the confusion in party records. As early as June 1933 a Central Committee investigation revealed that 75 of the 623 communists on the records of a works committee in Vitebsk "had gone no one knows where, without being taken off the records," while similar disorders were discovered in party records in the Kolchugino Metal Plant.[16] In the early months of 1935 such reports became commonplace and culminated in a Central Committee instruction dated May 13, 1935, which stated that inadequate security precautions with party documents had led to the infiltration of the party by "enemies," and ordered that the documents of all members be "verified."[17] While some of the more bizarre accounts of irregularities in the issuing and recording of party documents[18] may have been exaggerated, there is no reason to doubt that party records at this period left much to be desired. At the same time, it is an open question whether the "verification" was motivated by a genuine belief that carelessness with party documents had allowed many enemies to escape the purge (a belief that might have found support in the discrepancy we have noted between the declared object of the purge and the available data on its results), or whether the

[16] *SPR*, No. 8, pp. 306-307.

[17] *WKP* 500, p. 308. Cf. *KPSS v rez*, Vol. II, p. 822. While all other accounts date the verification from the decision of May 13, 1935, a recent party history states that it began as early as October 1934. See B. N. Ponomarev et al., *Istoriia Kommunisticheskoi Partii Sovetskogo Soiuza* (Moscow, 1959), p. 463. No contemporary evidence to "support" this version has been brought to light, but perhaps a decision was made in principle to undertake the "verification" in October 1934. Cf. Armstrong, *Totalitarianism*, pp. 27-28.

[18] See e.g. Brzezinski, *Purge*, p. 59.

whole issue was merely being employed by Stalin as a pretext to take the purge a step further. In any case, there is evidence that the "verification" was conducted in an atmosphere of rising hysteria in which the question of documents receded into the background and the smallest "suspicious" item in a member's biography provided an excuse for denunciation.[19] A review of progress published in August 1935 attacked those party officials who had underestimated the political importance of the "verification," and stressed its "enormous role in the matter of unmasking enemies of the party—white-guardists, Trotskyites and adventurers, who penetrated the party by way of deception and forged party cards, and exploited the gullibility, complacency and blunting of vigilance in certain echelons of the party apparatus."[20]

By December 1, 1935, four-fifths of all party members were said to have been verified, and 9 percent of those checked had been expelled (the rate was said to have been 7.5 percent in areas that had undergone the *chistka* in 1933-1934, compared with 13.4 percent in areas that had missed it).[21] No overall analysis of communists expelled in the "verification of documents" has been published. However, figures are available for one area—the Western oblast. Here two-fifths of those removed were described as "alien and

[19] See Fainsod, *Smolensk*, pp. 223-229.

[20] "Proverka partdokumentov—serëznoe ispytanie partiinykh kadrov" (The Verification of Party Documents Is a Serious Test of the Party's Cadres), *PS*, No. 15, August 1935, pp. 1-5. A further review published some weeks later stated that "the verification is helping the party to purge its ranks of crooks, kulaks, white-guardists, counterrevolutionary Trotskyites and Zinovievites, double-dealers and other enemy elements." *Ibid.*, No. 17, September 1935, p. 2.

[21] "Glavnye uroki proverki partdokumentov" (Chief Lessons of the Verification of Party Documents), *ibid.*, No. 2, January 1936, pp. 9-23. Those checked comprised 93 percent of the full members and 53 percent of the candidate members of the CPSU.

hostile elements," while a further one-third were said to be "degenerate elements, alienated from the party." The largest number of them held administrative or managerial jobs.[22] These figures indicate both the sharper political edge of the "verification" as compared with the *chistka*, and the shift of focus from the rank-and-file workers and peasants to the lower levels of the authority structure.

Although the "verification of documents" was conducted in an atmosphere of rising menace, suspicion and foreboding in which it became ever easier to imagine an "enemy" behind every ambiguous fact, some party officials remained slow in reacting to this atmosphere. These were roundly rebuked at a conference of chiefs of oblast ORPO (Leading Party Organs) departments held in 1935 under the chairmanship of Central Committee Secretary Ezhov. Condemning "opportunist, liberalistic elements" in the party apparatus who considered that, since they had already completed one purge, there were very few people left in their organizations who needed purging, Malenkov, then head of ORPO of the Central Committee, declared: "It must be precisely and clearly explained that no previous work, no matter how good it was, may be used now to justify the fact that they are uncovering too few crooks, too few rogues . . . there is no room for discussion on this."[23]

At the end of 1935, when the "verification" was said to be almost completed, a Central Committee plenum approved the issue of new party cards in February-April 1936. It was made clear, however, that this would be more than a mere

[22] See I. Rumiantsev, "Povtornaia proverka partdokumentov" (A Repeated Verification of Party Documents), *ibid.*, No. 17, September 1935, pp. 20-21. For the results of the "verification" in Smolensk city and raion, which formed part of the Western oblast, see Fainsod, *Smolensk*, pp. 229-231.

[23] *PS*, No. 18, October 1935, p. 65.

technical operation. "The chief lesson to be drawn from the experience of verifying party documents is that party members and organizations are as yet far from having mastered the repeated directives of the CC CPSU on increasing bolshevik vigilance and discipline among the members of the party."[24] In this situation "it should be borne in mind that in exchanging party cards, party organizations may decline to issue cards to members of the party, even if they have passed the verification of party documents, should these members not deserve the lofty title of party member." It was anticipated however, that, in contrast to the "verification of documents," most of those to be refused new cards would be "passive" rather than "hostile" elements.[25] The exchange of cards thus became a third purge operation. How many expulsions it involved is not known. All told, the membership of the party declined by about 300,000 in 1935, and 200,000 in 1936.[26]

Thrice purged in three years, the CPSU, one might have thought, was now due for a spell of consolidation and nor-

[24] *KPSS v rez*, Vol. II, p. 823.

[25] *Ibid.*, p. 827.

[26] In the Kirov oblast, where there were 2,350 full members and 2,533 candidates, 107 exclusions were reported during the exchange of cards (about 2 percent). See *PS*, No. 9, May 1936, p. 56. Similar proportions are reported from Smolensk. See Fainsod, *Smolensk*, p. 232. In Uzbekistan, when allowance is made for those reinstated on appeal up to January 15, 1937, the proportion of the party membership excluded in the exchange of documents came to 1.98 percent. See *Kommunisticheskaia Partiia Uzbekistana v tsifrakh: sbornik statisticheskikh materialov: 1924-1964 gody* (Tashkent, 1964), compiled by N. D. Bezrukova, p. 60 (cited hereafter as *KP Uzbekistana v tsifrakh*). In some areas, however, up to 50 percent were excluded as "passive," and the Central Committee was forced to issue a decision condemning wholesale labeling of members as "passive" and requiring a substantial proportion to be rehabilitated. See *PS*, No. 11, June 1936, p. 42; No. 17, September 1936, p. 21.

malcy. That, indeed, seemed a reasonable expectation from the experience of previous purges. Instead, hysteria was now raised to an unheard of pitch, and the country passed into the inferno of the "show trials" and the *Ezhovshchina*. In June 1936, a few weeks before the first "show trial" (of Zinoviev, Kamenev and fourteen others), a letter was sent out to local party organizations stating that "in present circumstances the inalienable quality of every bolshevik should be to recognize an enemy of the party, however well he may be masked." The letter made the grotesque accusation that "the Trotskyite-Zinovievite monsters unite all the most hostile and accursed enemies of the working people of our country—the spies, provocateurs, diversionists, white-guardists, kulaks, etc.—in their struggle against the Soviet state," and warned that failure of vigilance had allowed many enemies to slip through the "verification of documents."[27] These points provided the insistent theme of a redoubled search for enemies in the ensuing months, yielding a new flood of denunciations, expulsions and arrests.[28]

The final turn of the screw was the plenum of the Central Committee held in late February and early March 1937. On the eve of the plenum its tone was set by a leading article in the Central Committee's organizational journal: "Our Leninist-Stalinist party demands again and again that every party official and every communist should be able to identify and unmask, mercilessly and promptly, the masked enemies of the people, the rotten double-dealers and Trotskyite-Zinovievites, no matter how cunning the masks they have contrived."[29] The plenum heard reports from Stalin, Molotov,

[27] See *WKP* 499, pp. 322-328.

[28] See Fainsod, *Smolensk*, pp. 233-237.

[29] "Po-bol'shevistski raspoznavat' i razoblachat' vragov sotsializma" (Identify and Unmask in Bolshevik Fashion the Enemies of Socialism), *PS*, No. 2, January 1937, p. 15.

Zhdanov and (according to Khrushchev's 1956 "secret speech") Ezhov, the recently appointed NKVD commissar.[30] Despite doubts among a section of the Central Committee membership, Stalin and his henchmen forced through a resolution authorizing a further intensification of the hunt for "enemies of the people."[31] According to Khrushchev, arrests on charges of counterrevolutionary crimes increased tenfold between 1936 and 1937, and, while declining significantly after the Central Committee plenum of January 1938, they remained numerous for another year after that.[32]

It is this final and most terrible operation of the purge series—the *Ezhovshchina*—that non-Soviet writers usually have in mind when they refer to the "great purge." It has frequently been noted that the *Ezhovshchina*, while claiming victims in all sections of the population, appeared to take its greatest toll among the elite of Soviet society—administrative and managerial personnel at all levels, intellectuals, army officers, prominent minority nationals and so on.[33]

This impression of focusing on the elite derives powerful

[30] Stalin's speech, "Deficiencies in Party Work and Measures for the Liquidation of Trotskyites and other Double-Dealers," was published on March 29, 1937. Molotov's report, entitled "Lessons of Wrecking, Sabotage and Espionage by Japanese-German-Trotskyite Agents," appeared on April 21, 1937. Ezhov's report does not appear to have been published. See *The Anti-Stalin Campaign and International Communism*, p. 27. Armstrong (*Totalitarianism*, p. 57) has established that Kaganovich also addressed the plenum on the same subject, and suggests that the report printed by *Pravda* as Molotov's may have been identical with the one attributed by Khrushchev to Ezhov.

[31] *The Anti-Stalin Campaign and International Communism*, pp. 29-30.

[32] *Ibid.*, pp. 30, 38.

[33] See Brzezinski, *Purge*, p. 106. For a valuable examination of the evidence pertaining to the *Ezhovshchina*, see Armstrong, *Totalitarianism*, Chaps. IV and V.

211

support from the data on party membership changes at this period. During 1937, when the bulk of the arrests appear to have occurred, the party membership declined by only 60,000.[34] Since new recruits totaled less than 40,000, the number of *current party members* who were "purged" during 1937 must have been under 100,000. Taking the whole period between the renewal of recruitment in November 1936 and the Eighteenth Congress in March 1939, the growth in total party membership fell short of the number of candidates admitted by only about 180,000,[35] and this appears to be the maximum number who could have been "purged" during this period, not allowing for deaths of members from natural causes (probably very few in a predominantly youthful membership). Of course, vast numbers of people who were not members of the party also fell victim to the *Ezhovshchina*, including a large (but unknown) proportion of the million and a half communists who had been expelled from the party before the mass arrests began: these, whatever the original reason for their expulsion, were now the most obvious candidates for "unmasking" as "enemies." However, our concern here is with those communists who were still in the party when the *Ezhovshchina* began: in view of the abundant evidence of the wholesale replacement and arrest of prominent party members at all levels, who must have made up a very substantial proportion of the 100,000 lost to the party in 1937, it begins to look as if the surviving *rank-and-file* communists were now *relatively* immune from arrest.

Looking at the period 1933-1938 as a whole, one gets the

[34] *PZh*, No. 20, October 1947, p. 81.
[35] Calculated from comparison of figures in *ibid., BSE* (2nd edn.), Vol. IX, p. 149, and Barsukov and Iudin, in *Politicheskoe samoobrazovanie*, No. 6, June 1965, p. 29.

strong impression that, as each phase of the purge unfolded itself, the focus of the attack moved ever closer to the centers of power: while the *chistka* of 1933-1934 struck mostly at the rank-and-file, leaving the apparatus virtually untouched, and the "verification" and exchange of party documents in 1935 affected particularly the lower functionaries, the *Ezhov-shchina* was aimed primarily at the directing cadres and the intelligentsia, with the rank-and-file figuring now much more as accusers and informers than as victims. Or to view it from another angle, whereas most of the victims in 1933-1934 were simple, apolitical men and women accused of exploiting their party membership for personal ends, and those of 1935-1936 were communists suspected of connection with the various opposition groups of the 1920's or antibolshevik groups of an earlier period, in 1937-1938 the edge was turned against the Stalinists themselves, against those who had unwaveringly followed the General Secretary in all his struggles and been rewarded for their pains with office and privilege, only to be "unmasked" at last as Trotskyite-Zinovievites, spies and wreckers. And at each stage the accusers of yesterday became the accused of today. One is reminded here of Stalin's proclivity, often noted by his biographers, of destroying his enemies by setting them at each others' throats.

Was this all in accordance with a grand design, conceived by the dictator years before its denouement and aiming not only at the removal of his enemies, actual and potential, but at clearing the way for a new following, more suitable to his present purposes? At first glance the notion seems too diabolical to be plausible. One might alternatively hypothesize that the purge, once it reached a certain level, developed a momentum of its own, as communists, to save their skins and advance themselves, sought to outdo each other in vigilance

213

and denunciations. It could also be argued that it was the evidence of wavering support among Central Committee members at the February-March plenum that made Stalin turn against his own followers in 1937. As against this, the Central Committee letter of June 1936 and the show trials beginning in August are hard to understand except in the light of what happened in 1937. There is also Shaumyan's assertion that there were moves against Stalin in "his" Central Committee as early as 1934, and his linking of this with the murder of Kirov, which marked the beginning of the terror.[36] Finally, there is the telegram sent by Stalin and Zhdanov in September 1936, stating that the political police were now four years behind in the unmasking of enemies,[37] thus directly linking what was about to happen with the whole sequence of events since the original mooting of the *chistka*. While final conclusions must await further evidence (which may, or may not, be forthcoming), it now seems likely that something like the *Ezhovshchina* was planned well in advance by Stalin, and that the earlier purge operations, although they served other purposes, were also designed to *make possible* the *Ezhovshchina*.

Replenishing the Ranks

It was the Central Committee plenum of January 1938 that marked the turning of the tide. The leadership now condemned in scandalized tones the "heartless and bureaucratic attitude toward communists" accused of being "enemies of the people," blaming it on "careerist" officials anxious to protect themselves from charges of lack of vigilance or to gain

[36] See *P*, February 7, 1964.
[37] *The Anti-Stalin Campaign and International Communism*, p. 26.

promotion by supplanting falsely accused superiors.[38] Although the terror persisted for several more months, the rate of arrests fell off sharply. This change was reflected in party membership movements. Not only did the expulsion rate decline, but expelled members began to be rehabilitated and recommended expulsions were quashed by higher committees.[39] Meanwhile a substantial recruitment campaign was set in motion.

The ban on new party admissions, instituted in January 1933, lasted almost four years—by far the longest moratorium on recruitment in the history of the party. During these years, as we have noted, suitable applicants were supposed to be admitted to "sympathizers' groups" pending the renewal of recruitment. However, these groups seem never to have functioned very satisfactorily,[40] and it is doubtful if they played more than a marginal role in the process of restocking the party's depleted ranks following the purges. The December 1935 plenum of the Central Committee, after justifying the delay in renewing recruitment by reference to the confusion in party records, announced that enrollments could recommence on June 1, 1936.[41] In actual fact, the sig-

[38] See *KPSS v rez*, Vol. II, pp. 849-858.

[39] See Armstrong, *Totalitarianism*, pp. 71-72.

[40] More than a year after they were decreed by the Seventeenth Congress, sympathizers' groups were not even in existence in a majority of organizations, and where they did exist were often given no training whatsoever. At the other extreme, some organizations recruited members of sympathizers' groups on a mass scale, or gave them unconstitutional organizational functions. See "Protiv kampaneishchiny v priëme sochuvstvuiushchikh" (Against Campaign Methods of Recruiting Sympathizers), *PS*, No. 22, November 1934, pp. 40-41; V. Donskoi, "Protiv nedootsenki vazhneishego ukazaniia partii" (Against Underestimation of a Most Important Directive of the Party), *ibid.*, No. 9, May 1935, pp. 8-12.

[41] *KPSS v rez*, Vol. II, pp. 825, 828.

nal to start was delayed till September 29, and enlistments finally recommenced in November 1936.[42] The plenum decision of December 1935 had strongly warned against "turning the enrollment of new party members into a mass recruitment campaign," and this warning was underlined on the eve and in the early months of renewed enlistments. Local committees who gave the renewal of admission undue publicity or who forced the pace of recruitment were rebuked and acidly told that it was precisely this approach to recruitment which had necessitated the current purges.[43]

Generally speaking, local communists were probably only too willing to proceed with the greatest caution. Even before November 1936, difficulty was being experienced in building up the "sympathizers' groups," because of the unwillingness of communists to recommend their acquaintances as candidates in case they should be subsequently unmasked as "hostile elements."[44] In 1937 the chances of being compromised in this way were incomparably greater and the sanctions proportionately more fearful. Some local committees reacted to this situation by surrounding the admission process with formidable formalities. In Kiev, for example, the applicant had to appear in person before a plenary meeting of the raikom, while his sponsors had to address not only this meeting, but also a session of the raikom bureau, a general meeting of the applicant's cell, and in large cells, a meeting of the cell committee. Such elaborate precautions were subsequently denounced as inventions of "enemies of the peo-

[42] See *PS*, No. 19, October 1936, pp. 3-5. It is worth noting that the Seventeenth Congress had originally resolved to renew recruitment from the second half of 1934. See *KPSS v rez*, Vol. II, p. 769.

[43] See, for example, *PS*, No. 19, October 1936, pp. 3-5; No. 20, October 1936, pp. 4-7, 35-36, 44-45; No. 5, March 1937, pp. 63-64.

[44] See *ibid.*, No. 18, September 1936, pp. 27-28.

ple," but they were clearly encouraged by the pressures exerted by the Central Committee.[45]

In the course of 1937 and 1938 recruitment was progressively accelerated by a series of Central Committee decisions. The first, dated June 28, 1937, called for energetic enrollment of komsomol members and, while stressing the continued need for approaching each individual application with proper caution, condemned "those for whom bolshevik vigilance has become petty bourgeois cowardice."[46]

On March 4, 1938, a decision entitled "On the Work of Party Organizations in Admitting New Members into the Party" criticized local committees which had "as yet scarcely started recruitment" and condemned red tape in considering applications.[47] These criticisms were repeated in a further decision dated July 14, 1938,[48] and on August 22 a decision was issued clarifying and streamlining recruitment procedures.[49]

As a result of these efforts, the number of new candidates rose from 12,000 in the eight months November 1936 to June 1937, to 28,000 in the second half of 1937,[50] to 109,000

[45] See Z. Serdiuk, "Priëm v partiiu v kievskoi partorganizatsii" (Admission into the Party in the Kiev Organization), *ibid.*, No. 22, November 1938, pp. 54-57.

[46] *PS*, No. 14, July 1937, pp. 42-44.

[47] *Ibid.*, No. 6, March 1938, p. 61.

[48] "O kurse priëma novykh chlenov v VKP(b)" (On Progress in Admitting New Members into the CPSU), *ibid.*, No. 15, August 1938, pp. 63-64.

[49] "Voprosy priëma novykh chlenov v VKP(b)" (Problems of Admission of New Members into the CPSU), *ibid.*, Nos. 19-20, October 1938, p. 79. See *ibid.*, p. 80, for a further measure aimed at expediting enrollments.

[50] *Ibid.*, No. 6, March 1938, p. 61. This source also gives data on candidates raised to full membership. M. Shamberg, "Protiv volokity v priëme novykh chlenov v VKP(b)" (Against Red Tape in Admit-

217

in the first half of 1938,[51] and in the second half of that year apparently totaled over 400,000.[52] This acceleration continued after the Eighteenth Congress in March 1939, and the

---

ting New Members into the CPSU), *ibid.*, No. 7, April 1938, p. 17, confirms these figures, giving a slightly more precise version of them (12,373 candidates in November 1936-June 1937 and 28,451 in July-December 1937). Figures given by later sources imply a somewhat lower recruitment—about 33,000—for this fourteen-month period. See *ibid.*, No. 15, August 1938, p. 63, and D. Bakhshiev, *Partiinoe stroitel'stvo v usloviiakh pobedy sotsializma v SSSR* (Party Construction in Conditions of the Victory of Socialism in the U.S.S.R.), (Moscow, 1954), p. 65. Cf. Brzezinski, *Purge*, p. 99, where admissions during 1937 are estimated at 90,000. It seems likely that the data just quoted were not available when this estimate was made, and it was evidently based on a June 1938 source, which stated that "since the renewal of the admission of new members into the ranks of the CPSU, over 200,000 people have put in applications on their wish to enter the Communist Party." See L. Tandit, "Bol'shevistskoe vospitanie molodykh kommunistov" (The Bolshevik Training of Young Communists), *B*, Nos. 10-11, 1938, p. 62). Brzezinski may have taken this to mean that over 200,000 had already been *admitted* to the party by that date. However, there were at this time some scores of thousands of applicants for admission whose applications were awaiting consideration by party committees (see *PS*, No. 15, August 1938, p. 63). It is possible, though extremely improbable, that party authorities deliberately understated the rate of admissions at this period in order to conceal the scale of expulsions. No other cases of such large-scale falsification of party membership figures have been detected and it is hard to see how the numerous contemporary and subsequent data could have been squared so as to conceal such a falsification indefinitely. If contemporary sources are accepted, they indicate a total recruitment of under 40,000 in 1937.

[51] *PS*, No. 15, August 1938, p. 63.

[52] No official figure of recruitment in the second half of 1938 has been found. The estimate of over 400,000 was calculated as follows. Total recruitment from November 1936 through February 1939 was 775,000 (Barsukov and Iudin, in *Politicheskoe samoobrazovanie*, No. 6, June 1965, p. 29). In January-February 1939 the total party membership grew by 170,693 (cf. *PZh*, No. 20, October 1947, p. 81 and *BSE* [2nd edn.] Vol. IX, p. 149), and this suggests an intake of perhaps 200,000 candidates in these two months. When this number is added to the roughly 150,000 admitted up to mid-1938 (see

party grew by the record number of 1,100,000 in that year.[53] As the *Ezhovshchina* receded into the past, local committees became steadily less cautious and inhibited in their recruitment efforts. This is evidenced by the growing proportion of applicants granted admission as candidates—two out of five in the first half of 1938, and seven out of eight from April to October in 1939.[54]

By the closing months of 1939, party membership approached the high point reached in the last period of mass recruitment, on the eve of the 1933-1934 *chistka*. Apparently this was close to the limit currently set by the leadership, for at this point the brakes were applied. A Central Committee decision issued on November 16, 1939 stated that, while the recruitment record of recent months was generally satisfactory, there were signs that many local organizations were beginning to ignore the "individual approach" to applicants and to indulge in an indiscriminate chasing after numbers.[55] The admissions rate began to decline immediately. However, local organizations, while relaxing their drive

footnotes 50 and 51), and subtracted from the total recruits in November 1936-February 1939, the balance for the second half of 1938 comes to about 425,000. A contemporary source (*PS*, No. 23, December 1938, p. 59) stated that 135,000 candidates had been admitted in the previous three-month period and over 300,000 since the renewal of recruitment. This issue of the journal was set in type on November 23, 1938, which indicates that the three months referred to were probably July-September, while the figure of "over 300,000" probably includes recruitment in October. This points to a great acceleration of recruitment in the last quarter of 1938 to something like the 1939 level of about 100,000 a month.

[53] *PZh*, No. 20, October 1947, p. 81.

[54] Compare figures in *PS*, No. 15, August 1938, p. 63 and No. 22, November 1939, p. 12.

[55] *Ibid.*, No. 21, November 1939, pp. 59-60. As early as July 1939, an obkom was rebuked by the Party Control Commission for allowing local committees to rubber-stamp the recommendations of primary organizations, without verification. *Ibid.*, No. 14, July 1939, p. 61.

for recruits, continued to admit almost all who applied, and only 3 to 4 percent of applicants were rejected in the early months of 1940.[56] This prompted a further decision, issued in July 1940, which strongly condemned the continued wholesale rubber-stamping of admissions in many organizations, and regional organizations which failed to react promptly were singled out for severe rebuke.[57] This had its effect. Whereas 1,127,802 persons were admitted to candidate membership in the fourteen months from April 1, 1939, to June 1, 1940, only 138,728 were admitted in the eight months from June 1940, up to the opening of the Eighteenth Party Conference in February 1941;[58] that is, the monthly recruitment rate fell from about 80,000 to well under 20,000. The total membership was now 3,900,000 and it probably rose very little above this figure before the German invasion in June.[59]

[56] See *ibid.*, No. 13, July 1940, pp. 3-7.

[57] *Ibid.*, pp. 3-7; also No. 17, September 1940, p. 66.

[58] Compare figures in *B*, Nos. 15-16, 1940, and Nos. 3-4, 1941. The increased rate of rejection of applicants, though considerable, evidently accounted for only a fraction of this reduced intake. In the Moscow oblast 2,752 applicants were accepted as candidates out of 3,258 who applied in the period July 1940 to March 1941. See V. Sorokin, "Priëm novykh chlenov v VKP(b)" (Enrollment of New Members in the CPSU), *PS*, No. 9, May 1941, p. 14. In Kazakhstan the rejection rate increased from 12 percent to 33 percent between June and October 1940 (see Beisembaev and Pakhmurnyi, *op.cit.*, p. 234). On stricter measures to limit recruitment in this republic, see *ibid.*, pp. 234-238. The main reason for the decline in the recruitment rate was an abrupt reduction in applications as local committees switched over from a policy of stimulating enrollments to one of restricting them.

[59] See Shatalin's report to the Eighteenth Conference, *B*, Nos. 3-4, February 1941. For a useful discussion of CPSU recruitment in 1939-1941, see Bakhshiev, *op.cit.*, pp. 80-87. Bakhshiev, along with a number of other authors, states that the party increased its membership by over 1,600,000 in the course of World War II. Since

The Best People

What was the character of these post-purge recruits, who made up about half of the total party membership by the outbreak of the Soviet-German war? Although only fragmentary evidence is available as to their social composition, it is sufficient to reveal a complete break with the proletarian bias which dominated recruitment in 1921-1932. Henceforth recruitment was focused—to use the constantly repeated official formula—on the "best people."

The proletarian bias had been reaffirmed in the revised party rules adopted by the Seventeenth Congress in 1934, which reshuffled the system of recruitment categories as follows:

1) industrial workers with a record of no less than five years in production;
2) industrial workers of less than five years standing, agricultural workers, Red Army men drawn from the working class and collective farmers, and engineering-technical workers, employed directly in production workshops or sectors;

---

membership has been estimated at about 5,700,000 at the end of the war, this implies a figure significantly in excess of four millions in June 1941. However, there is some doubt about the accuracy of the 1945 figures, which calls this conclusion into question, and it is hard to square it with available data about the rate of recruitment on the eve of the war. For instance, recruitment in the Kirov oblast in the first half of 1941 amounted to only about 2 percent of the existing membership in the oblast. See *Kirovskaia oblastnaia partiinaia organizatsiia v gody Velikoi Otechestvennoi voiny: sbornik dokumentov* (The Kirov Oblast Party Organization in the Years of the Great Patriotic War: Collection of Documents), (Kirov, 1961), pp. 284-285. If this level of recruitment was typical, it would indicate a total party recruitment of only about 80,000 for January-June, 1941. The fact that recruitment averaged under 20,000 per month in June 1940-February 1941 would tend to confirm this.

3) collective farmers, members of industrial artels and elementary school teachers;

4) other white-collar workers.[60]

The discrimination between categories as to the number of recommendations required and the standing of those making recommendations was further widened. Although the distinction made between different groups of white-collar workers, some of them being placed in a relatively favored recruitment position, gave signs of a new approach, there was little here to prepare members for the drastic shift of emphasis which was apparent from the beginning of the renewal of recruitment in November 1936. An article describing how "the best and foremost people" were being enlisted in the Leningrad party organization showed that up to September 1937, about 40 percent of the new candidates and 50 percent of those transferred from candidate to full membership were scientists, teachers, engineers and technicians, doctors, students, and office workers.[61] This trend appears to have been intensified by the Central Committee decision of July 14, 1938, which, as we saw above, had been important in stimulating a great increase in the rate of recruitment. The July 14 decision reproved local party organs for not concentrating their efforts sufficiently on the "best people," and was later quoted by a Georgian official as authorizing a great acceleration of enrollments among the "rural intelligentsia" and ad-

[60] *KPSS v rez*, Vol. II, p. 776.

[61] P. Aleksandrov, "Priëm v nashu partiiu luchshikh liudei nashei rodiny" (Admission to the Party of the Best People of Our Motherland), *PS*, No. 1, January 1938, pp. 49-51. The Central Committee instruction on renewing recruitment had stated that recruitment should be focused on "the best people of our country, drawn first of all from the workers, but also from the peasantry and the intelligentsia, people proven in the various sectors of the struggle for socialism" (see *PS*, No. 19, October 1936, pp. 3-5).

ministrative personnel. This delegate compared figures of rural recruitment in Georgia for the twenty months prior to the July 14 decision and the eight months following it; these figures indicated an increase of four and a half times in the number of collective farm "brigadiers" and heads of livestock farms recruited, a fivefold increase in the number of chairmen of collective farms and of village soviets, and an elevenfold increase in the number of agronomists, schoolteachers and doctors. By comparison, the *total* number of recruits probably increased only about threefold.[62]

The radical change which the 1930's brought to the social orientation of CPSU recruitment is shown in Table 9,[63] where

TABLE 9: CLASS COMPOSITION OF POSTPURGE RECRUITS, COMPARED WITH 1929 RECRUITS

	1929 enrollments	Enrollments Nov. 1936- March 1939
	Percent of all enrollments	
Workers	81.2	41.0
Peasants	17.1	15.2
Intelligentsia and white-collar workers	1.7	43.8

the class composition of candidates admitted from November 1936 to March 1939 is compared with the figures for 1929, when the proletarian bias was at its height.

[62] See Dzhashi's speech in *XVIII s"ezd Vsesoiuznoi Kommunisticheskoi Partii(b)*, (Moscow, 1939), p. 577 (cited hereafter as *XVIII s"ezd*).

[63] SOURCES: The figures for 1929 are from *BSE* (1st edn.), Vol. XI, col. 534; those for 1936-1939 are from Barsukov and Iudin in *Politicheskoe samoobrazovanie*, No. 6, June 1965, p. 29. For separate figures for Georgia and Azerbaidzhan, showing a considerably higher peasant intake and lower worker intake than the national average, see *XVIII s"ezd*, pp. 544, 577.

Theoretical justification for this change of orientation was offered at the Eighteenth Congress in March 1939, which abolished the discriminatory four-category regulation of recruitment. The relevant decision of the congress, stressing the fundamental changes which had taken place in Soviet society and hence in the character and mutual relationships of its constituent classes, described the Soviet intelligentsia as "yesterday's workers and peasants and the sons of workers and peasants promoted to commanding posts." Henceforth equal opportunities to join the party should be given to all, irrespective of class; discriminatory provisions regarding the number of recommendations required and the length of service of those making recommendations were abolished; and there was to be a universal probationary (candidate) period of one year.[64]

Despite the sharp acceleration of recruitment after the Eighteenth Congress, there was an even more drastic reduction in the intake from the humbler social strata. Workers made up only 24 percent of recruits in the period from 1937 to June 1941.[65] Since they constituted 41 percent in November 1936-March 1939, this means that in the period between the Eighteenth Congress and the German invasion their share of total recruitment must have been under 20 percent. Comparable data on the intake of peasants during this period is not available for the country as a whole, but the reduction in peasant recruitment seems to have been similar to that for workers. One indication of this is the data from Kazakh-

[64] See *KPSS v rez*, Vol. II, pp. 909-910. Despite the encouragement given in practice to the recruiting of the "intelligentsia," the four-category system was retained right up to the Eighteenth Congress, although its implementation was certainly liberalized (see *PS*, No. 23, December 1938, pp. 61-62).

[65] M. Shamberg, "Nekotorye voprosy vnutripartiinoi raboty" (Some Questions of Intra-Party Work), *PS* No. 4, February 1946, p. 28.

stand and Kirgizia reproduced below in Table 11. Another is provided by figures of enlistments in the Cheliabinsk oblast (Table 10)[66] in the period January 1941-February 1942.

TABLE 10: New Enrollments and Transfers to Full Membership in Cheliabinsk Oblast, January 1941-February 1942—Social Class

	Transferred to full membership		New candidates	
	Number	Percent	Number	Percent
Workers	909	18	600	21
Collective farmers	399	8	289	10
Intelligentsia and white-collar workers	3,515	74	2,035	69

These cover not only newly enlisted candidates but also communists transferred from candidate to full membership, most of whom would have joined as candidates in the previous year, so it gives us an idea of the composition of those joining during 1940 as well as 1941. Since the Cheliabinsk oblast is a fairly typical provincial industrial area with a grain-growing and stock-raising hinterland, and without any exceptional concentration of administrative or intellectual activities, its recruitment pattern was probably not untypical of the country as a whole at this period, and this hypothesis derives support from the fact that the proportion of worker recruits did approximate the national average. It would seem, therefore, that workers constituted under 20 percent of all recruits to the CPSU in 1939-1941, peasants under 10 percent and intelligentsia and white-collar workers over 70 percent.

[66] SOURCE: See *P*, April 22, 1942. Cf. Fainsod, *How Russia Is Ruled*, pp. 263-264. In Kirgizia 71.7 of all recruits in the first half of 1941 were intelligentsia–white-collar workers; *KP Kirgizii*, p. 158.

It was in this period that the party made its biggest strides among the technical and professional intelligentsia. By 1939 only the fringe of many professions had been absorbed into the party, and local organizations seem to have been under pressure to remedy this as soon as possible. In March 1940, a raion party conference in Moscow was told that "the work of political education is clearly inadequate among the intelligentsia. Only four of the 400 doctors in the raion and 17 of the 500 teachers have so far been enrolled as candidates."[67] These efforts achieved striking results. Between January 1939 and January 1941 the proportion of CPSU members and candidates trained in various engineering, agricultural, scientific and other specialties rose from 16.3 percent to 34.1 percent.[68]

In 1938 the proportion of communists classified as workers by social class was 64.3 percent,[69] which was only 1 percent less than the proportion in 1932 (cf. Table 8, p. 199). Since, however, only 24 percent of those joining the party between 1937 and the German invasion were so classified, and the party doubled in size over this period, this must have reduced the proportion of "workers" to less than half the party membership for the first time since the Lenin enrollment.[70] Mean-

[67] *I*, March 3, 1940.

[68] V. M. Donskoi, ed., *Velikaia partiia Lenina: (K 60-letiiu II s"ezda RSDRP)*, (Moscow, 1963), p. 301.

[69] *Ibid.*, p. 293.

[70] Apart from the data from Central Asia, data is available from two industrialized oblasts in the Urals. In the Cheliabinsk oblast in 1940, 57.4 percent of the full members and only 36.5 percent of the candidates were workers. By 1941 the proportion of all communists in this oblast who were workers was 44.3 percent. See A. V. Mitrofanova, *Rabochii klass Sovetskogo Soiuza v pervyi period Velikoi Otechestvennoi voiny* (The Working Class of the Soviet Union in the First Period of the Great Patriotic War), (Moscow, 1960), p. 36. In the Perm oblast in June 1941, 44.3 percent of the membership were workers, 17.4 percent peasants, and 38.3 percent white-collar work-

while, the proportion of "peasants" evidently sank to something like 15 percent, about the same as at the beginning of mass collectivization. Moreover, as these classifications refer to "basic employment" prior to enlistment, it is safe to assume that, as in the past, many—perhaps a majority—of the "workers" and "peasants" recruited had already been "promoted to commanding posts" or were to be promoted soon after enlistment.[71] As for those still left in manual occupations, the main emphasis was upon recruiting: in industry, "Stakhanovites" and skilled workers such as fitters, boilermakers, coal-cutting machinists, and molders; and, in farming, tractor and combine drivers, agricultural brigade leaders, and heads of livestock farms.[72]

There are three republics for which we have relatively detailed data on the composition of the party membership in the purge and postpurge period. For Kazakhstan and Kirgizia we have annual figures for the three basic "social" or "class" categories, and these are summarized in Table 11.[73]

---

ers and others. See A. T. Naumova, *Permskaia partiinaia organizatsiia v gody Velikoi Otechestvennoi voiny* (The Perm Party Organization in the Period of the Great Patriotic War), (Perm, 1960), p. 4.

[71] In Georgia only 11,359 out of the 28,500 "peasant" communists in 1939 were actually employed on farms, and many (perhaps a majority) of these were undoubtedly in such "leading" posts as kolkhoz chairman, head of livestock farm, brigadier, etc. See *XVIII s"ezd*, p. 578.

[72] See, for example, *PS*, No. 21, November 1939, pp. 59-60; *I*, October 24, 1940, and December 19, 1940; speeches by Fedorov and Burmistenko at the Fifteenth Ukrainian Party Congress, *SU*, May 16, 1940.

[73] SOURCES: *KP Kirgizii*, p. 276; Beisembaev and Pakhmurnyi, *op.cit.*, pp. 175, 239, 250. Because of the big changes in total party membership, the absolute figures bring out other aspects not apparent in the comparison of percentages. In Kirgizia the workers decreased from 7,584 to 2,384 between 1933 and 1938, and increased to 4,631 by 1941. The corresponding figures for peasants were 11,107; 2,862; 5,868; and for white-collar workers and others: 1,241; 783; 7,445.

TABLE 11: SOCIAL COMPOSITION OF CPSU MEMBERSHIP IN KIR-
GIZIA AND KAZAKHSTAN, 1933-1941

| | | | *Percent on January 1* | | | |
| | 1933 | | 1938 | | 1941 | |
	Kir.	Kaz.	Kir.	Kaz.	Kir.	Kaz.
Workers	38	38	39	41	26	28
Peasants	56	52	48	48	32	36
White-collar workers and others	6	10	13	12	42	36

For Uzbekistan we have annual breakdowns, in broad categories, of the *current* occupation of the party membership,
which are reproduced in Table 12.[74] The social and occupational composition of the party in these republics differed
substantially from the U.S.S.R. average, in particular by containing far more peasants and far less workers. These figures

---

Thus while the number of workers and peasants doubled between
1938 and 1941, the number of white-collar workers increased nearly
tenfold.

[74] SOURCE: Compiled from data in *KP Uzbekistana v tsifrakh*, pp.
43, 45, 47, 55, 58, 61, 67, 71, 75. The main reason for the declining
percentage lumped together as "others" was the steady reduction in the
number of students, from 8.8 percent in 1932 to 2.3 percent in 1941.
In 1937 "minor service personnel" (*melkii obsluzhivaiushchii personal*) were shown for the first time as a separate category, constituting 3.7 percent of all communists in Uzbekistan. It is possible
that many of the persons included in this category were previously
shown as "workers" or "white-collar workers." In subsequent years
the proportion of "minor service personnel" steadily declined, and
was only 0.9 percent in 1941. Agricultural workers (i.e. those employed in manual occupations in state farms and MTS's) are included in the "worker" column of Table 12. Between 1933 and 1936,
when breakdowns were given of the "worker" category, agricultural
workers declined from 3.1 to 1.5 percent of the republic's party membership.

TABLE 12: MAIN OCCUPATIONAL CATEGORIES OF CPSU MEMBERSHIP IN UZBEKISTAN, 1932-1941

Jan. 1	Total membership	Percent of CPSU membership			
		Workers	Collective farmers	White-collar workers	Others
1932	68,494	25.4	34.6	25.5	14.5
1933	81,612	22.8	40.1	26.7	10.4
1934	56,702	14.6	45.2	31.7	8.5
1936	28,458	11.8	31.4	47.9	8.9
1937	29,934	13.6	24.4	50.4	11.6
1938	30,233	12.6	24.8	54.3	8.3
1939	35,087	14.7	24.3	54.2	6.8
1940	63,847	14.5	28.3	51.6	5.6
1941	72,068	12.8	27.4	53.3	6.5

are primarily of interest for the *trends* they reveal, and both the direction and scale of these can be taken as indicative of trends in the party as a whole. It is instructive to compare changes during the period of purges and falling membership (1933-1938) with those during the period of large-scale recruitment and expanding membership (1938-1941).

Examining Table 11, we see that communists officially classed as workers fell slightly between 1933 and 1938, those classed as peasants fell more substantially, and those classed as white-collar workers and others rose considerably. Between 1938 and 1941 the proportion of workers and peasants both fell by about a third, while the proportion of white-collar workers trebled.

Turning to the information from Uzbekistan, it is first worth noting that the increased representation of white-collar workers and, even more so, of kolkhozniks, at the expense of workers, which we have observed in the party at large between 1930 and 1932, continued in Uzbekistan be-

229

tween 1932 and 1934 (the gap between workers and peasants in 1934, however, was probably exaggerated by the fact that the *chistka* was more advanced in urban than in rural areas). But what is most interesting in these figures is that the big change in the relative representation of the main occupational groups, involving a doubling of the proportion of white-collar workers, occurred *before* the *Ezhovshchina* and the renewal of recruitment. From 1937 to 1941, though the membership increased by 140 percent, the representation of the main occupational groups fluctuated around the same percentages. One conclusion that may be drawn from this is that these percentages roughly corresponded with the percentages *recruited* in this period (i.e. over 50 percent of recruits were employed as white-collar workers, roughly 40 percent as manual workers and kolkhozniks). Another conclusion emerges, however, when these figures are compared with those from Kazakhstan or Kirgizia on "social position." If, as seems reasonable, we assume that main trends were similar in the three republics, comparison of Tables 11 and 12 suggests that the great increase in the proportion of CPSU members registered as white-collar workers by "social position" was compounded of two distinct elements: (1) an increase (in Uzbekistan from a quarter to a half) in the proportion of party members *currently employed* as white-collar workers; and (2) among those party members employed as white-collar workers a sharp reduction in the proportion previously employed as workers or peasants and so registered by "social position"; the latter undoubtedly reflected the far greater prominence, among white-collar communists, of persons recruited from the new soviet trained intelligentsia.

The social character of the party being created in the years preceding World War II was almost the direct antithesis of

230

that officially aimed at and in part achieved in the decade following Lenin's death. Supplanting the ideal of a thoroughly proletarian organization with rank-and-file workers and poor peasants forming the vast majority, there was implicit in postpurge recruitment policies the concept of an elite organization of men and women invested with authority, whether by virtue of their commanding position, their expertise, or their productive skill and energy. Meanwhile, as early as 1939, only one party member in five was a survivor from Stalin's years of struggle against the oppositions of the 1920's.[75] Stalin's old following, with the exception of a minority who had managed to adapt themselves, were now "on the scrap-heap of history," and new men, products of the emergent socialist society, had taken their place.

Party Weakness in the Countryside

By the time of the 1933-1934 *chistka* the party had managed to establish a widespread network in the collective farms. In October 1933 there were 790,000 communists in rural areas, grouped in 80,000 party cells and candidate groups, 50,000 of which were located in the kolkhozes. Half of the country's kolkhozes now contained at least one communist.[76] During 1933 further efforts were set in train to strengthen party influence among the collective farmers, by sending more party workers from the cities and concentrating communists in the crucial sectors of production,[77] and by the creation of Political Departments, which functioned in the Machine and Tractor Stations from January 1933 to Novem-

[75] Cf. pp. 351-352.
[76] See Glazyrin, *op.cit.*, pp. 89-90.
[77] See A. Abramov, *Organizatorskaia rabota partii po osushchestvleniiu leninskogo kooperativnogo plana* (Moscow, 1956), pp. 151-152.

ber 1934.[78] However, rural party organizations, as we have seen, were among the chief targets of the *chistka*, which largely undid the numerical expansion achieved during the collectivization era.

One legacy of the Political Departments was a further shift of the center of gravity from village-based cells to kolkhoz cells—a process which had gone a long way in the collectivization era itself.[79] To help these departments stimulate and control political activity in the kolkhozes, it was decided to withdraw all remaining collective farmers from village cells, with the aim of setting up a party cell or candidate group in each kolkhoz, or, at the very least, a "party-komsomol nucleus," consisting of communists, "sympathizers" and komsomol members. Kolkhozes lacking any communists at all were to be sent a party organizer to set up a so-called sympathizers' group.[80]

These arrangements led to a further dispersal of the limited human resources available to the party in the countryside. This may have made sense at the time of active recruitment. However, membership was now rapidly declining and continued to do so for four years. Moreover, with the abolition of the MTS Political Departments in November 1934 neither the raikoms nor the newly appointed Political Deputy-Directors in the MTS's seem to have achieved the same close direction of party work in the kolkhozes as had been exercised by the departments.

[78] On the role of these Political Departments and their relations with the district party committees, see Armstrong, *Totalitarianism*, pp. 12-14.

[79] See p. 93.

[80] See CC Decision, "O rabote politotdelov MTS, o kolkhoznoi iacheike, i o vzaimootnosheniiakh politotdelov i raikomov" (On the Work of the Politotdels of MTS's, on the Kolkhoz Cell, and on the Interrelationships of Politotdels and Raikoms), *PS*, No. 12, June 1933, pp. 1-3. See also comments by M. Volin, *ibid.*, pp. 4-9.

232

The result was that a substantial proportion of rural communists, intended to serve as nuclei for a great expansion of party strength in the countryside, found themselves isolated in remote farms and villages, belonging to no party cell and without any effective guidance from above. Such communists, who totaled nearly half the rural party membership in some areas,[81] were obviously of little value as a channel between the party and the peasantry, and this helps to account for a certain reduction of the party's impact on the peasantry in the mid-1930's. This may perhaps be regarded as the obverse side of the emergent political stabilization—or *modus vivendi*—in the villages, whose most striking exemplification was the model kolkhoz statute of 1935.

In January 1937 only 187,000 kolkhoz members and 52,000 state farm employees were in the party.[82] Although direct evidence on the employment of rural communists is meagre at this period, there can be little doubt that the overall contraction of membership involved an increasing con-

[81] In 1935 "isolated" communists were 11 percent of all rural communists in Bashkiria, 14 percent in the Western oblast, 28 percent in the Ivanovo oblast, and 47 percent in the Sverdlovsk oblast. See F. Iosifov, "Partiinaia rabota s kommunistami-odinochkami" (Party Work with Isolated Communists), *PS*, Nos. 1-2, January 1935, p. 44. In some areas they constituted 50 to 70 percent of all rural communists (*PS*, No. 3, February 1935, p. 6). In Belorussia 57 percent of all kolkhoz communists were "isolated"; in the Leningrad oblast, 53 percent; and in the Kirov oblast, 45 percent. The effectiveness of communists in "candidate groups" and "party-komsomol groups," which lacked statutory rights, was often little better than that of "isolated communists." In many areas these two categories also included a substantial number of kolkhoz communists, for example: in Bashkiria, 29 percent and 7 percent respectively; in Kazakhstan, 34 percent and 13 percent. See F. Chivirev, "K voprosu o rabote s kommunistami-odinochkami" (On the Question of Work with Isolated Communists), *ibid.*, No. 14, July 1935, pp. 30-34.

[82] *PZh*, No. 19, October 1967, p. 17.

233

centration of party members in "key" jobs.[83] Despite a substantial growth of party membership in rural areas after 1937, the main emphasis seems to have been on recruiting the "rural intelligentsia," so that kolkhoz organizations remained extremely weak. From November 1936 to March 1939, collective farmers made up only 1,177 of the 7,201 recruits to the party in the *rural* areas of the Leningrad oblast.[84] In the Moscow oblast only 334 of the 27,000 recruits to the party in 1938 were collective farmers.[85] At the beginning of 1939 only 12,000 of the country's quarter million collective farms possessed party organizations, and they contained a mere 7 percent of all party members.[86]

The massive enlistments in 1939 and 1940 brought some improvement in this situation. In the Moscow oblast there

[83] The only figures obtained on the employment of rural communists in the mid-1930's apply to "isolated" communists only in the Western and Ivanovo oblasts in 1935. Details are as follows:

	Western oblast	Ivanovo oblast
Chairmen of village soviets	312	195
Chairmen of kolkhozes	655	593
Chairmen of consumer-coops	70	21
Other *non* rank and file	282	155
Rank-and-file kolkhozniks	329	577
Total	1648	1541

SOURCE: *PS*, Nos. 1-2, January 1935, p. 45.

The proportion of rank-and-file kolkhozniks in these two samples was thus 20 percent and 37 percent repectively. This was probably a *lower* representation of rank and filers than in kolkhozes containing more than one communist. As against this, it must be remembered that a substantial proportion of rural communists occupied administrative jobs *outside* the kolkhozes.

[84] *P*, March 21, 1939.

[85] Bakhshiev, *op.cit.*, p. 86.

[86] See Andreev's speech at the Eighteenth Party Congress. *XVIII s"ezd*, p. 109. Andreev put the membership of kolkhoz party organizations at 153,000.

were party organizations in only 304 out of 6,556 kolkhozes at the beginning of 1939, but by early 1940 the party had formed almost 2,000 new kolkhoz organizations.[87] By the beginning of 1941 the number of rural party organizations had risen to 82,956, of which 29,723 were based on kolkhozes.[88] It is highly doubtful, however, if rural membership, particularly on the farms, yet approached the levels achieved on the eve of the 1933-1934 purge.[89]

Thus by the outbreak of the Second World War, when practically all social and occupational groups were covered with a substantial crust of party members, in the countryside and especially on the collective farms this crust remained wafer-thin, and in places was scarcely visible.

Despite more than a decade of headlong industrialization, two-thirds of the Soviet population still lived in rural areas. At the same time, the bulk of the party membership continued to be concentrated in the towns. In the villages, the party seemed little better prepared to meet the challenge of the war than it had been to meet the challenge of collectivization eleven years earlier, and this was one of the factors making for the regime's relatively permissive policies towards the peasantry during the Second World War.

[87] Bakhshiev, *op.cit.*, p. 86. For Central Committee criticism of inadequacies in building up party organization in the Smolensk oblast, see *PS*, No. 20, October 1939, p. 53.

[88] Bakhshiev, *op.cit.*, p. 87.

[89] Exact comparison is not possible, because the 50,000 cells in October 1933 included candidate groups. However, there were already 30,-000 party organizations in kolkhozes in January 1932 (see p. 189), and it is known that the number of kolkhoz communists greatly increased between then and October 1933. In Uzbekistan, there were 38,000 kolkhozniks in the party in 1933, and only 19,000 in 1941 (see *KP Uzbekistana v tsifrakh*, pp. 45, 75).

Chapter 7

World War II: Party and Army

THE 1930's provided the mold in which the fluid society of postrevolutionary Russia finally set, acquiring features which have remained basically unchanged ever since: the centrally planned and hierarchically directed economy, with rewards sharply differentiated for skill and responsibility, the comprehensive party-state controls over all aspects of social and intellectual life, the facade of pseudo-representative institutions, the technically trained administrative and managerial elite. The 1930's also completed the drift to personal dictatorship, with arbitrary police terror and the cult of Stalin as its twin supports.

The War

The initial successes of the German invasion placed this whole structure in jeopardy, and temporarily threw Stalin into despair.[1] But before Hitler could clinch his victory, the Russians rallied and the invading armies were stopped, mauled and pushed relentlessly back. Victory meant the survival of the Soviet sociopolitical system, the establishment of Soviet control over vast areas of Central and Eastern Europe, and the emergence of the U.S.S.R. as one of the two world superpowers.

World War II produced a cataclysmic effect on the membership of the CPSU exceeding even the 50 percent turnover of the years 1933-1939. It also brought drastic, if temporary, changes in party recruitment policy.

[1] See *The Anti-Stalin Campaign and International Communism*, p. 85.

From 1941 to 1945 the key determinant of all decisions on the recruitment and distribution of party members was the task of winning the war. Military and security considerations dictated the maximum concentration of communists in areas of greatest vulnerability, which meant primarily at the front. They also dictated recruitment policies which would help to bind the population to the regime, and to this end the party shifted to an open-door approach paying minimal attention to social and ideological criteria and focusing on such criteria as patriotism and service to the war effort.

The importance of a substantial leavening of communists in the armed forces to strengthen morale and discipline is obvious. A divisional party conference held in November 1941 resolved as follows:

> It is considered the chief task of every party organization [to carry on] a tireless struggle for the establishment of strict revolutionary order and iron military discipline, to put a stop to all manifestations of laxity and carelessness, of cowardice and panic, which are intolerable in a military unit. By their personal example, communists are obliged to ensure the precise and immediate execution of the commands and regulations of chiefs and commanders, strengthening their authority in every way.[2]

The vital importance in the military context of the party membership's role in mobilization, rule application and internal order maintenance is vividly expressed in this and similar statements of the period.

At the same time, as in the case of the Civil War, World War II afforded excellent opportunities for recruitng "de-

[2] I. I. Sidorov et al., eds., *Iaroslavtsy v gody Velikoi Otechestvennoi voiny: sbornik dokumentov* (People of Yaroslavl Oblast in the Years of the Great Patriotic War: Collection of Documents), (Yaroslavl, 1960), p. 331.

pendable elements," on the assumption that irresponsible, careerist or secretly hostile individuals would scarcely volunteer for the additional risks which being a communist involved for Soviet citizens in the war with the Nazis. The force of this consideration is clearly apparent in speeches and articles of contemporary spokesmen and in later discussions by party historians, where appropriate Civil War quotations from Lenin are frequently invoked. On the other hand it was of the utmost political concern to the party that the hundreds of thousands of servicemen and civilians who manifested leadership qualities under war conditions should be integrated into the established elite and not allowed to develop as a separate focus of prestige and initiative. While this concern was obviously not one to be constantly flaunted in party propaganda, it occasionally emerged fairly frankly. M. I. Kalinin, for instance, then President of the Presidium of the Supreme Soviet, posing for himself the question why the party placed special emphasis on recruiting new members at the front, gave the following explanation.

Because everyone feels that it is necessary to strengthen the party. Everyone knows that our party is the leader and that only a mighty, powerful army can ensure the people victory. And when the Red Army man sees that he is about to participate in a harsh battle, he puts in an application to join the party, wishing to go into battle a communist. That is the great strength of our party, and of the Soviet state. The masses well know that they share the same path as the party.[3]

[3] M. I. Kalinin, *O kommunisticheskom vospitanii* (Moscow, 1958), p. 315. One consequence of this policy of integrating war heroes into the party was the extremely high proportion of communists among those awarded decorations for gallantry. See V. S. Telpukhovskii, *Velikaia Otechestvennaia voina* (The Great Patriotic War), (Moscow, 1959), p. 202.

Similar considerations applied with respect to those citizens who emerged on the home front to take over responsible jobs vacated by communists who had entered the armed forces. During World War II, the white-collar class continued to supply recruits to the CPSU at a rate relative to its numbers far in excess of that shown by other classes. Nevertheless, compared with the immediate prewar years, there was a sharp drop in its predominance. In the party as a whole, i.e. both its civilian and military organizations, 32.1 percent of all wartime admissions were classified as workers, 25.3 percent as peasants, and 42.6 percent as white-collar workers or intelligentsia.[4] Recruitment was not to become so "democratic" again till the late 1950's.

Party Membership in the Armed Forces
Prior to World War II

Scant reference has so far been made to the question of party recruitment and representation in the armed forces. We have noted the salient facts about army service by communists in the Civil War, the role of the army as a recruiting ground for the party, and the related tendency of party recruitment of servicemen to raise the proportion of peasant communists. Discussion of other aspects has been delayed to this point, however, because the facts can best be appreciated if brought together in one place and considered for the period between the Civil War and World War II as a whole.

Table 13[5] summarizes most of the available data on the

[4] *PS*, No. 4, February 1946, p. 28; *K*, No. 13, September 1966, p. 47.

[5] SOURCES: Iu. P. Petrov, *Partiinoe stroitel'stvo v Sovetskoi armii i flote (1918-1961)*, (Party Construction in the Soviet Army and Navy—1918-1961), (Moscow, 1964), pp. 69, 107-108, 150, 154, 222-223, 225, 281, 283, 298, 312, 314, 316, 329, 352, 390, 393,

extent of overlap of the party membership with the armed forces between 1919 and 1945. As might be expected, these figures show wide fluctuations as between periods of war and peace, and a high positive correlation between the number of communists in army party organizations and the proportion of the whole party membership currently serving in the armed forces. Other data reveals that both the representation of nonofficers in military party organizations and the success attained in maintaining party cells (or primary organizations) at subunit level are highly dependent on the overall number of communists in the armed forces.

Throughout the period between the downfall of the tsarist

396-397 (cited hereafter as Petrov, *Partiinoe stroitel'stvo*); *Istoriia Velikoi Otechestvennoi voiny Sovetskogo Soiuza: 1941-1945* (Moscow, 1960), Vol. I, p. 98 and (Moscow, 1963), Vol. v, p. 45. Where dates are given as January, the source states January 1; where given as December, the source states "the end of the year"; the date given as "approximately mid-1934" was stated in the source as "in the aftermath of the Seventeenth Congress." Petrov's figures of armed forces communists in the 1920's appear to be more inclusive and in this sense more accurate than contemporary statistics. Cf. *Partiia v tsifrovom osveshchenii: materialy po statistike lichnogo sostava partii*, p. 30. In 1946, 25.9 percent of the army were in the party and the proportion of naval personnel continued to be a good deal higher. See K. V. Krainiukov, *Partiino-politicheskaia rabota v sovetskikh vooruzhennykh silakh v gody Velikoi Otechestvennoi voiny 1941-1945* (Party-Political Work in the Soviet Armed Forces in the Years of the Great Patriotic War, 1941-1945), (Moscow, 1963), pp. 514-515. B. N. Ponomarev et al., *Istoriia Kommunisticheskoi Partii Sovetskogo Soiuza* (History of the Communist Party of the Soviet Union), (Moscow, 1959), pp. 526, 548, 576, give the following figures for communists in the armed forces: end of 1941—1,300,000 (42.4 percent of all communists); 1942—over two million (54.3 percent); and at the end of the war—3,325,000 (60 percent). These figures are also quoted by a number of other writers, but Iu. P. Petrov, in the most recent systematic study of the topic, ventures the clear assertion that the 3,030,775 communists in the armed forces in December 1944, was the largest number for the whole war period. See Petrov, *Partiinoe stroitel'stvo*, p. 396.

TABLE 13: PARTY REPRESENTATION IN THE ARMED FORCES, 1919-1945

Date	No. of communists in armed forces	Armed forces communists as percent of whole party	Communists as percent of all armed forces personnel
March 1919	60,000	20	
March 1920	280,000	50	
August 1920	300,000		8
December 1921	73,000	14	5
March 1922			7.5
March 1923			10.5
September 1924	45,000		
December 1924			12
December 1925	57,700	5	
December 1926	78,250	6	14
January 1928	82,018	6	
January 1929	93,300	6	
January 1930	102,749	6	
January 1931	133,789	7	
December 1931	200,000	7	
Second half 1932	300,000	9	25+
Approx. mid-1934	269,000		24
December 1937	147,500	7	approx. 10
December 1938	230,000	10	
December 1939	435,000	13	
June 1941	560,800	15	13*
December 1941	1,127,000		
June 1942	1,413,870		
December 1942	1,939,327	50	
December 1943	2,702,500	56	
December 1944	3,030,775	53	23*
July 1945	2,984,750		

* Army only. In the navy the percentage was substantially higher, but inclusion of naval communists would raise the overall percentage by no more than 1 percent.

regime and the final victory of the bolsheviks over the "counterrevolution," a substantial proportion of the party membership was in uniform. The high point was reached in 1920, when every second communist, about 300,000 men altogether, were in the Red Army. At that time one Red Army man out of every twelve was a party member.[6] Over half a million communists saw service with the Red Army during the Civil War, roughly half of them sent into the army by civilian party organizations and half recruited by the party while on army service.[7] Some 200,000 communists lost their lives.[8] During 1919 and 1920, about half the communists serving in the Red Army were in combat units. [9]

In 1921-1923 the bulk of the Red Army was demobilized, and as early as December 1921 only one party member in seven was in the armed forces. Although efforts were made to maintain the level of party representation in the army,[10] the number of party members in the forces continued to decline, reaching an all-time low of 45,000 in September 1924. The 1921 purge, which resulted in the removal of some 10 percent of army communists[11] (compared with a quarter of the party as a whole), was not the main reason for this decline, which was apparently due for the most part to the current restriction of recruitment. Since at all times a large proportion of the communists in the armed forces have been con-

[6] Petrov, *Partiinoe stroitel'stvo*, pp. 107-108.

[7] Estimated from data given in *ibid.*, pp. 88, 107-110.

[8] *Ibid.*, p. 110. Other sources differ, however, on the number of communists killed during the Civil War. A figure as low as 50,000 is given by N. Kuklev, "Partiia v period inostrannoi voennoi interventsii i grazhdanskoi voiny" (The Party in the Period of Foreign Military Intervention and the Civil War), *Kommunist Sovetskoi Latvii*, No. 11, November 1965, p. 54.

[9] Petrov, *Partiinoe stroitel'stvo*, pp. 69, 101-107. For a more detailed account of party membership in the Red Army during the Civil War, see Iu. P. Petrov, *KPSS—rukovoditel' i vospitatel' Krasnoi armii (1918-1920gg.)*, (The CPSU—Leader and Educator of the Red Army, 1918-1920), (Moscow, 1961), especially Chaps. II and IV.

[10] Petrov, *Partiinoe stroitel'stvo*, p. 154.

[11] *Ibid.*, p. 150.

scripts who joined the party after commencing their military service, periods of restricted recruitment have always seen a disproportionate reduction in the size of military party organizations, as compared with civilian organizations.

During the Civil War, the party had discovered the advantages of establishing cells at a level low enough to capitalize on face-to-face relationships, which in the army meant at the company or battery level. By early 1920 a network of company-level cells had become firmly established in the Red Army. One effect of the declining party membership after 1921 was that company-level cells ceased to be viable, and for the most part they were absorbed by cells based on battalion headquarters.[12]

The power struggles of the mid-1920's had strong repercussions on army-party relations. The efforts of Stalin and his allies to remove Trotsky from control of the Red Army, which began during the Civil War, came to a head in 1923-1924. In January 1924 Trotsky's ally Antonov-Ovseenko was removed as chief of the Army Political Directorate, and soon afterwards Stalin's friend Frunze was made Deputy Commissar for War, virtually supplanting Trotsky, who was finally removed as War Commissar in January 1925.[13] Between 1924 and 1926 radical changes were made in the organization of the army, motivated partly by a concern to modernize and stabilize the Soviet military machine and partly by the aim of entrenching the new regime and eliminating the influence of Trotsky. These changes included the introduction of unified command (in place of dual command by combat and political officers), the large-scale replacement of upper-class "military specialists" by "Red com-

[12] *Ibid.*, p. 149.
[13] See Schapiro, *The CPSU*, Chap. 18, and John Erickson, *The Soviet High Command 1918-1941* (London, 1962), Chaps. 5 and 7.

manders" of worker and peasant origin, and an expansion of the proportion of party members both among military cadres and the rank and file.

Between 1924 and 1926 the number of communists in the armed forces rose sharply, regaining the level of late 1921. In the later 1920's the growth continued, but more slowly. The proportion of servicemen who were in the party was now about three times what it had been in 1921.

Particularly significant was the increased party "saturation" of the higher echelons. Between October 1923 and October 1924 the percentage of communists in the central military administration rose from 12 to 25 percent.[14] During the Civil War, because of reliance on "military specialists," only one officer in ten had been a party member. The proportion increased sharply during the demobilization period and was given further impetus by the defeat of Trotsky: from 30 percent in 1923 it rose steadily to over 50 percent in 1929.[15] By 1927 two-thirds of the divisional commanders were communists and 95 percent of the corps commanders.[16]

Apart from policies specifically connected with the struggle against Trotsky, party recruitment practices in the armed forces during the 1920's also reflected in other ways the current struggles between Stalin and his rivals. For example, in February 1926 the Army Political Directorate ordered more active enlistment of peasant soldiers in the party in line with Stalin's current pro-Right policies. Following Stalin's break with the Right, however, when he moved to a policy of restricting peasant enlistment and concentrating on recruiting workers, the Directorate instructed political officers to raise

[14] Erickson, *op.cit.*, p. 175.
[15] See Bubnov, in *BSE* (1st edn.), Vol. xi, col. 542. Cf. *XV s"ezd*, Vol. i, pp. 441-442, where somewhat higher percentages are given.
[16] Petrov, *Partiinoe stroitel'stvo*, p. 192.

the worker intake to between 65 and 80 percent of all servicemen admitted to the party and the proportion of working class members among army communists rose to 58 percent in 1929 and to 63 percent in 1930.[17]

One of the results of the contraction of party representation during the demobilization period was that army party cells came to consist overwhelmingly of officers and political staff. At the end of 1921 privates and N.C.O.'s constituted 50 percent of all army communists, but by 1924 they were down to 20 percent.[18] This trend was reversed, however, by the new policies associated with the removal of Trotsky. The Thirteenth Congress resolved that special attention should be given to the recruitment of rank-and-file soldiers and seamen;[19] in 1925 the proportion of privates and N.C.O.'s in army cells rose to 30 percent and in 1926 to 40 percent.[20] Meanwhile the changeover to unitary command led to a steady decrease in the ratio of political officers in army party cells. The net result of these changes was a significant rise in the representation of rank and filers. However, as can be seen from Table 14,[21] the majority of members of army party cells continued to be men occupying positions of some degree and kind of authority, and the most striking change over the period was the increased predominance of regular (nonpolitical) officers and N.C.O.'s.

[17] *Ibid.*, pp. 223-225, 281.

[18] *Ibid.*, pp. 150, 224.

[19] *KPSS v rez*, Vol. I, p. 819. On subsequent moves by the Orgburo to stimulate the enlistment of rank-and-file soldiers in the party, see I. B. Berkhin, *Voennaia reforma v SSSR (1924-1925)*, (The Military Reform in the USSR [1924-1925]), (Moscow, 1958), pp. 407-409.

[20] Petrov, *Partiinoe stroitel'stvo*, p. 224. At the end of 1927 the figure was 42 percent (*ibid.*, p. 225). For further details on party membership in the armed forces during the 1920's, see Erickson, *op.cit.*, pp. 796-798.

[21] SOURCE: Bubnov, in *BSE* (1st edn.), Vol. XI, col. 542.

TABLE 14: Positions Held by Military Communists, 1925 and 1929

| Positions held | 1925 | | 1929 | |
	No.	Percent	No.	Percent
Officers and N.C.O.'s	18,106	31.4	45,419	48.8
Political officers (politsostav)	14,155	24.5	11,266	12.1
On course or in higher educational establishments	11,909	20.6	10,774	11.6
Privates (krasnoarmeitsy)	9,412	16.3	21,936	23.6
Others	4,105	7.2	3,578	3.9
Totals	57,687	100.0	92,973	100.0

Connected with the drive in the mid-1920's to raise party membership among enlisted men was the campaign to revive company-level cells. A new general instruction on the work of party cells in the armed forces issued by the Central Committee in December 1924 stated that henceforth cells were to be based on companies, batteries, squadrons or ship's companies, so long as they contained at least three communists.[22] Company-level cells increased from 2,264 in July 1924[23] to 4,318 in October 1925, and continued to rise till they reached 6,800 in 1929, by which time practically

[22] Berkhin, op.cit., pp. 405-406. The instruction appeared in Izv Ts K, No. 4, 1925, and the sections pertaining to company-level cells are available in V. N. Manin and V. P. Moskovskii, eds., KPSS o Vooruzhënnykh Silakh Sovetskogo Soiuza: sbornik dokumentov (The CPSU on the Armed Forces of the Soviet Union: Collection of Documents), (Moscow, 1958), pp. 268-273.

[23] Berkhin, op.cit., p. 402.

all infantry companies and subunits of comparable strength in other branches of the armed forces possessed party cells.[24]

As in the 1921 purge, party cells in the armed forces suffered relatively little loss of membership during the purge of 1929-1930, the rate of expulsion being only half that for the party as a whole.[25] In the early 1930's the growth of party membership in the armed forces was sharply intensified, outstripping the unprecedentedly high overall growth rate of the party. The ratio of party members who were in the armed forces, having remained steady at 5 to 6 percent since 1925, rose to 9 percent between 1930 and 1932. At this time over a quarter of the members of the armed forces were communists, a proportion which was not to be reached again until the final stages of World War II. It is unclear whether this represented a deliberate policy of preferential party recruitment in the armed forces, or whether it merely reflected the fact that general party recruitment policy at this time concentrated on those groups who made up the bulk of army conscripts, namely young workers and collective farmers. The proportion of Red Army officers who were party members or candidates continued to rise in the early 1930's and reached 68 percent in 1934.[26]

The exaggerated way in which changes in the ratio of party members in the armed forces reflected fluctuations in the overall party membership is again seen in the contraction of

[24] Petrov, *Partiinoe stroitel'stvo*, p. 226.

[25] *Ibid.*, p. 229.

[26] Erickson, *op.cit.*, p. 374. In 1933 all corps commanders and commanders of military districts were in the CPSU, as were 93 to 95 percent of divisional commanders and 88 percent of commanders of rifle regiments (*ibid.*). For more on party membership among Red Army officers up to the mid-1930's, see D. A. Voropaev and A. M. Iovlev, *Bor'ba KPSS za sozdanie voennykh kadrov* (Struggle of the CPSU for the Creation of Military Cadres), (2nd edn., Moscow, 1960).

membership in the mid-1930's. By 1937 only one service-man in ten was a communist. Once more the ratio of officers to other ranks in army party organizations rose sharply, and company-level cells began to collapse. In 1935 the Central Committee bowed to the inevitable and shifted the basis of the military cell from the company to the regimental level.[27] The pattern of the early 1920's was now repeating itself. The sharp drop in party representation in the armed forces was due not so much to expulsions as to the exaggerated impact of the cessation of recruitment on the membership of military cells. Only 3.5 percent of armed forces communists were expelled and 2.4 percent reduced to candidates or sympathizers during the 1933-1934 purge, compared to 17 and 6 percent respectively in the party as a whole. Army cells seem to have suffered relatively a greater loss of membership during the verification and exchange of party documents in 1935-1936.[28] Nevertheless the main factor was that the military cells lost a substantial proportion of their members with the discharge of each conscript age group, and these could not be replaced by enlistments among the new age group, because of the general ban on party recruitment.

The *Ezhovshchina* hit the armed forces in the middle months of 1937. Its impact varied in direct proportion to rank. Thus, while one-fifth to one-half of all officers are estimated to have been purged, the proportion of higher officers

[27] See *SPR*, No. 9 (1935), p. 115. Efforts were made to salvage something of the party's former impact on enlisted men by creating candidates' groups and party-komsomol groups at company level (see Petrov, *Partiinoe stroitel'stvo*, p. 286).

[28] Petrov, *Partiinoe stroitel'stvo*, p. 284. Erickson considers that the military command, acting in the interests of efficiency, successfully intervened to moderate the impact of the 1933-1934 purge on the Red Army. See Erickson, *op.cit.*, p. 374.

has been calculated at 65 percent.[29] What proportion were communists is not known, but of course the incidence of party membership also increased with rank. The number of army communists purged during the *Ezhovshchina* must have been at least 15,000, and it may have been very much higher. Meanwhile the terror was also inhibiting recruitment. In the middle of 1937 the Central Committee decreed that 20,000 komsomol members of the armed forces were to be enlisted in the party. However, up to the beginning of 1938 only 4,000 had actually been admitted, and a Soviet historian has attributed this to the reluctance of party members either to make recommendations or to approve applicants for fear that they would subsequently be compromised. Total recruitment by party cells in the armed forces was only 7,500 in 1937.[30]

The turning point came in February 1938 when the Central Committee issued a decision entitled "On Admitting Red Army men into the Party," which relaxed formal admission requirements and procedures. There was a sevenfold increase in the admission rate. In the first nine months of 1938, 57,170 members of the Red Army were enlisted as candidates for the party, including 12,770 privates and 27,160 N.C.O.'s. The total membership of party cells during the year increased by nearly a third, compared with under a fifth for the party as a whole. Nevertheless enlisted men still made up only a quarter of all military and naval communists.[31] The admission rate doubled again in 1939, and was given a further impetus by the Soviet-Finnish War, when entry was made especially easy for troops in the Leningrad

[29] Armstrong, *Totalitarianism*, pp. 63-64. Cf. Erickson, *op.cit.*, Chaps. 14 and 15, especially pp. 505-506.
[30] Petrov, *Partiinoe stroitel'stvo*, p. 312.
[31] *Ibid.*, pp. 313-314.

Military District.[32] By 1940 the total strength of party cells in the armed forces was three times what it had been in 1937. The July 1940 decision ordering more selective recruitment (see above, p. 220) was given effect in the armed forces as elsewhere. The proportion of applicants rejected by primary organizations or by divisional party commissions rose from 11 to 25 percent between the first and second half of 1940.[33] In the six months before the German invasion only 34,000 servicemen were admitted to the party compared with 165,000 in 1939.[34]

Despite the enormous expansion of military party organizations between 1937 and 1941, this fell well short of making good the damage done during the purge years. It should be recalled that the overall membership of the armed forces also doubled or trebled during this period. At the time of the German invasion, the proportion of servicemen who were in the party was only half what it had been in 1932-1934. Despite vigorous efforts to revive company-level organizations, less than half of all companies had them in June 1941. Party membership remained particularly low among privates and N.C.O.'s, who between them constituted less than a third of all military communists.[35]

Party and Armed Forces During World War II

In the first six months of the war over 1,100,000 communists were called up for military service.[36] Some 100,000 of them were individually chosen by local committees, which were required to meet quotas of party and komsomol members for service as *politbortsy* ("political warriors"—in-

[32] See *V I KPSS*, No. 11, 1963, p. 65.
[33] Petrov, *Partiinoe stroitel'stvo*, p. 328.
[34] *Ibid.*, pp. 328, 361.
[35] *Ibid.*, p. 329.
[36] *Ibid.*, p. 352.

tended as a stiffening for key front-line detachments),[37] while the remainder merely fell into the appropriate call-up age groups. There were over half a million casualties among party members during these months.[38]

Meanwhile, although the invasion brought a sharp increase in party recruitment in the armed forces, the number joining was insufficient to make up for losses in action. By the end of 1941 total party membership had fallen to 3,064,000,[39] compared with about 4,000,000 at the time of the German invasion. Since the number of communists *killed* was only 400,000 up to mid-1942, Armstrong has concluded that large numbers of communists must have surrendered or been cut off in occupied areas.[40] One of the main obstacles to more rapid recruitment was the rule that applicants were to present recommendations from three persons who had themselves been in the party for at least three years and who had known the applicant at his place of employment for at least twelve months.[41] Under war conditions would-be candidates for party membership often found it impossible to secure three such recommendations. To meet this situation, the Central Committee resolved on August 19, 1941 that in the case of applicants "who had distinguished themselves in battle" those recommending them might have been in the party for as little as one year, and the requirement that they

[37] L. M. Spirin, "Partiinye i komsomol'skie mobilizatsii v Krasnuiu Armiiu v gody Velikoi Otechestvennoi voiny" (Party and Komsomol Mobilizations for the Red Army during the Great Patriotic War), *V I KPSS*, No. 3, 1963, pp. 34-46.

[38] *Ibid.*, p. 36.

[39] *PZh*, No. 19, October 1967, p. 9.

[40] Armstrong, p. 40. This author's excellent and well-documented reconstruction of wartime party membership movements (*Totalitarianism*, Chap. 10) should be considered in conjunction with the present account.

[41] See *KPSS v rez*, Vol. II, p. 925.

should have known the applicant for at least a year was waived. In such cases the application was to be supported by a reference from the political officer of the applicant's unit, covering his military record.[42] It was also resolved that the bureaus of military party organizations could formally admit candidates without holding a meeting of the party organization, as was normally required, subject to the approval of the Party Commission of the formation.[43] In December 1941 a further decision was made permitting battle-tried servicemen to be admitted to full membership after only three months as candidates.[44] These decisions gave a tremendous impetus to recruitment. Army party organizations enlisted 126,000 new candidates in the second half of 1941, 432,000 in the first half of 1942, 640,000 in the second half of 1942 and 646,000 in the first half of 1943. Altogether 2,232,000 servicemen applied for admission to the party during these two years, and 1,845,000 were actually admitted. The difference was said to have been due not to the rejection of applicants, but mainly to their being lost in action

[42] The August 19 decision is available in *Kommunisticheskaia partiia v period Velikoi Otechestvennoi voiny: dokumenty i materialy* (The Communist Party in the Period of the Great Patriotic War: Documents and Materials), (Moscow, 1961), pp. 95-96. It has been discussed by a number of Soviet authors, e.g. Petrov, *Partiinoe stroitel'stvo*, p. 360; S. S. Kultyshev, in *V I KPSS*, No. 2, 1958, p. 60; *PZh*, No. 20, 1947, p. 82; E. A. Rafikov, "Ukreplenie partiinykh organizatsii Krasnoi Armii v pervyi period Velikoi Otechestvennoi voiny" (Strengthening of Party Organizations in the Red Army in the First Period of the Great Patriotic War), *V I KPSS*, No. 3, 1964, p. 70. Rafikov and Petrov state that the initiative for these relaxed entry requirements came from certain front-line Political Directorates, and Rafikov adds that the actual decision was based on a submission forwarded to the Central Committee by the Chief Political Directorate of the Army on August 16. On September 1 the provisions of the August 19 decision were extended to the navy.

[43] E. A. Rafikov, in *V I KPSS*, No. 3, 1964, p. 72.

[44] Malin and Moskovskii, *op.cit.*, p. 364.

before the completion of admission procedures.[45] Large-scale recruitment continued through 1944, taking the number of communists in the armed forces to about three millions by the end of the year.

Party representation was far from uniform in different branches of the services. While generally speaking it was higher in combat than noncombat units,[46] it remained relatively low in the infantry throughout the war, despite special recruitment efforts aimed at correcting this.[47] Thus at the end of 1944, when almost a quarter of all soldiers were in the party, the proportion among infantry soldiers was under 10 percent. The largest concentrations of communists were found in the artillery, tank units, engineers and air force: in these arms the proportion of communists sometimes reached 40 percent.[48] In the navy, party representation was persistently higher than in the army, and it reached its maximum among submarine crews, 56 percent of whose members were said by one source to have been communists at the end of the war.[49]

[45] Petrov, *Partiinoe stroitel'stvo*, p. 392.

[46] The intake of candidates in front-line units increased by 24 percent in the second half of 1941 and by 45 percent in the first half of 1942, while in rear units the increases in these periods were 12 percent and 14 percent respectively (E. A. Rafikov, in *V I KPSS*, No. 3, 1964, p. 75).

[47] See E. A. Rafikov, in *V I KPSS*, No. 3, 1964, p. 73. Failure of party representation in the infantry to keep pace with that in other branches was evidently due in part to a higher casualty rate, but there were other reasons as well. Although in the first eighteen months of the war the infantry's share rose from 21 percent to 41 percent of all candidates admitted in the army, it remained low on a per capita reckoning (*ibid.*, p. 76).

[48] Petrov, *Partiinoe stroitel'stvo*, p. 396.

[49] *Istoriia Velikoi Otechestvennoi voiny Sovetskogo Soiuza: 1941-1945* (Moscow, 1963), Vol. v, p. 226. Cf. K. V. Krainiukov, *op.cit.*, pp. 514-515. This source gives a far lower party membership figure for submarine crews—42 percent—about the same as for cruisers and destroyers.

The mass enlistment of servicemen in the party beginning in late 1941 facilitated the restoration of company-level cells. On December 29, 1941 the Chief Political Directorate issued a directive calling for the establishment of "full-blooded party organizations" in infantry companies and corresponding units in other arms.[50] Such cells existed in an absolute majority of units by the middle of 1942 but, owing to difficulties in building up party representation in the infantry, the objectives of the December 1941 directive were not fully achieved until the final stages of the war.[51]

As on previous occasions, there was a close connection between the establishment of company-level cells and the increased recruitment of nonofficers. This was apparent in the December 1941 directive on company-level cells, which laid particular stress on the enlistment of N.C.O.'s and privates.[52] In the first quarter of 1942 the proportion of privates among newly admitted candidates was 37 percent—twice what it had been a year earlier[53]—and by the second half of 1943 privates and N.C.O.'s between them made up three-quarters of all recruits.[54] This produced a marked change in the composition of military cells. At the outbreak of the war 12 percent of their members were privates and 16 percent N.C.O.'s. By mid-1942 these proportions had risen to 24 and 18 percent respectively,[55] and at the end of the war privates and N.C.O.'s constituted 57 percent of all members of army party organizations while 34 percent were officers, 7 percent on training courses and 2 percent were civilians.[56]

[50] E. A. Rafikov in *V I KPSS*, No. 3, 1964, p. 73.
[51] *Ibid.*, p. 76.   [52] *Ibid.*, p. 73.   [53] *Ibid.*, p. 75.
[54] *Istoriia Velikoi Otechestvennoi voiny Sovetskogo Soiuza: 1941-1945* (Moscow, 1961), Vol. III, p. 230.
[55] E. A. Rafikov, in *V I KPSS*, No. 3, 1964, p. 75.
[56] Petrov, *Partiinoe stroitel'stvo*, p. 394. For the percentage of officers, N.C.O.'s and private soldiers among the candidates admitted

Unfortunately, available data does not permit precise calculation of the proportion of soldiers holding rank as privates, N.C.O.'s and officers who were party members. However, such data is available for the navy, and is set out in Table 15.[57]

TABLE 15: PARTY REPRESENTATION IN THE SOVIET NAVY, 1941 AND 1945

	Percent of party members and candidates		
	Among ordinary seamen	Among leading seamen and petty officers	Among officers
At beginning of war	6.4	28.1	62.5
At end of war	19.3	55.7	73.2

These figures show that, while there was an increase in the proportion of communists at all levels, and a marked positive correlation persisted between rank and the incidence of party membership, the rate of growth increased faster at the lower echelons, and consequently the gap between the representation of officers and other ranks (particularly N.C.O.'s) was sharply reduced. Approximate calculations suggest that the same general pattern applied in the army as well, although there it is doubtful whether the contrast between the repre-

by army party organizations between 1942 and 1946, see *V I KPSS*, No. 5, May 1965, p. 66. Officers fell from 24 percent of admissions in 1942 to 19 percent in 1944, and then began to rise, reaching 28 percent in the first half of 1946. Meanwhile, privates reached their maximum in 1944, when they made up 40 percent of all admissions; by the first half of 1946 their share had fallen to 24 percent.

[57] SOURCE: *Istoriia Velikoi Otechestvennoi voiny Sovetskogo Soiuza: 1941-1945* (Moscow, 1963), Vol. v, p. 226.

sentation of officers and N.C.O.'s was reduced as much during the war years as in the navy.

As victory approached, the Central Committee took its first steps towards decelerating party recruitment in the armed forces. A directive issued by the Chief Political Directorate on October 14, 1944 and approved by the Orgburo, called for more serious observation of the principle of individual selection of party candidates, and warned that ignoring this principle could result in the admission of "suspicious" people.[58] At the same time the Central Committee stressed that the August 1941 decision easing entry requirements for applicants "who had distinguished themselves in battle" should not be extended indiscriminately to all servicemen.[59] There was an immediate and sharp drop in the admissions rate. In November it was 32,000 and in December, 30,000,[60] compared with an average of 70,000 in the first eight months of 1944.[61] On December 8 both the August 1941 decision easing enlistment of candidates and the December 1941 decision on accelerated transfer of servicemen from candidates to full members were revoked.[62] For a time the total number of com-

[58] *Ibid.* (Moscow, 1962), Vol. IV, pp. 646-647.

[59] In May 1942 the "Central Committee" (presumably in the form of the Orgburo or the Politburo) rejected a proposal by the Chief Political Directorate of the Armed Forces to broaden the provisions of the August 1941 decision to include also those whose service (whatever its nature) had helped to ensure the success of military operations. Nevertheless it is a clear implication of the October 1944 decision that the reduced entry requirements were generally applied in the armed forces and not restricted to battle heroes (see Petrov, *Partiinoe stroitel'stvo*, p. 395).

[60] *Ibid.*, p. 396.

[61] *Ibid.*, p. 394. Admissions to the party in the Red Army fell from 1,328,359 in 1943 to 896,500 in 1944, to 215,738 in the first half of 1945 and to 84,296 in the second half of 1945. See *V I KPSS*, No. 5, May 1965, p. 66.

[62] Petrov, *Partiinoe stroitel'stvo*, p. 442.

munists in the armed forces continued to grow, but by the middle of 1945 it had sunk significantly below the maximum of a few months earlier.[63] It was given a final boost between June and August by intensified recruitment on the Transbaikal and Far Eastern fronts, stimulated by the hostilities against Japan.[64] But already there was a trickle of army communists back into civilian life, and within a few months the trickle had become a flood.

Underground and Home Front

As the Soviet army and administration withdrew before the German advance in the early period of the war, party committees selected small groups of members to stay behind as an underground obkom, gorkom and raikom apparatus, the main purpose of which was to organize and direct a partisan struggle against the Germans. In the Ukraine alone, the communist underground left in the rear of the German armies between June and September 1941 numbered 26,000. In areas where the German advance was too rapid for the underground to be organized before the Soviet withdrawal, party workers were infiltrated later. For instance, some 800 communists were sent into the occupied areas of the Western Ukraine in July 1941.[65] The casualty rate among these under-

[63] According to one source (*Istoriia Velikoi Otechestvennoi voiny Sovetskogo Soiuza: 1941-1945*, Vol. v, p. 46) party membership reached its high point "at the beginning of 1945," and the context implies that this referred to some date in February. This statement is not inconsistent with other available data, but the actual figure given (3,325,000) is significantly higher than the figure that one would infer from Petrov (*Partiinoe stroitel'stvo*, pp. 396-397), and it is possible that the two authors were employing slightly different measures. Cf. footnote 5, p. 240.

[64] Petrov, *Partiinoe stroitel'stvo*, pp. 396-397.

[65] K. K. Dubina, "Kommunisticheskaia partiia Ukrainy v gody Velikoi Otechestvennoi voiny" (The Communist Party of the Ukraine in the Years of the Great Patriotic War) in F. P. Ostapenko, ed.,

ground communists was of course formidable, but reinforcements continued to be brought in throughout the occupation. While the partisan struggle was the chief preoccupation of the party underground, it is important not to imagine it as simply the CPSU element in the partisan movement. Of the 986 communists selected to staff the communist underground in the Kirovograd oblast, for instance, only 392 were assigned to organize and participate in partisan detachments.[66]

The efforts of the underground apparatus to generate partisan activity in the early months of the war met with only modest success. As time went on, however, the partisan bands were joined by large numbers of regular Soviet troops who had eluded capture after being encircled by the advancing Germans, and later by recruits from the local population, especially after the tide of war turned in 1943.[67] These troops and civilians joining the partisans included very few communists, and although the party committees in partisan units actively recruited new members,[68] Armstrong estimates that

Voprosy istorii KPSS perioda Velikoi Otechestvennoi voiny (Problems of the History of the CPSU in the Period of the Great Patriotic War), (Kiev, 1961), p. 42. On the organization of the communist underground and partisan movement in the occupied areas of the Leningrad oblast, see A. V. Karasev, *Leningradtsy v gody blokady 1941-1943* (Leningraders in the Years of the Blockade, 1941-1943), (Moscow, 1959), p. 49.

[66] See the account by M. M. Skirda, former secretary of the Kirovograd underground obkom, in Ostapenko, *op.cit.*, p. 296.

[67] Western scholarship has not yet caught up with the vast material on the partisan movement that has been published in the Soviet Union in recent years. The best available study is John A. Armstrong, ed., *Soviet Partisans in World War II* (Madison, 1964). For an excellent brief account, see Armstrong, *Totalitarianism*, Chap. 10.

[68] The 4,900 members of Kovpak's famous brigade, for instance, included 832 communists, about a half of whom joined the party while serving with the brigade. See Iu. G. Panin (secretary of the party committee in Kovpak's brigade) in Ostapenko, *op.cit.*, p. 295. About 1,500 candidates were enlisted by underground party organiza-

the proportion of communists in the partisan movement as a whole did not exceed 7 or 8 percent.[69] There were about 15,000 communists among the partisans operating in the Ukraine,[70] and 25,000 in Belorussia.[71] These republics included the main partisan areas. Nonetheless, in estimating the total size of the communist underground, we must remember that partisans were also operating in the occupied areas of the R.S.F.S.R., and that there were many underground communists who were not members of partisan units.[72] Perhaps a total figure in the vicinity of 100,000 would not be far wrong, but the high turnover must be borne in mind, and the underground organizations cannot have contained anything like this number at any one time.

The membership needs of civilian party organizations were of course not diminished by war conditions, and the enlistment of some 1,600,000 communists in the army, two-thirds of them during the first six months of the war,[73] put a severe strain on party organizations on the home front. Attempts to make good their depleted membership by recruitment proved for some time a labor of Sisyphus, since members continued to depart for the front almost as fast as new ones were enlisted. Civilian party organizations evidently admitted about

---

tions in the occupied areas of the Leningrad oblast. See S. P. Kniazev et al., *Na zashchite Nevskoi tverdyni* (In Defense of the Neva Redout), (Leningrad, 1965), p. 624.

[69] Armstrong, *Totalitarianism*, p. 163.

[70] *PZh*, No. 12, June 1958, p. 58.

[71] T. Kiselëv, "40 let Kommunisticheskoi partii Belorussii" (Forty Years of the Communist Party of Belorussia), *PZh*, No. 23, December 1958, pp. 8-14.

[72] In the occupied western areas of the Kalinin oblast, for instance, there were 3,000 members and candidates in the party underground. See I. M. Shliapin et al., *Kommunisticheskaia partiia v period Velikoi Otechestvennoi voiny* (The Communist Party in the Period of the Great Patriotic War), (Moscow, 1958), p. 109.

[73] Petrov, *Partiinoe stroitel'stvo*, p. 352.

370,000 candidates in the first eighteen months of the war, and a further 460,000 in 1943.[74] All told they recorded about 1,450,000 admissions during the war.[75] Meanwhile the membership of these organizations fell from about 3,500,000 at the time of the German invasion to 1,900,000 at the end of 1941, and did not begin to pick up significantly until

[74] Calculated by subtracting the number of party admissions in the armed forces, as given by Petrov, *Partiinoe stroitel'stov*, pp. 392-393, from total admissions as given by G. D. Komkov, *Ideino-politicheskaia rabota KPSS v 1941-1945gg.* (Ideological-Political Work of the CPSU in 1941-1945), (Moscow, 1965), p. 291; but see also footnote 75.

[75] Telpukhovskii, in Levitin, *op.cit.*, p. 160, states that the party admitted 5,319,000 candidates during the war and 3,615,000 members. Petrov, *Partiinoe stroitel'stvo*, p. 397, states that admissions in the armed forces were 3,869,200 and 2,511,900 respectively. Thus civilian party organizations must have admitted the other 1,450,000 candidates. On the face of it this conflicts with Petrov's statement (*ibid.*) that four-fifths of all those entering the party during the war were admitted while on military service. A partial explanation is that considerable numbers of battle heroes were evidently admitted to full membership without passing through the candidate's stage, an honor which, under normal conditions, is bestowed only rarely and then upon particularly distinguished citizens, but there remains some contradiction between the apparent level of recruitment by civilian organizations and claims made about the proportion of wartime recruits admitted in the armed forces. Civilian recruitment of the order calculated here is certainly indicated by available data on the number of candidates admitted by a number of particular organizations. Thus 97,000 were admitted in Moscow (P. Andreev, in Levitin, *op.cit.*, p. 186); 67,000 in Leningrad and 34,000 in the Kuibyshev oblast (S. S. Kultyshev, "Rost riadov partii v 1945-1950 godakh" [Growth of the Party's Ranks in 1945-1950], *V I KPSS*, No. 2, 1958, p. 61); 14,000 in the Kirov oblast (*Kirovskaia oblastnaia partiinaia organizatsiia v gody Velikoi Otechestvennoi voiny: sbornik dokumentov*, p. 284); 28,000 in Yaroslavl oblast (Sidorov, *op.cit.*, p. 8); and 129,000 in Kazakhstan (Beisembaev and Pakhmurnyi, *op.cit.*, p. 256): thus these six organizations alone, containing in 1941 perhaps one-fifth of the whole civilian membership of the CPSU, admitted about 370,000 candidates during the war.

1943. By the end of 1944 it had recovered to about 2,700,000.[76]

All civilian organizations underwent cataclysmic changes of membership during the war, but these were greatest, of course, in areas that experienced a period of enemy occupation. At the beginning of the war the western districts of the country immediately threatened by German invasion sent exceptionally large contingents of party members into the army. Thus, while about a quarter of the CPSU membership entered the armed forces in the first few months of the war, the proportion was 40 to 60 percent in many western and southwestern oblasts.[77] In the Ukraine over 50 percent of the CPSU membership were stated to have left for the front "in the first days of the war."[78] Of those who did not join the military forces, the party attempted to evacuate the majority as their areas came under attack. At the time of the battle for Smolensk, only 8,000 communists were left of the 32,000 in the oblast on the eve of the war.[79] By September 1941, when the enemy was at the gates of Odessa, all but

[76] Figures calculated from data given in Petrov, *Partiinoe stroitel'stvo*, pp. 329, 390-397, of the number of communists in the armed forces and the percentage they represented of the total party membership.

[77] See A. D. Kiselëv, *op.cit.*, p. 40.

[78] F. P. Ostapenko and N. E. Kostritsa, in Ostapenko, *op.cit.*, p. 28. This source states that 90 percent of communists in Sevastopol joined the army. In the Krasnodar krai 40 percent of all communists left for the armed forces in the first four months of the war. See G. P. Ivanov, ed., *Dokumenty otvagi i geroizma: Kuban' v Velikoi Otechestvennoi voine 1941-1954gg: sbornik dokumentov i materialov* (Documents of Courage and Heroism, the Kuban in the Great Patriotic War of 1941-1945: Collection of Documents and Materials), (Krasnodar, 1965), p. 7.

[79] P. I. Kurbatova, *Smolenskaia partiinaia organizatsiia v gody Velikoi Otechestvennoi voiny* (The Smolensk Party Organization in the Years of the Great Patriotic War), (Smolensk, 1958), p. 20.

1,908 of the 21,692 Odessa communists had joined the army or been evacuated.[80] In the Kursk oblast, a front-line area for much of 1942 and 1943, the party organization numbered only 5,000 in April 1943, compared with 40,000 on the eve of the war.[81] It is interesting that the party managed to continue a modest recruitment in these areas under enemy attack. In the first quarter of 1942, for instance, 57 persons joined the CPSU in the besieged city of Sevastopol.[82]

Those communists who failed to withdraw in time and found themselves in occupied territory stood a poor chance of survival, since it was German policy to shoot captured communists. Some, as we have seen, were assigned to stay behind to man the party underground. An unknown number was simply cut off before they could make their escape, and some of these (the number is again unknown) succeeded in concealing their party membership and either eventually making contact with the underground or avoiding such contact in the interests of their personal survival.

As each area was liberated from the enemy, the party immediately set about restoring its shattered organization and building up the membership required to perform its manifold functions. The nucleus of this restored membership consisted of two parts: the underground members who had survived the occupation, and new cadres who came in with the Soviet Army. Out of such elements, for instance, a party nucleus of 7,000 members was formed in the liberated Smolensk oblast in 1943.[83] Such nuclei were then augmented from three sources: (a) local recruitment—on a very cautious and modest level at first; (b) evacuated communists

---

[80] S. A. Vol'skii, in Ostapenko, op.cit., p. 91.
[81] V. M. Plotnikov, in ibid., p. 117.
[82] S. L. Klimenko, in ibid., p. 108.
[83] See Kurbatova, op.cit., p. 113.

returning from the eastern regions of the country; and (c) demobilized servicemen, some of whom had not lived in the area before the war—these last supplied the main party reinforcements beginning in 1945.

This process can best be illustrated from the example of the Ukraine. In 1940 this republic contained 521,000 communists.[84] The whole of the Ukraine passed under German control in the first year of the war; the eastern half was reconquered in the summer and autumn of 1943, and the western half in the succeeding months. By November 1, 1943, there were 16,816 communists in the six easternmost oblasts of the Ukraine first liberated from the Germans, and these formed the nucleus for restoring the party organization of the republic. The same day the Central Committee of the Communist Party of the Ukraine issued a decision "On the Creation of Party Organizations in Districts of the Ukraine Liberated from the Germans, and Improving Leadership of the Latter." As each town or district was retaken the newly installed gorkom or raikom was to carry out a registration of all communists who had lived under the German occupation and the status of their membership was to be weighed "on a strictly individual basis." Meanwhile groups of party members were formed in the liberated areas ready to be installed as the party nucleus in areas awaiting liberation further west. Party cadres for the Lvov oblast, for instance, were formed and held in readiness in the Rovno and Ternopol oblasts.[85]

In 1943 candidates enlisted by party organizations in the liberated areas of the Ukraine amounted to only a few hundred. In 1944 they numbered 4,600 and in the first half of 1945 6,993.[86] A more important source of reinforcements

[84] Armstrong, *The Soviet Bureaucratic Elite*, p. 135.
[85] F. A. Petliak, In Ostapenko, *op.cit.*, p. 159.
[86] *Ibid.*, p. 161.

was the return of Ukrainian evacuees from the eastern districts of the country. As early as January and February of 1943 the Central Committee of the CPSU recalled some 9,000 Ukrainian communists from Kazakhstan, Uzbekistan, Bashkiria, and the Sverdlovsk, Novosibirsk, Orenburg, Kuibyshev, Cheliabinsk and Omsk oblasts, for reposting to those areas of the Eastern Ukraine where they had worked before the invasion.[87] Altogether up to April 1945 49,000 Ukrainian cadres had been brought back from the eastern regions, nearly a half of them communists.[88] How many party members who had survived the occupation passed the test of reregistration we do not know. Nor do we know how many communists discharged from the armed forces joined the Ukrainian party organization in the later stages of the war. These included both servicemen discharged with wounds and political officers reposted to civilian jobs. The beginnings of demobilization in the second half of 1945 added 125,000 to the strength of the Communist Party of the Ukraine, which by January 1946 had recovered to about three-fifths of its prewar level. The progress of this recovery is indicated by the following figures of the total number of members and candidates in the republic:[89]

[87] N. A. Butsko, in *ibid.*, p. 165.

[88] Petliak, in *ibid.*, p. 161.

[89] *Ibid.*, pp. 159-161. The Stalino oblast in the Donbass, which before the war had contained 83,000 communists, began its recovery at the time of its liberation with 200 CPSU members. By June 1944 its members had been built up to 16,417, and by January 1945 to 22,146. See N. Ia. Omel'ianenko, *Kommunisty Donbassa v Velikoi Otechestvennoi voine* (Communists of the Donbass in the Great Patriotic War), (Stalino, 1959), pp. 160, 165. Other occupied areas made similar efforts to restore their membership after liberation, but without regaining anything like their prewar levels. Belorussia, for example, contained 56,000 communists at the end of the war, which was 20 percent less than at the time of the Eighteenth Congress,

October 1943	5,615
November 1943	16,816
January 1944	55,931
June 1944	97,902
July 1944	115,595
January 1945	164,743
July 1945	195,764
January 1946	320,307

Front-line areas that escaped actual occupation by the enemy also underwent an extremely high turnover of party members. Two such areas of special interest are Moscow and Leningrad. On the eve of the war, the party organizations of Moscow city and oblast contained 330,000 members and candidates. By November 1941, with the German advance to the outskirts of the capital and the withdrawal of government departments to Kuibyshev and other cities of the Volga and Urals area, membership had fallen to 87,000. Vigorous recruitment in the ensuing months restored it to 157,000 by the end of 1942. All told the Moscow party organization enlisted 97,000 candidates in the war years—more than its total membership at the time of the battle of Moscow—and with the return of the government departments to the capital, the prewar level was regained.[90] In Leningrad, encircled by the enemy for 872 days, army enlistments, evacuation and casualties took membership down from 153,351 at the outbreak of the war to 43,893 in January 1943. From then on it began to re-

---

before the mass recruitment of 1939-1940. See Komkov, *op.cit.*, p. 377. The Krasnodar krai, which suffered a shorter period of occupation, contained 28,034 communists in January 1945, compared with 61,777 in July 1941. See G. P. Ivanov, ed., *op.cit.*, p. 267. See also *Istoriia Velikoi Otechestvennoi voiny Sovetskogo Soiuza: 1941-1945*, Vol. VI, p. 370.

[90] See P. Andreev, in Levitin, *op.cit.*, pp. 183-186.

cover, and reached 84,898 in September 1945.[91] Altogether some 70,000 Leningrad communists joined the armed forces, and party organizations in the city enlisted 67,356 candidates in the course of the war, about 46,000 of them during the blockade.[92] In 1943, when the number of Leningrad communists was at its lowest, almost two-thirds of them were members who had joined during the war.[93] The Murmansk oblast provides a third and less cataclysmic example of a front-line area. Here the mobilization and evacuation of communists in the first months of the war reduced party membership from 6,899 to 3,165. However, subsequent recruitment brought in 3,640 new candidates and the total number of communists must have approached the prewar level by 1945.[94]

Areas remote from the front followed a very different pattern. They also were hard hit by army enlistments in the early stages of the war, but these losses were often substantially offset by the arrival of evacuees, and subsequent enlistments sufficed to take membership up to or above prewar levels even before demobilization began. The Kirov oblast provides an example. Party membership here totaled 23,496 on July 1, 1941. In the first six months of the war the oblast lost 10,375 communists to the armed forces, but gained 6,119 evacuated from front-line or occupied areas, and there were 637 enrollments. Between 1942 and the end of the war, a further 6,851 joined the armed forces, but meanwhile

[91] Kniazev, op.cit., p. 497.

[92] N. Ia. Ivanov et al., eds., Leningrad: Kratkii Istoricheskii ocherk (Leningrad: A Brief Historical Sketch), (Leningrad, 1964), p. 524.

[93] Kultyshev, in V I KPSS, No. 2, 1958, p. 61.

[94] V. A. Konovalov, "Murmanskaia partiinaia organizatsiia v period oborony zapoliar'ia" (The Murmansk Party Organization in the Period of the Defense of the Polar Area), V I KPSS, No. 6, June 1966, pp. 75, 80.

13,717 new candidates were enrolled. Membership on July 1, 1945 was 26,583, or 13 percent higher than at the outbreak of the war.[95] Similarly, the Khabarovsk krai, which began the war with 33,951 communists and lost 16,539 to the armed forces, ended it with 41,552.[96] The Kuibyshev oblast had 34,481 communists at the beginning of the war and 44,768 at the end, the Chkalov oblast 28,228 and 32,357 respectively, and the picture was similar in the Central Asian republics and in other areas of the upper and middle Volga, the Urals and Siberia.[97]

At the beginning of this chapter we noted the substantial democratization which took place in recruitment to the CPSU during World War II. However, this affected civilian organization somewhat differently than those in the armed forces. From published annual breakdowns of candidates admitted in the army between January 1942 and June 1945, it can be calculated that workers averaged 33.8 percent, peasants, 23.4 percent and white-collar workers, 42.8 percent. Exact figures are not available for civilian recruits, but by comparing these percentages of candidates admitted by army organizations with those for all recruits to the party during the war (see p. 239), and allowing for the ratio of military to civilian admissions (approximately 3 to 1), it can be calculated that about 27 percent of candidates admitted by civilian party organizations during the war were workers, 31 percent were peasants and 42 percent were white-collar work-

[95] *Kirovskaia oblastnaia partiinaia organizatsiia v gody Velikoi Otechestvennoi voiny: sbornik dokumentov*, p. 284.

[96] N. A. Gogolev et al., eds., *Khabarovskaia Kraevaia partiinaia organizatsiia v period Velikoi Otechestvennoi voiny (1941-1945 gody): sbornik dokumentov i materialov* (The Khabarovsk Krai Party Organization in the Period of the Great Patriotic War [1941-1945]: Collection of Documents and Materials), (Khabarovsk, 1964), pp. 6, 22.

[97] Komkov, *op.cit.*, p. 380.

ers.[98] Since there were far more peasants than workers in the Soviet Army, it is evident that the latter were much more likely to join the party. On the other hand, the relatively heavy recruitment of peasants by civilian party organizations probably reflected the exceptional shortage of party cadres experienced in rural areas during the war.

When we recall that less than 20 percent of all recruits in 1939-1941 were officially classified as workers and only about 10 percent as peasants, it is clear that a big change took place after the German invasion. Local committees were instructed to broaden their recruitment efforts, especially among production workers, and to eliminate bureaucratic procedures hindering higher enlistments.[99] To encourage enrollments, especially among less highly educated groups, they were told to stop examining potential candidates on such matters as party history.[100] The results may be illustrated by a few examples. In the cities of the Southern Urals, workers comprised 13 percent of all recruits in the second quarter of 1941, 19 percent in the third quarter, and continued to rise till they formed 33 percent of those recruited in the fourth

[98] See *Istoriia Velikoi Otechestvennoi voiny Sovetskogo Soiuza: 1941-1945*, Vol. vi, p. 365, and *V I KPSS*, No. 5, May 1965, p. 66. The approximate character of the breakdown of civilian candidates is due to lack of information about the small number of candidates admitted in July-December 1941, and about candidates in the Soviet Navy. Nonetheless this breakdown is accurate to within a few decimal points.

[99] See A. I. Pol'skaia, ed., *Astrakhanskaia partiinaia organizatsiia v gody Velikoi Otechestvennoi voiny 1941-1945 gg: sbornik dokumentov i materialov* (The Astrakhan Party Organization in the Years of the Great Patriotic War of 1941-1945: Collection of Documents and Materials), (Astrakhan, 1962), pp. 172-174.

[100] See *Rost riadov VKP (b) vo vremia Otechestvennoi voiny* (Growth of the Ranks of the CPSU(b) during the Patriotic War), (Kuibyshev, 1942), pp. 10-14.

quarter of 1942.[101] In Kirgizia workers and peasants together constituted 28 percent of those enrolling in the first half of 1941, 31 percent in the second half, and 39 percent in the first half of 1942.[102] During 1942 workers made up 29 percent of all recruits in Moscow, 32 percent in Novosibirsk, and 31 percent in the Chelyabinsk oblast.[103]

At the same time, this impression of democratization calls for certain qualifications. In the first place, despite the prewar concentration of recruitment on white-collar and intelligentsia groups, particularly after 1939, the overall membership of the party on the eve of the war still contained a lower percentage officially classed as white-collar workers and intelligentsia than did the wartime recruitment, and the representation of this category therefore continued to rise, though far more slowly than before the war. In Kazakhstan, for instance, this category increased from 11 percent to 36 percent of the party membership in the five years 1936-1941, and from 36 to 44 percent in the five years 1941-1946.[104]

Secondly, in these years, no less than in other periods, a large proportion of the recruits classified as "workers" and "peasants" in terms of their "basic occupation" in the past had already been placed in administrative or supervisory jobs at the time of joining the party, or were in line for such appointments. Indeed, the wartime democratization of recruitment was in part a reflection of the desperate shortage of personnel which obliged the party, in exercising its po-

[101] A. F. Vasil'ev, "Partorganizatsii Iuzhnogo Urala vo glave perestroiki promyshlennosti na voennyi lad" (Party Organizations of the Southern Urals at the Head of the Reorganization of Industry onto a War Footing), *V I KPSS*, No. 1, January-February 1960, p. 69.

[102] *K P Kirgizii*, p. 158.

[103] V. M. Donskoi, ed., *Velikaia partiia Lenina* (The Great Party of Lenin), (Moscow, 1963), p. 302.

[104] See Beisembaev and Pakhmurnyi, *op.cit.*, pp. 203, 250, 281.

litical recruitment function, to cast its net more widely and be satisfied with qualifications inferior to those it had previously been in a position to require. An important aspect of this was the vast number of women workers and collective farmers called upon during the war to bear managerial or administrative responsibilities for the first time (cf. p. 361). This gap between the official social classification of members and their actual employment may again be illustrated by data from the Kirov oblast. At the beginning of 1943, 38 percent of the oblast party membership were classified as workers, 17 percent as peasants and 45 percent as white-collar workers. Over the previous year there had been a very slight increase in the proportion of workers and white-collar workers and a slight decrease in the proportion of peasants. Yet only 16 percent of recruits in 1942 were actually employed as workers and 13 percent as collective farmers. The main employment groups in January 1943 were as follows: workers—12 percent, collective farmers—9 percent, white-collar workers—69 percent and pensioners and housewives—7 percent. The employment pattern had shown a slight increase in the percentage of workers, collective farmers *and* white-collar workers over the previous year, offset mainly by a drop in the pensioners and housewives.[105] Such patterns appear to have been typical of civilian party organizations in 1942-1945. They may be summed up as a

[105] *Kirovskaia oblastnaia partiinaia organizatsiia v gody Velikoi Otechestvennoi voiny*, p. 284. On party membership trends in rural areas during the war, see Iu. V. Arutiunian, *Sovetskoe krest'ianstvo v gody Velikoi Otechestvennoi voiny* (The Soviet Peasantry in the Years of the Great Patriotic War), (Moscow, 1963), pp. 50-58. Arutiunian adduces data demonstrating the widespread collapse of kolkhoz party organizations in the early stages of the war, and the extreme paucity of rank and file kolkhozniks in the party, as the few remaining communists in the villages became concentrated in managerial and administrative jobs. I am indebted to Mr. Sandford Lieberman for drawing my attention to this source.

marked slowing down of the trend towards predominance of those classified by their basic occupation prior to enlistment as white-collar workers, combined with relative stability in the current employment distribution of members.

The 1945 Membership

World War II was the last of that series of profound crises that shook the CPSU in the sixteen years beginning in 1929. Unlike the earlier crises of collectivization and the purges, it tended to strengthen, rather than weaken, the links between the party, the regime and the Soviet people, particularly the Great Russians. It is, moreover, the only one of these crises in which a substantial proportion of the present membership of the CPSU, including perhaps a majority in the intermediate levels of the party and government bureaucracies, were active participants. Small wonder, then, that the experiences of World War II continued in the 1960's to dominate the political imagination in the Soviet Union to an extent unknown in the other major belligerents, including Germany. For these reasons, it is important to realize that the nature of these experiences, and the part they played in their lives and careers, was far from being the same for all Soviet communists whose membership dates from prior to 1945. It may therefore be useful to conclude this chapter with a breakdown of the 1945 membership in terms of the relationship between their party membership and the war. The main groups were these:

1. Prewar members who had remained in their own localities, often assuming much greater responsibilities throughout the war. These probably did not number much more than one million of the nearly six million members and candidates in 1945.

2. Prewar members evacuated from occupied and frontline areas to more easterly regions, most of them returning

271

to their original localities after the enemy's withdrawal. These comprised perhaps a quarter to a half million members in 1945.

3. Wartime recruits who remained in their own localities during the war. These probably totaled about a million, roughly half of them were women, and for most of them the war probably gave them their first taste of authority and responsibility.

4. Members recruited in civilian organizations during the war who subsequently joined the armed forces—perhaps a quarter million in 1945.

5. Prewar members who survived their military service— probably not more than half a million. Most of these were probably commissioned or noncommissioned officers, many of them serving as political workers.

6. Wartime members enlisted while on military service. These formed by far the largest group in the 1945 membership, numbering about two and a half million or over 40 percent of all communists. Over a third of them were commissioned officers, but more than half were privates or N.C.O.'s, and most of them had probably never exercised authority in a civilian capacity.

7. A small group, number unknown (perhaps 50,000?) who had been in the communist underground in occupied areas.

At the end of the war the party apparatus was faced with the task of welding together these disparate groups and allocating among them the various tasks, responsibilities and opportunities adhering to party membership. The tensions and conflicts of outlook and interest which this must have generated remain one of the unexplored problems of postwar Soviet political history.

Chapter 8

Postwar Consolidation

FOR THE U.S.S.R., victory in World War II was won at a stupendous cost, which included over 20 million dead, the devastation of vast areas and the destruction of a large part of the Soviet production machine. In 1945 Stalin was faced with the task of rebuilding his shattered economy through the medium of an exhausted and decimated population. In the interests of morale, moreover, this population had been encouraged to expect far-reaching postwar changes in the direction of greater freedom and attention to consumer needs: expectations which Stalin was unable or unwilling to satisfy. Internationally, the collapse of the axis powers and the upheavals and confusion of the postwar years afforded tempting opportunities for the extension of communist power, but these opportunities could not be exploited without turning Stalin's wartime allies into formidable opponents.

Stalin's solutions to these postwar dilemmas were entirely in character: internally they amounted to reimposing—all the more implacably for the relaxations of the war years—the full rigors of the Stalinist system of the 1930's; externally they meant the Iron Curtain and the Cold War with the West, which again were all the harsher for the warmth of the wartime alliance. Any tendency to complaint or resistance was now crushed under the weight of ever more mendacious propaganda, ever more rigid controls, and intensified police terrorism, with its fabricated "plots" and constant prophylactic arrests. A new ingredient in all this was the dictator's incipient senility which intensified his morbid suspicion, his megalomania and resistance to outside influence and change, while provoking vicious infighting within the bureaucracy as his lieutenants jostled to improve their succession prospects.

In spite of political stagnation and reaction, forces for change were nevertheless accumulating in Soviet society. Rapidly rising educational levels were matched by an economy growing fast in scale, complexity and technical level. The crude, repressive and obscurantist politico-administrative system of Stalinism contrasted ever more grotesquely with the society it had created.

Whether Stalin was capable of recognizing the fundamental obsolescence of his regime seems highly doubtful. One aspect, however, which he did appear to see was the obsolescence of the politico-administrative elite. In the early 1950's, despite war losses, the middle and upper levels of the bureaucracy were still full of men in early middle age who had begun their political or managerial careers during the 1930's.[1] The years of terror, war and forced-pace reconstruction had left this generation very much the worse for wear, both physically and morally, and its shortcomings became increasingly apparent as the demands of administration grew in scale and complexity. At the same time, thousands of fresh, better educated young men were kept marking time at the lower levels of the various hierarchies. All this was reminiscent of the situation in the early 1930's, when also the bureaucracy had been packed with men in early middle age unfitted by their training and experience to cope with the changing problems of administering the state and the economy, and obstructing advance by the new intelligentsia emerging in increasing numbers from technical training in-

[1] Of the 1,192 delegates to the Nineteenth Party Congress in 1952, 6 percent were aged under 30, 18 percent were in their thirties, 61 percent in their forties, and 18 percent were over 50. Eighty percent had joined the party before World War II, but only 7 percent during Lenin's lifetime. See *P*, October 9, 1952.

stitutions. There is evidence that Stalin, just before his death, was planning to deal with this situation in the same way he had dealt with it 15 or 20 years earlier: by sweeping away a whole generation of the administrative-managerial elite and replacing them with new men. Khrushchev has confirmed the estimate of contemporary Western observers that the "doctors' plot" allegations and other developments in Stalin's last months were the dictator's first steps towards purging the older generation of leaders.[2] It is most unlikely that he intended to limit this to the inner leadership, and it may well have led to massive changes in the composition of the party had his death not intervened in March 1953.

Quality, Not Quantity

The CPSU emerged from the war with a minority of tried and experienced members and masses of raw recruits. The wartime wastage had amounted to at least three and a half millions.[3] Only one-third of the party's six million full and

[2] See *The Anti-Stalin Campaign and International Communism*, p. 85.

[3] *Pravda*, May 9, 1965, put the figure for party losses during the war at three millions. Other data, however, suggest a substantially higher figure. Party membership at the end of the war was 5.8 millions (see V. S. Telpukhovskii, "Kommunisticheskaia partiia— vdokhnovitel' i organizator pobedy sovetskogo naroda v Velikoi Otechestvennoi voine" [The Communist Party: The Inspirer and Organizer of Victory in the Great Patriotic War] *V I KPSS*, No. 2, 1958, p. 55), a wartime increase of approximately 1.8 million. However, between 5.1 and 5.3 million new candidates had been admitted during the war. (Cf. *PZh*, No. 19, October 1967, p. 11 and V. S. Telpukhovskii, in *Kommunisticheskaia partiia v period Velikoi Otechestvennoi voiny*, p. 160.) This gives a minimum wastage of approximately 3.5 millions, to which figure must be added a figure equal to those (number unknown) who were admitted to full membership without passing through the candidate's stage. Cf. Armstrong, *Totalitarianism*, p. 379, footnote 88. Perhaps the *Pravda* figure excludes "dishonorable" losses—communists captured by the Germans or expelled for wartime misconduct.

candidate members in January 1946 had been in the party before the German invasion,[4] and of these at least half had less than three years' previous experience of party membership under peacetime conditions. Few communists had received any significant indoctrination in Marxism-Leninism, the content of wartime party propaganda having been strongly patriotic rather than ideological. It was this party, however, which was now called upon to serve the dictator as his main instrument for dragooning the population into forced-pace reconstruction while accepting a further indefinite deprivation of the material and spiritual benefits for which they had worked and suffered. It was this party which was now expected to maintain the discipline and orthodoxy vitally necessary in a situation where the only rewards for loyalty and sacrifice were promises validated by the official ideology. Small wonder, then, that the Central Committee now began to apply the brakes to recruitment and to shift the emphasis to training and indoctrinating its millions of new members.

We have already noted the October 1944 decision of the Chief Political Directorate of the Armed Forces initiating a more careful admissions policy in army party organizations (see p. 256). Evidence of changes of recruitment policy in a number of local areas suggests that a similar decision affecting civilian organizations may have been taken at about the same time. We have, for example, the text of a decision of the Vokzal raikom in Tomsk, dated November 23, 1944, which orders a strict observance of the principle of individual recruitment and the termination of simplified admissions procedures and the practice of admitting all who apply. This decision indicates that recruitment efforts should focus on workers in "leading trades," engineers, technicians, the in-

4 *PS*, No. 4, 1946, p. 28.

telligentsia and komsomol activists—that is on the "best people" of the 1937-1941 recruitment period. It also calls for a radical change in the training of new recruits, involving a sharp intensification of ideological indoctrination, based on the *Short Course on the History of the CPSU,* and a more active deployment of young communists in party-directed activities.[5]

In January 1945, a combined meeting of the Leningrad obkom and gorkom is reported to have criticized the excessive rate of recruitment and to have emphasized that the growth in numbers must not outrun the party's ability to train new members.[6] In Moscow, new admissions to the party fell from 17,078 in 1944, to 10,212 in 1945, and to 7,393 in 1946.[7]

This drop in recruitment, however, must have been largely offset by the cessation of war losses, and many party organizations were said to be still expanding rapidly. The situation was exacerbated by the slowness of local officials in breaking with wartime practices. The party organization in one Machine Tractor Station, for instance, is reported to have

[5] *Tomskaia gorodskaia partiinaia organizatsiia v gody Velikoi Otechestvennoi voiny* (The Tomsk City Party Organization in the Years of the Great Patriotic War), (Tomsk, 1962), pp. 357-358. For a similar decision from Kazakhstan, see Beisembaev and Pakhmurnyi, *op.cit.,* pp. 260-268. The renewed emphasis on the indoctrination of young communists formed part of a general re-emphasis on the official ideology now that the end of the war was in sight. The guidelines for this were laid down in a Central Committee decision on "mass political and ideological work" in the Tatar regional organization, issued in September 1944 (see *Kommunisticheskaia partiia v period Velikoi Otechestvennoi voiny (iiun' 1941 goda-1945 god): dokumenty i materialy* (The Communist Party in the Period of the Great Patriotic War [June 1941-1945]: Documents and Materials), (Moscow, 1961), pp. 222-227.

[6] See *Propagandist,* No. 5, 1945, p. 36. For a similar decision in Kirgizia, issued on December 8, 1945, see *KP Kirgizii,* pp. 161-166.

[7] Kultyshev, in *V I KPSS,* No. 2, 1958, p. 64.

277

adopted a decision obliging every communist to prepare two persons for admission to the party within a two-year period.[8] Attacking indiscriminate admission practices, an authoritative party spokesman on organizational matters indicated in 1945 that both the uncritical acceptance of all applicants and the adoption by raikoms and gorkoms of decisions stimulating recruitment by primary organizations were still widespread.[9] By 1946 the difficulties experienced by the local party machine in assimilating, training and deploying these new recruits were redoubled by the arrival of a flood of untrained young communists discharged from the armed forces.

It was against this background that the Central Committee issued its decision "On the Growth of the Party and Measures for Strengthening Party-Organizational and Party-Political Work among Those Newly Admitted to the Party," on July 26, 1946, a decision which was destined to set the tone for party recruitment policies for the remainder of the Stalin era. The July 1946 decision emphatically reaffirmed the principles embodied in earlier party statements and local decisions: that organizations must return to an individual consideration of each separate applicant and stop accepting as candidates all who applied. Local party bodies were told they must satisfy themselves in each particular case "of the capacity of the applicant for admission to the party to really justify the lofty calling of a communist." The whole emphasis of party work was to shift from expansion to consolidation

[8] *Ibid.*, p. 63.

[9] L. Slepov, "Priëm v partiiu i regulirovanie eë sostava" (Admittance to the Party and the Regulation of Its Composition), in *Voprosy organizatsionnogo stroitel'stva bol'shevistskoi partii* (Moscow, 1945), pp. 46-49.

of membership, and to this end there was to be a further intensification of indoctrination and training programs.[10]

While the July 1946 decision was followed within a few months by reduced recruitment levels in many areas, it was not till 1948 that its effects were fully felt. In Georgia, for instance, 11,959 candidates were accepted in 1947 and only 1,555 in 1948.[11] The decline in admissions reflected not only the lifting of recruitment pressures on primary organizations but also a sharp increase in the proportion of applicants rejected by raikoms. In Moscow, for instance, the Bauman raikom refused to endorse only 25 of the 793 applicants in the first half of 1946, while the Timiriazev raikom admitted

[10] See *P*, August 8, 1946. An additional, though subsidiary motive for curtailing recruitment after the war was simply to take stock of the existing membership. There is evidence of a degree of confusion in party membership records at this time. Official party statistics show a fall in membership in 1945, although reports from local organizations indicate that there must have been a significant increase. This is probably partly due to the fact that the fate of numerous communists killed or captured before January 1945 was only established in the course of the year, allowing them to be removed from the party records. Another reason, however, appears to have been the double counting of many communists who had shifted from one area to another during the war, and such double counting was evidently not wholly eliminated even by 1946. The Kazakh Central Committee, for instance, reported in February 1946 that 3,000 communists shown in republic party statistics could not be located and they were thought to have left the republic. If most of these were alive and registered in other party organizations as well, and if this was typical of the party as a whole, it would suggest an overstatement of party membership figures by perhaps 100,000. See Beisembaev and Pakhmurnyi, *op.cit.*, pp. 293-296.

[11] Charkviani, First Secretary of the Georgian Central Committee, reporting to the Fourteenth Congress of the Georgian Communist Party, *ZV*, January 28, 1949. There was at least one republic, namely Kazakhstan, where a further decision requiring even more restrictive recruitment was adopted in 1948. See Beisembaev and Pakhmurnyi, *op.cit.*, pp. 288-289.

all 402 of its applicants. In 1947, however, the raikoms in Moscow rejected 22 percent of all applicants, and in 1948 rejections rose to 47 percent.[12]

Party membership now showed a tendency to decline: it fell by 38,000 in 1948 and 12,000 in 1949. This, however, was evidently not the Central Committee's intention but rather "a consequence of the incorrect understanding of the CC CPSU's directives on the part of certain local organizations which, not wanting to bother making careful selections, stopped admissions altogether."[13] Between 1949 and 1951 such organizations frequently came under fire at regional and local conferences. The Tbilisi party conference in January 1951, for instance, resolved that "it is impossible to regard as normal the fact that 691 primary party organizations have not admitted a single person as candidate for the party in the last two years. . . ."[14] While the principles of the July 1946 decision were frequently reiterated, there was thus a

[12] Kultyshev, in *V I KPSS*, No. 2, 1958, p. 65.

[13] *K P Kirgizii*, p. 187.

[14] *ZV*, January 14, 1951. Fragmentary data for the period 1948-1953 from various districts indicate some local variations within the same overall pattern. In Moscow there appears to have been a significant decline in membership between 1949 and 1951 (see *MP*, April 1, 1951). In Uzbekistan the party membership fell by 2 percent in 1948 and 0.5 percent in 1949 (see *KP Uzbekistana v tsifrakh*, pp. 107, 111, 116). In Kirgizia the admission of new candidates, who numbered 829 in the second quarter of 1947, fell off sharply in the second half of the year, and in the third quarter of 1948 only 60 new candidates were admitted in the whole republic. There were seven raions in Kirgizia where not a single candidate was admitted during 1948 (*KP Kirgizii*, p. 187). In this republic there was a 0.4 percent reduction of membership in 1948 and a 2.3 percent reduction in 1949 (*ibid.*, p. 208 and appendix). Both in Uzbekistan and Kirgizia there was a small rise in membership in 1950. In Kazakhstan there was a drop of 0.2 percent in 1948 and 2 percent in 1949, and a 1 percent increase in 1950. See Beisembaev and Pakhmurnyi, *op.cit.*, pp. 306, 309, 312, 315.

modest effort to reflate recruitment, and between 1950 and 1953 party membership grew by about half a million. Even this, however, represented an annual increase of only 3 percent, which was less than at any period in the party's history, other than periods of suspended recruitment or mass purge. And this brings us to the question of expulsions. A considerable number of individual expulsions has occurred at all stages of the party's history, as indeed is to be expected in a party which requires of its members certain levels of activity and ideological commitment. At this period, however, expulsions from the CPSU averaged at least 100,000 a year,[15] a level comparable with that reached during the 1921-1922 and 1929-1930 purges, and exceeded only during the purges of the mid-1930's.[16]

[15] Calculated from figures given in "KPSS v tsifrakh" (The CPSU in Figures), *PZh*, No. 1, 1962, p. 47. The source stated that over 200,000 were expelled "over the last six years" (i.e. presumably 1956-1961 inclusive), and that the number excluded and dropping out in the five years preceding the Twentieth Congress (held February 1956) was two and a half times greater than in the five years preceding the Twenty-Second Congress (held October 1961). This suggests that the number expelled in 1951-1955 must have approached half a million. However, there was almost certainly a drop in the expulsion rate after 1953. See Beisembaev and Pakhmurnyi, *op.cit.*, p. 342, for evidence of reduced expulsions in Kazakhstan. The 1951-1955 average of close to 100,000 per year can therefore be regarded as a minimum for 1951 to March 1953. The 1948 data from Georgia indicates that this high expulsion rate was already a fact several years before 1951.

[16] Compare figures on pp. 97 and 180. There is probably no way of fixing on a "normal" rate of expulsion. It would be useful to compare the expulsion figures in the postwar period with those for the period between the end of the *Ezhovshchina* and the German invasion, but only fragmentary evidence on this period is available. Between February and July 1940, published lists of members expelled from party organizations in the city of Moscow totaled 238. If this figure were complete and if it were typical of the party at large, it would imply a rate of expulsion from the CPSU of about 10,000 a

Many of those expelled during these years no doubt fell victim to the numerous purges of local areas and branches of the administration and intellectual life, associated with "plots" and "cases" fabricated by the political police, which were a feature of this period; *how* many, however it is impossible to say. There is only one partial breakdown of expulsions during these years, and that was for the 2,871 expelled in Georgia in 1948. Of these, 22 percent were held to be guilty of "isolating themselves from party life and an indifferent attitude towards their membership in the party," 9 percent were expelled for losing party documents, 12 percent for embezzlement and other criminal offences, and 2 percent for the practice of religion.[17] Political offences, real or concocted, formed an unknown proportion of the remaining 55 percent.

In the light of this high expulsion rate, it is clear that the slow growth of the postwar years concealed a significant recruitment level or, to put the matter in its contemporary political setting, recruitment was maintained at a high enough level to offset and perhaps partly to mask the scale of expulsions during the period. The Georgian case is again instructive in this connection. In 1948 expulsions were running at almost twice the rate of enlistments, and this was followed by efforts by the republic leadership to modestly increase recruitment. Seen in a wider perspective, the postwar years figure as an era of consolidation of membership, comparable with other phases of consolidation following on periods of

---

year. These, however, are big "ifs" and other evidence is insufficient either to corroborate or disprove this estimate. For data see *Propagandist*, No. 11, 1940, pp. 31-32; Nos. 13-14, 1940, pp. 47-48; No. 15, 1940, pp. 30-31; No. 16, 1940, pp. 31-32. There were 88 expulsions reported in Moscow in January 1941 and 78 in May 1941 (see *ibid.*, No. 9, 1941, pp. 30-32).

[17] *ZV*, January 28, 1949.

rapid growth, such as the years 1921-1923 or 1933-1934, and differing from these only in that the purging, which was an essential feature of such consolidation, became a regular part of normal political life rather than a temporary campaign.

Like many other policies of the late Stalin era, the policy of membership consolidation persisted for a certain period after the dictator's death. At the Nineteenth Party Congress in October 1952, Malenkov had reaffirmed the postwar decision "to sift admissions to the ranks more carefully, to be more exacting regarding the qualifications of applicants" in order to counteract the discrepancy which had arisen "between the numerical strength of the party and the level of political enlightenment of its members and candidates." He went on to say that this task "cannot be regarded as fully accomplished. We must therefore continue the line of restricting admissions to the party and improving the political enlightenment and party training of communists, since it is not only in its numbers that the strength of the party lies, but also, and chiefly, in the quality of its members."[18]

Malenkov thus spoke only of continuing the precongress line on recruitment, but a number of statements made at republic party congresses on the eve of the Nineteenth Congress of the CPSU suggest that henceforth the line was to be applied more stringently. Party First Secretaries in at least seven of the sixteen union republics condemned local party bodies for "chasing after numbers" and "putting quantity before quality in their recruitment practice."[19] This implied that

[18] G. M. Malenkov, *Report to the Nineteenth Party Congress on the Work of the Central Committee of the CPSU(b)*, (Moscow, 1952), pp. 110-111.

[19] See *S Lit*, September 30, 1952; *SK*, September 21, 1952; *K(A)*, September 21, 1952; *ZV*, September 18, 1952; *SM*, September 20, 1952; *SE*, September 17, 1952; *S Lat*, September 26, 1952.

even the moderate recruitment since 1950 was now considered too high, and there are indications from many areas that after the congress there was a further drastic restriction of admissions. One can only speculate on the relationship of this policy to the political purge which Stalin was evidently preparing at this period. In any case, this highly restrictive approach to recruitment persisted for about a year after Stalin died, as is evidenced by data made public in the course of the republic party congresses in January and February 1954. In the seventeen months before these congresses the party grew by only 1.2 percent in Belorussia, 1.8 percent in Georgia, and 0.8 percent in Tadzhikistan. In Kazakhstan it fell by 1.8 percent. The Ukraine was the only area where a significant increase (3.1 percent) was reported.[20] N. S. Patolichev, the Belorussian Party Secretary, commented that "certain raikoms of the party and secretaries of primary party organizations, misunderstanding the demand of the party for more careful recruitment into the ranks of the CPSU have completely terminated accepting people into the party. . . ."[21] It was only in 1954 that the postwar policy of membership consolidation was significantly

[20] See *SB*, September 22, 1952 and February 13, 1954; *KT*, January 24, 1954; *KP*, September 21, 1952 and February 17, 1954; *ZV*, September 18, 1952 and February 18, 1954; *PU*, September 26, 1952 and March 24, 1954. In the Ukrainian figure, allowance is made for the incorporation of the Crimea, with its roughly 35,000 members and candidates. Data subsequently published shows that in Kirgizia there was a drop in membership of approximately 1 percent in 1953 (*KP Kirgizii*, pp. 222, 226) and in Uzbekistan a drop of 0.7 percent (*KP Uzbekistana v tsifrakh*, pp. 132, 137). On Kazakhstan, cf. Beisembaev and Pakhmurnyi, *op.cit.*, pp. 323 and 326. Overall CPSU membership figures show a drop of 32,000 in 1953 (see *PZh*, No. 19, October 1967, p. 9).

[21] N. S. Patolichev's report to the Twenty-First Congress of the Belorussian Communist Party, *SB*, February 13, 1954.

284

changed, and a new approach inaugurated which will be examined in the next chapter.

The "Best People" Again

Although only fragmentary data is available on the social orientation of postwar recruitment to the CPSU, certain general trends may be established. During the war, as we have observed, there was a marked democratization of party recruitment. Since this was particularly the case in the armed forces, the demobilization of army communists—some 1,830,000 men and women were transferred from military to civilian party organizations from mid-1946 to mid-1947[22]— involved a further broadening of the social composition of the local party membership.

Meanwhile, however, the new policy of restricting admissions was beginning to exert pressures in the opposite direction. The effective exercise of the party's social and political role demands that the overwhelming majority of those wielding economic, administrative or cultural authority above certain levels should be subject to the obligations and discipline of party membership. Consequently the day-to-day recruitment and promotion of young citizens to such positions prevents the enlistment of persons from the white-collar and intelligentsia categories from falling below a certain level. The more restrictive party recruitment policy becomes, the greater the percentage which this base level of white-collar/ intelligentsia admissions represents of total enrollments. We have seen the force of this factor even at a time when party membership policies were unequivocally worker-orientated (see p. 39). In some areas, at least, this was beginning to happen as early as 1946.[23] Small wonder, then, that it exerted

[22] See Petrov, *Partiinoe stroitel'stvo*, p. 442.
[23] In February 1946 the Bureau of the Kazakh Central Committee, noting a drop in the proportion of workers and peasants among new

a powerful influence in the postwar years when it had no mystique of proletarianization to inhibit it. By 1948, when the full force of the policy of restricting recruitment was first making itself felt, the proportion of "workers" and "peasants" admitted had fallen drastically from wartime levels, and admissions were again heavily concentrated, as they had been on the eve of the war, on the white-collar and intelligentsia categories. Beginning in 1949, however, there seems to have been a deliberate effort to moderate this process and broaden the social basis of recruitment, which met with varying success in different areas of the country. Finally, the even closer restriction of enrollments after the Nineteenth Congress (October 1952) led to a renewed narrowing of the social basis. These trends can be best documented with respect to Belorussia (see Table 16).[24]

---

enlistments, instructed local organizations to try and effect a reduction in the general level of recruitment without a further fall in worker and peasant representation (see Beisembaev and Pakhmurnyi, *op.cit.*, pp. 293-296). In the first half of 1946, however, only 11 percent of all candidates enlisted in this republic were currently employed as workers, and a further decision of the Kazakh CC Bureau, issued in response to the CPSU Central Committee decision of July 26, 1946, while stressing even more strongly the need to restrain recruitment, markedly weakened the qualification about the need to maintain worker and peasant representation (*ibid.*, pp. 296-300). In Latvia the class composition of candidates recruited in 1945 was given as 23 percent workers, 6 percent peasants and 72 percent white-collar workers and others (*Kommunist sovetskoi Latvii*, No. 4, April 1965, p. 64), but the Baltic states, currently undergoing their second campaign of sovietization, were scarcely typical of the U.S.S.R. as a whole. In the Army, the cutback in admissions to the CPSU was accompanied by a rise in the proportion of white-collar workers among those admitted from 40 percent in 1944 to 48 percent in 1945 (see *V I KPSS*, No. 5, 1965, p. 66).

[24] SOURCE: Based on figures published in *SB*, September 22, 1952 and February 13, 1954. There were certain raions where recruitment in 1953 had been entirely limited to white-collar workers (*ibid.*, February 17, 1954).

TABLE 16: Class Status of Candidates Admitted in Belorussia, 1948-1953

Year	Workers and collective farmers Percent	White-collar workers and intelligentsia Percent
1948	18.8	81.2
1949	40.4	59.6
1950	42.4	57.6
1951	43.9	56.1
January-June 1952	49.8	50.2
October 1952-January 1954	42.7	57.3

Scattered information from other areas of the country affords some confirmation of the Belorussian picture. Membership data given in a number of provincial organizations between 1949 and 1951 showed that "workers" ranged from 11 to 27 percent of new admissions.[25] In Uzbekistan the proportion of communists *employed* as white-collar workers reached the lowest point since before the purges in January 1946 (47.2 percent), but then started rising again, reaching a maximum of 53 percent at the end of 1954. The rise, however, was not steady, the main jumps being made in 1946, 1948 and 1953.[26] In Kazakhstan the official figures on the social composition of the party membership show a rise of 1.9 percent in the proportion of white-collar workers in

[25] See Fainsod, *How Russia Is Ruled*, p. 270. In Kishinev only 7 percent of recruits in 1945-1946 were workers. See *Ocherki istorii Kommunisticheskoi Partii Moldavii* (Kishinev, 1964), p. 309. In the city of Moscow the proportion of workers among new recruits was 32 percent in the first half of 1948 (Kultyshev, in *V I KPSS*, No. 2, 1958, p. 66), and rose slightly to 34 percent in 1949-1950 (*MP*, March 21, 1951).

[26] *KP Uzbekistana v tsifrakh*, pp. 97, 102, 107, 111, 116, 122, 127, 132, 137, 142.

1946-1948, a decline of 0.2 percent in 1949, a rise of 0.5 percent in 1950-1951, and a sharper rise of 2.0 percent in 1952-1953.[27] In Georgia, party officials in the town of Staliniri were rebuked early in 1951 because 70 percent of recruits in the previous two years had been drawn from office workers or intelligentsia—the proportion was said to be too high.[28] In Kirgizia 53.5 percent of all recruits in 1953 were white-collar workers, compared with an average of 50.5 percent in 1940-1949.[29] In Georgia during 1953, only 19 of the 83 recruits in industrial Kutaisi and 40 of the 194 in the port of Batumi were workers.[30] In the country at large, the recruitment of farmers was said to have virtually stopped after the Nineteenth Congress, and there were many areas where new enrollments were wholly restricted to white-collar workers.[31]

The social orientation of postwar recruitment broadly resembled what we discovered in the period following the purges of the 1930's. The proletarian ideal which had informed CPSU membership policies up to the early 1930's remained very much in the background, and instead the proper source of recruits was identified as "the best people," as it had been during the heavily intelligentsia-oriented recruitment of 1937-1941. In those years when recruitment was most restricted, namely in 1948 and 1952-1953, the predominance of white-collar enrollments reached the extreme level previously experienced on the eve of the German invasion. Taking the postwar years as a whole, however, the objective seems to have been a modest inflow of recruits,

[27] Beisembaev and Pakhmurnyi, *op.cit.*, pp. 281, 303, 306, 309, 312, 313, 315, 319, 323, 326.

[28] *ZV*, February 2, 1951.

[29] *KP Kirgizii*, pp. 188, 237.

[30] *ZV*, February 18, 1954.

[31] See *P*, March 21, 1954; *SB*, February 18, 1954; *PU*, March 24, 1954.

made up roughly half-and-half of officials and intelligentsia on the one hand and skilled, "activist" workers and farmers on the other. The policy was aimed at sustaining the party saturation of the bureaucracy and the intelligentsia at the necessary levels, offsetting the constant stream of expulsions, while ensuring a reinforcement of workplace representation sufficient to make good the upward leakage of communists from manual jobs. Later we shall see some of the shortcomings of this policy, and in the Conclusion we shall attempt to place it in a wider perspective.

The party organizations hardest hit by the restrictive recruitment policies of the postwar years were those in the armed forces. The wartime arrangements easing party admission procedures in the army were revoked in December 1944, in which month the number of admissions was less than half what it had been in July. By 1947 the majority of communists in the armed services had returned to civilian life. Meanwhile, very few of the conscripts called up in the postwar years joined the party during their service. Here the effects of restrictive party recruitment policies were accentuated by the extreme youth of postwar conscripts: in 1939 the call-up age had been lowered, and because of the war there were now far fewer older men in the services. In 1949 the number of enlisted men who joined the party was only one-eighteenth of what it had been in 1940. This abrupt contraction in party membership in the army had the usual effects on the structure and composition of army party organizations. The majority of company-level organizations again collapsed, and officers again came to predominate, so much so that by 1948 only 3 percent of army communists held the rank of sergeant or below.[32]

[32] See Petrov, *Partiinoe stroitel'stvo*, pp. 442-443.

Success in the Kolkhozes

The postwar years saw one important achievement in the distribution of party members: for the first time the party attained a significant representation in the collective farms. On the eve of World War II only one collective farm in eight possessed a party organization.[33] By 1953 the proportion was five out of six.[34] This transformation was effected in three phases:

1. 1945-1946: Demobilization brought back to the villages large numbers of young communists who had joined the party while serving in the armed forces.

2. 1947-1949: Party forces in the countryside were redistributed and rural cells reorganized so as to transfer the greatest possible number of communists to kolkhoz cells.

3. 1950-1952: The reorganization of the collective farms, which enlarged them in size and membership and drastically reduced their number, greatly increased the average strength of collective farm cells.

We saw in the previous chapter how the mass recruitment of 1939-1940 effected a striking improvement in party representation in the villages, falling short, however, of the peak strength on the eve of the purges. This improvement was swiftly undone by the mobilization of communists in 1941-1942. In the Tiumen oblast in Western Siberia, for instance, only 45 of the oblast's 2,874 kolkhozes (under 2 percent) still had party cells in June 1942. Most kolkhoz communists, scattered about the farms in ones and twos, were

[33] B. N. Ponomarev et al., *Istoriia Kommunisticheskoi Partii Sovetskogo Soiuza*, p. 634.
[34] N. S. Khrushchev, *O merakh dal'neishego razvitiia sel'skogo khoziaistva SSSR* (Moscow, 1953), pp. 4, 72.

now concentrated in village cells covering substantial farming areas, as they had been before collectivization and again in the mid-1930's.[35] Nor did the large scale civilian recruitment after 1942 greatly help this situation. In the Krasnodar oblast in January 1945, only one collective farmer in every 170 was in the party.[36]

The influx of communists into the villages following demobilization, testified to in many sources, is best illustrated by an analysis of rural party organizations in the Orël oblast in 1945-1946 (see Table 17).[37]

TABLE 17: RURAL PARTY ORGANIZATIONS IN ORËL OBLAST, 1945-
1946

Type of party organization	Number of organizations		Number of members	
	Jan. 1945	April 1946	Jan. 1945	April 1946
Kolkhoz organizations	34	253	298	1,582
MTS organizations	73	89	557	996
"Village territorial" organizations	259	536	2,072	7,539
Total	366	878	2,927	10,117

[35] See Iu. Vasil'ev, *Tiumenskie Kommunisty v Velikoi Otechestvennoi voine* (Tiumen Communists in the Great Patriotic War), (Tiumen, 1962), p. 70. For similar evidence from the Yaroslavl oblast, see Sidorov, *op.cit.*, p. 15. See also Iu. V. Arutiunian, *Sovetskoe krest'ianstvo v gody Velikoi Otechestvennoi voiny*, pp. 50-53.

[36] See G. P. Ivanov, *op.cit.*, p. 268. Due no doubt to their relatively large area and membership, the proportion of Krasnodar kolkhozes with their own party organizations was comparatively high—about 20 percent.

[37] SOURCE: Based on figures given by I. Afanas'ev, "Ob ukreplenii pervichnykh partiinykh organizatsii v kolkhozakh" (On the Reinforcement of Primary Party Organizations in the Kolkhozes), *PS*, Nos. 7-8, April 1946, p. 22.

The two striking facts which emerge from this table are first, a threefold increase in the number of rural communists in this fifteen-month period, and secondly, the continued predominance of organizations based on the village administration rather than the kolkhozes, despite a great proportional increase in kolkhoz organizations. The same pattern was repeated elsewhere. In the Kalinin oblast, for example, only 10 percent of the collective farms had party organizations in early 1947, although this was already over three times the wartime number; meanwhile the great majority of kolkhoz communists were still enrolled in village organizations, where they made up over half the total membership.[38] In the country as a whole, less than a quarter of all collective farms had their own party organizations at the beginning of 1947.[39]

Starting in 1946, there was an intensive campaign to achieve what had been twice abortively attempted in the 1930's, namely to shift the main focus of rural party organizations from village to kolkhoz cells, with the ultimate object of providing the party machine with a base in every collective farm. In some areas—the Orël oblast is again an example—this campaign achieved substantial successes as early as 1946.[40] However, the main organizational effort, which took the form of large-scale transfers of party members from

[38] See *PZh*, No. 7, April 1947, p. 14. For further data relating to the Ukraine and to the Molotov, Kaluga and Briansk oblasts of the R.S.F.S.R. see *PZh*, No. 9, May 1947, pp. 3, 43 and No. 11, June 1947, pp. 22, 34.

[39] See *P*, March 13, 1947, and *B*, No. 6, April 1947, p. 7. The latter source stated that there were 139,434 primary party organizations in the rural districts, of which 61,211 were based on collective farms.

[40] Between April 1, 1946, and March 1, 1947, the number of collective farms in Orël oblast with their own party organizations rose from 253 to 458, and their membership from 1,582 to 3,091. See *PZh*, No. 5, March 1947, p. 27.

administrative to farm jobs and from farm to farm, so as to secure the necessary quorum of communists to form a separate cell in the maximum number of collective farms, was concentrated in 1947. In that year the number of rural party organizations grew by 32,000, and 26,000 of these were in collective farms. Kolkhoz cells now made up over half the rural party organizations, and more than a third of all collective farms had their own cells.[41]

The year 1949 marked the end of the second phase of the postwar program for expanding party membership in the kolkhozes. Figures made public at party conferences and congresses early that year give some indication of the achievements to that point. In the Moscow oblast, kolkhoz cells had increased from 153 before the war to 1,048 in 1948.[42] In the Ukraine, the increase was from 3,156 to 13,280,[43] and in Georgia from 1,339 to 3,200.[44] The number of kolkhoz cells, however, was expanding at a far greater rate than the number of kolkhoz communists. Thus, while the number of collective farm organizations in the Ukraine had quadrupled since before the war, their total membership had scarcely more than doubled.[45] In Tadzhikistan the number of party organizations in industry grew by 150 percent between 1940 and the end of 1948, while those in collective farms rose by 352 percent, yet the increase in total membership was prac-

---

[41] *PZh*, No. 5, March 1948, p. 21. In many areas over half the collective farms had their own cells by early 1948, and in some the proportion was as high as 85 percent (*ibid.*). There was one raion of Stalingrad oblast where cells existed in all collective farms but one (*ibid.*, p. 20).

[42] See G. M. Popov's report in *MB*, February 2, 1949.

[43] See Khrushchev's report to the Sixteenth Congress of the Ukrainian Communist Party, *P*, January 26, 1949.

[44] See Charkviani's report to the Fourteenth Congress of the Georgian Communist Party, *ZV*, January 28, 1949.

[45] *P*, January 26, 1949.

tically identical—297 percent in industry and 319 percent in the kolkhozes.[46] These facts indicate the relative weakness of many of the new collective farm cells, and confirm that the great increase in their number between 1947 and 1949 was due less to the recruitment of new party members than to a judicious disposal of those communists already available in the rural areas.

The third phase, which was a side effect of the campaign to amalgamate the smaller collective farms, began in 1950. By October 1952 the number of kolkhozes had declined from over a quarter of a million to 97,000. This automatically led to a large increase in the proportion of farms with their own party organizations, a proportion which probably exceeded three-quarters by the time of the Nineteenth Congress.[47] It also entailed a big increase in the average size of kolkhoz cells, reflected in the proliferation of party groups in the labor brigades and livestock farms of the kolkhozes, and the steadily rising number of collective farm organizations with the necessary 15 members to elect a bureau as well as a secretary.[48]

This period saw a particularly large increase in party membership in the rural areas of the recently acquired Western borderlands, connected with the collectivization of agriculture in these areas in 1949-1952. In Moldavia, for instance, the number of communists working in the countryside increased by 4,211 between April 1951 and September 1952, while those working in industry rose by only 1,029.[49] In Belorussia, 14,008 of the 17,887 new members admitted from

[46] KT, December 22, 1948.

[47] It was 76,000 out of 94,000 in September 1953. P, September 15, 1953.

[48] See e.g. P, August 22, 1952, and Niiazov's speech in PV, September 20, 1952.

[49] See SM, September 20, 1952.

294

1949 to 1952 were enrolled in the party organizations of collective farms or MTS's.[50]

However, the picture we have sketched of the proliferation of party organizations in the kolkhozes and the rise in their average membership after 1950 calls for one qualification. These results could be achieved without there necessarily being any increase in the *total* number of communists on the farms, and in fact this total number probably fell significantly in this period, because of slow recruitment and the draft of peasant communists into administrative jobs. Positive evidence of this is available from only one area, namely the North Ossetian autonomous oblast, where party membership on the farms declined by a quarter between 1949 and 1954,[51] and this area cannot necessarily be taken as typical of the country at large. Nonetheless, on the analogy of other periods of static party membership, it would be very surprising if some overall wastage of communists from the farms did not occur in these years.

The ideal of a strong party organization in every collective farm was not fully achieved in the Stalin period. But it was the energetic pursuit of this ideal in the early postwar years which made possible its attainment in the next phase of the party's growth.

[50] See *SB*, September 22, 1952.

[51] See A. M. Musaev, "Iz opyta raboty partiinykh organizatsii Severnogo Kavkaza po rasstanovke kommunistov v sel'skokhoziaistvennom proizvodstve (1953-1958 gg)" (From the Experience of the Work of Party Organizations of the North Caucasus in the Assignment of Communists in Agricultural Production [1953-1958], *V I KPSS*, No. 6, June 1967, p. 75.

Chapter 9

The Khrushchev Enrollment

THE DEATH of Stalin opened up broad possibilities of change in the stagnating Soviet politico-administrative system.

In the period that followed, however, change was cautious and limited, and many important features of the Stalin regime were retained, including the command economy, the centralized and hierarchically structured distribution of power, the facade of pseudo-democratic institutions and procedures, and the close control of public discussion and intellectual life. Nonetheless, the personal dictatorship itself was not restored, despite the ascendancy achieved by Khrushchev after 1957, and along with the dictatorship went the leadership cult and the arbitrary police terror. The cloud of fear, fantasy and mendacity which had permeated the atmosphere of daily life and public discussion was substantially (though not wholly) dissipated, and policy formation became more responsive to public needs, moods and pressures, including those emanating from the technological, scientific and intellectual elites.

The role of the CPSU was one major aspect of the Soviet political and social system which underwent only minor change in the first post-Stalin period. The party continued to participate in the various functions of the political system along the lines sketched out in the Introduction. It continued to provide an apparatus of overall coordination and supervision at each echelon of the power hierarchy, to exercise disciplinary and ideological control over the administrative-managerial and other elites, and to act as the principal guardian and purveyor of official values in each occupational group and in society at large. Change was limited to fluctuations in

296

the jurisdiction of the party in relation to the other more specialized power agencies.

Such a high degree of continuity in the role of the party was by no means inevitable in post-Stalin Russia. The inherited character and pattern of party activities stemmed in large part from the General Secretary's successful struggle against his rivals in the 1920's. While this pattern prejudiced the post-Stalin succession struggle in favor of the new First Secretary, Khrushchev's victory was, nonetheless, not a foregone conclusion. At various stages between 1953 and 1957, the fortunes of the succession struggle might well have led to a sharp accession of power to the political police, the central government or the armed forces, at the expense of the party. Had this occurred, a long-term shift in the political and social role of the party might have followed. The fact that such changes did not occur helps to explain why modifications in party membership policies in the post-Stalin era, significant though they were in some respects, were nevertheless not such as to make the party a radically different one in scale or the character of its membership.

Party Expansion 1954–1964

The keynote speeches at three of the republic party congresses held early in 1954 contained the first public criticism of the narrowly restrictive recruitment practices of the late Stalin era.[1] This criticism was taken up by Khrushchev, the recently appointed First Secretary of the Central Committee. Speaking at a meeting of the Central Committee on February 13, 1954, Khrushchev, who was concerned on this occasion primarily with the ill-effects of overrestrictive recruitment on

[1] The republics were Belorussia, the Ukraine and Georgia. See *SB*, February 18, 1954, *PU*, March 24, 1954, and *ZV*, February 18, 1954.

the party's strength in the kolkhozes, stated that "many raikoms are paying no attention whatsoever to the question of recruitment. It is well known that in recent years the party has been conducting a policy of restricting admissions, but this does not mean that the admission of the foremost kolkhozniks should be stopped altogether. . . . This shortcoming must be eliminated."[2]

Thus was initiated the sharpest change in party recruitment policies since 1946. The rate of enrollments soon showed a marked increase. Party membership, having dropped by 32,000 in 1953, rose by 92,000 in 1954 and 166,000 in 1955 (see p. 52). In the Ukraine, Belorussia, Azerbaidzhan, Georgia, Armenia, Uzbekistan, Tadzhikistan and Kirgizia—the eight union republics for which comparative figures are available—the average increase in party membership between September 1952 and February 1954 was 1.2 percent, while between February 1954 and January 1956 it was 6.6 percent.[3]

There are signs, however, that Khrushchev's policy of membership expansion ran into some initial resistance. The February 1954 congress in Kirgizia, far from attacking the existing policy of restricting recruitment, reendorsed it in the following emphatic terms: "It is essential for us to continue strictly carrying out the demands of the Nineteenth

[2] *P*, March 21, 1954.
[3] Based on a comparative analysis of figures given in the republic press. Percentage increases in the individual republics for the periods before and after February 1954 were as follows: Ukraine: before 3.19, after 7.49; Belorussia: before 1.25, after 12; Georgia: before 1.8, after 4.9; Azerbaidzhan: before 1.6, after 5.5; Armenia: before 2.2, after 5.3; Uzbekistan: before − 0.4, after + 5.9; Kirgizia: before − 0.5, after + 4.6; Tadzhikistan: before 0.8, after 7.3. Party membership in Kazakhstan fell by 1.6 percent in 1953 and rose by 3 percent in 1954. See Beisembaev and Pakhmurnyi, *op.cit.*, pp. 323, 326, 349.

Congress that it is necessary not to force the growth of the party's ranks, but to concentrate attention on raising the political level of communists."[4] In this republic there was a further fall in membership in 1954, and it was only in 1955 that a substantial expansion began.[5] In Uzbekistan, party membership began to grow in 1954, but the rate of increase was trebled in 1955.[6] Since these are the only two areas (apart from Kazakhstan, where the position was complicated by arrivals connected with the "virgin lands" campaign) for which data on membership changes are available for 1954 and 1955 separately, we cannot say how widespread this pattern was. Even if localized, however, this delay in implementing a policy to which the First Secretary of the Central Committee was publicly committed would scarcely have occurred without some encouragement from within the top party leadership. This raises the question whether Malenkov was continuing to espouse the restrictive recruitment policy for which he had been the spokesman at the Nineteenth Congress. This speculation gains some *prima facie* support from the fact that no further signs of resistance to Khrushchev's expansion policy have been discovered after January 1955, when Malenkov was finally defeated in his struggle for the position of *primus inter pares*, and his protégé Shatalin was removed from the Central Committee Secretariat.

Following the Twentieth Party Congress in February 1956, the enrollment rate continued to accelerate. New candidates in 1956 totaled 381,000—more than twice the intake in 1953.[7] Thereafter there were substantial increases in enrollments every year except 1960 (when there was a slight reduction), until in 1964 the number of new candidates ad-

[4] *KP Kirgizii*, p. 234.
[5] *Ibid.*, pp. 226, 244 and appendix.
[6] *KP Uzbekistana v tsifrakh*, pp. 137, 142, 147.
[7] *K*, No. 7, May 1966, p. 4.

mitted reached 879,000.[8] By the middle of 1965 the party membership figure had passed the 12 million mark.[9] This represented an increase of over 70 percent since the death of Stalin.

Although in absolute terms the party's growth in the Khrushchev era was far greater than at any period in the party's history, the ratio of the annual intake to the existing membership, which varied between 1:17 and 1:11, was only a fraction of what it had been, for example, during the Lenin enrollment, the collectivization period, 1938-1940 or World War II. Consequently it did not occasion such acute difficulties of absorption and training as were apparent in these earlier phases of rapid growth. However, it did raise problems of another order. Even when allowance is made for population changes, the decade from 1954 saw a sizeable increase in the proportion of Soviet adults who were members of the CPSU. If this were to continue, it could not fail to affect the political and social significance of party membership in the U.S.S.R. However, although the post-Stalin expansion was linked, as we shall see, with policy shifts on the social composition of the party, nothing like a general reevaluation of what was involved in being a party member seems to have been contemplated at this stage.

The new party rules adopted at the Twenty-Second Congress in 1961 included a number of amendments to the list of rights and duties of party members, but these were not such as to imply significant changes in the social and political role of the party membership.[10] Nor, in this connection, was

[8] See *PZh*, No. 1, 1962, pp. 45-46 and No. 10, 1965, p. 9.

[9] *P*, June 5, 1965.

[10] Cf. Section I, par. 3 of the rules adopted by the Nineteenth Congress, with Section I, par. 2 of those adopted by the Twenty-Second Congress. For discussion of the 1961 changes in the party rules, see Leonard Schapiro, "The Party's New Rules," *Problems of Communism*, Vol. IX, No. 1 (January-February), 1962. The most

great importance to be attached to the doctrine that the CPSU was now a party of the whole people, and not specifically of the proletariat. The regulations providing for preferential treatment for workers in party admission procedures had been removed as long ago as 1939 (see above, p. 224), while the amendments to the party rules endorsed by the Nineteenth Congress in 1952 had dropped the formula "vanguard of the working class," and defined the party as "a voluntary militant union of like-minded communists, organized of people from the working class, toiling peasants and working intelligentsia." Compared with this change, the modifications introduced in the 1961 formulation[11] were of minor significance. Likewise the one paragraph devoted to the party membership in the 100 pages of the revised party program of 1961 was a concoction of hoary clichés which gave little indication of any new thinking on this question.

In the period of the large-scale building of communism, the role and responsibility of the party member are raised even higher. The communist is obliged in all his conduct in productive work, in his public and private life, to set lofty examples of struggle for the development and strengthening of communist relationships, and to observe the principles and norms of communist morality. The CPSU will reinforce its ranks with the most conscious and active toilers and keep pure and hold high the title of communist.[12]

---

important official statement on the membership aspects of the 1961 rules is contained in Party Secretary Kozlov's report to the Congress, *XXII s"ezd* (Moscow, 1962), Vol. III, pp. 7-12.

[11] The preamble to the 1961 party rules defines the CPSU as "the militant, experienced vanguard of the Soviet people, uniting on a voluntary basis the advanced and most conscious part of the working class, the kolkhoz peasantry and the intelligentsia of the U.S.S.R."

[12] See *XXII s"ezd*, Vol. III, p. 333.

In the absence of any new doctrine or regulations on the role of the party member, it seemed only a matter of time before the rapid post-1954 expansion would begin to arouse fears of a possible dilution of the significance of party membership in Soviet society.

Broadening the Base

The great expansion of the CPSU under Khrushchev was accompanied by significant changes in the social orientation of recruitment. Criticisms of the restrictive admissions policy inherited from the Stalin era which were voiced in 1954 focused on the fact that it resulted in hardly any workers or peasants being recruited (see above, pp. 146, 153). Khrushchev followed this up at the Twentieth Congress (February 1956) by rebuking local party officials for "weakening their attention to the regulation of the party's growth, and especially to increasing the working class core of the party."[13] His fellow Central Committee secretary Mikhail Suslov spelt out this point, giving examples of recruitment figures from particular oblasts where an insufficient number of workers or collective farmers had been admitted, and asserting: "Party organizations must . . . achieve a decisive increase in the relative weight of workers and collective farmers among those admitted to the party."[14] And finally, the resolution of the congress laid down the line in the following terms: "the congress obliges party organizations to intensify their concern for the individual recruitment of front-rank people, choosing

[13] XX s"ezd Kommunisticheskoi Partii Sovetskogo Soiuza: stenograficheskii otchët (Moscow, 1956), Vol. I, p. 109 (cited hereafter as XX s"ezd). For a 1954 decision of a republic Central Committee calling for greater attention to recruitment, and stressing the enlistment of kolkhozniks, see Beisembaev and Pakhmurnyi, op.cit., pp. 343-344.
[14] Ibid., p. 279.

them first and foremost from the ranks of the workers and collective farmers."[15]

This line, which firmly directed the main focus of the party's recruitment efforts *away from* officialdom and the intelligentsia, remained in force for a number of years. In 1961, however, formulae used at the Twenty-Second Congress indicated a significant relaxation of this emphasis. Khrushchev stated in his report that "it is necessary to continue to accept into the party front-rank people of the working class, the kolkhoz peasantry and the Soviet intelligentsia, the best of the Soviet people."[16] From now on the stress shifted from

[15] *Ibid.*, Vol. II, p. 425. For examples of statements reiterating this line see *P*, April 6, 1956, *MP*, July 8, 1958, *KP*, June 7, 1957, and *Kommunist Turkmenii*, No. 9, September 1958, p. 40. Such statements make it clear that wherever local committees weakened their efforts to stimulate worker and peasant recruitment, the proportion of white-collar enlistments immediately showed a sharp rise.

[16] *XXII s"ezd*, Vol. I, p. 112. Khrushchev's speech also contained a justification of the recruitment of white-collar workers in terms reminiscent of those used in the 1930's (see pp. 191, 224). "And what does the category of white-collar workers (*sluzhashchie*) admitted to the party represent in our day? Almost two-thirds of them are engineers and technicians, agronomists, zootechnicians and other specialists. One must say that the very conception of white-collar workers has now changed. In the first years of Soviet power the intelligentsia consisted for the most part of people who had been connected with the propertied classes before the revolution. It was for this reason that certain restrictive measures were applied to the white-collar category. Now the position is entirely different: at the present time the overwhelming majority of white-collar workers are former workers or peasants or their children. And that is precisely why the attitude towards the white-collar worker has changed. In the process of development of science and technology, and the automatization and mechanization of production the category of people whom we call white-collar workers will play a bigger and bigger part in production. In time we will have no need to divide party members into workers, kolkhozniks and white-collar workers, since class differences will have entirely disappeared and all will be workers (*truzheniki*) of communist society" (*ibid.*, p. 111). Here Khrushchev seemed

increasing the proportion of workers and kolkhozniks to simply increasing the proportion of party members working "in the sphere of material production." The effects of these policy shifts are clearly shown in published data on the social composition of recruits to the party during the Khrushchev era. Between the Twentieth and Twenty-Second Congresses (roughly 1956-1961) 40.7 of all recruits were workers at the time of joining the party and 22.7 percent were kolkhozniks,[17] a marked change from the pattern of recruitment on the eve of and immediately after Stalin's death. When this data is related to breakdowns for recruitment for particular years (available for 1955, 1960, 1963 and 1964) a number of additional points emerge (see Table 18).[18] We see that the white-collar worker/intelli-

clearly to be preparing the party for an increased intake of white-collar workers/intelligentsia in the ensuing years. V. N. Titov, Chairman of the Credentials Commission, stated: "The indissoluble link between the CPSU and the working people finds expression in the constant flow into the party of the best and most advanced representatives of the working class, the kolkhoz peasantry and the intelligentsia" (ibid., p. 423). F. R. Kozlov, in his report on the new party rules, put it this way: "The party will continue to replenish its ranks from among the most conscious and active members of our society, and keep pure and hold high the title of communist" (ibid., Vol. III, p. 7). This was a paraphrase of the formula used in the new party program (see above, p. 301).

[17] P, May 26, 1964.

[18] SOURCES: Based on figures in PZh, No. 1, January 1962, p. 45, No. 4, February 1963, p. 21 and No. 10, May 1965, p. 9; K, No. 8, May 1962, p. 12 and No. 18, December 1964, p. 57; and P, May 26, 1964.

A later source (PZh, No. 19, October 1967, p. 11) gives a significantly different breakdown for the years 1956-1961 inclusive, namely: workers, 40.6 percent; kolkhozniks, 19.4 percent; and white-collar workers and others, 40.0 percent. The differences are probably due to subsequent reclassifications, particularly those connected with the transfer of farm personnel from collective to state farms and the abolition of the MTS's, but this is uncertain. This source is valuable

gentsia had sunk to under half of all recruits as early as 1955, and it continued to decline sharply during the later 1950's, but recovered significantly in the early 1960's. The workers' share of recruitment rose throughout the period, but whereas

in giving a comparative breakdown of candidates enlisted in the years 1952-1955, as follows: workers, 27.2 percent; kolkhozniks, 16.4 percent; white-collar workers and others, 56.4 percent. Comparison of these percentages with those for 1955 only shown in our table indicates that the "democratization" of recruitment had already begun before 1956. Further indications of developments in the pre-1956 period are available in data from certain of the republics. In Kazakhstan 28 percent of those joining the party in 1954-1955 were workers, compared with 17 percent in "the preceding period," which evidently meant 1952-1953 (*KP*, January 26, 1956; see also Beisembaev and Pakhmurnyi, *op.cit.*, 342). In Uzbekistan the proportion of party members *employed* as white-collar workers was still increasing in 1954, but fell significantly in 1955, and continued to decline thereafter. In this republic, however, there was a significant increase in the number of workers in the party, and a drop in the kolkhozniks, in 1953-1954. See *KP Uzbekistana v tsifrakh*, pp. 132, 137, 142. Other figures from the *rural* districts of Uzbekistan show that white-collar workers accounted for 44 percent of recruits in 1949-1953 and 35 percent in 1954-1958. See B. A. Tulepbaev, *Kompartiia Uzbekistana v bor'be za krutoi pod"ëm sel'skogo khoziaistva* (Tashkent, 1959), p. 120. In Estonia the percentage of workers and peasants among those admitted to the party in 1956-1957 was two and a half times greater than in 1954-1955 (*SE*, January 29, 1958). A less sharp change is indicated by the following figures from Tadzhikistan:

Percent of New CPSU Candidates in Tadzhikistan

	1954-1955	1956-1957
Workers	16	24
Peasants	21	25
White-collar workers and others	63	51

SOURCE: S. A. Radzhabov and Iu. A. Nikolaev, eds., *Istoriia Tadzhikskogo naroda* (Moscow, 1965), Vol. III, p. 162.

In Turkmenia 19 percent of recruits were workers in 1954 and 8 percent were collective farmers. In 1955 these percentages rose to 20 and 16 respectively. In 1957 workers and collective farmers to-

TABLE 18: SOCIAL COMPOSITION OF CPSU RECRUITS, 1955-1964

Occupation on joining party	Percent of all recruits					
	1955	1956-61	1960	1961	1963	1964
Workers	30.4	40.7	43.1 ⎫	63.3	45.0	45.3
Kolkhozniks	21.3	22.7	21.7 ⎭		14.4	15.1
Intelligentsia/ white-collar workers	46.2	35.6	34.3 ⎫	36.7	39.1	38.6
Students and others	2.1	1.0	0.9 ⎭		1.5	1.0

the rise was rapid up to 1960, it tended to level out thereafter. By 1955 kolkhozniks accounted for just over a fifth of all admissions to the CPSU, and they fluctuated around that level for the next six years. After the Twenty-Second Congress however, the kolkhoznik share of recruitment fell by about a third.

Party statisticians explain this relative decline in party recruitment in the kolkhozes after 1961 in terms of two factors: the overall reduction in the agricultural labor force and the transfer of a significant part of the rural population from collective to state farms, which involved an automatic reclassification from peasants (kolkhozniks) to workers.[19] This appears to be part of the story but not the whole story. Between 1960 and 1963 the number of kolkhoz workers declined from 22.3 million to 19.4 million, while the number of state farm workers rose from 6.3 million to 7.9 million.[20]

gether made up 58 percent of all recruits in this republic. See E. Kasimov, "Regulirovaniiu rosta riadov KPSS—neoslabnoe vnimanie" (Unflagging Attention to Regulating the Growth of the CPSU's Ranks), *Kommunist Turkmenii*, No. 9, September 1958, p. 40.

[19] See *PZh*, No. 10, May 1965, p. 10.

[20] *Narodnoe Khoziaistvo SSSR v 1963 godu: statisticheskii ezhegodnik* (Moscow, 1965), p. 363. These figures include relatively small numbers employed in "subsidiary" (*podsobnye*) rural enterprises processing agricultural products.

However, the fall in party recruitment in the kolkhozes was proportionately much sharper than the decline in the kolkhoz share in the labor force, while the increased recruitment on the state farms barely kept pace with the increase in the state farm share of the labor force.[21] In other words, non-white-collar agricultural labor evidently contributed a significantly smaller proportion of those who joined the party in 1963-1964 than in previous years.[22]

At the risk of trying the reader's patience with a rather complicated line of argument, it is also worth noting the implications for the interpretation of recruitment figures up to 1961 of the social reclassifications of farming personnel which were occasioned by Khrushchev's agricultural reorganizations. The ratio of state to collective farm workers increased considerably faster *before* 1960 than afterwards.[23]

[21] State farm employees constituted 10 percent of all "workers and white-collar workers" (*rabochie i sluzhashchie*) in 1960, and 11 percent in 1964 (*Narodnoe khoziaistvo SSSR v 1964 godu: statisticheskii ezhegodnik* [Moscow, 1965], p. 546). Meanwhile state farm workers constituted 15 percent of all workers who joined the party in 1960, and 16 percent in 1964 (*PZh*, No. 1, January 1962, p. 45 and No. 10, May 1965, p. 9).

[22] The slight increase in kolkhoz recruitment from 1963 to 1964 may have reflected a decision to arrest this decline. The party statisticians point out that in *absolute* terms kolkhoz recruitment did not decline: it was 101,553 in 1964 as against 99,603 in 1961 (*PZh*, No. 10, May 1965, p. 9). As we have argued, however, these figures need to be seen in the light of total recruitment, which was 23 percent higher in 1964 than in 1961. Incidentally, these absolute figures indicate levels of kolkhoz recruitment considerably lower than the official percentage breakdown reproduced in Table 18. The explanation is probably that the latter include kolkhozniks joining the party while on military service, and the absolute figures do not.

[23] State farm employees increased from 2.8 million in 1955 to 6.3 million in 1960 (*Narodnoe khoziaistvo SSSR: statisticheskii sbornik* [Moscow, 1956], p. 190); from 1960 to 1963 there was a further increase to 7.9 million (*Narodnoe khoziaistvo SSSR v 1963 godu: statisticheskii ezhegodnik* [Moscow, 1964], p. 475).

Even more pertinent were the changes which took place in the status of farm machinery operators. In October 1953 some two million of these were transferred from membership of the kolkhozes to the MTS payroll, and automatically became "workers"; in 1958, however, with the abolition of the MTS's, most of them reverted to the status of kolkozniks.[24] Now, the proportion of farm machinery operators admitted to the party is far higher than that of other rural employees. In 1955, when they were "workers," 13,578 of them joined the party; in 1960, when they were "kolkhozniks," 31,976 joined.[25] The latter figure represented over 5 percent of all recruits to the CPSU, which is probably typical for these years.[26] This means that the achievements of the party in building up the recruitment level in the kolkhozes were considerably more impressive up to 1958 than is apparent from Table 16, because the latter was based on figures of kolkhoz recruitment which in 1955-1958 did not include farm machinery operators. But it also means that the number of kolkhozniks recruited other than farm machinery operators must have been considerably less in 1960-1961 than in 1955-1958. In other words, the decline in farming recruitment, which Table 16 suggested as having begun after 1961, was apparently already under way by 1960.[27]

[24] See *Narodnoe khoziaistvo SSSR: statisticheskii sbornik* (1956), p. 190 and *Narodnoe khoziaistvo SSSR v 1961 godu: statisticheskii ezhegodnik* (Moscow, 1962), p. 467.

[25] *PZh*, No. 1, January 1962, p. 46. The number of recruits to the party in 1955 is not known, but it is probable that the 13,578 farm machinery operators recruited represented *at least* 5 percent of the total.

[26] In 1964, 40,731 farm machinery operators were admitted, or 4.6 percent of all recruits (*PZh*, No. 10, May 1965, p. 10).

[27] The extent of this decline is obviously difficult to quantify: it is impossible to establish on present data whether it began in 1960 or 1959, although it almost certainly did not begin later and is un-

Expulsions, Withdrawals, Deaths

From the early 1930's till some years after Stalin's death the Central Committee published no statistics on the number of party members and candidates who were expelled, dropped out of the party voluntarily, or died. At the Twenty-Second Congress, Khrushchev stated that something over 200,000 persons had been expelled "for various reasons" in the preceding six years.[28] It was later revealed that the rate at which

---

likely to have begun earlier. According to figures which evidently exclude kolkhozniks recruited while on military service and are therefore not strictly comparable with the percentages in Table 18, 99,139 kolkhozniks joined the party in 1960 and 99,603 in 1961, a rise of one-half of one percent (see *PZh*, No. 1, January 1962, p. 46 and No. 10, May 1965, p. 9. Cf. footnote 22). However, overall recruitment to the party was about 6 percent higher in 1961 than 1960. It would seem, therefore, that the percentage of kolkhozniks among admissions to the party was lower in 1961 than in 1960, and we may estimate the reduction at about 1 percent. Now, given that kolkhozniks averaged 22.7 percent of all recruits between 1956 and 1961, that they represented 21.7 percent in 1960 and about 20.7 percent in 1961, and allowing for differences in the annual recruitment rate, kolkhoz recruitment appears to have averaged about 23.7 percent in 1956-1959. If one were to assume that the decline in kolkhoz recruitment (other than farm machinery operators) began in 1959, this would mean that the average kolkhoz recruitment for 1956-1958 was significantly higher than 23.7 percent, and if one assumed that it began in 1958, the 1956-1957 figure would be higher still, at a time when the farm machinery operators were not members of the kolkhozes, and this seems improbable. From these considerations it seems fairly safe to conclude that (a) the decline began in 1959-1960, and (b) unless there was an extraordinarily high recruitment of kolkhozniks in 1958-1959, recruitment was significantly higher in 1956-1957 than in 1960-1961, despite the fact that the farm machinery operators had gone back on the strength of the kolkhozes in the meantime. Another approach to this question would be to compare the figures for kolkhozniks recruited other than farm machinery operators. This would produce a series something like this: 1955—21.3 percent; 1960—16.5 percent; 1964—10.5 percent.

[28] *XXII s"ezd*, Vol. I, p. 112.

people were expelled or dropped out of the party in the five years before the Twenty-Second Congress (i.e. presumably 1957-1961) was only 40 percent of what it had been in the five years before the Twentieth Congress (1951-1955).[29] More precise figures are available for expulsions and withdrawals in the years 1958-1960 and 1962-1964. Although the number of deaths was not given, this may be calculated by subtracting the number who were expelled or dropped out from the difference between the net growth of the party and the number of admissions for the year. It should be noted that formal resignation from the party, which was a frequent occurrence during the 1920's, seemed to be no more regarded as a feasible action under Khrushchev than it had been during the Stalin era. Only two ways were recognized of withdrawing from the party (*vybyvat' iz partii*). One was to be refused acceptance as a full member on completion of one's probation as a candidate, which amounted to a form of expulsion. The other was to be adjudged as having "lost contact with the party," after failing to pay membership dues for three months in a row. Both forms of "withdrawal" were qualified as "automatic."

Looking first at the figures for deaths (see Table 19)[30] the average death rate for party members over this period, 7 per 1,000, is approximately what one would expect given the age structure of the membership and the death rates of different age groups in the population at large; in other words, there appears to be no marked difference between the death rate of party members and others.[31] It is doubtful if

[29] *PZh*, No. 1, January 1962, p. 47. Cf. Chapter 8, footnote 15.
[30] SOURCES: Calculated from figures given in *PZh*, No. 1, January 1962, pp. 44-45, 47, and No. 10, May 1965, pp. 8-10. Ratios are based on the total party membership on January 1 of the year concerned.
[31] See *PZh*, No. 10, May 1965, p. 13 and *Narodnoe khoziaistvo SSSR v 1963 godu: statisticheskii ezhegodnik*, p. 32.

TABLE 19: Deaths, Expulsions and Withdrawals, 1958-1964

Year	Died Number	Per 1,000 of party	Expelled or withdrew Number	Per 1,000 of party
1958	31,270	4	53,302	7
1959	56,420	7	53,456	7
1960	65,387	8	40,333	5
1962	98,948	10	65,163	7
1963	66,612	6	69,454	7
1964	74,858	7	68,770	6

much significance should be placed on the annual fluctuations shown in Table 19, as the figures for deaths are residual ones which have to bear the full weight of any lack of synchronization in the three sets of figures from which they are derived.[32]

Further details have been published on those who were expelled or withdrew in 1962-1964 (though not in 1958-1960) and these are reproduced in Table 20.[33] They indicate that the annual rate of "hard-core" expulsions (category a) was a mere 3 per 1,000. These figures also bring out the tiny

[32] Two factors which would help to account for the *direction*, though not the scale, of the trends shown in the table are: (a) the average age of party members appears to have risen somewhat up to 1962, and to have fallen from 1963 (see p. 356); (b) the death rate in the Soviet population was 0.3 per 1,000 higher in 1962 than in 1961 or 1963 (see *Narodnoe khoziaistvo SSSR v 1963 godu: statisticheskii ezhegodnik*, p. 30).

[33] SOURCE: *PZh*, No. 10, May 1965, p. 10. Very little data is available on the grounds for expulsion during this period. Of the 327 communists expelled in Turkmenia in 1960-1961, 75 were expelled on grounds such as abuse of official position, deception of superiors, submission of false performance reports and embezzlement, and 54 on grounds such as "feudal" attitude towards women, polygamy and moral depravity. No information was given about the other 198. See *TI*, September 15, 1961.

TABLE 20: ANALYSIS OF EXPULSIONS AND WITHDRAWALS, 1962-1964

	1962	1963	1964
Total who were expelled or withdrew	65,163	69,454	68,770
Of whom: (a) Full members	33,582	36,797	34,525
(b) Candidates	31,581	32,657	34,245
Breakdown of expulsions and withdrawals:			
(a) Expelled for various misdemeanors, incompatible with the title of communist	31,370	34,045	30,763
(b) Classified as withdrawn by virtue of having lost contact with the party organization	13,614	14,422	15,877
(c) Classified as withdrawn by virtue of having been refused admission as full members on completion of probation as candidates	20,179	20,987	22,130

number (about one in seven hundred each year) who voluntarily or through carelessness dropped out of the party. Further, it is worth noting the high figures for candidates relative to full members. This also applied in 1958-1960. (The rise in the proportion of candidates among those who were expelled or withdrew, however—from 34 percent in 1958 to 50 percent in 1964—simply reflected the increased ratio of candidates to full members.) True, about two-thirds of the candidates concerned come under the special category of people who had failed to leap the hurdle from candidate to full membership. Even if these are subtracted, however, the chances of a candidate being expelled from the party or dropping out during these years appear to have been about five times those for a full member.

Although Khrushchev spoke of the 200,000 expulsions

between the Twentieth and Twenty-Second Congresses as a good thing which had strengthened the party,[34] there is no doubt that the leadership during these years was most concerned to show a reduced level of expulsions which would compare reassuringly with the level under Stalin. In 1962 *Partiinaia Zhizn'* made this comparison explicitly, and commented:

> The reestablishment of Leninist norms of party life, development of democratic principles in the work of party organizations, and the strengthening of the Marxist-Leninist training of communists has had a favorable effect in heightening the consciousness of party members and candidates and strengthening party discipline. All this has found expression, in particular, in the reduction of the number of people who have been called before the party's tribunals (*privlekaemye k partiinoi otvetstvennosti*) and expelled from the CPSU.

And the journal went on to announce proudly that the number expelled from or leaving the party had been lower in 1960 than it had been for twenty years.[35] All this explains the reluctance which local organizations are reported to have shown to recommend expulsions, fearing it would "spoil their statistics" and arouse the displeasure of higher party echelons. This almost shamefaced attitude towards expulsions reached the point where even in the case of persons expelled following criminal convictions many local organizations added the rider that they might be recommended for readmission within a year.[36] It was not till after the removal of Khrushchev, however, that such attitudes came strongly

[34] *XXII s"ezd*, Vol. I, p. 112.
[35] *PZh*, No. 1 January 1962, p. 47.
[36] *K*, No. 14, September 1965, p. 89.

313

under fire, and party statements began to foreshadow an intensification of expulsions.

Applying the Brakes

In his report to the Twenty-Second Congress, Khrushchev made a strong statement on the party's need to guard itself against those who were interested in membership solely for careerist purposes.[37] For some time thereafter, this subject received little publicity. In April 1963, however, an article was published by V. Zasorin, an official of the Party Organs Department of the Central Committee, which struck a new note of caution on party recruitment. Zasorin indicated that regional officials were systematically pressurizing local organizations into keeping up their admissions. "Sometimes the decisions adopted by obkoms and kraikoms in endorsing [party] statistical returns boil down to counting up the number admitted in the various organizations, and the number of organizations which have failed to grow in the quarterly period concerned. Then out go warnings to their leaders instructing them to ensure there is continuous recruitment in every organization." A refinement of this was the action of the Alma-Ata gorkom, which had rebuked some of its subordinate raikoms for allowing their growth in the third quarter of 1962 to fall below that in the previous quarter. Zasorin stressed that, just because the CPSU was now "the party of the whole people," this did not mean that local organizations should admit all who applied; on the contrary, their task was to select from the applicants "the best of the best."[38] As an example of how lightly some people were beginning to take the question of recruitment, he cited the case of a kolkhoz

[37] *XXII s"ezd*, Vol. I, p. 112.
[38] V. Zasorin, "Priëmom v partiiu nado rukovodit' " (Admissions into the Party Must be Guided), *PZh*, No. 8, April 1963, p. 15.

driver, who was duly enrolled as a candidate by the primary organization secretary and endorsed by the raikom, without, however, his ever being consulted or informed.[39]

If the facts disclosed by Zasorin carried the unavoidable implication that regional officials had themselves been subject to pressures from above to keep up recruitment, his article clearly indicated that such pressures were now being eased, and that, if anything, the brakes were being applied. During the next eighteen months, party publications and spokesmen kept up a moderate but persistent campaign against the indiscriminate admission of applicants, "chasing after numbers," and the relaxing of standards of personal and public probity expected of communists.[40]

In spite of this campaign, new admissions in 1964 reached their highest level since World War II. There are a number of possible reasons. The least likely is that there were divided counsels in the central apparatus, with A saying one thing and B doing the opposite; there are no signs of the muted polemic which one would expect to accompany such divisions. Another possibility is that local officials were sim-

[39] *Ibid.*, p. 17.

[40] The following are some of the highlights in this campaign:

(a) The widely publicized rebuke of a raikom which merely rubberstamped the admission of a candidate against whom a substantial minority of his primary organization had voted because of his suspicious past (see *PZh*, No. 20, October 1963, pp. 47-50).

(b) Criticism of lax recruitment activity in the reports of a number of republic first secretaries in their republic congress reports (see *S Lat*, December 25, 1963, *SE*, January 8, 1964, *K(A)*, January 8, 1964 and *ZV*, January 30, 1964).

(c) A leading article in the Central Committee's organizational journal, entitled "Show Thought and Seriousness in Recruitment to the Party" (Ser'ëzno, vdumchivo otbirat' v partiiu), *PZh*, No. 16, August 1964, pp. 3-5). For a typical example of the treatment of this issue by republic party journals in 1964, see *Kommunist Sovetskoi Latvii*, No. 6, June 1964, pp. 67-69.

ply manifesting that tardiness of response to central policy changes on the scale of recruitment, which is something we have seen recurring several times in the history of the party (see, e.g. pp. 217, 220, 277). Perhaps the most likely explanation is that the campaign at this stage was intended not so much to reduce recruitment as to prevent it growing even faster than it in fact did. While references to greatly increased public interest in joining the party after the Twenty-Second Congress[41] lend some weight to this supposition, the absence of any data on the number of applications and the rate of rejection by primary organizations and raikoms unfortunately renders it unverifiable.

Be this as it may, the campaign for more careful and selective recruitment appears to have been intensified soon after Khrushchev's removal in October 1964. A series of articles appeared in February 1965 stressing the responsibility, authority and persistent activity which should go with party membership. Lenin was quoted as saying: "It is better for ten who work not to call themselves party members (those who really work do not chase after rank) than for one chatterbox to have the right and opportunity to be a party member. . . . We should try to raise the title and importance of the party member higher, higher and higher."[42] This dictum was to provide the keynote for discussions of party membership questions in the following months.

In August 1965 the party organizational journal *Partiinaia Zhizn'* printed a Central Committee decision "On Serious Shortcomings in the Work of the Kharkov Oblast Party Organization on the Acceptance into the Party and Training of Young Communists." The publication of Central Committee documents criticizing subordinate committees for their

[41] See, e.g. *PZh*, No. 8, April 1963, p. 14.
[42] See *P*, February 1, 5 and 25, 1965.

direction of some field of party activities is a standard device for signaling clarifications or modifications of the party line, and this decision was perhaps the most important official statement on party membership questions since Khrushchev's remarks in 1954 which initiated the rapid expansion program. It rebuked the Kharkov obkom for forgetting that "the chief thing for the party is not the admission of new members in general, but the replenishment of its ranks with genuine fighters for the cause of communism." In their concern to keep up the number of recruits, gorkoms, raikoms and primary organizations were failing to check the personal and public qualities of applicants, sometimes admitting in effect all who applied. Higher committees were encouraging this "chasing after numbers" by the stress they placed on the scale of recruitment in evaluating the organizational and political-educational efforts of subordinates. (These practices, incidentally, lend further support to the view that in 1963-1964 the leadership was concerned simply to keep the expansion of recruitment within bounds rather than to reduce it.) A number of committees had laid down quotas for the recruitment of different social categories which were obligatory on all subordinate organizations. "This sometimes leads to abnormal situations: for instance, in certain scientific institutions there are few scientists and technicians among recruits to the party, while in a number of large production collectives there are insufficient workers amongst those admitted." The decision stressed the need for more energetic and systematic indoctrination and training of young communists. Then, indicating that higher standards were to be required not only of future recruits, but of the existing membership as well, it stated: "There must be a decisive end to the existing indulgence and liberalism shown towards

317

members and candidates of the CPSU, whose actions are incompatible with their belonging to the party."

In its condemnation of insufficient care in scrutinizing applicants and of "chasing after numbers," the August 1965 decision on the Kharkov obkom was reiterating points which had been frequently stressed since 1963; however, it did so with a new firmness and urgency. "The numerical growth of party organizations is not an end in itself. . . . In selecting people for the party it must be borne in mind that even isolated cases of accepting into the CPSU people who are unworthy of the title of communist do harm to the party, sully its ranks, and reduce the authority and fighting capacity of party organizations." Moreover, the decision was breaking new ground in its condemnation of inflexible social category quotas, and its call for more energetic weeding out of "unworthy" people from the existing membership.[43]

A few weeks later the chief party ideological journal *Kommunist* followed up with a discussion of recruitment questions in the course of a statement on "the Leninist norms of party life." It stressed the need for a far more critical attitude towards applicants for admission. To illustrate the widespread irresponsibility shown towards party membership questions, it cited an obkom plenum which was presented with a report analyzing recruitment over the first half of 1965; despite glaring irregularities indicated by the report, the plenum did not discuss it, but simply noted it. The article told of cases where applicants who performed badly at the meeting of their primary organization held to consider their entry were told "we'll take you, but see you prepare yourself

[43] *PZh*, No. 15, August 1965, pp. 23-25. For comment and other examples of lax recruitment practices in this period, see article by Petr Kruzhin, *Bulletin* (Institute for the Study of the USSR), Vol. XII, No. 11, November 1965, pp. 48-56.

better when you go before the gorkom bureau." *Kommunist*'s scandalized correspondent remarked, "As if one can arrive at the appropriate convictions in a week or two!"[44]

Then a new note was struck: there were still people joining the party for careerist motives. The article told of a party member who was informed by an acquaintance of his intention to join the party. "The communist knew him to be a hypocritical and crude person with a marked acquisitive bent. Naturally, he was amazed by what he had heard. 'You must be joking,' he cautiously remarked, 'After all, everyone knows you inside-out.' The man gave a self-satisfied smirk and, rummaging in his pocket, pulled out a couple of carelessly folded sheets of paper: they were recommendations. 'Well, you see, a nice little job has turned up,' he said offhandedly, 'and I want to get in the swim.' 'But what has the party got to do with it?' questioned the astonished communist. And the other answered, 'Let's put it this way: it's that sort of job. You've got to have authority. A man must move on, understand.' " In this case, it was reported, the unworthy applicant was rejected. But there were other careerists who were managing to join the party, as a result of the relaxation of vigilance.[45]

On January 1, 1966 the party membership totaled 12,357,308,[46] and in Brezhnev's report to the Twenty-Third

[44] "Leninskie normy partiinoi zhizni" (Leninist Norms of Party Life), *K*, No. 14, September 1965, pp. 88-90.

[45] *Ibid.*, p. 92. Cf. the example reported on p. 75 of a job-motivated application for party membership quoted on the eve of the 1919 "reregistration." For examples of articles in republic party journals urging more cautious recruitment in the post-Khrushchev period, see *Kommunist Sovetskoi Latvii*, No. 10, October 1965, pp. 53-56; *Kommunist Moldavii*, No. 10, October 1965, pp. 24-31 and No. 7, July 1966, pp. 3-8; *Kommunist Belorussii*, No. 1, January 1967, pp. 60-66.

[46] Calculated from figures given in *PZh*, No. 7, April 1967, p. 7.

Congress, delivered on March 29, it was put at 12,471,000.[47] This meant that the rate of increase since the beginning of 1965 had gone down by 20 percent as compared with 1965. Statements made at a number of the republic party congresses preceding the Twenty-Third Congress suggested that the policy of more restricted recruitment would continue,[48] and the policy was duly reaffirmed in emphatic terms both in Brezhnev's keynote report to the Congress and in a congress resolution. Brezhnev again quoted Lenin's aphorism that it is better for ten who work to be left out of the party than for one chatterbox to be let in.[49] The relevant passage in the Congress Resolution on the Report of the Central Committee read as follows:

The Congress observes that the growing authority of the CPSU is strengthening the aspiration of Soviet people to link their lives with the party ideologically and organizationally, to enter its ranks. At the same time the Congress considers it incorrect that in certain party organizations the principles of individual selection have been violated, and there has been a lowering in the requirements made of persons entering the party. The Congress obliges all party organizations to approach admissions to the party more carefully. It is necessary to admit to the ranks of the CPSU, in strict accord with the party-rules, advanced and conscious workers, kolkhozniks, and members of the intelligentsia, who are actively participating in the building of communism. Moreover, workers should continue to

[47] P, March 30, 1966.

[48] See SM, March 2, 1966; KT, March 3, 1966; BR, February 25, 1966; S Lit, March 4, 1966; S Lat, March 3, 1966; K(A), March 4, 1966; and PU, March 16, 1966. Most of these republic party spokesmen invoked the Central Committee decision on recruitment in Kharkov.

[49] P, March 30, 1966.

320

occupy the leading position in the social composition of the party.[50]

A more cautious approach to recruitment was also indicated by three of the changes in the party rules approved by the Congress. In votes taken in primary party organizations on the admission of new candidates, a two-thirds majority of those present was now required for the applicant to be admitted. Those recommending applicants now had to be party members of at least five years standing, instead of three years, as previously. In the past applicants aged between 18 and 20 had to be members of the komsomol for their applications to be considered. This requirement was now extended to all applicants aged up to 23.[51] This last change would appear to indicate dissatisfaction with the level of ideological and organizational discipline displayed by the younger adults who had been joining the party.[52]

Other decisions of the Twenty-Third Congress were designed to put teeth into the campaign, which had been run-

[50] *P*, April 9, 1966. The final sentence about workers continuing to occupy the leading position is of some interest in view of the concept of the CPSU as a "party of the whole people." In fact, of course, workers had not constituted the largest segment of the party membership since the early 1930's, although for some years they had provided the largest category of recruits. In view of the tendency whenever recruitment is restricted for the proportion of white-collar workers to increase at the expense of the workers and kolkhozniks, this statement may have been intended as an assurance that the leadership would seek to avoid this consequence on this occasion. For evidence of the speedy appearance of this consequence in many areas and of the leadership's desire to counter it, see *PZh*, No. 18, September 1966, p. 6.

[51] *P*, April 9, 1966.

[52] Brezhnev justified this amendment on the grounds that "this will heighten the role of the komsomol as a reserve of the party, and will make for the recruitment to the party of the most active part of youth, who have undergone a school of training in the ranks of the Leninist Young Communist League" (*P*, March 30, 1966).

ning since February 1965, to heighten party discipline generally and remove unsuitable members. The Resolution on the Report of the Central Committee emphasized the importance of "concern for the purity of the party's ranks, that every communist should bear with honor and justify the title of member of the party of Lenin." A passage was inserted in the introductory section of the party rules to the effect that "the party frees itself of persons who violate the program or rules of the CPSU and compromise by their conduct the lofty title of communist." The rules were also amended so that decisions of primary organizations expelling CPSU members or candidates entered into force upon endorsement by the gorkom or raikom, without requiring, as previously, endorsement by the obkom, kraikom or republic central committee.[53]

The statements and decisions on party membership and recruitment made at the Twenty-Third Congress did not imply anything like a cessation of recruitment or systematic purge of the membership. Nor was it apparent at this stage whether they were intended to prepare the ground for radical decisions of this order. It appeared, however, that the new leadership was bringing to a close the phase of rapid membership expansion initiated by Khrushchev, and that a new phase in the history of the party membership was beginning. In 1966 the number of candidates accepted into the party was 510,955, which was only 58 percent of the number accepted in 1964. Meanwhile the rate of expulsions rose sharply. In 1966, 62,868 were removed "for various misdemeanors, incompatible with the title of communist," compared with 30,763 in 1964. As a result, the party grew by only 326,825 (to 12,684,133) during 1966, as compared with 599,139 in 1965 and 734,800 in 1964. In the Conclusion we discuss the possible long-term implications of this latest change in party membership policy. For the time being

[53] *P*, April 9, 1966.

we will merely note its immediate effects on the social composition of new recruits. The Twenty-Third Congress injunc-
tions about the continued priority for workers was reflected
in the 1966 recruitment figures, which showed that 46.8 percent of the new candidates were workers, compared with
45.3 percent in 1964 and 40.7 percent in 1956-1961 (see
p. 158). This increase was achieved, however, at the expense
of the peasants, who made up 12.6 percent of all recruits in
1966, as against 15.1 percent in 1964 and 22.7 percent in
1956-1961. The intelligentsia/white-collar category (including students "and others") supplied 40.6 percent of all recruits in 1966, compared with 39.6 percent in 1964 and 36.6
percent in 1956-1961.[54]

In 1967 the jubilee of the "proletarian revolution" was
seen as warranting some relaxation of the restrictions on enrollments and special efforts to maximize the proportion of
worker recruits. "In connection with preparations for the
fiftieth anniversary of Great October," reads a statement by
the Central Committee's Department of Organizational Party
Work, "there has been a strengthening of the aspirations of
advanced people in our society to link their lives organizationally with the communist party, to enter its ranks. In considering the applications to join the party [which] they have
been receiving, party organizations are ensuring a worthy reinforcement of the party on the basis of individual recruitment." In the first half of 1967, 339,000 candidates were enrolled, which represents an enlistment rate 30 percent higher
than in 1966, and 51.4 percent of them were classified as
workers.[55] There was every indication, however, that the
leadership intended to return to more restricted recruitment
when the jubilee was over.

[54] See *PZh*, No. 10, May 1965, pp. 9-10 and No. 7, April 1967,
pp. 7-8.
[55] *Ibid.*, No. 19, October 1967, pp. 11-12.

Chapter 10

A Party of the Whole People

GIVEN THE scale of admissions to the CPSU in the post-Stalin period, it is obvious that the marked changes in the social orientation of recruitment must have significantly modified the class composition of the party.

In CPSU statistics the concept of "social position" usually does service for that of class, and this is determined by "basic occupation at the time of joining the party." In previous chapters we have noted the difficulties of interpreting party "social position" breakdowns: the minor difficulty that we are unsure just where the line is drawn in certain borderline categories, such as junior supervisory personnel; and the major difficulty that occupation at the time of joining the party may bear little relation to the member's position in society during the greater part of his party career. Nonetheless, so long as these limitations are borne in mind, such breakdowns do give some idea of crude trends in the social composition of the party.

Analyses of the party membership in terms of "social position" have been published for the years 1956, 1961, 1964, 1966 and 1967 (see Table 21).[1] These show a sig-

[1] SOURCES: *BSE* (1st edn.), Vol. XI, col. 534; *PS*, No. 21, November 1932, p. 48; *PZh*, No. 1, January 1962, p. 47, No. 10, May 1965, p. 11 and No. 7, April 1967, p. 8; *P*, March 30, 1966. It is uncertain to which month the 1964 figures apply. It is also unknown whether the 1956 and subsequent figures are adjusted to take account of reclassifications of sections of the rural labor force. While no class breakdown of the party as a whole is available for the late Stalin period, such breakdowns were given for two of the smaller republics, Georgia and Kirgizia, in 1952. In Georgia 14.6 percent of the CPSU membership were classified as workers, 26.5 percent as kolkhozniks and

A PARTY OF THE WHOLE PEOPLE

TABLE 21: "SOCIAL POSITION" OF CPSU MEMBERSHIP, 1956-1967, COMPARED WITH 1924-1932

| | Percent of all members and candidates | | | | | | |
	Jan. 1924	Jan. 1930	July 1932	Jan. 1956	July 1961	1964	Jan. 1966	Jan. 1967
Workers	44.0	65.3	65.2	32.0	34.5	37.3	37.8	38.1
Peasants	28.8	20.2	26.9	17.1	17.5	16.5	16.2	16.0
White-collar workers and others	27.2	14.5	7.9	50.9	48.0	46.2	46.0	45.9

nificant decline in the proportion of the CPSU membership who had joined the party as white-collar workers/intelligentsia, and a rise in the proportion who had joined as (manual) workers. Both these trends, and particularly the former, tended to level out with the cut-back in recruitment after 1964. Relatively small changes—a rise at first, and then a decline—also occurred in the representation of peasants. Limited though their utility may be, these figures have the interest of being the first official class analyses of the party membership since the early 1930's. For the sake of comparison, therefore, we have included in Table 21 the figures for certain earlier years, which may serve as a reminder of the vast changes which took place in the social composition of the party during the Stalin era.

58.9 percent as white-collar workers / intelligentsia (*ZV*, September 18, 1952). In Kirgizia the figures were 25.2 percent, 31.8 percent and 41.4 percent respectively (*SK*, September 21, 1952). Both of these republics are predominantly agricultural, so the percentage of peasants was undoubtedly far above, and the percentage of workers below, the national average. However, these local breakdowns do not provide a basis for calculating the class composition of the party as a whole at this time.

[2] A glance at section 3A of the Bibliography is instructive in this regard.

Main Fields of Employment

Fortunately we do not have to rely exclusively on statistics of "social position" for our picture of how the CPSU membership was distributed through Soviet society in the post-Stalin period. Information about the current employment of party members, which had been extremely fragmentary since the 1930's, became steadily more abundant after 1953 and particularly after 1961.[2]

Percentage breakdowns of party members "employed in the national economy" (i.e. in regular civil employment) have been published for the years 1947, 1957, 1961, 1964, 1965 and 1967. These are assembled in Table 22.[3] For the years 1947, 1957 and 1967 absolute figures are also available for certain categories of employment, and by comparison of these with the percentages they represent one can calculate the absolute numbers in other categories, as well as the proportion of the total party membership not included in the breakdowns (i.e. not in regular civil employment).

[2] A glance at section 3A of the Bibliography is instructive in this regard.

[3] SOURCES: *PZh*, No. 1, January 1962, p. 50, No. 10, May 1965, p. 14, No. 7, April 1967, p. 8 and No. 19, October 1967, p. 17; *K*, No. 18, December 1964, p. 59. The agriculture category includes forestry. It is unknown whether fishing is included under industry or agriculture. Category 4 includes retail and wholesale trade, "material-technical supply and procurement" and agricultural procurement, as well as public catering. Category 6 is listed as "organs of state and economic administration and the apparatus of party and voluntary organizations." In the 1961 breakdown category 7 is shown as "communal economy [i.e. civic services] and other fields." In the breakdowns for 1947, 1957 and 1967 category 7 is split into two: other branches of material production (1.8, 0.4 and 1.1 percent respectively) and housing, communal economy and personal services (1.0, 1.2, and 1.3 percent respectively). For comparison of trends in one particular republic, see *KP Kirgizii*, pp. 245, 274. The absolute figures (for industry, construction, transport and agriculture) are in *PZh*, No. 19, October 1967, p. 17.

TABLE 22: COMMUNISTS IN CIVIL EMPLOYMENT, 1947, 1957, 1961, 1964, 1965, 1967

Field of employment	Percentage of all employed communists					
	Jan. 1947	Jan. 1957	July 1961	Jan. 1964	Jan. 1965	Jan. 1967
1. Industry and construction	28.5	32.6	33.5	35.4	35.9	36.6
2. Transport and communications	9.3	10.1	9.2	9.2	9.2	9.0
3. Agriculture	23.4	23.6	23.3	22.7	22.6	22.2
4. Trade and materials-handling	6.4	5.0	5.4	4.9	4.7	4.4
5. Science, education, health, culture	11.1	12.8	15.6	16.3	16.5	16.5
6. Government, economic and party bureaucracy, etc.	18.5	14.3	10.8	9.5	9.1	8.9
7. Other fields	2.8	1.6	2.2	2.0	2.0	2.4

The principal trends revealed by Table 22 are an increasing proportion of party members employed in industry and construction and in science, education, health and culture and a decreasing proportion employed in the government, party and other bureaucracies. Further points emerge when one allows for that part of the membership not in civil employment, who accounted for about one-quarter of all members and candidates in 1947 and one-sixth in 1957 and 1967, the reduction probably being due to a fall in the number of communists in the armed forces and police agencies. Since the percentages shown in the table for 1947 represent a smaller proportion of the total party membership than those for 1957-1967, one may deduce that the share of categories 1 (industry and construction) and 5 (science, education, etc.) increased faster between 1947 and 1957 than is suggested by the table, while that of category 6 (the bureaucracies) declined *more slowly* than suggested. By the same token one may deduce a substantial increase in the proportion of party members employed in agriculture in 1957 as compared with

327

1947, which the table fails to bring out.[4] As we saw in the previous chapter much stress has been placed during the 1960's on building up the proportion of the party employed in "material production" (categories 1-4 and part of category 7 in Table 22). This is another point on which one needs to allow for the changing numbers of party members not in civil employment in order to get an accurate picture of trends. In fact, the proportion of communists employed in "material production" appears to have been 51 percent in 1947, 59 percent in 1957 and 61 percent in 1967. Thus the progress achieved on this point in the early Khrushchev period subsequently dwindled to insignificance, suggesting that the attention paid to it during the 1960's may have been actuated by a concern to prevent an actual decline rather than any real expectation of effecting a further substantial increase.

We shall now examine the principal occupational groups in the party since 1953 in closer detail, and attempt at the end of this chapter to summarize the occupational composition of the CPSU as it stood on the eve of the 50th anniversary of the October Revolution.

Industry

Communists engaged in industry (including manufacturing and mining, construction, transport and communications) increased their numbers by about a third (876,000) between January 1956 and July 1961, thus roughly keeping pace with the overall growth of the party in these years.[5]

---

[4] The postwar expansion of party membership on the farms was still under way in 1947. Subsequently there may have been some decline before a further sharp expansion in the early post-Stalin years.

[5] *PZh*, No. 1, January 1962, p. 50. In some branches, including construction and construction-materials, tool- and instrument-making, chemicals and electrical and radio equipment, the growth was far above the general industrial average.

Between 1961 and 1967 they increased from 42.7 to 45.6 percent of all communists in the national economy. Substantial changes took place in the size and composition of enterprise cells (see Table 23).[6] Fragmentary data from the late

TABLE 23: INDUSTRIAL PARTY ORGANIZATIONS, 1956-1965—SIZE OF ORGANIZATIONS AND PROPORTION OF WORKER MEMBERS

Type of enterprise	Average size of organizations			Percent of workers in organizations		
	1956	1961	1965	1956	1961	1965
Industry	38	61	78	46.0	53.3	53.5
Construction	26	39	42	42.2	52.2	52.5
Transport				52.2	61.0	62.6

Stalin period suggest that managerial, technological and office employees normally constituted at least half the membership of industrial party organizations.[7] This was still the situation in 1956. Within the next five years, however, there was a substantial increase in the proportion of workers in these

[6] SOURCES: *PZh*, No. 1, January 1962, pp. 51, 54, No. 10, May 1965, pp. 14, 17.

[7] Of the 1,675 communists employed in the machine-tool industry of Baku in 1945, 55 percent were workers. The context indicates that this was higher than average (see *PS*, Nos. 3-4, February 1945, p. 19). Of the industrial employees who joined the party in Moscow between 1949 and 1951, 52 percent were production workers (*MP*, March 31, 1951). However, promotions consequent on joing the party make it probable that the percentage of workers among all communists in enterprise organizations was less than the percentage among their recruits. Moscow, moreover, was an area of higher than average worker recruitment. In the Chkalov oblast in 1955 only 4,000 of the 11,000 communists in industrial jobs were employed "in the decisive sectors of actual production." In one large mill only 36 of the 207 communists worked on the factory floor. In construction 470 out of the 1,000 communists were working "directly in production" (*PZh*, No. 17, September 1955, p. 25).

329

organizations, ranging from 7 percent in industry proper to 10 percent in construction. Between 1961 and 1965 there was little further change, indicating that white-collar staff shared almost on equal terms with workers in the growth of industrial party organizations during these years. Meanwhile there was a sharp increase in the average size of party organizations, which began to level out, however, after 1961. Unfortunately we have no information on the proportion of worker members of industrial cells who exercised minor supervisory responsibilities. Nor have we any breakdown into trades or into degrees of skill, although on the latter score educational data affords us some clues (see pp. 408-410).

Agriculture

Turning now to agriculture, we may note first that the small decline in the ratio of party members in this field between 1961 and 1965, which we observed in Table 22, followed a somewhat larger rise in the preceding years. In 1954, 21.8 percent of communists employed in the national economy were working in agriculture, in 1956, 22.6 percent, in 1961, 23.3 percent, in 1965, again 22.6 percent and in 1967, 22.2 percent.[8] These changes reflect alterations in the pattern of recruitment which we have already discussed.

The concern and publicity devoted to agricultural problems in the post-Stalin era resulted in more statistical information being revealed about communists employed in this field than in any other. Between 1953 and 1967 the number of CPSU members and candidates working in agricultural enterprises increased from 1.2 millions to 2.3 millions (see Table 24).[9] At the same time there was a marked shift in the

[8] *Ibid.*, No. 1, January 1962, p. 51, No. 10, May 1965, p. 14 and No. 7, April 1967, p. 8.

[9] SOURCES: Figures given in the following sources, or based on comparisons of data provided in these sources; *PZh*, No. 1, January

distribution of party members as between the two main kinds of agricultural enterprise. The number of communists on the state farms multiplied sevenfold over this period, whereas in the kolkhozes the increase was only 60 percent, despite the influx of some 200,000 communist farm machinery operators after the abolition of the MTS's in 1958. The state farms' share of the farming section of the party membership rose from one-tenth to over a third.

In September 1953 there were still something like one-fifth of Soviet collective farms which had no party organization. By 1958 there were hardly any.[10] Four factors contributed to this result: (a) the transfer to the kolkhozes of some tens of thousands of communists from the towns and from rural administrative posts;[11] (b) recruitment; (c) enlargement of the farms through further amalgamations;[12] (d) abolition of the MTS's in 1958. The Stavropol krai was one area where all 171 of its kolkhozes possessed party organizations by 1958. After the transfer of farm machinery operators the number of kolkhoz communists in the krai jumped from

---

1962, pp. 51-54, No. 10, May 1965, pp. 15-17 and No. 19, October 1967, p. 17; N. S. Khrushchev, *Stroitel'stvo kommunizma v SSSR i razvitie sel'skogo khoziaistva* (Moscow, 1962), Vol. 1, pp. 8, 281, Vol. 3, pp. 427-428.

[10] *Ibid.*, Vol. 3, pp. 427-428.

[11] On the role of the so-called thirty-thousanders as a stimulus to the growth of rural party organizations in 1955-1958, see A. N. Karamelev, "Dvizhenie tridtsatitysiachnikov i ukreplenie kolkhozov" (The Thirty-Thousanders Movement and the Strengthening of the Kolkhozes), *V I KPSS*, No. 1, 1962, p. 125.

[12] The number of kolkhozes was reduced from 93,300 at the end of 1953, to 69,100 at the end of 1958 and to 39,500 at the end of 1963 (*Narodnoe khoziaistvo SSSR v 1961 godu: statisticheskii ezhegodnik*, p. 291 and *Narodnoe khoziaistvo SSSR v 1963 godu: statisticheskii ezhegodnik*, p. 226). This was partly due to the transformation of collective into state farms, but mainly to the amalgamation of farms. The average number of households per kolkhoz increased from 220 in 1953 to 411 in 1963.

TABLE 24: PARTY MEMBERSHIP IN FARMS, 1953-1967

Date	Membership of farm and MTS organizations				Communists working in agriculture			
	Kolkhozes	State farms	MTS	Total	Kolkhozes	State farms	Others	Total
Sept. 1953	825,000 -900,000							1,190,000
Feb. 1954	930,000	130,000	240,000	1,300,000				
Jan. 1956	1,040,000	145,000			817,000	120,000	353,000	1,290,000
Jan. 1957					931,340	132,762	378,469	1,442,571
Dec. 1958	1,350,000							
July 1961	1,400,000	665,000		2,065,000		557,800		1,790,000
Jan. 1962					1,154,045	578,516	107,740	1,840,301
Jan. 1963					1,193,259	622,680	124,875	1,940,814
Jan. 1964					1,229,945	668,440	137,188	2,035,573
Jan. 1965	1,530,000	905,000		2,435,000	1,285,077	733,710	145,468	2,164,255
Jan. 1967					1,330,316	837,543	168,553	2,336,412

7,570 to 9,746. By this time only two farm organizations had less than 15 communists, while almost half of them had over 50.[13] Special efforts were devoted to building up party numbers in the rural areas of the Western borderlands, where they still lagged well behind the rest of the country. In Belorussia, for example, the proportion of kolkhozes with party organizations rose from 51 percent in September 1953 to 92 percent in December 1955 and to 100 percent in December 1958.[14] Despite these efforts, there were still pockets of the U.S.S.R. where many kolkhozes lacked party organizations; in Lithuania such farms numbered 535 (almost a third of the total) in 1956,[15] and still over 400 in 1960.[16] During the next two years there appears to have been a drive to eliminate these pockets of backwardness, and by the beginning of 1962 all but about 200 of the country's 41,000 kolkhozes possessed their own party organizations.[17]

Parallel with this there was a striking growth in the size of farm party organizations, substantially exceeding the growth in any other major field. The average membership of kolkhoz organizations increased from 13 in January 1956 to 34 in July 1961 and to 40 in 1965, while that of state farm organizations grew from 25 to 74 to 78 respectively.[18] It is worthy

[13] *K*, No. 10, 1958, p. 55.
[14] *KPB v bor'be za dal'neishee razvitie narodnogo khoziaistva respubliki v poslevoennye gody* (Minsk, 1961), pp. 206-207. For data on Estonia see *SE*, January 1, 1956 and January 29, 1958, and for the Ukraine see *PZh*, No. 12, June 1958, p. 20.
[15] *S Lit*, January 26, 1956.
[16] *P*, March 4, 1960.
[17] At the end of 1961 the number of kolkhozes was 41,300 (to the nearest hundred), of which 40,500 were farming collectives and the rest fishing collectives (*Narodnoe khoziaistvo SSSR v 1961 godu*, p. 291). On January 1, 1962 there were 41,119 kolkhoz party organizations (*PZh*, No. 10, May 1965, p. 16).
[18] *PZh*, No. 1, January 1962, p. 54 and No. 10, May 1965, p. 17.

of note that again the main improvement took place in the latter 1950's, with the early 1960's figuring more as a period of consolidation.

There were also substantial changes in the relative weight of different occupational groups within the farm organizations. In 1948 kolkhoz communists were employed as follows:[19]

	percent
Kolkhoz chairmen	13.8
Heads of livestock departments	4.7
Brigade leaders	10.1
Farm machinery operators	5.4
Other farm workers (including team leaders)	47.9
Miscellaneous (including specialists, store and office personnel)	18.1

Unfortunately no equivalent breakdowns were published in the post-Stalin period, but these figures nonetheless provide some basis for comparison. By 1956 the proportion of chairmen among kolkhoz communists had fallen to about 10 percent and by 1965 to about 3 percent.[20] Meanwhile the pro-

[19] *Ibid.*, No. 5, March 1948, p. 21. In Moldavia, of the 6,707 villagers who joined the party between the end of the war and January 1952, 680 were kolkhoz chairmen, 1,076 brigade leaders, 1,165 team leaders and 390 heads of livestock farms. Thus farm supervisory personnel accounted for half the total. What proportion were village soviet officials, teachers, storekeepers and other non-farming personnel was not stated. There were 1,034 tractor drivers and farm machinery operators. See *Ocherki istorii Kommunisticheskoi Partii Moldavii*, p. 357.

[20] Calculated on the basis of the number of kolkhozes and the percentage whose chairmen were party members. The latter rose from 80 percent in 1953 to 91 percent in 1956 and to 94 percent in 1959. By 1965 there could have been very few kolkhoz chairmen who were not in the party (see *Sel'skoe khoziaistvo SSSR: statisticheskii sbornik* (Moscow, 1960), p. 474).

334

portion of farm machinery operators rose to about 20 percent in 1961[21] and to 25 percent in 1965.[22] This graphically indicates the main trend in the composition of kolkhoz party organizations after 1953, which was away from the kolkhoz office and out into the fields. A further illustration of the same trend is provided by Table 25,[23] which compares kolkhoz communists in "nonproductive" posts with those "directly engaged in production." The latter are shown as rising from two-thirds to five-sixths of all kolkhoz communists between 1956 and 1965. The data on which this table is based, unfortunately, gives no information on the ratio of supervisory to nonsupervisory personnel among those "directly engaged in production." Undoubtedly a large proportion of the communists in production brigades are brigade leaders, and those in livestock are heads of kolkhoz livestock sectors.[24] Furthermore, the sharp reduction of peasant recruit-

[21] *PZh*, No. 1, January 1962, p. 51.

[22] *Ibid.*, No. 10, May 1965, p. 15.

[23] SOURCES: *Ibid.*, and No. 1, January 1962, pp. 51-52. The following breakdown was given of kolkhozniks joining the party in 1964 (*ibid.*, No. 10, May 1965, p. 10).

Occupation	Number	Percent
Fieldwork, fruit and vegetable growing	22,729	22.4
Livestock	19,514	19.2
Farm machinery operators	40,731	40.1
Other production brigades	2,510	2.5
Agronomists and other specialists	6,491	6.4
Others	9,578	9.4
Total	101,553	100

[24] In 1965 there were about 450,000 communists in kolkhoz production brigades and 250,000 in livestock sectors. In 1959 the kolkhozes contained 283,000 production brigades and 126,000 livestock sectors (*Sel'skoe khoziaistvo SSSR: statisticheskii sbornik*, p. 471; by 1965 the numbers were probably somewhat less). This means there was an average of two communists per livestock sector or production brigade. It should hardly surprise us that in many

335

TABLE 25: Composition of Kolkhoz Party Organizations, 1956-1965

Nature of work	Percent of all kolkhozniks		
	1956	1961	1965
Fieldwork, fruit and vegetable growing			30.7
Livestock			17.9
Farm machinery operators		20*	25.1
Other production brigades			3.7
Agronomists and other specialists	3*	5*	5.3
Total "directly engaged in production"	66.7	77.4	82.7
Administrative and other "nonproduction" work (incl. pensioners)	33.3	22.6	17.3

* Approximation

ment in the 1960's must have slowed down the trend towards more production workers, and may even have reversed it. Little has been published on the employment of state farm communists. Our only concrete data are that in

cases one of these two was the livestock sector head or brigade leader, while many other communists in kolkhoz production sectors held minor supervisory jobs such as team leader or timekeeper. Of the 20,-000 communists transferred to the collective farms in the Ukraine following the January 1961 Central Committee plenum, 1,500 became farm chairmen, while 11,000 were appointed as brigade or team leaders or heads of livestock sectors (*PU*, September 29, 1961). Meanwhile an analysis of collective and state farm party organizations in one oblast of Uzbekistan showed that most of the communists in field brigades were brigade leaders or timekeepers (B. A. Tulepbaev, *Kompartiia Uzbekistana v bor'be za krutoi pod''ëm sel'skogo khoziaistva*, p. 122). In Belorussia in 1958 about a third of the heads of kolkhoz livestock sectors and a quarter of the field brigade leaders were party members or candidates, and the proportion had undoubtedly risen by 1965 (*KPB v bor'be za dal'neishee razvitie narodnogo khoziaistva respubliki v poslevoennye gody*, pp. 239-240). At a conservative estimate, at least a half of the communists in collective and state farm production sectors have held supervisory responsibilities of some kind.

336

1962 about 24 percent of them were farm machinery operators, and in 1965, 27 percent.[25]

White-Collar/Intelligentsia Groups

We have already noted one important post-Stalin development touching the white-collar sections of the party membership: their numbers first showed a considerable decline relative to manual workers, both urban and rural, and then recovered substantially after the Twenty-Second Congress. A second development relates to changing ratios within the white-collar "class." This may be roughly summarized as a marked trend in favor of professionally trained specialists and at the expense of line officials and clerical staff. We have already noted that the percentage of communists employed in education, health services and the arts steadily increased in the post-Stalin era, while the percentage working in the party-state bureaucracy declined (see p. 327). In our discussion of kolkhoz party organizations, we saw evidence of a reduced representation of administrative and office staff, and some increase in the representation of agricultural specialists (see p. 336). Another fact which is probably related to the same trend is that between 1956 and 1961 the proportion of communists in industry who were employed at administrative levels higher than the plant management (that is in economic councils, ministries, trusts, directorates, etc.) sank from 130 per 1,000 to 46 per 1,000.[26] Table 26,[27] which gives a break-

[25] Calculated from figures in *PZh*, No. 10, May 1965, p. 15, where it was also stated that "in the party organizations of the state farms the majority of communists are also [i.e. as in the kolkhozes] working in the decisive production sectors."

[26] *Ibid.*, No. 1, January 1962, p. 51.

[27] *Ibid.*, p. 48, No. 10, May 1965, p. 11 and No. 19, October 1967, p. 13. Category 1 is shown in the sources as "leaders of organizations, institutions, enterprises, state farms and their structural subdivisions." In the 1962 source category 4 specifically included

337

down of communists classified by "social position" as white-collar workers (*sluzhashchie*) offers a more general illustration of this trend. In considering this table, it should be borne in mind that it is not based on complete figures for the employment categories represented since it excludes persons classified by "social position" as workers or peasants who were promoted to white-collar posts after joining the party; such persons probably became less numerous over the period, because of rising educational requirements in numerous classes of work, and there was undoubtedly a higher proportion of them among line officials and office staff than among other white-collar/intelligentsia groups. With this qualification, a comparison of categories 1 and 2 with categories 4 and 5 in Table 26 provides some measure of the trend from "bureaucrats" to "specialists" among the CPSU's white-collar members. Between 1956 and 1965 the former fell from 27.4 percent to 18.6 percent, while the latter rose from 38.9 percent to 55.8 percent. Between 1965 and 1967, however, there was no further reduction in the proportion of line administrators and executives.

Communists Not Employed in the Economy

So far we have been concerned mainly with that part of the CPSU membership which is "employed in the national economy." This still leaves, however, something like one-sixth of the party membership, or over two million members and candidates in 1967. Practically no official information is forthcoming about this section of the membership, and the

---

architects and economists, and category 6 was shown as "Other white-collar workers" (communications, communal economy, etc.). The latter probably includes a sizeable number of police and possibly military as well. Category 3 includes public catering. The 1967 data did not give separate percentages for "control, records and clerical staff" and "others."

338

TABLE 26: OCCUPATIONAL CHANGES AMONG WHITE-COLLAR COM-
MUNISTS, 1956-1967

Field of employment	Percent of all white-collar communists			
	Jan. 1956	July 1961	Jan. 1965	Jan. 1967
1. Line administrators and executives	14.2	10.2	7.8	7.9
2. Control, records and clerical staff	13.2	11.9	10.8	
3. Trade and materials-handling	4.7	4.9	5.8	5.5
4. Engineers, technologists, agricultural specialists	20.1	29.2	32.5	34.9
5. Science, education, health, arts	18.8	21.5	23.3	23.6
6. Others	29.1	22.3	19.8	

researcher is obliged to use roundabout methods to arrive at some estimate of its composition. It undoubtedly consists largely of members of the armed forces, pensioners and students, probably in that order of numerical importance. Apart from these, we are left with two large groups of the population, namely dependent housewives of working age (over eleven millions in 1959)[28] and members of kolkhoz families working full time on family plots (nearly ten millions in 1959),[29] and one smaller group, namely household servants and personal chauffeurs. Although the life-styles of these groups are more or less in conflict with the concept of the party member, they undoubtedly include some party members (and especially, perhaps, the housewives), who par-

[28] *Itogi vsesoiuznoi perepisi naseleniia 1959 goda: SSSR*, p. 99. No figures have been discovered on the proportion of housewives in the party membership since the party census of 1927, when 1.4 percent of the candidates and 0.5 percent of the full members were housewives. See *Kommunisty v sostave apparata gosuchrezhdenii i obshchestvennykh organizatsii* (Moscow, 1929), p. 10.
[29] *Itogi vsesoiuznoi perepisi naseleniia 1959 goda: SSSR*, p. 96.

ticipate in the party's functions mainly by activity in voluntary public organizations.

The number of military representatives attending party congresses suggests a method of calculating how many communists there are in the armed forces. On this basis the number has been estimated at 580,000 in January 1956[30] and 700,000 in October 1961.[31] While the possibility cannot be excluded that military representation at congresses is deliberately manipulated so as to conceal the actual proportion of party members in the armed forces, this is unlikely. One indication that figures of the order just quoted are, at least, not gross underestimates, is the report that 23 percent of the 640,000 demobilized from the army on the eve of the Twentieth Congress were communists.[32] Since a large proportion of these would have joined the party in the course of their military service, the *average* party "saturation" of the armed forces must have been far less than this, i.e. totaling well under a million. It is unlikely, therefore, that we will be going far wrong if we accept the estimates just quoted as approximately correct.

The growth of party membership in the armed forces between 1956 and 1961 was thus quite impressive if one allows for the considerable cuts in the Soviet army in this period. An important factor here was the drive to strengthen party influence in the army after the removal of Marshal

[30] See A. Avtorkhanov, "Politicheskie itogi XX s"ezda KPSS i perspektivy kollektivnogo rukovodstva" (Political Results of the Twentieth CPSU Congress and the Perspectives for Collective Leadership), *Vestnik Instituta po izucheniiu SSSR*, No. 2, 1956, p. 7.

[31] See Nikolai Galay, "The Soviet Armed Forces and the Twenty-Second Party Congress," *Bulletin* (Institute for the Study of the USSR), Vol. IX, No. 1 (January), 1962, p. 4.

[32] *P*, February 17, 1956.

Zhukov in October 1957. In 1958-1959 the party recruited 60 percent more candidates in the armed forces than in 1956-1957,[33] compared with a 38 percent increase in recruitment in the party at large. This growth continued, and led to two developments which we learned in Chapter Six to expect in periods of rapid party expansion in the armed forces. Party organizations at company level were reestablished; in 1957 only a third of all company-level units had party organizations, in 1960, two-thirds,[34] and by 1963, all of them.[35] And meanwhile there was a sharp increase in the ratio of N.C.O.'s and enlisted men among army communists: between 1957 and 1960 this ratio increased twofold in the case of the former and almost fivefold in the case of the latter. Even then, however, only 10.5 percent of military and naval communists were N.C.O.'s and 4.3 percent were enlisted men.[36] Thus officers still accounted for about six-sevenths of all communists in the armed forces. In 1964, 65 percent of all platoon commanders were communists and 90 percent of all

[33] Petrov, *Partiinoe stroitel'stvo*, p. 475. In 1959 the number of communists in the army and navy was said to have increased by 8 percent (*ibid.*).

[34] *Ibid.*, pp. 475-476.

[35] A. A. Epishev, "O vozrastaiushchei roli KPSS v rukovodstve Vooruzhënnymi Silami" (On the Growing Role of the CPSU in the Leadership of the Armed Forces), *V I KPSS*, No. 2, 1963, p. 13. See also P. Efimov, "Sviazi armii i naroda nerazryvny" (The Links of the Army and the People Are Indissoluble," *PZh*, No. 3, February 1962, p. 13.

[36] Petrov, *Partiinoe stroitel'stvo*, p. 475. This implies that in 1957 a mere 5 or 6 percent of military communists were N.C.O.'s and under 1 percent were enlisted men! The increased representation of nonofficers seems to have been greatest in line units. By 1964, 30 to 40 percent of the party members in such units were said to be N.C.O.'s and enlisted men. See N. Egorov, "Armiia i formirovanie novogo cheloveka" (The Army and the Forming of the New Man), *PZh*, No. 9, May 1964, p. 33.

company and battery commanders.[37] At higher levels the party saturation must have been virtually complete.

When the Twenty-Third Congress convened in March 1966 there were 352 military delegates, representing approximately 890,000 party members and candidates.[38] As at previous congresses, these military delegates were stated to include in addition to regular army and navy personnel, representatives of the border guards, who may more accurately be regarded as militarized police. Whether they also included delegates from other branches of the political police (who also carry military ranks) is unknown. This raises the difficult question of police representation in the CPSU. Guesses at the total size of all branches of the political police range from half a million to a million, indicating the lack of reliable information on this question. The majority are probably party members, but, understandably, no official breakdowns of the membership have ever grouped police personnel in a separate category. A substantial proportion are undoubtedly shown under "military," others are probably categorized as

[37] I. P. Prusinov, "Povyshenie vliianiia partii v Vooruzhënnykh Silakh" (Increasing the Party's Influence in the Armed Forces), *V I KPSS*, No. 2, 1965, p. 11. At the same time the official magazine of the Chief Political Directorate of the Armed Forces spoke critically of "units where they try to get every single officer into the party at all costs." See Petr Kruzhin, in *Bulletin* (Institute for the Study of the U.S.S.R.), Vol. XII, No. 11 (November), 1965, p. 51. The fact that a third of the platoon commanders remained outside the party is accounted for by the youth of most of these junior officers. There is little doubt that the great majority of nonparty platoon commanders were still komsomol members. In 1962 some 90 percent of all officers were in either the party *or the komsomol* (see *P*, October 25, 1962).

[38] *XXIII S"ezd Kommunisticheskoi Partii Sovetskogo Soiuza 29 marta-8 aprelia 1966 goda: stenografickeskii otchët* (23rd Congress of the CPSU—29 March-8 April 1966: Stenographic Report), Vol. I, p. 283.

state officials, others again (including undercover agents) may be distributed among various categories—industry, culture, etc. The miscellaneous, unclassified members shown in most breakdowns probably also include police personnel. Our ignorance as to the number of police communists therefore has the effect of distorting our picture of certain other categories, especially the military and the government bureaucracy, up to a quarter of whom may be employees of various police agencies.

In 1959 there were over twelve million Soviet citizens dependent on state pensions as their sole or principal source of income.[39] These included certain groups, such as retired military and naval officers and persons severely incapacitated in World War II, who probably contained a fairly high proportion of party members.[40] In the largest group, however, the old-age pensioners, party saturation was probably rather low, firstly because these people spent their youth and early middle age (when the CPSU takes in most of its recruits) at a time when recruitment was at a lower level than later, and secondly because of the high wastage rate of party members (due to heavy expulsions and a death rate higher than that of the population at large), especially between 1933 and 1945. In 1967, 23 percent of the party membership was aged over 50.[41] If the age distribution curve were the same in the party as in the adult population at large, this would imply about 10 to 11 percent over the retiring age of 60 for men and 55 for women. As we have just noted, however, the curve

[39] *Itogi vsesoiuznoi perepisi naseleniia 1959 goda: SSSR*, p. 96.

[40] For a breakdown into different kinds of pension, see *Narodnoe khoziaistvo SSSR v 1963 godu; statisticheskii ezhegodnik*, p. 513. This, however, includes all persons in receipt of pensions, irrespective of the degree of their dependence on their pension, and is therefore of limited value for our purposes.

[41] *PZh*, No. 19, October 1967, p. 16.

probably dipped more sharply among communists than non-communists, and in addition a considerable proportion of communists aged over 60 were doubtless still working. In Uzbekistan the proportion of party members aged over 60 rose from 2 percent in 1955 to 3.1 percent in 1959 to 4.2 percent in 1964.[42] Since the proportion aged over 50 was about one-seventh lower than in the CPSU as a whole, the percentage of all CPSU members over retiring age was probably higher than this, but is unlikely to have been much over 5 percent.

In the middle of World War II, 7 percent of all communists in the Kirov oblast were pensioners, housewives and other nonemployed persons (apart from students).[43] If one allows for half the CPSU membership being in the armed forces and assumes the Kirov figures to have been roughly typical of other civilian party organizations, these groups would appear to have accounted for 3 to 4 percent of the total party membership at this time. However, during the war, there was, of course, great pressure on all persons capable of working to join the labor force, so the peacetime figure would undoubtedly have been greater. Moreover, the proportion of older people in the party has considerably increased since then (see p. 354). By subtracting our estimates of other groups from the total party membership in the mid-1960's, we are left with a residue of 7 to 9 percent for all these nonemployed groups other than students. There is supporting evidence for a percentage of this order from Latvia, where these categories made up 9.3 percent of the party membership in 1962.[44] The estimate for these groups most

[42] See *KP Uzbekistana v tsifrakh*, pp. 142, 162, 189.
[43] See *Kirovskaia oblastnaia partiinaia organizatsiia v gody Velikoi Otechestvennoi voiny*, p. 284.
[44] *Kommunist Sovetskoi Latvii*, No. 7, July 1962, p. 61.

consistent with our other data and calculations would be about 900,000 in 1965. Perhaps two-thirds of these were pensioners, and the majority of the remainder were housewives, including wives of kolkhoz members.

No data is available on the number of full-time students in the party since the early 1930's. In 1927, 5.1 percent of all communists were students[45] and in 1932, 7.5 percent.[46] A large proportion of these, however, were communists of mature years attending courses of secondary education, and this has now long been a thing of the past.[47] In 1933, 22 percent of the 491,000 students in higher educational establishments (VUZ'es) were in the CPSU.[48] This represented something over 2 percent of the party membership. Subsequently, however, the proportion of younger communists, of the age groups now providing most VUZ students, has greatly declined (see pp. 354-355), while on the other hand VUZ students now constitute about four times the proportion of Soviet adults that they did in 1933. These changes were certainly the most important ones affecting the percentage of CPSU members who were students, and they may have more or less canceled each other out, but we would not be justified in assuming this.

Fortunately, annual figures are available on the number of students among the CPSU membership in one union republic, namely, Uzbekistan. Since these show levels of student representation very close to the all-CPSU levels during the

[45] *Kommunisty v sostave apparata gosuchrezhdenii i obshchestven-nykh organizatsii*, p. 10.

[46] *PS,* No. 21, November 1932, p. 46.

[47] On the effects of the falling age levels of students on the party "saturation" of the student body during the 1930's, see V. V. Ukraintsev, *KPSS—Organizator revoliutsionnogo preobrazovaniia vysshei shkoly* (Moscow, 1963), pp. 240, 243-244.

[48] *XVII S"ezd*, p. 528.

late 1920's and early 1930's, it seems reasonable to suppose that they were also not very different in later years, when figures for the CPSU as a whole are not available, especially as local differences in social structure have tended to narrow, rather than widen.

The Uzbek figures show a sharp drop in the proportion of party members who were on full-time courses, from 7 to 8 percent in the early 1930's to 2.3 to 2.7 percent in the period 1937-1941. This was undoubtedly due to the reorientation in party recruitment policies: instead of getting its qualified members by recruiting workers and then sending them to secondary and tertiary training, the party was now concentrating on recruiting the products of the burgeoning Soviet technical and professional training program. During the war the proportion of Uzbek communists on study courses contracted sharply, but then soon returned to prewar levels, fluctuating between 2.2 and 2.5 percent of the republic's party membership in the years 1949-1955. The mass recruitment of the Khrushchev era had the effect of reducing this percentage: it declined steadily to 1.1 percent in 1961, but then began to increase again, reaching 1.4 percent in 1964.[49]

If the levels and trends of student representation in Uzbekistan were still close to those in the party as a whole, this would indicate a total of about 200,000 students among the CPSU's 12.7 million communists in 1967.[50] Supporting

[49] KP Uzbekistana v tsifrakh, pp. 20, 25, 36, 43, 45, 47, 50, 55, 58, 61, 67, 71, 75, 79, 83, 87, 92, 97, 102, 107, 111, 116, 122, 127, 132, 137, 142, 147, 152, 157, 162, 167, 172, 177, 182, 188.

[50] It is easier to point to factors which might tend to make the proportion of students in the Uzbek party membership differ from that in the CPSU as a whole than to estimate the effect of such factors. At the time of the 1959 census the proportion of the adult population who were students was considerably higher in Uzbekistan than in the country at large (see Itogi perepisi naseleniia 1959 goda:

346

evidence is forthcoming from Latvia (an area of relatively low membership), where 1.1 percent of all communists in 1962 were students, i.e. the same percentage as in Uzbekistan in 1961.[51] Nonetheless, the very approximate character of this estimate must be stressed.

Employment of Party Membership in 1967

The foregoing discussion may be summarized by essaying a breakdown of how the whole party membership was employed in 1967, and this we do in Table 27. These figures are not all offered with equal confidence. Official absolute figures are available only for categories 6-11 of our table, and these are reproduced here rounded to the nearest thousand. Percentages only are available for categories 1-5 and 12, but fairly precise numerical equivalents may be calculated. As for categories 13-16, all that we can be reasonably confident about is their combined total, while the distribution between them must be regarded as a rough approximation. The figure for category 13 (armed forces) is probably fairly well grounded, but the other three are little more than informed guesses.

There remain some tantalizing gaps. We know something of the relative numbers of line executives, experts and office personnel in the party at large, but we have few clues as to how these are distributed through the various fields of employment. We do not know how many communists are em-

---

SSR, pp. 54-55; *Narodnoe khoziaistvo SSSR v 1963 godu: statisticheskii ezhegodnik*, pp. 569, 572) probably because of the younger age structure of the population and because students from other Central Asia republics also come to study in Tashkent. This, however, would need to be set against other factors, such as the influence of national, geographical and economic differences on the social composition of the party membership.

[51] See *Kommunist Sovetskoi Latvii*, No. 7, July 1962, p. 61.

TABLE 27: OCCUPATIONAL COMPOSITION OF CPSU, 1967

Field of employment	Number	Percent
1. Government, economic, party etc. bureaucracies[52]	936,000	7.4
2. Science, education, health, culture	1,740,000	13.7
3. Trade and materials-handling	463,000	3.7
4. Housing, civic and personal services	136,000	1.1
5. Communications	109,000	.9
6. Transport	838,000	6.6
7. Industry	3,196,000	25.2
8. Construction	666,000	5.2
9. Kolkhozes	1,330,000	10.5
10. State farms	838,000	6.6
11. Miscellaneous agricultural and related branches	166,000	1.3
12. Other branches of economy	116,000	.9
13. Armed forces (including border guards)	890,000	7.0
14. Pensioners	760,000	6.0
15. Students	200,000	1.6
16. Housewives and miscellaneous	300,000	2.3
Total	12,684,000	100.0

ployed in various police agencies, and where they fit into our occupational breakdown. We know approximately how many communists work on the factory floor and out in the fields of collective and state farms, but cannot say what proportion of these bear supervisory responsibilities. Despite such gaps in our information, however, we now have a fuller picture of how the CPSU membership is employed than at any time since the first Five Year Plan. Some of the implications of this picture will be considered in a later chapter.

[52] Little hard data is available on the number of Communists employed in the party bureaucracy itself. Western estimates for the late Stalin era range about 200,000 to 250,000, and there has probably been some contraction since then. See Armstrong, *Totalitarianism*, pp. 325-326 and Fainsod, *How Russia Is Ruled*, pp. 205-207.

Part Two

Some Special Aspects

Chapter 11

Turnover, Age and Sex

Turnover

A BASIC consideration in relating any elite formation to the social or political system in which it functions is its stability of size and composition. For most of its history the CPSU has been marked by a very low level of membership stability, although this position has been considerably modified since World War II. Wars, purges and a series of recruitment campaigns, each more massive than the last, have combined to produce a situation where at any one time recent recruits have usually formed a majority of the membership, while the proportion of survivors from earlier phases of recruitment has dropped drastically with each successive phase.

In the course of 1919 the party halved its membership and then doubled it again. In the next two years it was doubled once more, only to fall by a third in 1921-1923. The following decade saw an eightfold increase. In 1933-1938 it was again halved, and in 1938-1941 again doubled. There was an even greater turnover during World War II. The years 1947-1954 were the only period of relatively little movement. In 1955-1965 the membership again almost doubled. Taking the membership in January 1919 as 1, the index rose by 1921 to 3, by 1933 to 14, by 1945 to 23, by 1956 to 28, and by 1966 to 50.

In 1922 over 40 percent of the CPSU membership were recruits of the previous two years. At the time of the 1927 party census almost 60 percent had been in the party for three years or less. In 1939 candidates made up more than a third of all communists, while only one party member in

351

five had been in the party for ten years or more. In 1946 two-thirds of all communists were wartime or postwar recruits. Of the 24,000 "undergrounders," who were bolsheviks at the beginning of 1917, about 12,000 were still in the party in 1922, 8,000 in 1927 and under 5,000 in 1939. Of the 430,000 party members at the beginning of 1920 (over 90 percent of them aged under 40), only 225,000 were still there in 1922, 135,000 in 1927 and 90,000 in 1939.[1]

At the end of World War II the proportion of party members who had been in the CPSU for 11 years or more (i.e. since before the purges of the 1930's) can have been no more than about 15 percent. The trend to greater stability of membership in the postwar period is indicated by the fact that this proportion rose to 34 percent by 1952 and to 58 percent by 1956 (see Table 28).[2] Subsequently this trend was slowed down and then partly reversed by the resumption of large-scale recruitment, the effects of which, however, were partly offset by a reduced expulsion rate.

Despite the mass recruitment of the post-Stalin period, the proportion of CPSU members who had been in the party a decade or less was still considerably lower in 1966 than in 1952 (though we should qualify this by noting that recruits from the preceding three years made up only 18 percent of the party in 1956 and 24 percent in 1961).[3]

Meanwhile, significant changes were taking place in the 10-30 years group. Between 1957 and 1967 the proportion who had been in the party for 10-20 years fell from 45 to 21 percent, while members of 20-30 years standing increased

[1] The figures given in this paragraph are calculated from data appearing in *Izv Ts K*, Nos. 7-8, August-September 1923, p. 60; *BSE* (1st edn.), Vol. xi, col. 537; *XVIII s"ezd*, pp. 147-148; and *PS*, No. 4, February 1946, p. 28.

[2] SOURCE: *PZh*, No. 1, January 1962, p. 49, No. 10, May 1965, p. 13 and No. 19, October 1967, p. 15.

[3] *Ibid.*, No. 1, January 1962, p. 49 and No. 10, May 1965, p. 13.

TABLE 28: LENGTH OF PARTY MEMBERSHIP, 1952-1967

No. of years in party	Percent* of members in			No. of years in party	Percent of members in			
	1952	1956	1961		1957	1962	1965	1967
Up to 11	66	42	40	Up to 10	44.2	39.0	42.8	48.3
11-25	29	51	52	10-30	51.9	56.2	51.3	46.7
Over 25	5	7	8	Over 30	3.9	4.8	5.9	5.0

* Rounded in original

from 7 to 26 percent.[4] In the late 1960's the reduced recruitment rate and the maturing of those recruited in the Khrushchev period will lead to a big increase in the 20-30 age group at the expense of the 10-20 age group, and the overall trend to greater stability and maturity of membership is likely to be resumed.

Age

Youthful recruits have been the main targets of all major recruitment drives. A sample analysis of 20,000 communists during the Civil War showed that over half were under 30 and 90 percent were under 40.[5] In the first half of 1925 less than a fifth of all candidates admitted were aged over 35, while more than a third were under 24.[6] Komsomol members were prominent among new candidates admitted in the later 1930's, and young soldiers during World War II. Komsomol members made up roughly half the nearly seven million candidates admitted in 1956-1964.[7]

When these facts are seen in relation to the patterns of

[4] *Ibid.*, No. 1, January 1962, p. 46.
[5] *Izv Ts K*, No. 15, March 24, 1920.
[6] *Ibid.*, No. 41, October 26, 1925.
[7] *PZh*, No. 1, January 1962, p. 46, and No. 10, May 1965, p. 10; *P*, March 30, 1966.

353

membership growth and turnover discussed in the previous section, it becomes obvious why the CPSU has always been a party of the young and younger middle-aged.

Nonetheless there has been a secular trend towards a maturer membership (see Table 29).[8] This trend probably

TABLE 29: Age Structure of the Party, 1927-1967

	1927	1941	1945	1965	1967
Percent aged:					
Up to 25	25	9	18	7	5
Up to 30	54				
Up to 35			64		
Up to 40	86			54	52
Up to 50	97			79	77

began in the early 1930's, was interrupted by the youthful recruitment of the late 1930's and war years, proceeded apace in the postwar decade, and was moderated but not halted, by the mass recruitment under Khrushchev.

The relatively extensive data on the age structure of the party membership in Uzbekistan, reproduced in Table 30,[9] show the same broad trends as in the CPSU as a whole, and very similar proportions in those years for which nationwide

[8] SOURCES: Based on data appearing in *BSE* (1st edn.), Vol. XI, col. 541; *PS*, No. 4, February 1946, p. 28; *PZh*, No. 10, May 1965, p. 13; *P*, March 30, 1966. The only figures available for the 1930's, apart from those from Uzbekistan, relate to the Tula oblast in 1935, when only 3 percent of the membership were aged under 25 and 27 percent under 30 (see S. Fridberg, "Iz opyta raboty s partaktivom" (Experience in Working with the Party Active), *PS*, No. 10, May 1935, p. 26. These are close to the Uzbek figures in 1937 shown in Table 30.

[9] SOURCE: *KP Uzbekistana v tsifrakh*, pp. 58, 61, 67, 71, 75, 83, 87, 92, 102, 107, 111, 116, 122, 132, 137, 142, 152, 162, 167, 172, 177, 182, 189.

data is available.[10] It therefore seems fairly safe to use them to amplify the very patchy data available on the party at large.

The CPSU membership in Uzbekistan showed a gradual decline in the younger age groups (aged up to 30) after World War II. In the Khrushchev period the percentage aged up to 24 more than doubled, but when these are taken with the 25-30 year-olds, the combined increase was only from 20 to 24 percent, compared with over 30 percent in the early postwar period. Meanwhile the older membership (aged over 50) after contracting to a minimum of 4 percent during the postpurge recruitment, increasing during the war and then suffering a further setback with demobilization, grew continuously from a level of 6 percent in the late 1940's to nearly 20 percent in the early 1960's.

Of no less interest are the changes which have taken place in the middle age groups (31-60), since communists in these

[10] In 1926, 20 percent of the Uzbek Communist Party were aged up to 25 and 50 percent up to 30 (*KP Uzbekistana v tsifrakh*, p. 25), compared with 25 percent and 54 percent respectively in the whole CPSU in 1927. In 1941, 7.4 percent of the Uzbek membership was aged up to 24, while 9 percent of the whole party membership was aged up to 25. The Uzbek figures in 1964 compare with those for the whole CPSU in 1965 as follows:

	Uzbekistan 1964	CPSU 1965
Aged up to 25	8	7
Aged up to 40	61	54
Aged up to 50	82	79

Thus, wherever comparable figures are available, the similarities are close, with the party membership in Uzbekistan showing a somewhat older than average age structure in the mid-1920's, and a somewhat younger than average age structure in the mid-1960's. The wartime figures are not comparable, since a large proportion of the party membership were then registered with military party organizations, and not shown in the figures of territorial party organizations.

TABLE 30: Age Structure of Party Membership in Uzbekistan, 1941-1964

		Percent of party membership in age groups				
Date	Up to 24	25-30	31-40	41-50	51-60	over 60
January 1, 1937	1.5	27.6	51.8	15.1	3.6	0.5
January 1, 1938	0.7	22.0	55.1	17.3	4.3	0.6
January 1, 1939	3.4	22.4	51.4	17.3	4.7	0.8
January 1, 1940	9.2	29.2	44.8	13.0	3.2	0.6
January 1, 1941	7.4	29.1	45.8	13.8	3.4	0.6
January 1, 1943	5.1	18.4	46.1	22.6	6.5	1.3
January 1, 1945	9.6	18.2	44.2	21.9	5.2	1.0
January 1, 1947	9.6	20.3	43.4	21.2	4.7	0.9
January 1, 1948	9.5	20.4	42.9	21.8	4.9	0.8
January 1, 1949	7.2	21.6	41.7	23.4	5.3	0.9
January 1, 1950	4.8	21.3	41.2	25.5	6.1	1.0
January 1, 1951	4.5	21.3	39.7	27.1	6.2	1.2
January 1, 1953	4.2	20.9	37.0	28.4	8.0	1.4
January 1, 1954	3.4	20.0	36.2	29.9	9.1	1.6
	Up to 25	26-30				
January 1, 1955	4.2	16.9	36.1	30.4	10.5	2.0
January 1, 1957	3.7	16.8	34.8	29.7	12.6	2.4
January 1, 1959	4.6	15.8	36.0	27.1	13.6	3.1
January 1, 1960	5.6	14.5	36.8	25.7	14.1	3.4
January 1, 1961	6.7	15.7	36.2	24.0	14.1	3.3
January 1, 1962	7.9	14.8	37.1	22.4	14.1	3.6
December 10, 1962	8.3	15.9	36.9	21.3	13.7	3.9
January 1, 1964	7.9	15.6	37.7	20.4	14.1	4.2

age groups fill the great majority of administrative and other authority positions in the U.S.S.R. The purges of the 1930's and subsequent recruitment produced a heavy concentration in the younger middle-aged groups. In 1940 the ratio of communists in their thirties, forties and fifties was 45:13:3. This imbalance was still marked after World War II. In 1947 the ratio was 43:21:5. This meant that an extraordinary number of authority posts were occupied by younger men, while

356

very few posts were becoming vacant through their occupants reaching retiring age, thus rendering upward mobility very difficult. By the early 1950's the ratio between communists in their thirties and those in their forties had become more normal, but the proportion aged in their fifties remained very small. In 1951 the ratio of 41-50 year-olds to 51-60 year-olds was more than 4:1, the same as it had been in 1947. Many communists aged in their forties had now been languishing in the lower and middle reaches of the various authority structures for many years, and the prospects for advancement to the upper levels were still extremely limited. The likely relevance of this situation to the major purge that Stalin was evidently preparing on the eve of his death has already been indicated (see p. 275).

In the Khrushchev period these trends were reversed. On the one hand the 31-40 year-olds again came to heavily outnumber the 41-50 year-olds. One would expect this to be accompanied by accelerated rejuvenation of the lower levels in the various authority structures, and there is ample evidence that this did in fact take place.[11] On the other hand, however, something like a normal balance was approached between communists in their forties and those in their fifties, and for the first time a significant number of party members were reaching retiring age. This meant that, while the majority of younger communists recently placed in the more junior authority posts could not expect rapid advancement, the prospects for somewhat older and more senior cadres to make progress through the intermediate and upper levels were considerably enhanced. If this applies generally throughout the CPSU, as appears likely, it is a fact of con-

[11] See, e.g. F. R. Kozlov, in *K*, No. 8, May 1962, p. 16; M. Polekhin, in *PZh*, No. 1, January 1964, p. 26; *P*, January 14, 1962 and February 6, 1965.

siderable political interest. It means that we can expect, barring purges, wars or basic institutional changes, that frustrated ambition and competition for position in the upper levels of the Soviet system should be considerably moderated during the next decade or so.[12]

Despite the trend to greater maturity of membership, the age structure of the CPSU remained considerably younger than that of the Soviet adult population as a whole. In 1961, for instance, over two-thirds of the party membership were people who had spent their whole life under the Soviet regime, compared with only half the total population of the U.S.S.R. aged over 20.[13] This gap could be eliminated, however, if the reduction of recruitment initiated in 1965 were to continue for a few years. At the same time, a prolonged slowdown in recruitment would jeopardize another achievement of the Khrushchev era. Despite the overrepresentation of the 31-40 year-olds, the age structure of the CPSU was now more representative of the adult Soviet population as a whole than at any period in the party's history.[14] A sharp, prolonged cutback would result in underrepresentation of the generation currently aged in their late 'teens and early twenties. In order to progress simultaneously towards greater maturity of membership and an age structure more representative of the population at large, the party would need to pursue a policy of fairly brisk recruitment (though slower than under Khrushchev), concentrated mainly on young men and women aged in their twenties.

[12] This may not apply to the top political posts, however, since there are ample precedents for their occupants continuing in office well beyond the normal retiring age.

[13] See *PZh*, No. 1, January 1962, p. 50 and P. A. Pod'iachikh, *Naselenie SSSR* (Moscow, 1961), p. 29.

[14] Cf. Table 28 with data shown in *Itogi vsesoiuznoi perepisi naseleniia 1959 goda: SSSR*, pp. 54-55.

The age structure of the CPSU membership has implications which deserve closer attention by students of the Soviet political system, since it must obviously affect the atmosphere and work-style of primary organizations, the relations between the latter and the "nonparty masses," career patterns and opportunities, and the climate of attitudes and experience within which the party apparatus itself functions.

The Sexes

Despite the Soviet ideological commitment to equality of the sexes, there are sharp differences in the pattern of participation of men and women in Soviet society. While women predominate in all except the topmost levels of the medical profession, for instance, they are overwhelmingly outnumbered among managerial and administrative personnel.[15] Since the latter have always provided a large section of the CPSU membership, it will not surprise us to find women in a minority in the party. Nonetheless the persistent *extent* of male predominance in the CPSU is striking. Moreover, although increasing female representation has always been held up as a desirable objective, at no time since the 1920's has it been treated as a matter of great weight or urgency except in certain (mainly Muslim) areas of exceptionally low female representation.[16]

---

[15] In 1959 women held 26 percent of all "line" posts in government, party and similar organizations and 12 percent of all "line" posts in production enterprises. Their share of these posts had approximately doubled since 1939 (see *Itogi vsesoiuznoi perepisi naseleniia 1959 goda: SSSR*, pp. 168-169). They tended to become less numerous at progressively higher levels and such key categories as obkom first secretaries and U.S.S.R. ministers were practically all men.

[16] In 1927, ten years after the Revolution, women formed 4.7 percent of the Tatars, 2.5 percent of the Bashkirs, 2.1 percent of the Kazakhs and 0.7 percent of Tadjiks in the CPSU, compared with

On the face of it, Table 31[17] tells a fairly simple story. During the first 16 or 17 years of the Soviet regime the proportion of women in the party rose steadily, advancing from one in twelve in the early 1920's to one in six in the mid-1930's. At this point, however, the advance stopped. The middle and later 1930's saw some decline in female representation, which, however, was made good in the war years, so that the position in 1945 approximated to what it had been 11 years earlier.[18] In the early postwar years women increased their

12.1 percent of the party as a whole (see *Sotsial'nyi i natsional'nyi sostav VKP(b)*, p. 139). In 1925 only 3 of the 1,401 Kirgiz in the party were women (see *KP Kirgizii*, p. 47). The campaign to recruit women to the party in such areas formed part of the long-term struggle for the emancipation of women and for asserting the values of communism against traditional Islamic values. In the period since World War II the representation of women in former Muslim areas has been raised to approximately average party levels (see, for instance, *TI*, September 15, 1961, *PV*, February 28, 1961, *BR*, January 27, 1956).

[17] SOURCES: *Izv Ts K*, No. 1, January 1923 and No. 7, November 1924; *Sotsial'nyi i natsional'nyi sostav VKP(b)*, p. 24; F. Rizel', "Priëm zhenshchin v partiiu" (Admitting Women into the Party) in *God raboty po regulirovaniiu rosta VKP(b)*, p. 26; "O rabote partorganizatsii sredi zhenshchin" (The Work of Party Organizations among Women), *B*, No. 1, January 1951, p. 11; *XX S"ezd*, Vol. 1, p. 238; S. Smidovich, "Zhenshchina: zhenshchina v SSSR" (Woman—Woman in the U.S.S.R.), *Malaia sovetskaia entsiklopedia* (2nd edn.), Vol. IV (1935), col. 311 (I am indebted to Miss Louise Luke for this reference, as well as for the figure for 1939, which Miss Luke calculated from data given by Aristov in *XX S"ezd*, Vol. 1, pp. 238-239); *P*, January 30, 1961; *PZh*, No. 7, April 1967, p. 8, No. 10, May 1965, p. 13, and No. 19, October 1967, p. 15. The last-named source gives the following additional percentages of female representation: January 1961—19.5 percent, January 1963—19.7 percent, January 1964—19.9 percent. A figure of 18.7 percent women in 1945 is given in *Istoriia Velikoi Otechestvennoi voiny Sovetskogo Soiuza: 1941-1945*, Vol. VI, p. 377. For a possible explanation for the discrepancy between this percentage and that reproduced in the table, see p. 279.

[18] The increased male representation in the later 1930's was probably due to the vast influx of young men into managerial and ad-

360

TABLE 31: Sex Structure of CPSU Membership, 1922-1967

Date	Men Percent	Women Percent
1922 (January)	92.2	7.8
1924 (August)	90.1	9.9
1927 (January)	87.9	12.1
1929 (October)	86.3	13.7
1932 (July)	84.1	15.9
1934 (January)	83.5	16.5
1937 (January)	85.2	14.8
1939 (March)	85.5	14.5
1941 (January)	85.1	14.9
1945 (January)	83.0	17.0
1947 (January)	81.8	18.2
1950 (July)	79.3	20.7
1952 (October)	80.8	19.2
1956 (January)	80.4	19.6
1957 (January)	80.3	19.7
1959 (January)	80.5	19.5
1962 (January)	80.4	19.6
1965 (January)	79.8	20.2
1967 (January)	79.1	20.9

share of the party membership by 4 percent.[19] About 1950, however, the advance again came to a halt, and in the following 15 years there were only minor fluctuations in a male-female ratio of four to one.

ministrative posts during these years. The wartime increase in the percentage of women communists occurred despite the heavy concentration of recruitment in the armed forces, and is accounted for by the extraordinary proportion of women among those recruited on the home front. Women made up 41 percent of all recruits to the party outside the armed forces during the war years. See M. Shamberg, "Nekotorye voprosy vnutripartiinoi raboty" (Certain Questions of Intra-Party Work), *PS*, No. 4, February 1946, p. 28.

[19] The reasons for the significant rise in female representation between 1945 and 1950 are not clear, but they may be connected with

This, however, is not the whole story, for trends since the middle 1930's appear somewhat differently when one takes account of changes in the sex structure of the population. Although women substantially outnumbered men even before World War II,[20] the war vastly accentuated this imbalance. As late as the 1959 census, adult females outnumbered males by about 40 percent, while in those age groups which were subject to military service during World War II there were about five women to every three men.[21] This means that the increased percentage of women in the party after World War II did not necessarily mean a commensurate increase in the relative chances of a woman being in the party. In 1959 these chances were about one in eight for a man and one in forty for a woman, and this ratio of 5:1 was approximately the same as that existing in 1934. On the other hand by the later 1950's the ratio of males to females in the Soviet population was rapidly growing more normal, especially among the young adults who supply the largest group of recruits to the party. This meant that the near-stationary *percentage* of women among party members during this period concealed an improvement in the relative *chances* of women being in the party. This improvement has continued. In the first half of 1965, 23.2 percent of all recruits were women, and in the first half of 1966, 25.3 percent.[22] How is this to be explained? Was it a consequence of the increased influx of women into administrative and managerial posts? Or did it rather reflect

the fact that wartime losses were compelling the employment of large numbers of women in jobs which would normally have been occupied by men. By the 1950's such pressures were easing.

[20] The 1939 census showed that there were 89 million females and 82 million males (see F. Lorimer, *The Population of the Soviet Union: History and Prospects*, Geneva, 1946, p. 141).

[21] See *Itogi vsesoiuznoi perepisi naseleniia 1959 goda: SSSR*, p. 50.

[22] *PZh*, No. 18, September 1966, p. 5.

the increasing percentage of party members *not* occupying managerial and administrative posts during the Khrushchev era? Since separate occupational breakdowns for male and female party members are not available, this question must remain open. Taking a longer perspective, however, there is no doubt that the improvement in female representation in the party has lagged far behind the increased participation of women in work involving authority and expertise, since the 1930's.[23]

The history of male and female membership of the CPSU obviously raises a number of complex issues which cannot be adequately explored within the specialized framework of the present work. The apparently anomalous trends since the 1930's may be explained in terms of the *levels* at which women are employed as administrators and experts. Alternatively, they may be related to more elusive factors of social psychology. In any case these facts clearly need to be set in the context of a systematic study of the social position of women in the U.S.S.R., which still remains to be written.

[23] Between 1939 and 1959 the proportion of women among judges and procurators rose from 13 to 33 percent, among advocates from 13 to 36 percent, among economists and statisticians from 48 to 77 percent, among directors of theaters, clubs and other cultural establishments from 33 to 45 percent, among agricultural specialists from 14 to 34 percent, among chairmen and secretaries of village soviets from 7 to 33 percent, and among heads of health establishments from 39 to 52 percent. It is worth noting that by contrast, the proportion of women among full-time secretaries of primary organizations in the party, komsomol, trade unions and similar organizations increased by only 1 percent over this period. (See *Itogi vsesoiuznoi perepisi naseleniia 1959 goda: SSSR*, pp. 167-170.) See also footnote 15.

Chapter 12

Nationality

THE SOVIET UNION inherited from the tsarist "prison-house of peoples" an ethnic composition of unrivalled complexity. Among the 209 million people recorded in the 1959 census 114 million were Russians, 37 million were Ukrainians, there were 17 nationalities numbering from one to eight millions, 29 numbering from 100,000 to a million, and dozens of smaller groups.[1]

Soviet policies towards the non-Russian peoples of the U.S.S.R. have remained essentially unchanged since 1917. They may be summarized as follows: on the one hand, equal opportunity for participation in all aspects of social life, preservation of national languages and cultures, and structuring of regional administration to reflect national groupings; and on the other, suppression of all separatist tendencies, assimilation of all social activities to a uniform and centralized institutional pattern, and limitation of national traditions and cultural expression to what the party leadership holds to be consistent with the socialist order and the general interests of the U.S.S.R. These policies rest on the assumption that national differences under socialism will naturally fade and eventually disappear but that this process should not be unduly forced.

For the non-Russian nationalities these policies often meant a great widening of opportunities as compared with the tsarist period, but they did not mean either political emancipation or the disappearance of assimilationist pres-

[1] See A. A. Isupov, *Natsional'nyi sostav naseleniia SSSR* (Moscow, 1964), pp. 15-16.

364

sures. Such pressures, operating particularly at the institutional and ideological levels, were in fact sharply intensified under the Soviet system. No assimilationist policies, however enlightened, can offer identical satisfactions to members of the majority and minority nationalities concerned, and their impact on the latter will depend on the history, level of economic and cultural development, and sense of national identity of each particular nationality.[2]

These general aspects of the Soviet nationalities situation are clearly reflected in the structure and composition of the CPSU. In keeping with the pseudo-federal structure of the Soviet state, the party organizations in the various non-Russian union republics are called "the Communist Party of Armenia," "the Communist Party of Belorussia," and so on, yet both in theory and practice these form an integral part of the centralized and unitary CPSU, with no more autonomy than have the various regional organizations of the party in the R.S.F.S.R., and the individual communist is officially a member *of the CPSU*, not of his republic party organization. At the same time, despite constant efforts to build up party membership in non-Russian areas, most of these remained relatively underrepresented in the party even 50 years after the Bolshevik Revolution, some of them grossly so.

From Revolution to World War II

Despite the great many non-Russians active in the Bolshevik leadership in the early years of the Soviet regime, the predominance of Great Russians in the mass membership was greater then than it has been at any subsequent period.

---

[2] See, e.g., Walter Kolarz, *Russia and Her Colonies* (London, 1952), Richard Pipes, *The Formation of the Soviet Union* (2nd edn.), (Cambridge, Mass., 1964), and R. Conquest, *The Soviet Deportation of Nationalities* (London, 1960).

This reflected both the existence of separatist movements among many of the non-Russian peoples and the fact that Soviet power was most firmly established in the central areas of European Russia during the Civil War, while the White armies and foreign troops were active mainly on the periphery. At the same time, those minority nationalities which were prominent in the leadership, namely the Jews, Georgians, Armenians, Poles and Latvians, were, like the Russians, also overrepresented in the mass membership of the party. Table 32[3] shows how strongly marked were these differences, and also how they were substantially moderated between 1922 and 1927.

TABLE 32: NATIONAL COMPOSITION OF THE CPSU, 1922-1927

| Nationality | Percent of party | | Percent of population |
	1922	1927	1926
Great Russians	72.0	65.0	52.9
Ukrainians	5.9	11.7	21.2
Belorussians	1.5	3.2	3.2
Poles, Latvians and other Baltic peoples	4.6	2.6	0.7
Jews	5.2	4.3	1.8
Minority peoples in R.S.F.S.R.	2.0	2.3	4.3
Transcaucasian peoples	3.4	3.6	2.5
Central Asians (incl. Kazakhs)	2.5	3.5	7.0
Others	2.9	3.8	6.4

[3] SOURCES: *Izv Ts K*, Nos. 7-8, August-September 1923, p. 61, *Sotsial'nyi i natsional'nyi sostav VKP(b)*, p. 114, Lorimer, *op.cit.*, pp. 55-61. The 1922 figures cover members and candidates, the 1927 figures, members only. For additional details on national representation at this period, see Fainsod, *How Russia Is Ruled*, p. 219. On the growth of party organizations in minority areas between 1922 and 1927, see *Sotsial'nyi i natsional'nyi sostav VKP(b)*, p. 117.

It will be noted that the biggest increases during the mid-1920's were made by the Belorussians and Ukrainians. Improvements in the representation of non-Slavic minorities, though significant, were more modest. This was in spite of quite intense efforts to recruit members among these peoples, and the relaxation of admission requirements for many of them.[4]

The problem of the "underrepresented" nationalities cannot be fully understood without noting the close interconnection of national differences with social and economic factors. The minority areas were predominantly rural and their populations sometimes semi-nomadic or semi-tribal. Russian settlers often outnumbered local nationals in the towns, especially where there was industrial development. Yet the CPSU was predominantly a party of townsmen, with an ideological preference for industrial workers. There was obviously a tension here between the need to put down roots among the minority peoples and the danger of swamping the local organizations with "nonproletarian elements."

Not surprisingly, therefore, membership policies in these areas represented a compromise. The January 1929 decision intensifying working class recruitment, for instance (see p. 167) was extended to the non-Russian republics, but here the working class quota was fixed at 60 percent, compared with 90 percent in the industrial areas and 70 percent in the agricultural areas of Russia proper. Or to take another example, in Kirgizia, one of the areas where easier admission requirements were laid down for local nationals, the rejection

[4] For a Central Committee circular laying down easier conditions for admission as candidates and for transfer to full membership in 29 national minority areas in the North Caucasus, the Volga area, Siberia and Central Asia, see *KP Kirgizii*, pp. 32-33. For examples of special measures adopted to encourage the enlistment of Kazakhs, see Beisembaev and Pakhmurnyi, *op.cit.*, pp. 53, 119-120.

rate among applicants for admission was nevertheless far higher among Kirgiz than among Russians (about 50 percent as against 30 percent during the "October Recruitment" of 1927-1928),[5] while Kirgiz were more likely than Russians to be expelled (a quarter of the Kirgiz members were expelled during the 1929 purge, compared with an eighth of the Russians).[6] In both these cases, the ratio between Kirgiz and Russians correlated closely with the ratio between peasants and workers.

The connection between social and national differences is well illustrated by the data of the 1927 party census. They show that the proportion of manual workers in the party organizations of the autonomous republics and oblasts of the R.S.F.S.R. was just over half that for the CPSU as a whole, while the proportion of farmers was twice the national average.[7] Even more pertinent, they show that *within* the party organizations of nearly all non-Russian areas (including the Ukraine and Belorussia), local nationals were far more likely than Russians to be farmers and less likely to be workers.[8]

In spite of the complexities of the problem, the party managed during the 1920's to improve the position of most of

[5] *Ibid.*, p. 67.
[6] *Ibid.*, p. 72.
[7] *Sotsial'nyi i natsional'nyi sostav VKP(b)*, p. 127.
[8] *Ibid.*, p. 128. For data on the relation between social and national differences among party members in 1922, see *Izv Ts K*, Nos. 7-8, August-September 1923, pp. 58-59. The interplay of these two factors in party membership policy was not always as straightforward as we have pictured it here. In Buryat Mongolia, for instance, where the communists were hard put to overcome local nationalists entrenched in the soviets, examination of party membership data shows that the party relied mainly upon members recruited among Russian *peasant* settlers to enforce its control. See B. M. Mitupov, in *Iz istorii partiinoi organizatsii Buriatii*, pp. 52-58.

the "underrepresented" nationalities not only in relation to the party membership as a whole, but also in relation to non-natives in their "own" organizations, as we can see from Table 33.[9] Nonetheless, party successes in this matter were

TABLE 33: REPRESENTATION OF LOCAL NATIONALS IN MAJOR NON-RUSSIAN AREAS, 1922-1930

Area	Percent of natives in population 1926	Percent of natives in party organization		
		1922	1927	1930
Ukrainian SSR	79.8	23.6	47.0	53.0
Belorussian SSR	80.4	21.0	46.7	55.5
Georgian SSR	62.2	61.7	55.0	64.0
Armenian SSR	84.7	89.5	92.3	89.0
Azerbaidzhan SSR	64.2	39.5	31.7	39.5
Uzbek SSR	75.6		36.5	48.5
Tatar ASSR	48.3	19.8	32.4	36.3
Crimean Tatar ASSR	25.1	2.5	4.8	10.7
Bashkir ASSR	23.7	17.8	15.6	17.8
Chuvash ASSR	74.6	61.4	57.6	62.7
Mari ASSR	51.4	37.6	37.6	39.7
Volga German ASSR	66.4	67.5	26.9	35.2
Komi Aut. Oblast	92.2	84.9	85.4	82.1
Votyak Aut. Oblast	52.3	15.2	12.9	16.9
Kalmuck Aut. Oblast	75.6	30.8	64.8	68.9

[9] SOURCES: *Sotsial'nyi i natsional'nyi sostav VKP(b)*, p. 18, and V. Vlasov, "Za uluchshenie sostava natsorganizatsii" (For an Improvement in the Composition of National Organizations), *PS*, Nos. 19-20, October 1930, p. 21. Kazakhstan and Turkmenia, which are not included because of incomplete information, also showed an improvement in local representation. For developments in Kirgizia, see pp. 372, 394. The continued Ukrainization of the Ukrainian Communist Party shown in this table was referred to by a recent writer, who put the proportion of Ukrainians at 43 percent in 1926 and 53 percent in 1930. See F. E. Sherstiuk, "Ukreplenie rabochego iadra KP(b)U v period industrializatsii" (Strengthening of the Worker

patchy and incomplete. Apart from Georgia and Armenia (where most of the nonnative communists were, in any case, other Caucasians rather than Russians), local nationals remained everywhere underrepresented, and there were some areas where little or no improvement had been effected. In the Ukraine and Belorussia the intensified stress on proletarian recruitment after 1927 slowed down the "nativization" of the party membership, and in 1930 Russians in these republics were still about twice as likely to be communists as were the Ukrainians and Belorussians.

A priori it might be expected that the processes of nativization of party organizations in non-Russian areas and equalization of national representation in the CPSU would be advanced by the mass recruitment of the early 1930's, with its expanded peasant intake, but then retarded or even reversed in later years, due to the effects of the 1933-1934 purge, which fell most heavily on rural cells, and to the heavily intelligentsia-oriented recruitment of 1937-1941 (most non-Russian groups still being underrepresented in the intelligentsia because of their lower level of urbanization and legacy of educational backwardness). There is a good deal of evidence to confirm these expectations. Between

---

Core of the Ukrainian CP in the Period of Industrialization) *V I KPSS*, No. 5, 1960, p. 123. One contemporary source, however, showed the level of Ukrainization as virtually unchanged between 1927 and 1930. According to this source, the increase in the percentage of Ukrainians in the Communist Party of the Ukraine was only from 52.0 percent to 52.3 percent, while Russian members increased from 27.5 to 28.4 percent and members of other nationalities declined from 20.5 to 19.3 percent. See *Natsional'naia politika VKP(b)* (Moscow, 1930), pp. 144-145. This source also stated that the percentage of native communists in *all* national minority areas increased from 46.6 to 49.1 percent, while the percentage of Russians in these organizations increased from 30.0 to 31.4 percent (*ibid.*, p. 152).

January 1931 and April 1932 the proportion of local nationals in the 34 main non-Russian areas increased from 50.9 to 53.8 percent.[10] No overall figures were published for later years, but data is available for the Ukraine, Kazakhstan and three of the four Central Asian republics.

Table 34[11] shows that the Ukrainization of the Com-

TABLE 34: Ukrainians and Russians in the Ukrainian Communist Party, 1930-1940

	Percent of all Communists in Ukrainian SSR		
	June 1930	October 1933	April 1940
Ukrainians	54	60	63
Russians	27	23	19
Others	19	17	18

munist Party of the Ukraine was accelerated in the early 1930's, but then slowed down markedly. It can further be calculated that Ukrainians constituted about 11 percent of the whole CPSU membership in 1930, 13 percent in 1933

[10] See *PS*, No. 16, August 1932, p. 9.

[11] Sources: *P*, January 24, 1934, *SU*, May 18, 1940. It is noteworthy that by April 1940 the incorporation of the western oblasts of the Ukraine had already added large populations in which ethnic Ukrainians outnumbered Russians more heavily than in the republic as a whole. This obviously stood to assist Ukrainization of the party membership, but it is doubtful if there had yet been significant recruitment in these areas. Another source indicates that the proportion of Ukrainians in the Communist Party of the Ukraine fell from 60 percent to 57 percent between 1933 and 1937, before rising to 63 percent in 1940. See N. A. Barsukov, A. R. Shaidullin and I. N. Iudin, "KPSS—Partiia internatsional'naia" (The CPSU—an International Party), *V I KPSS*, No. 7, July 1966, p. 12. This shows that the setback to the indigenization of the party in this republic during the 1930's was caused by the purges, and that the process of indigenization was renewed at its previous level during the succeeding mass recruitment.

and were back to 11 percent in 1940.[12] Table 35[13] also reveals rapid indigenization in the Central Asian party membership in the early 1930's, but here the percentage of native com-

TABLE 35: "NATIVE" COMMUNISTS IN CENTRAL ASIA, 1927-1941

Year	CP of Uzbekistan Percent Uzbeks	CP of Tadzhikistan Percent Tadzhiks	Percent Uzbeks	CP of Kirgizia Percent Kirgiz
1927	37	49	21*	50
1930	49			48
1931	52			51
1933	61	53	22	59
1937	52			50
1940	50	45	18	
1941	49			44

* Also includes some smaller local Central Asian groups.

munists actually began to decline in the middle 1930's, so that by the outbreak of World War II it was lower than it had been a decade or so earlier. In Kazakhstan the pattern was similar but the setback to indigenization in the 1930's not quite so severe. The percentage of Kazakhs in the party membership of the republic followed the following course: 1927—

[12] These calculations are based on the sources cited in footnote 11, and assume that the incidence of party membership among Ukrainians living inside and outside the borders of the Ukrainian republic was roughly the same; allowance is made for the tendency of an increasing number of Ukrainians living in non-Ukrainian areas to identify themselves as Russians (see Lorimer, op.cit., pp. 51, 138-139).

[13] SOURCES: KP Uzbekistana v tsifrakh, pp. 41, 44, 60, 72, 76; Ocherki istorii Kommunisticheskoi Partii Tadzhikistana, pp. 44, 100, 189; KP Kirgizii, pp. 66, 77, 90, 120, 276; Sotsial'nyi i natsional'nyi sostav VKP(b), p. 18; V. Vlasov, in PS, Nos. 19-20, October 1930, p. 21. See also Ia. Peters, in B, No. 3, 1935, p. 23, especially for Turkmenia in the early 1930's. Peters gives figures for 1935 which appear to be approximations.

38.2; 1930—43.0; 1933—53.1; 1937—48.8; 1940—51.8; 1941—51.0.[14]

No official data on the proportion of Jews in the CPSU has been published since the 1920's. However, later figures are available from the Ukraine, where half the Jewish population of the U.S.S.R. were living prior to World War II. In 1940, 13.4 percent of all communists in the Ukraine were Jews.[15] If the incidence of party membership among Jews in other areas of the U.S.S.R. was the same as in the Ukraine, this would mean that Jews constituted 4.9 percent of the CPSU in 1940.[16] Even if the proportion of Jews joining the party was lower outside the Ukraine (which there seems no reason to suppose), it can scarcely have been lower enough to reduce the proportion of Jews in the CPSU as a whole below the 1927 level of 4.3 percent (see p. 366). The apparent success of Soviet Jews in holding their own in the party

[14] See Beisembaev and Pakhmurnyi, op.cit., pp. 142, 146, 176, 206, 247, 251. The purges also caused a setback to the indigenization of the party membership in Belorussia, and the Tatar, Mari, Chuvash and Komi ASSR's. Compare Table 3 with data in Barsukov, Shaidullin and Iudin, op.cit., pp. 9, 12.

[15] See SU, May 18, 1940.

[16] In calculating the incidence of party membership among Jews in the Ukraine, the 1940 ethnic percentages have been applied to the 1939 population, in order to avoid the distorting effects of including the areas acquired in 1939-1940. The assumption here is that the proportion of party members in the Ukraine living in the new territories must have been so small in 1940 that any difference in ethnic ratios there compared with the rest of the republic cannot have affected the overall position significantly. In connection with the question whether the incidence of party membership among Jews was the same in the Ukraine and elsewhere, it is worth noting that the incidence of party membership among the *whole* population of the Ukraine was very close to the average for the U.S.S.R. as a whole (see Table 36, p. 379; Lorimer, op.cit., p. 162). In Uzbekistan the percentage of Jews in the party membership was 1.5 in 1925, 1.75 in 1937, and stayed steady at 1.7 percent between 1939 and 1941. See *KP Uzbekistana v tsifrakh*, pp. 19, 60, 68, 72, 76.

membership over this period seems remarkable when one considers the relatively greater increase of non-Jews in the urban population, the worsening of official attitudes towards the Jews from the middle 1930's, and the striking drop in the number of Jews in the upper levels of the party.[17] On the other hand, it might be argued that the greatly increased re-cruitment of the "intelligentsia" at the expense of the manual workers and peasants should have favored the Jews, and their apparent failure to achieve a substantial *improvement* in their representation under these circumstances bears wit-ness to discrimination against them in party recruitment. It is doubtful if this question can be fully clarified on the basis of available information.

Since World War II

For an impression of trends in the national composition of the CPSU during the 1940's and 1950's, we are mainly de-pendent on such indirect evidence as is provided by the strength of delegations from the various republics to CPSU congresses (see Table 36).[18] There are serious limitations to

[17] See Salo W. Baron, *The Russian Jew under Tsars and Soviets* (New York, 1964), pp. 241-243; S. M. Shvarts, *Antisemitizm v Sovetskom Soiuze* (New York, 1952), pp. 110-122. At the Sixteenth Congress of the CPSU in 1930, 10.9 percent of the delegates were Jews, i.e. over twice the proportion of Jews in the CPSU as a whole (see *XVI s"ezd*, p. 600). No national breakdown was given at the Eighteenth Congress in 1939, but at the Fifteenth Congress of the Communist Party of the Ukraine, Jews made up only 6 percent of the delegates, which was under half the proportion of Jews in the party organizations of the republic at that time (see *SU*, May 18, 1940).

[18] SOURCES: The 1939 and 1961 figures are derived from a count of delegates as listed in *XVIII s"ezd* and *XXII s"ezd*; the 1952 figures are calculated from lists of delegates published in the republic Russian-language press in the weeks preceding the Nineteenth Con-gress, supplemented by data given at the Congress, *P*, October 7,

TABLE 36: Size of Republic Delegations to CPSU Congresses, 1939-1952-1961

Republic	Percent of U.S.S.R. population		Percent of Congress delegates		
	1939	1959	XVIII Cong. 1939	XIX Cong. 1952	XXII Cong. 1961
R.S.F.S.R. districts	63.9	55.9	65.8	about 65.0	63.1
Ukraine	18.2	20.0	18.0	12.8	16.3
Belorussia	3.3	4.1	2.9	2.2	2.9
Georgia	2.1	1.9	2.5	2.7	2.1
Azerbaidzhan	1.9	1.8	2.5	1.9	1.6
Armenia	0.8	0.8	1.0	1.1	0.8
Uzbekistan	3.7	3.9	1.5	2.1	2.5
Turkmenia	0.7	0.7	0.4	0.7	0.6
Kirgizia	0.9	1.0	0.3	0.7	0.7
Tadzhikistan	0.9	0.9	0.3	0.5	0.6
Kazakhstan	3.6	4.5	2.5	3.5	3.9
Karelo-Finland[a]				0.3	
Estonia[b]		0.6		0.5	0.5
Latvia[b]		1.0		0.8	0.9
Lithuania[b]		1.3		0.6	0.7
Moldavia[c]		1.4		0.6	0.7

[a] Constituted union republic only during the years 1940-1955.
[b] Incorporated in the U.S.S.R. in 1940.
[c] Made union republic in 1940.

the value of this evidence for our present purposes. The congress delegations include representatives from the armed forces and border and other security troops stationed in the republics as well as from local organizations, and their relative size therefore does not exactly correspond with the relative strength of the republic organizations themselves; more

1952. Voting delegates (representing full members) and nonvoting delegates (representing candidates for the party) are both included for 1939 and 1961, but the 1952 figures include only the former. Since candidates made up only 13 percent of the total party membership in 1952, their exclusion should not materially distort our impression of the ratios between the size of republic organizations.

seriously, there is no indication in this evidence as to the percentage of native members in the republic organizations. Nonetheless, it seems reasonable to interpret the marked changes which have occurred in the relative size of delegations as *prima facie* evidence of the following trends in the national composition of the party:

1. a big increase in the degree of overrepresentation of Great Russians in the 1940's, which *may* have been somewhat moderated in the 1950's;

2. a big increase in the degree of *under*representation of the Ukrainians and Belorussians in the 1940's, which was partly but not wholly repaired in the 1950's;

3. a reduction in the degree of underrepresentation of the Central Asian nationalities (but see below, pp. 393-399);

4. in the Transcaucasian republics, the Georgians and Armenians improved their already strong position in the 1940's, but then fell back considerably in the 1950's; the relative strength of the party in Azerbaidzhan declined over the whole period;

5. the weakness of the party among the Baltic nationalities and Moldavians was slightly eased in the 1950's.

These changes were mainly due to the unequal effects of the war on party membership in different areas (see Chapter 7)[19] and to the slow recruitment rate in 1946-1953.

[19] The way in which defense of the Soviet motherland was identified with Great Russian patriotism during World War II (cf. Armstrong, *Totalitarianism*, Chap. XI) had its counterpart in heavily Russian-oriented party recruitment. For figures indicating very low relative recruitment of major non-Russian nationalities during the war, see V. K. Molochko, in K. I. Suvorov et al., ed., *Partiia i massy* (Moscow, 1966), p. 82. In September 1942 the Central Committee, evidently disturbed at the lengths to which this had gone in the armed forces, prescribed measures to stimulate recruitment among non-Russian soldiers, and some success has been claimed for these measures. See A. D. Kiselëv, *op.cit.*, pp. 112-113, 125.

When it comes to the 1960's, we are on much firmer ground. Figures are available as of July 1961, January 1965 and January 1967 for the number of communists of those nationalities possessing "their own" union republics. We have reproduced the 1961 and 1965 figures in Table 37[20] and

[20] SOURCES: Calculated from party membership figures given in *PZh*, No. 1, January 1962, p. 49 and No. 10, May 1965, p. 49, and from estimates of the U.S.S.R. population, given in *Ezhegodnik BSE: 1961*, p. 5 and *Ezhegodnik BSE: 1965*, p. 11. Estimates of the population of each nationality in 1961 and 1965 are derived simply by applying the U.S.S.R. rate of increase to the 1959 figures of these nationalities (the only ones available), i.e. no allowance is made for differences in the rate of natural increase. In fact, such differences are significant. Between 1957 and 1961 the various republics showed the following average annual natural increase per 1,000: U.S.S.R.—17.5, R.S.F.S.R.—15.4, Ukraine—13.2, Belorussia—17.5, Baltic republics —9.0, Moldavia—22.6, Transcaucasia—27.6, Central Asia—33.8 and Kazakhstan—29.7 (see G. S. Nevel'shtein, "Territorial'nye razlichiia estestvennogo dvizheniia naseleniia SSSR" [Territorial Differences in the Natural Movement of the Population of the USSR] in E. N. Pavlovskii, ed., *Geografiia naseleniia v SSSR: osnovnye problemy* [Moscow, 1964], p. 151). The main element in these regional differences is undoubtedly differences of birthrate among the major nationalities of these areas. However, no satisfactory formula has been devised for correcting the estimates in Table 37 to allow for such birthrate differences, and it is important to note therefore that our estimates (particularly for 1965) slightly deflate the actual ratio of party membership to population among those nationalities of relatively low birthrate (especially Latvia and Estonia) and slightly inflate the ratio of party membership to population among those nationalities of relatively high birthrate (especially Azerbaidzhan, Armenia and Central Asia). It is due to this problem of demographic changes that we have compared the 1961 figures in our table with the 1965 figures, rather than the more recent 1967 figures published in *PZh*, No. 19, October 1967, pp. 14-15. The latter, however, indicate that changes between 1965 and 1967 continued in the same direction as between 1961 and 1965, though at a somewhat reduced rate, e.g. the Russians declined further to 61.88 percent, the Ukrainians increased to 15.63 percent, the Belorussians to 3.34 percent, the Uzbeks to 1.73 percent, etc.

TABLE 37: NATIONAL COMPOSITION OF CPSU, 1961-1965

Nationality	Nationality as percent of population 1959	Number of communists		Percent of CPSU membership		Communists per 1,000 of national population		Party membership rate as percent of U.S.S.R. average	
		July 1, 1961	Jan. 1, 1965	1961	1965	1961	1965	1961	1965
Russians	54.65	6,116,700	7,335,200	63.54	62.39	52	58	118	114
Ukrainians	17.84	1,412,200	1,813,400	14.67	15.42	36	44	82	86
Belorussians	3.79	287,000	386,000	2.98	3.28	35	44	80	86
Georgians	1.29	170,400	194,300	1.77	1.65	61	65	139	127
Armenians	1.34	161,200	187,900	1.67	1.60	55	61	125	120
Azerbaidzhanis	1.41	106,100	141,900	1.10	1.21	35	44	80	86
Kazakhs	1.73	149,200	181,300	1.56	1.54	38	45	86	88
Uzbeks	2.88	142,700	193,600	1.48	1.64	23	29	52	59
Turkmen	0.48	27,300	32,400	0.28	0.28	26	29	59	59
Kirgiz	0.46	27,300	35,000	0.28	0.30	27	33	61	65
Tadzhiks	0.67	32,700	41,900	0.34	0.36	22	29	50	59
Latvians	0.67	33,900	44,300	0.35	0.38	23	29	52	59
Lithuanians	1.11	42,800	61,500	0.44	0.52	18	24	41	47
Estonians	0.47	24,400	33,900	0.25	0.29	25	31	57	61
Moldavians	1.06	26,700	40,300	0.28	0.34	12	17	27	33
Other nationalities	10.15	866,100	1,035,300	9.00	8.90	39	44	89	86
Whole population	100.00	9,626,700	11,758,200	100.00	100.00	44	51	100	100

related them to population. They reveal most of the trends which Table 36 suggested were probably already under way during the 1950's and which may be summarized as a generalized narrowing of the contrasts between better- and poorer-represented nationalities. The most significant changes over these three and a half years were made by the Ukrainians, who advanced about a quarter of the way towards parity of representation, and the Belorussians and Azerbaidzhanis who advanced a third of the way towards parity.

The lack of any recent data on those nationalities not represented by union republics results in some serious gaps in our picture of long-term trends. These nationalities totaled about 23 million in 1965, the largest groups being the Tatars (about 5.5 millions) and the Jews (about 2.5 millions), followed by about 1.75 million Germans and 1.5 million Poles; the various Finno-Ugrian and Turkic peoples (other than the Tatars) of the Volga-Urals area totaled about 6 million. There is little point in attempting to estimate the number of communists among most of these peoples on the extremely flimsy evidence available, and we shall confine ourselves to a brief note on the four largest of them (see Tables 38a,[21] 38b,[22] 38c,[23] 38d[24]).

[21] SOURCES: The 1959 population figures are taken from *Itogi vsesoiuznoi perepisi naseleniia 1959 goda: SSSR*, p. 206; the 1962 population figure is from *Ezhegodnik BSE; 1962*, p. 116; the party membership figures from *Kamunist Belorusi*, No. 5, May 1962, p. 57. In this table, as well as Tables 38b and 38d, calculation of the party membership rate relative to the population of each ethnic group assumes identical pro rata population growth. The distortion due to this assumption is unlikely to be significant at the level of accuracy attempted here, with the possible exception of the estimates for Kazakhstan, which may understate the Russian and Ukrainian membership rates and overstate the Kazakh rates by perhaps 1 per 1,000.

[22] SOURCES: 1959 population figures are taken from *Itogi vsesoiuznoi perepisi naseleniia 1959 goda: SSSR*, p. 207. Party membership figures are from *Ocherki istorii Kommunisticheskoi Partii Moldavii*

TABLE 38a: BELORUSSIA—PARTY (1962) AND POPULATION (1959),
ETHNIC COMPOSITION

Nationality	Population 1959		Party 1962		Communists per 1,000 population 1962
	Number	Percent	Number	Percent	
Belorussians	6,532,035	81.1	168,300	67.4	25
Russians	659,093	8.2	49,800	19.9	73
Poles	538,881	6.7	2,700	1.1	5
Jews	150,084	1.9	16,000	6.4	103
Ukrainians	133,061	1.7	11,000	4.4	80
Others	41,494	0.4	1,900	0.8	
Totals	8,054,648	100.0	249,700	100.0	30

Population in 1962: 8,316,000

On the Poles we have data from Belorussia, where only 5 per 1,000 were party members in 1962—only one-ninth the average level for the Soviet population as a whole (see Table 38a). Since one-third of all Poles living on Soviet territory are resident in Belorussia, these extravagantly low figures, suggestive of widespread and profound alienation from the Soviet regime, may well be typical of the Soviet Polish population as a whole.

An indirect clue to the level of German representation is

(Outlines of the History of the Communist Party of Moldavia), (Kishinev, 1964), p. 488. The estimate of total population is taken from *Ezhegodnik BSE: 1963*, p. 139.

[23] SOURCES: Population figures: *Itogi vsesoiuznoi perepisi naseleniia 1959 goda: SSSR*, p. 207; party membership: *KP Uzbekistana v tsifrakh*, p. 163.

[24] SOURCES: 1959 population figures: *Itogi vsesoiuznoi perepisi naseleniia 1959 goda: SSSR*, p. 206; party membership: Beisembaev and Pakhmurnyi, *op.cit.*, p. 359; 1960 population estimate: *Ezhegodnik BSE: 1961*, p. 106 (assuming uniform growth between January 1959 and March 1961).

380

TABLE 38b: MOLDAVIA—PARTY (1963) AND POPULATION (1959),
ETHNIC COMPOSITION

Nationality	Population 1959 Number	Percent	Party 1963 Number	Percent	Communists per 1,000 population 1963
Moldavians	1,886,566	65.4	26,201	34.6	13
Russians	292,930	10.2	23,620	30.9	73
Ukrainians	420,820	14.6	17,837	23.5	38
Belorussians	5,977	0.2	875	1.2	133
Jews	95,107	3.3	4,742	6.3	45
Gagauzy	95,856	3.3	1,042	1.4	10
Bulgars	61,652	2.1	1,369	1.8	20
All others	25,569	0.9	114	0.2	4
Totals	2,884,477	100.0	75,800	100.0	24

Population in 1963: 3,172,000

TABLE 38c: UZBEKISTAN—PARTY AND POPULATION 1959,
ETHNIC COMPOSITION

Nationality	Population Number	Percent	Party membership Number	Percent	Communists per 1,000 of population
Uzbeks	5,038,273	62.1	92,878	49.5	18
Karakalpaks	168,274	2.1	3,885	2.1	23
Tadzhiks	311,375	3.8	5,585	3.0	18
Turkmen	54,804	0.7	788	0.4	14
Kirgiz	92,725	1.1	1,231	0.7	13
Kazakhs	335,267	1.1	7,799	4.2	23
Tatars	444,810	5.4	10,200	5.4	23
Russians	1,090,728	13.5	44,132	23.5	40
Ukrainians	87,927	1.1	5,691	3.0	65
Belorussians	9,520	0.1	620	0.3	65
Jews	94,344	1.2	5,422	2.9	57
All others	377,657	4.7	9,310	5.0	24
Totals	8,105,704	100.0	187,541	100.0	23

TABLE 38d: KAZAKHSTAN—PARTY (1960) AND POPULATION (1959), ETHNIC COMPOSITION

Nationality	Population 1959 Number	Percent	Party 1960 Number	Percent	Communists per 1,000 population 1960
Kazakhs	2,794,966	30.0	115,357	36.3	40
Russians	3,974,229	42.7	138,147	43.4	34
Ukrainians	762,131	8.2	35,373	11.1	43
Tatars	191,925	2.1	6,656	2.1	33
Uzbeks	136,570	1.5	2,725	0.8	19
Uigurs	59,840	0.6	1,425	0.5	24
All others	1,390,186	14.9	18,819	5.8	13
Totals	9,309,847	100.0	318,502	100.0	33

Estimated population in 1960: 9,750,000

provided by party membership figures from Kazakhstan. Official analyses of the ethnic composition of the Kazakh population published on the basis of the 1959 census left almost a million (over 10 percent) unaccounted for,[25] and at least half of these were Germans.[26] Meanwhile the ethnic breakdown of the 1960 party membership reproduced in Table 38d omitted nationalities representing nearly 15 percent of the population, and these nationalities showed a party

[25] See *Itogi vsesoiuznoi perepisi naseleniia 1959 goda: Kazakhstan,* p. 162.

[26] Half the 1.6 million Germans in the U.S.S.R. in 1959 were living in the R.S.F.S.R. (*ibid.,* p. 184). How the remainder were distributed is, however, unknown, as Germans were omitted from the ethnic breakdowns of the other republics in both the U.S.S.R. and republic volumes of the *Itogi vsesoiuznoi perepisi naseleniia 1959 goda.* The total population omitted from these breakdowns was about 1.3 million, of whom almost a million were in Kazakhstan. Since the number of Germans unaccounted for was about 800,000, it is evident that a minimum of 500,000 of them were living in Kazakhstan. The most likely figure is probably 600,000 to 700,000.

membership rate of only 13 per 1,000 or less than a third the rate for the Soviet population as a whole. The Germans among them can scarcely have fared much better than the average for these omitted nationalities, and they may have fared worse.[27]

The Soviet Tatars are a much dispersed and socially diverse people, less than a third of whom live in the Tatar Autonomous Republic. We have CPSU membership figures for the 8 percent of them living in Uzbekistan (1959) and the 3 percent living in Kazakhstan (1960), showing a party-population ratio of 23 per 1,000 and 33 per 1,000 respectively—in both cases the average for the whole population of the republic (see Tables 38c and 38d). If the membership rate for all Tatars is nearer the Kazakhstan than the Uzbekistan level, this would make them the fifth largest ethnic group in the CPSU, and they are probably at least the seventh largest.

Turning to the Jews, we may begin by recalling their apparent success in retaining their high CPSU membership levels in the 1930's, despite the beginning of restrictions on Jewish cultural activities and on the access of Jews to senior party and government positions (see p. 373). Recent data on Jewish party membership is available from three republics, namely Belorussia, Moldavia and Uzbekistan (see Tables 38a, 38b, 38c), which in 1959 contained between them some 340,000 or 15 percent of the Soviet Jewish population.[28] Belorussia and Moldavia are important traditional areas of Jewish settlement, but earlier demographic and oc-

[27] The other nationalities involved included some, notably Belorussians and Jews, who probably had a relatively high party membership rate, and others, such as Poles and Moldavians, who probably had a low one.

[28] See *Itogi vsesoiuznoi perepisi naseleniia 1959 goda: SSSR*, pp. 184, 206, 207.

cupational patterns were of course disrupted by World War II. Jewish numbers were drastically depleted, and the present population consists partly of the few survivors from the German occupation (proportionately probably greater in Moldavia) and partly of Jews who were evacuated during the war or served in the Red Army. By contrast, the Jewish population of Uzbekistan consists almost entirely of immigrants from the European areas of the U.S.S.R. during the Soviet period, and particularly during World War II, and this was reflected in the movements of Jewish party membership in the republic. The few Central Asian ("Bukhara") Jews among Uzbek communists were greatly outnumbered by newcomers from Europe as early as the 1920's. In the prewar years Jews made up just about 2 percent of the Uzbek party membership. The wartime evacuation from the Ukraine, Belorussia and other Western areas brought a large influx of Jewish communists into Uzbekistan, where by 1943 they constituted 12 percent of all party members. At the end of the war many of these Jewish communists left Central Asia, but the net increase from those who remained was considerably higher than was the case with the Ukrainians and Belorussians. In January 1941 the Uzbek party membership included about 2,500 Ukrainians and 1,200 Jews. In January 1943 the figures were about 6,000 and 9,000, and in January 1947, 4,500 and 5,000 respectively.[29] These differences in the recent history of the Jewish population in the three areas in question need to be borne in mind.

Two things stand out when we compare the percentage of communists in the Jewish population of these republics: it is very high in all of them, but the differences between them are marked. In Moldavia the proportion of party members in the

[29] *KP Uzbekistana v tsifrakh*, pp. 76, 84, 103.

Jewish population was nearly twice that for the total population of the republic, in Uzbekistan two and a half times, and in Belorussia over three times. On this evidence it seems reasonable to suppose that the party membership rate in the Jewish population of the U.S.S.R. as a whole is still very high. However, the range shown by the membership rate in these three areas (from 45 per 1,000 in Moldavia to 103 per 1,000 in Belorussia), precludes any firm estimate of the rate in the country at large. We must therefore confine ourselves to a little cautious deduction.

By totaling the Jewish party members in these three republics, we get an average membership rate among their 340,000 Jewish residents of 77 per 1,000; allowing for differences of population and party membership in the years recorded, this implies a rate of at least 80 per 1,000 in the mid-1960's. The two republics containing the majority of Soviet Jews are the Ukraine (840,000 in 1959)[30] and the R.S.F.S.R. (875,000 in 1959).[31] The prewar positions and recent history of the Jews in the Ukraine being the same as those in Belorussia, it would be surprising if their party membership rates were very different, and indications of a very high membership rate among Ukrainian Jews are in fact to be found in a partial breakdown of the ethnic composition of the Ukrainian party membership published in 1958. This shows that the 6.3 percent of the republic's population who were neither Ukrainians nor Russians contained 11.5 percent of the party members.[32] Since Jews constituted almost a third of these 6.3 percent and the remainder consisted largely of such ethnic minorities as Poles, Moldavians and Hungarians,

[30] *Itogi vsesoiuznoi perepisi naseleniia 1959 goda: SSSR*, p. 206.
[31] *Ibid.*, p. 202.
[32] *PZh*, No. 12, June 1958, p. 58.

who probably contained a very small percentage of communists,[33] it seems likely that the Jewish population had a party membership rate at least twice and possibly three times as great as that for the republic's population as a whole. So far as the R.S.F.S.R. is concerned, we can only speculate. In areas occupied by the Germans during the war, communist Jews stood a far better chance of survival than noncommunist Jews, because of evacuation policies, and this would tend to leave a legacy of higher CPSU membership among Ukrainian and Belorussian Jews than those of the R.S.F.S.R. As against this, a high proportion of the Jews in the latter republic live in Moscow and Leningrad, where they are heavily represented among professional groups with high party membership levels.[34]

To sum up, then, the indications are that the proportion of communists among the Jewish population of the U.S.S.R. is at least as high as the average for the three republics from which recent data is available, that is 80 per 1,000. This would make the Jews easily the most party-saturated nationality in the country, and in terms of absolute numbers the largest non-Slavic group of communists, with the possible exception of the Tatars.

On the fact of it, then, the Jews have continued to do well in the CPSU membership, in spite of the vicissitudes of the Soviet Jewish community in the postwar years. In the latter connection, it is pertinent to note that the figures of Jewish

---

[33] *Itogi vsesoiuznoi perepisi naseleniia 1959 goda: SSSR*, p. 206.

[34] At the time of the 1959 census there were 239,000 Jews in Moscow and 162,000 in Leningrad (see *Itogi vsesoiuznoi perepisi naseleniia 1959 goda: RSFSR*, pp. 312, 316). These two cities contained almost a half of all Jews in the R.S.F.S.R. and nearly a fifth of all Jews in the U.S.S.R. Meanwhile 87 percent of all Jews in the R.S.F.S.R. had a secondary or higher education, compared with 45 percent of the Russians and 44 percent for the whole population of the republic. See *ibid.*, p. 416.

membership in the Communist Party of Uzbekistan show a drop from 3.8 to 3.0 percent in 1948-1949, a recovery to 3.4 percent in 1949-1951, and no further change till the mass recruitment of the later 1950's initiated a steady decline in the percentage of Jewish members.[35] It would appear then, that the intensification of official anti-Semitism between 1948 and 1953 probably had a significant though not drastic effect on Jewish representation in the party membership; as to what might have happened after that, had the processes dramatized by the "Doctors' Plot" affair been able to run their course, we can only guess.

When our estimates are compared with the prewar situation, however, a rather different picture emerges. At this time, if we ignore the some two million Jews living in the Western areas acquired in 1939-1940, extremely few of whom can have been admitted to the party prior to World War II, Jews constituted about 1.7 percent of the Soviet population. In 1965 the proportion was about 1.1 percent. Meanwhile the Jewish share of the party membership fell from about 5 percent in 1940 (see p. 373) to perhaps 1.5 or 1.7 percent in 1965. In April 1940 (again ignoring the newly annexed Western areas), the incidence of party membership among Ukrainian Jews was about 47 per 1,000, compared with about 15 per 1,000 in the Soviet population at large. Assuming that the party membership rate among Ukrainian Jews did not differ radically from the average for all U.S.S.R. Jews, we may conclude that the party saturation of the Soviet Jewish community fell from about 300 percent of the national average in 1940 to about 140 to 180 percent of the national average in 1965.

[35] See *KP Uzbekistana v tsifrakh*, pp. 103, 108, 112, 123, 128, 133, 138, 143, 148, 153, 158, 163, 168, 173, 178, 183, 189. Between 1955 and 1964 the proportion of Jews in the Uzbek party membership declined from 3.3 percent to 2.3 percent.

It is hard to say how far this trend is due to official discrimination, at its most marked in 1948-1953, but still in evidence, notably in the extreme paucity of Jews in high office. Certainly, there are also other factors involved. Firstly, there has been a general trend towards reducing the extremes of national over- and under-representation in the party which in turn has largely resulted from economic and educational progress as well as the increased sovietization of minority groups. Secondly, the extraordinary party membership rate among the Jews was partly a result of their high level of urbanization, and the doubling of the Soviet urban population since World War II has reduced their advantage in this respect. Meanwhile, the gap between the party saturation of the urban and rural population has been steadily reduced (see p. 491). And finally, as we have noted in the Uzbek case, the mass recruitment of the Khrushchev era probably made for a reduced relative representation of Jews. In considering the striking reduction in Jewish over-representation in the CPSU since World War II, we unfortunately lack the evidence to assign relative weights to these external factors on the one hand, and to discriminatory policies and attitudes on the other; nor is such evidence likely to be available in the foreseeable future.

Before leaving Tables 38a-d, a final point worth drawing attention to is the marked differences of party membership rate which members of the same ethnic group may show in different areas of the country—a point already encountered with respect to the Jews. This assumes considerable importance in considering the role in the CPSU of the three Slavic nationalities which together make up more than three-quarters of its membership. The general position is that communities of Russians, Ukrainians and Belorussians tend to have a higher membership rate outside "their own" republics than inside them, except where, for special reasons, they provide a large part of the manual work force (like the Russians and Ukrainians in the "virgin lands" farms and metal industry of Kazakhstan). This is presumably because they constitute such a large proportion of the cadres deployed through the country by central party and government agencies. The smaller the community of these basic Slavic nationalities, and the shallower its local roots, the larger the percentage of communists it tends to have. The most extreme case in our data is provided by the 6,000 Belorussians in Moldavia, one-eighth of whom (counting men, women and children) were in the party. Another startling case is the Ukrainian community in Belorussia (under 2 percent of the Belorussian population), 80 per 1,000 of whom were communists in 1962 compared with 20 per 1,000 of the Ukrainians resident in the Ukraine in 1958[36] (perhaps 25 by 1962). Russian residents in Moldavia (1963) were more than six times as likely to be members of the party as were ethnic Moldavians. The Russians in the Ukraine constitute a special problem, since most of them probably regard themselves as being as much natives of their areas as the Ukrainians. In 1958 Russians resident in the Ukrainian SSR were more than twice as likely to be communists as were Ukrainians.[37] This is the same ratio as in 1930 and, despite the heavy recruitment of Ukrainians since then, it was probably not much different in 1967. Probably the most important reason is that a large proportion of the Russians are found in the industrialized eastern oblasts, while the Ukrainians still contain a far higher proportion of peasants. A second reason is that the indigenous population of those western Ukrainian territories annexed by the Soviet Union in 1939-1945 still ap-

[36] *PZh*, No. 12, 1958, p. 58.
[37] *Ibid.* The membership rate was 43 per 1,000 for Russians and 20 per 1,000 for Ukrainians.

389

pears to show relatively low party membership levels—like the indigenous population in other border territories incorporated at this period. Here again socioeconomic and ethnic factors merge, frustrating any simple causative explanation. Nonetheless, however we weight the causes, *the effect* is that being in the party, or having relatives in the party, is a far more usual ingredient of the Russian pattern of life in the Ukraine than of the Ukrainian.

Perspectives

We will conclude this chapter by summarizing and elaborating on the main trends apparent at the time of writing. The trend towards equality of representation in the CPSU has been a slow one. It was helped by the mass recruitment of the Khrushchev era, but even then the ratio between the best- and worst-represented of those nationalities possessing a union republic of "their own" was almost four to one. We would do well at this point to recall the pertinence here of economic factors. These, however, are clearly inadequate to explain all the differences. Latvians and Estonians, economically among the most "advanced" peoples of the U.S.S.R., figured very badly in terms of party membership rates. The Turkmen, with a higher degree of urbanization than the Georgians, were less than half as well represented in the party. National attitudes and national psychology surely play a big part in these differences, and their influence appears to be most tenacious. Thus the persistence of very low membership levels in the Western borderlands 20 years after the close of World War II was presumably due in part to continued resentment over Russian dominance and to lack of identification with the Soviet system, while strong historical and cultural influences help to account for the other main area of party weakness, Central Asia.

390

Secondly, the predominance of the Great Russians in the mass membership of the CPSU was only slightly less in 1965 than in 1927, and their decline was more than offset by the increase in Ukrainians. As a result, the overall position of the non-Slavs worsened: in 1927 they constituted 22.6 percent of the population of the U.S.S.R. and 19.1 percent of the CPSU membership, while in 1965 the figures were 23.7 percent and 18.9 percent respectively.

Finally, some further observations on the relative position of natives and Russian settlers in the party organizations of non-Russian areas. We have noted that native communists improved their party representation in most local areas during the 1920's. After 1927, however, this process tended to slow down, was resumed in the early 1930's, and subsequently again slowed down and in some places was reversed. Social factors undoubtedly played a part in this, viz. the intensification of working class recruitment in the late 1920's and subsequently the stress on recruiting members of the managerial-technical intelligentsia. Another relevant variable here was probably the recruitment rate: there is some evidence that local nationals did relatively better at periods of large-scale recruitment and worse when admissions were more restricted or during purges. But a further factor of great importance was migration. Movements of population over the Soviet period have resulted in substantial dilution of the indigenous nationalities by Russians in many areas, particularly in Soviet Asia, without any commensurate dilution of Russians in traditional Great Russian areas.

In the years following World War II all these factors were operating, and combined to reduce the native representation in the party organizations of at least some non-Russian areas. In the Communist Party of Kirgizia the proportion of Kirgiz members fell from 38 to 34 percent between 1946 and 1953,

391

while the proportion of Russian members rose from 32 to 38 percent (see Table 40a). In Tadzhikistan only 39 percent of those admitted to the party between 1949 and 1952 were Tadzhiks,[38] compared with 68 percent in 1939-1940.[39] In Moldavia, where about two-thirds of the population were Moldavians, only 25 percent of the party membership were Moldavians in 1952.[40]

The mass recruitment of the Khrushchev period produced a widespread improvement in indigenous party membership in non-Russian areas. This may be illustrated by the official data reproduced in Table 39[41] which shows the percentage of

TABLE 39: PROPORTION OF NATIVES AMONG CPSU RECRUITS IN CERTAIN REPUBLICS, 1960-1964

Republic	Natives as percent of republic population 1959	Natives as percent of new CPSU candidates in republic 1960	1964
Azerbaidzhan	67.5	71.0	74.4
Armenia	88.0	91.7	91.8
Georgia	64.3		78.2
Lithuania	79.3	74.3	76.1
Estonia	74.6	60.7	61.0
Uzbekistan	62.2	63.5	60.3
Tadzhikistan	53.1	68.9	68.5
Ukraine	76.8	73.2	71.7
Belorussia	81.1	82.0	78.6

indigenous recruits in a number of republics in the years 1960 and 1964. The failure of the source to include data

[38] KT, September 20, 1952.
[39] B, Nos. 15-16, 1940, p. 2.
[40] SM, September 20, 1952.
[41] SOURCES: PZh, No. 1, January 1962, p. 49 and No. 10, May 1965, p. 12; Itogi vsesoiuznoi perepisi naseleniia 1959 goda: SSSR, pp. 206-208.

from Kazakhstan, Kirgizia, Turkmenia, Latvia and Moldavia probably reflects the fact that native recruitment was less favorable in these republics, but this does not necessarily mean that there was no improvement there in this period, as the case of Kirgizia indicates (see Table 40a)[42] In Moldavia the proportion of communists of Moldavian nationality appears to have risen by about 8 percent between 1952 and 1961.[43] In Latvia it was stated in 1958 that, due to inadequate political activity among ethnic Latvians, "few Latvians are being admitted to the party, especially in the towns";[44] between 1961 and 1965, however, the incidence of party membership among Latvians rose from 52 to 59 percent of the national average (see Table 37, p. 378).

Assuming a reasonable scale of recruitment, national inequalities in the incidence of party membership may be well on the way to elimination in a further 20 or 30 years. Meanwhile, however, the percentage of indigenous nationals in the population of many non-Russian areas will have been sharply reduced. The ethnic composition of the CPSU in these areas in the years to come will depend upon the balance between these two conflicting trends.

Fairly extensive data are available from Uzbekistan, Kirgizia and Kazakhstan on the national composition of party

[42] SOURCES: *KP Kirgizii*, pp. 224, 276; Lorimer, *op.cit.*, p. 64; A. A. Isupov, *Natsional'nyi sostav naseleniia SSSR*, p. 30.

[43] Calculated from data published in *SM*, September 20, 1952, and November 30, 1961, and *PZh*, No. 1, January 1962, p. 49, assuming equality of party membership rate among the 15 percent of Moldavians living outside the Moldavian S.S.R. with the 85 percent living in the republic.

[44] *S Lat*, January 24, 1958. It is perhaps not without significance that two compilations of party membership data for Latvia, unlike such compilations published for certain other republics, contain no statistical information about ethnic composition. See *Kommunist Sovetskoi Latvii*, No. 7, July 1962, and No. 4, April 1965.

TABLE 40a: Ethnic Composition of Communist Party of Kirgizia, 1925-1962

Year	Percent of party membership						Percent of republic population		
	Kirgiz	Other Asians	Total Asians	Rus-sians	Other Euro-peans	Total Euro-peans	Year	Kirgiz	Rus-sian
1925	64	16	80			20	1926	67	12
1933	59	9	68	26	6	32			
1938	46	13	59	28	13	41	1939	52	21
1941	44	13	57	31	12	43			
1946	38	15	53	32	15	47			
1953	34			38					
1959	35	13	48	38	13	51	1959	41	30
1962	36	12	48	38	14	52			

members from the mid-1920's on. These show two quite distinct patterns of interaction between the trends referred to in the preceding paragraph. The contrast can best be illustrated from the cases of Kirgizia and Uzbekistan (see Tables 40a and 40b).[45] In both cases there was a progressive dilution of the indigenous population by immigration, and at the same time improving relative representation of indigenous nationals in the party. However, in Kirgizia it was not until the 1950's that the rate of indigenous recruitment reached a level sufficient to halt the decline in Kirgiz representation in the local party membership, by which time the proportion of Kirgiz in the population had fallen so far as to exclude the possibility of their ever regaining a majority in "their" party organization; whereas in Uzbekistan the recruitment of indigenous communists, though still only half

[45] Sources for Table 40b: *KP Uzbekistana v tsifrakh*, pp. 21, 41, 44, 60, 68, 76, 84, 98, 112, 133, 148, 163, 173, 189; Lorimer, *op.cit.*, p. 64; Isupov, *op.cit.*, p. 30.

TABLE 40b: Ethnic Composition of Communist Party of Uzbekistan, 1925-1964

Year	Uzbek[a]	Other[b] Central Asian	Total Central Asian	Russian	Other non-Central Asian	Total non-Central Asian	Year	Uzbek	Russian
								Percent of republic population	
1925	42	10	52	40	8	48	1926	74	6
1931	52	12	64	29	7	36			
1933	61	13	74	20	6	26			
1937	52	11	63	26	11	37			
1939	49	12	61	27	12	39	1939	65	12
1941	51	13	64	25	11	36			
1943	36	10	46	27	27	54			
1946	48	13	61	24	15	39			
1949	45	13	58	27	15	42			
1953	49	13	62	25	13	38			
1956	50	13	63	25	12	37			
1959	52	14	66	24	10	34	1959	62	14
1961	53	13	66	23	11	34			
1964	54	14	68	22	10	32			

[a] Including Karakalpaks
[b] Including Kazakhs and Tatars

the average CPSU level, had sufficiently outrun the effects of immigration by the late 1950's to restore the absolute majority of Uzbek party members which had been lost during World War II.

Though long-term trends in Kazakhstan resemble those in Kirgizia, the ethnic history of the CPSU in the two republics shows some important differences (see Table 41).[46] Unlike Kirgizia, Kazakhstan has long been an important area of Russian and Ukrainian settlement, and Kazakhs were al-

[46] Sources: Beisembaev and Pakhmurnyi, op.cit., pp. 95, 98, 101, 144, 146, 176, 204, 240, 244, 251, 273, 279, 313, 320, 327, 353, 359; Isupov, op.cit., p. 29; Lorimer, op.cit., p. 64.

TABLE 41: ETHNIC COMPOSITION OF COMMUNIST PARTY OF KAZAKHSTAN, 1924-1960

Year	Percent of party membership				Percent of population			
	Kazakhs	Russians	Ukrainians	Others	Kazakhs	Russians	Ukrainians	Others
1924	8	54	12	26				
1925	29	51	6	14				
1926	36	44	8	12	57	20		
1928	38	38	11	13				
1930	43							
1933	53	38						
1936	53	33						
1938	47	34	10	9				
1939	49	33	10	8	38	40	11	11
1941	51	32	10	7				
1943	32	37	16	15				
1945	43	35	10	12				
1950	41	41	11	7				
1952	40	41	10	9				
1954	41	41	10	8				
1956	38	43	11	8				
1959					30	43	8	19
1960	36	43	11	10				

ready outnumbered before World War II. On the other hand, they have long been proportionately far better represented in the party than either the Kirgiz or Uzbeks (in 1965 their membership rate was 45 per 1,000 compared with 33 per 1,000 and 29 per 1,000 respectively, which incidentally made them even better represented than the Ukrainians and Belorussians, whose rate was 44 per 1,000). In Kazakhstan itself they had in 1959 a party membership rate well above the average for the republic, higher than the local Russian population, and only slightly lower than the Ukrainians (see Table 38d).[47] Thus both processes—dilution of the indige-

[47] J. W. Cleary, in his unpublished Ph.D. thesis, "Politics and Administration in Kazakhstan 1955-1964" (Australian National Uni-

nous population and increased relative representation of indigenous nationals in the CPSU—have proceeded much faster and farther in Kazakhstan than in Kirgizia. The net effects, however, have been much the same. The proportion of native Kazakhs among all communists in Kazakhstan soared from 8 percent in 1924 to over 50 percent in the early 1930's, fell off somewhat during the purges, and recovered during the postpurge recruitment.

After the drastic shake-up of the war, when evacuation temporarily lifted the proportion of Ukrainians and others (probably largely Jews and Belorussians) from 17 to 31 percent, the proportion of Kazakhs settled down in the postwar decade at about 10 percent lower than before the war. With the "virgin lands" campaign of the mid-1950's, however, the influx of European settlers was accelerated, and by 1960 Russian and Ukrainian communists in the republic were one and a half times as numerous as the Kazakhs.

Soviet writers envisage the eventual disappearance of distinct nationalities within the Soviet population as involving two long-term processes, which may be summarized as equalization and homogenization, the first generally preceding, but overlapping with, the second.[48] In this context, the trends

---

versity, Canberra, 1967), has shown that Kazakhs were also numerically overrepresented among the party elite of the republic during this period. The same applies at the middle levels of the party bureaucracy. In 1960 Kazakhs made up almost half of all obkom, gorkom and raikom secretaries in the republic, though they comprised only 36 percent of the party membership and 30 percent of the population. See Beisembaev and Pakhmurnyi, *op.cit.*, p. 339.

[48] See e.g. V. S. Lukoshko *Sblizhenie sotsialisticheskikh natsii v period razvernutogo stroitel'stva kommunizma* (Moscow, 1963), S. N. Stepin, *Natsional'nyi vopros v programme KPSS* (Moscow, 1963), and K. Kh. Khanazarov, *Sblizhenie natsii i natsional'nye iazyki v SSSR* (Tashkent, 1963).

397

we have noted in the national composition of the Communist Party of Kirgizia, and even more so of the Communist Party of Kazakhstan, appear quite proper and normal. However, it is clear that these trends are still far from universal. The great variety presented by trends in the national composition of the CPSU membership in different non-Russian areas may be reduced to four main patterns:

1. Where the indigenous nationalities have consistently maintained clear predominance in the local party membership. Georgia and Armenia are probably the only examples of this pattern.

2. Where the indigenous nationalities, although in the past strongly underrepresented in "their" party organizations, have managed to maintain or, as is the case of Uzbekistan, to regain, a numerical majority, and seem likely to maintain this majority for the foreseeable future. This applies most notably to the Ukraine and Belorussia. It probably applies to Azerbaidzhan, and the Dagestan and Chuvash Autonomous Republics. The Baltic republics and Turkmenia evidently also conform to this pattern, but they have shown some signs of lapsing into pattern 3.

3. Where the indigenous nationalities, though constituting a plurality or even an absolute majority of the local population, now appear unlikely ever to attain (or regain) a numerical majority in the party membership. This applies to Kirgizia and Moldavia, and probably also to the Kabardin-Balkar, North Ossetian, Tatar, Tuva and Yakut Autonomous Republics.

4. Where the indigenous nationalities are so heavily outnumbered in "their own" areas that their attainment of even a plurality in the local party membership seems out of the question—even in cases where their rate of party member-

ship is relatively high. This applies in Kazakhstan, and in the Bashkir, Buryat, Kalmuck, Karelian, Komi, Mari, Mordvin, Udmurt and Chechen-Ingush Autonomous Republics. The autonomous oblasts of the R.S.F.S.R. probably all conform to patterns 3 or 4.

Chapter 13

Party Membership and Education

IN AN education-oriented society like the Soviet Union, the educational qualifications of an individual constitute in themselves an important constituent of his social status. At the same time, however, these qualifications will to a greater or lesser extent determine the occupational opportunities open to him. Clearly, then, we will need some idea of major trends in the educational composition of the CPSU in relation to broad educational patterns in the population at large, before attempting, as we do in the next chapter, to consider the claims of the CPSU to be regarded as a (or *the*) Soviet elite.

The prerevolutionary Bolshevik Party, founded and led by *intelligenty*, setting great store by ideological purity and hence strongly oriented towards the printed word, was an essentially literate organization functioning in a semiliterate society.[1] This contrast remained marked for many years after the Revolution, and persists in a modified form today.

Table 42[2] summarizes the available data on the main educational groups in the CPSU between 1919 and 1967.

[1] In terms of the fairly stringent criteria of literacy employed by tsarist statisticians, the proportion of literate persons aged over 8 in the Russian Empire on the eve of World War I was only about 40 percent (see A. G. Rashin, *Naselenie Rossii za 100 let* [Moscow, 1956], p. 311). However, the percentage was higher in the towns than in the country, and among some groups of urban workers it reached 70 percent or more (see I. Yu. Pisarev, *Narodonaselenie SSSR* [Moscow, 1962], pp. 148-151).

[2] SOURCES: *Izv Ts K*, No. 15, March 24, 1920, No. 1, January 1923 and Nos. 47-48, December 31, 1927; *P*, March 15, 1939; *PZh*, No. 20, October 1947, p. 83, No. 1, January 1962, p. 48, No. 10, May 1965, p. 11, and No. 19, October 1967, p. 14. The last-named source

400

TABLE 42: Education of CPSU Membership, 1919-1967

Year	Higher Percent	Secondary Percent	Incomplete secondary Percent	Primary and less Percent
1919 (sample only)	5.0	8.0		87.0
1922	0.6	6.3		92.7
1927	0.8	7.9		91.3
1939	5.1	14.2		
1947	6.3	20.5	23.7	49.5
1956	11.2	25.8	29.6	33.4
1961	13.3	29.6	28.6	28.5
1965	15.0	32.7	27.9	24.4
1967	16.5	34.1	49.4	

Note: The 1919 percentages are based on a sample of 16,069 members as of October 1919, equal to about one-tenth of the whole party membership. All others are based on the whole party membership, including candidates. Primary education is normally completed in 4 years, incomplete secondary in 7 years and secondary in 10 years. Sixteen percent of those shown with primary education or less in 1919, however, had attended schools of the superior, "urban" kind. Percentages for those with secondary education include members who have commenced higher education courses but not completed them. In 1965 these amounted to 2.6 percent.

The percentages for 1919 call for some comment. In the light of subsequent data, the figure of 5 percent for members possessing higher education seems implausible, even on the hypothesis that unlike later figures, it includes all who

also includes breakdowns for 1937 and 1957 and gives slightly different percentages for 1927 and 1947. The following figures are also available for 1966 (*P*, March 30, 1966):

	percent
higher and incomplete higher education	18.2
secondary education	30.9
incomplete secondary education	27.5
primary education	23.4

401

had *commenced* a higher education, without necessarily completing it. On the other hand, the percentages for other educational categories *do* seem plausible, while the scale of recruitment and of membership losses between October 1919 and 1922 would have permitted sharp changes in the educational profile of the party between these dates. In publishing its analysis of the sample, the Information and Statistics Department of the Central Committee stated its opinion that it did not differ significantly from what would be obtained from data on the whole party membership.[3] What is known about the compilation of the sample moreover, would not lead us to expect any great bias in favor of the better-educated categories.[4] It seems probable, therefore, that there was a marked decline of educational standards in the CPSU after 1919, especially at the higher educational levels.

Between 1922 and 1927 there were slight increases in the percentages of party members with secondary and higher education. On balance, however, the educational composition of the party worsened during this period. The proportion of members who had completed at least four years of formal schooling (92 percent in the 1919 sample) declined from 82 percent in 1922 to 71 percent in 1927. Meanwhile there was an increase in the number of communists with bare literacy, acquired by self-instruction or through adult literacy classes,[5]

[3] See *Deviatyi s"ezd RKP(b): protokoly*, p. 571.

[4] See *ibid.*, p. 572. The sample comprises complete data on party members and candidates in the Samara, Ivanovo-Voznesensk, Riazan, Simbirsk and Vitebsk guberniyas, and data on the whole membership in most uezds of some nineteen other guberniyas, varying widely in their location and the character of their economies. Timofeevskii, *op.cit.*, p. 138, appears to err in treating this data as a sample of party membership at the time of publication (March 1920) rather than in October 1919.

[5] See *Izv Ts K*, No. 1, January 1923 and Nos. 47-48, December 31, 1927.

due to the mass intake of manual workers and peasants following the death of Lenin. It is unlikely that this trend was reversed, and it may even have been accentuated, during the mass recruitment campaigns of 1927-1932. These facts about the educational profile of the CPSU need to be borne in mind when considering the political history of this period, for the resolutions adopted and the delegates chosen by party cells throughout the country often played a significant part in the leadership struggles which culminated in the Stalin dictatorship. It is small wonder that the subtleties of a Trotsky or a Bukharin cut very little ice in the average party cell, of whose members six out of ten had received only a primary (four-year) schooling and a further three out of ten had received no formal education at all.

Despite the rudimentary education possessed by the majority of party members during the 1920's, the literacy level of the party still contrasted very favorably with that of the population at large. The 1926 census showed that one Soviet citizen in two aged over eight was illiterate, and as late as 1939 the proportion was one in five.[6] By contrast, the 1919 sample of party members revealed an illiteracy rate of only 3 percent, while the percentages in 1922 and 1927 were 4.6 and 2.4 respectively.[7] Educationally, then, the party was certainly proletarian in character, but it stood in the literate "vanguard" of the proletariat. While it would be difficult to quantify, it is safe to assume that there was a significant correlation between literacy and party membership among both

[6] See Pisarev, *op.cit.*, p. 152. In view of the unequal representation of men and women in the party, it is worth noting that 67 percent of Soviet men were recorded as literate in 1926, compared with 37 percent of women. In 1939 the percentages were 91 percent and 73 percent respectively.

[7] See *Izv Ts K*, No. 15, March 24, 1920, No. 1, January 1923 and Nos. 47-48, December 31, 1927.

workers and peasants during these years, with both variables also correlating positively with a third—upward occupational mobility.

Although illiteracy never reached significant proportions in the party as a whole, it was a major problem among certain nationalities and in certain areas. In 1927 the illiteracy rate among Kazakh, Uzbek, Kirgiz and Turkmen communists ranged from 27 to 46 percent.[8] In 1933, 21 percent of all communists in Central Asia were still illiterate.[9] The problem was reduced to minor proportions, however, during the purges of the 1930's. By 1939 only 3 percent of party members in Uzbekistan were illiterate,[10] and in Kirgizia the percentage was even smaller.[11] Nonetheless it proved difficult to eliminate illiteracy from the party entirely. Relatively com-

[8] See *Sotsial'nyi i natsional'nyi sostav VKP(b)*, p. 145.

[9] See *PS*, No. 20, October 1933, pp. 41-43. See also *ibid.*, Nos. 3-4, February 1932, pp. 21-22, and *Izv Ts K*, Nos. 43-44, November 16, 1925 and Nos. 5-6, February 14, 1927. Illiteracy was defined as unfamiliarity with the alphabet. Once a person had mastered the alphabet he was classed as "literate, but without primary education."

[10] *P*, March 22, 1939.

[11] *KP Kirgizii*, pp. 121, 152. Evidence from Tadzhikistan indicates that there, at least, it was in 1935-1936 that the drive against illiteracy achieved its greatest successes, after the relative failure of earlier efforts. In December 1931 the Tadzhik Central Committee opened a three-month campaign to eliminate "alphabet illiteracy" among Tadzhik communists. Although nearly 8,000 attended "Illiteracy Elimination" (*Likbez*) courses during this period, the campaign was declared in March 1932 to have been a failure, and the republic Central Committee then placed responsibility on the raikoms to make a "radical attack" on the problem. See *Ocherki istorii Kommunisticheskoi Partii Tadzhikistana*, pp. 100, 117). However, during the Verification of Party Documents in 1935, it was discovered that one-seventh of all communists in Tadzhikistan were still totally illiterate, whereupon these were promptly drafted to full-time "Illiteracy Elimination" schools specially set up for the purpose, and this was said to have virtually put an end to illiteracy among Tadzhik communists (*ibid.*, p. 138).

plete data is available on this point from Kirgizia, where the number of illiterate communists actually increased during the war to about 1.5 percent.[12] That party officialdom regarded this with concern is indicated by a January 1948 decision of the Kirgiz Central Committee making obkom and raikom secretaries personally responsible for eliminating illiteracy among party members in their areas within a year.[13] However, the number of illiterates among Kirgiz communists again increased during 1949,[14] and it was not till 1953 that it was reduced below prewar levels.[15]

If illiteracy among party members was always a fairly localized phenomenon, this was not true of semiliteracy. As we have seen, in 1927 over a quarter of all CPSU members and candidates were semiliterate, in the sense that they were familiar with the alphabet but had received less than four years' schooling.[16] It may be assumed that this proportion fell rapidly from the 1930's, but there are no party-wide figures on this. In Kirgizia and Uzbekistan about a half of all communists in 1937 were semiliterate in the sense defined.[17] In Kirgizia the proportion had fallen to one in five by 1943 and to about one in eight by 1955.[18] In Uzbekistan the proportion fell more gently at first—to 36 percent in 1941 and to 29 percent in 1945; it accelerated in the postwar years, slowed

[12] *KP Kirgizii*, pp. 180, 203.
[13] *Ibid.*, p. 198.
[14] *Ibid.*, pp. 206, 209.
[15] *Ibid.*, pp. 213, 217, 221, 224, 228. It was during this period that the remnants of illiteracy among Tadzhik communists also appear to have been eliminated. Though absolute figures are not available, there were said to have been only one-ninth as many illiterate communists in Tadzhikistan in September 1952 as there had been three and a half years earlier (*KT*, September 20, 1952).
[16] *Izv Ts K*, Nos. 47-48, December 31, 1927.
[17] *KP Kirgizii*, p. 121; *KP Uzbekistana v tsifrakh*, p. 59.
[18] *KP Kirgizii*, pp. 174, 243.

down in the early 1950's, and then fell precipitately from 15 percent in 1955 to 5 percent in 1959 to 2.5 percent in 1964.[19] In this republic, at least, the proportion of party members who had not completed primary school appears to have been no greater in the villages than the towns by the late 1950's.[20] Since these figures from Central Asia were almost certainly higher than the average for the CPSU as a whole, it may be concluded that semiliteracy among party members had been reduced to marginal proportions by the mid-1960's.

Turning again to Table 42, we see that the improvement in party educational levels since the 1920's has passed through four main phases. The first was the breakthrough of the technical intelligentsia in the 1930's. The proportion of party members with secondary education doubled between 1927 and 1939, while the proportion with higher education increased sixfold. Even in 1939, however, four out of five CPSU members were educated to less than the secondary level. In the second phase, corresponding with the war years, there were further substantial improvements but these were practically confined to the secondary level.[21] The decade following World War II constituted the third phase, when the proportion of communists with higher education doubled, and those with only primary education or less declined from a half to a third of all communists. The fourth phase was the era of mass recruitment under Khrushchev, when overall improvement continued, but at a considerably reduced rate. Whether the cutback in recruitment after 1964 signified a

[19] KP Uzbekistana v tsifrakh, pp. 77, 94, 123, 144, 164, 179, 190.
[20] Tulepbaev, op.cit., p. 121.
[21] Despite increased recruitment among lower occupational strata during the war, the proportion of recruits with secondary or higher education was said to have been twice that in the corresponding pre-war period (see M. Shamberg, in PS, No. 4, February 1946, p. 28).

new change in the educational profile of the CPSU was unclear at the time of writing. Despite revolutionary progress in Soviet levels of education, the contrast between the educational profile of the CPSU membership and that of the Soviet population at large shows little sign of narrowing. As may be seen from Table 43,[22] the likelihood in the early 1960's of a party member

TABLE 43: EDUCATION OF CPSU MEMBERSHIP AND SOVIET POPULATION

Level of education	Soviet population aged 20 or over, Jan. 1959 Percent	CPSU members and candidates Percent		Estimated party saturation Percent
		Jan. 1956	Jan. 1962	1959
Higher	2.9	11.2	13.7	27.0
Incomplete higher	1.2	⎰ 25.8	2.9	⎱ 14.0
Secondary	11.5	⎱	27.2	⎰
Incomplete secondary	19.6	29.6	28.4	9.5
Primary or less	64.7	33.4	27.8	0.3

possessing a higher education was nearly five times that of the average Soviet citizen, while the likelihood of his having completed secondary school was two and a half times the

22 SOURCES: *PZh*, No. 10, 1965, p. 11; *Itogi vsesoiuznoi perepisi naseleniia 1959 goda: SSSR*, pp. 74-75. In order to estimate the party "saturation" of different educational groups in 1959, it was first necessary to derive approximate figures for the educational distribution of the party membership in that year from the figures available for 1956 and 1962. In deriving these figures it was assumed that 40 percent of the difference between each pair of 1956 and 1962 figures had been achieved by January 1959, since approximately 40 percent of the 1956-1962 increase in total party membership had been achieved by that date. While this procedure obviously leaves room for error, such error is unlikely to be large enough to significantly affect the estimates of party "saturation" given in the table.

national average. Nearly two-thirds of the whole adult population of the Soviet Union had received less than seven years schooling, compared to a little over a quarter of the party membership. In 1959 approximately one-third of the adult population had not even completed primary (four-year) school, whereas, as we have seen, the number of party members to which this applied was now negligible.

Table 43 also shows us that the incidence of party membership rises sharply as one moves up the educational ladder. In 1959 only one adult in thirty with less than seven years schooling was in the party, whereas among graduates of higher educational establishments the proportion exceeded one in four. The big jumps in party "saturation" came with the completion of seven years' schooling and the obtaining of a higher education diploma. The contrast between the incidence of party membership as between those with incomplete (seven years) and completed (ten years) education is far smaller.

Unfortunately there is insufficient synchronized data to trace in detail changes in the rate of party membership among different educational strata since the 1920's. Enough is available, however, to show that the "saturation" of higher strata, after increasing sharply in the 1930's, thereupon tended to level out, and it has probably not changed much since World War II. Nicholas De Witt, in his monumental study on the education and employment of Soviet professionals, has calculated that the proportion of party members among persons with higher education employed in the national economy rose from 3.8 percent in 1929 to 15.1 percent in 1939 to 30.0 percent in 1947, but was still 30.5 percent in 1956 and 30.8 percent in 1959.[23] Meanwhile, official data are available

[23] Nicholas De Witt, *Education and Professional Employment in the USSR* (Washington, National Science Foundation, 1961), p.

on party membership among "specialists," a category that includes persons with a higher education and also graduates of *tekhnikumy*, pedagogical training schools and other specialized secondary schools, but excludes graduates of ordinary general secondary schools. The proportion of communists among all specialists employed in the economy rose from 1.2 percent in 1928 to 20.5 percent in January 1941. In the next sixteen years to December 1956, however, it rose only to 28.0 percent, while from 1956 to 1960 the increase was a mere one-half of 1 percent.[24] We may therefore conclude that the intake of graduates of higher and specialized secondary educational establishments into the party, large though it has been, has for many years only barely sufficed to maintain existing levels of party "saturation" of these groups.

This points up the dilemma which the rapid advance of Soviet educational levels presents for party recruitment policy. Unless the party is to steadily lose ground among the better-educated strata of the population, it must maintain a high level of recruitment among these strata. Yet these strata

---

534. Taking *all* Soviet citizens possessing a higher education (i.e. not only those employed in the economy), it appears that the proportion who are party members has actually declined since World War II. As already indicated, this proportion was a little over a quarter in the early 1960's whereas in 1945 it was one-third (404,513 out of 1,200,-000). See *Istoriia Velikoi Otechestvennoi Voiny Sovetskogo Soiuza: 1941-1945*, Vol. VI, p. 377.

[24] *PZh*, No. 1, January 1962, p. 48. From 1962 to 1965 the number of communists with higher or specialized secondary education increased by 848,000 (*ibid.*, No. 10, May 1965, p. 12). Since this was evidently little more than a third of the number of graduates from higher and specialized secondary institutions during this period (see *Narodnoe khoziaistvo SSSR v 1963 godu*, p. 574) it seems unlikely that the proportion of party members among all Soviet specialists increased more than marginally over the December 1960 level of 28.5 percent.

409

remain a small minority of the Soviet population, and they will continue to do so for many years to come. This means that heavy recruitment among the poorer-educated strata is also necessary if the unequal representation of different educational strata is not to become rapidly more marked. Clearly, there are built-in pressures here to maintain a high recruitment level, since the intake of new members cannot be reduced below a certain point without seriously harming either the representativeness of the party or existing levels of "saturation" of the educational elite. As we shall see below, the same kind of dilemma confronts the party in other forms as well.

Implicit in the way party educational statistics are presented in Soviet official sources is the high value which is placed on the recruitment of specialists. It is not surprising, therefore, that persons with a specialized secondary education are considerably more likely to join the party than persons with a general secondary education. Of all Soviet citizens in 1959 with a completed secondary education 44 percent had attended specialized secondary schools,[25] whereas among party members in 1962 the proportion was 58 percent. The graduate of a general ten-year school was in fact scarcely more likely to join the party than the graduate of a seven-year school, while the graduate of a specialized secondary school was about 60 percent more likely to do so.[26]

It would be a mistake to conclude from this, however, that the better-educated members of the CPSU are predominantly drawn from the "technical intelligentsia." In 1961 slightly less than half the "specialist" members of the CPSU had been trained in technical or agricultural specialties,[27] and the pro-

[25] *Itogi vsesoiuznoi perepisi naseleniia 1959 goda: SSSR*, pp. 74-75.
[26] Based on data in *PZh*, No. 10, May 1965, pp. 11-12. Cf. *ibid.*, No. 1, January 1962, p. 48.
[27] *Ibid.*, No. 1, January 1962, p. 48.

portion had not significantly increased by 1965.[28] Since until recently specialists in technical fields were being graduated at a far lower rate than in nontechnical fields (education, economics, law, medicine and arts),[29] the technical specialists were, it is true, better represented in the party in relation to their numbers in the population. Nonetheless, when nonspecialist secondary graduates are also taken into account, we see that less than a third of all party members in the early 1960's with a full secondary or higher education were drawn from the "technical intelligentsia."[30]

Finally, we should not be led, by the relatively high incidence of party membership among the better-educated strata of society, to exaggerate the degree of identity between the party and the educational elite of the country. To say that 27 percent of Soviet citizens possessing higher education are members of the CPSU is also to say that 73 percent of them are not. Clearly, there must be many fields of employment in the Soviet Union requiring a higher education which are not restricted to party members.

[28] *Ibid.*, No. 10, May 1965, p. 75.
[29] See *Narodnoe khoziaistvo SSSR v 1963 godu: statisticheskii ezhegodnik*, p. 577.
[30] No general figures are available on the proportion of party school graduates among communists with secondary and higher education, but this proportion appears to be small. In Uzbekistan in 1937, 2.7 percent of all communists were graduates from higher party schools and 3.0 percent were graduates from secondary party schools. By 1941 these proportions had fallen to 0.4 percent and 1.8 percent, and by 1951 to 0.2 percent and 1.1 percent respectively. In 1951 party school graduates constituted 3 percent of all communists in Uzbekistan with a higher education and 6 percent of those with a secondary education. No later figures were published. See *KP Uzbekistana v tsifrakh*, pp. 59, 77, 94, 123.

Chapter 14

A Representative Elite?

THE OFFICIAL formula that the CPSU comprises "the *best* representatives of the working class, the kolkhoz peasantry and the Soviet intelligentsia" imputes to it the quality of an elite, yet an elite of a rather peculiar kind: one in which representation is ensured for all major segments of Soviet society.[1] We are already familiar with the two distinct aspects which this "representative elite" concept acquires in practice. On the one hand it covers those individuals drawn originally from all strata of society who enjoy elite status because the *posts* they hold carry high prestige, remuneration or power; for them a party card is at the same time a pass to and a certificate of success in Soviet society. On the other hand, it includes a leavening of members currently located in all spheres and at all levels of employment, including those which are relatively low in prestige, remuneration or power; by virtue

---

[1] The term "elite" is used here in the nonnormative sense of groups enjoying high levels of power, income or prestige in a given society. A useful discussion of the elite concept, distinguishing between the analytical and ideological levels of its use in Western sociology over the last fifty years, will be found in T. B. Bottomore, *Elites and Society* (London, 1964). Reference to the CPSU as an elite is common in the literature on Soviet society. See, for instance, Alfred G. Meyer, *The Soviet Political System: An Interpretation*, p. 136, Fainsod, *How Russia Is Ruled*, p. 247, Duverger, *Political Parties*, p. 266. This usage needs to be carefully qualified, as the discussion in the present chapter indicates. John Armstrong prefers to restrict the term to those sections of the party membership who are involved in the decision-making process (*The Soviet Bureaucratic Elite*, Chap. 1; cf. his *Ideology, Politics and Government in the Soviet Union*, pp. 51-53 and Rigby, "The Selection of Leading Personnel in the Soviet State and Communist Party," Chaps. 4-6, 9).

412

of party membership these become, as it were, an elite of the non-elite, are invested with special responsibilities and prestige, and often acquire opportunities for influence, promotion or education which they would not otherwise enjoy. It is this basic ambiguity in the representative elite concept which prevents us from simply identifying the CPSU as *the* political (or social) elite of the U.S.S.R.

We cannot attempt here the massive task of identifying and characterizing the political (or social) elite (or elites) of the U.S.S.R. Our modest objective is simply to record the degree of reciprocal representation between the CPSU membership and those categories of Soviet citizens who *prima facie* stand high with respect to prestige, remuneration or power. There are two ways in which this may be expected to help Soviet elite studies; firstly by establishing how far various presumed elite categories are incorporated into the party, and secondly, since party membership is held to be reserved for "the best of the best," by using the criterion of its incidence in different social and occupational groups to help identify and rank various elite categories. At the same time we must realize its limitations. We have no right to assume *a priori* that the incidence of party membership taken alone is an adequate guide to elite status. There are also limitations of evidence. We simply do not know how many persons in certain social and occupational categories are in the party, while certain categories of the population which it would be interesting to investigate cannot readily be isolated from the available statistical data.

"Social Position" and Spheres of Employment

Despite the primacy of esteem accorded the working class in Soviet ideology, the workers appear always to have played second fiddle to the white-collar-intelligentsia "stratum" so

413

far as the incidence of party membership is concerned. Table 44[2] compares the percentages of party members registered as

TABLE 44: CLASS COMPOSITION OF SOVIET POPULATION AND CPSU

	Population 1959 Percent	CPSU 1956 Percent	CPSU 1961 Percent
Workers	48.2	32.0	34.5
Collective farmers	31.4	17.1	17.5
White-collar workers	20.1	50.9	48.0

workers, collective farmers and white-collar workers, with the distribution of these categories in the Soviet population. It shows that the chances of a worker entering the party were about twice those of a collective farmer, while the chances of a white-collar worker were six or seven times as great. This suggests that elite status was far more accessible (or attractive) to members of the white-collar-intelligentsia stratum than to other social groups, and least of all accessible (or attractive) to the collective farmer.

As the reader is already aware, party members transferred to white-collar jobs after joining the party usually continue to be shown as "workers" or "collective farmers" in party statistics. Such members have always been numerous, and class breakdowns like those shown in Table 44 therefore

2 SOURCES: *Itogi vsesoiuznoi perepisi naseleniia 1959 goda: SSSR*, p. 90; *PZh*, No. 1, January 1962, p. 47. For a useful recent discussion of the concepts *sluzhashchie* (white-collar workers) and "intelligentsia," see V. S. Semënov, "Ob izmenenii intelligentsii i sluzhashchikh v protsesse razvernutogo stroitel'stva kommunizma" (On Changes in the Intelligentsia and White-Collar Workers in the Course of the Full-Scale Building of Communism" in G. V. Osipov, ed., *Sotsiologiia v SSSR* (Sociology in the U.S.S.R.), (Moscow, 1965), Vol. I, p. 419.

seriously understate the preferential representation of the white-collar stratum. The degree of understatement, however, probably varies over time, though it can rarely be established from the available data, and this obviously limits the value of such breakdowns in deducing trends in the social composition of the party.

Many of the facts adduced in earlier chapters point to the bureaucracies of official and "voluntary" organizations as the sphere of heaviest party membership, and to agriculture as the sphere most weakly represented.

Details of the employment of the Soviet workforce and of party members which have appeared in recent years confirm these differences and enable us to allot approximate quantities to them (see Table 45).[3]

TABLE 45: PARTY MEMBERSHIP RATIO IN MAIN SPHERES OF CIVILIAN EMPLOYMENT, 1964

Sphere of employment	Percent of those in civil employment		Approximate ratio of party membership
	Population	Party	
Government, economic, party, etc. bureaucracies	2.0	9.5	4.8
Education, health, science, etc.	13.0	16.3	1.3
Trade and materials-handling	6.0	4.9	0.8
Transport and communication	8.0	9.2	1.2
Industry and construction	35.0	35.4	1.0
Agriculture and forestry	33.0	22.7	0.7
Other fields	3.0	2.0	0.7

[3] SOURCES: *PZh*, No. 10, May 1965, p. 14; *Narodnoe Khoziaistvo SSSR v 1964 godu: statisticheskii ezhegodnik* (Moscow, 1965), p. 543.

415

In the middle 1960's the ratio between the proportion of party members employed in the bureaucracies and the proportion of the Soviet civilian workforce so employed was nearly four times that for people employed in the educational, health, science and related fields, five times that for industrial employees and seven times that for agricultural employees. (It is important to realize that the education-health-science category includes not only professionals, but all the semiprofessionals and unskilled personnel employed by these institutions, who in some cases greatly outnumber the professional employees.)

Relating our data on the two variables examined, namely "social position" and field of employment, we may note first that members of the white-collar-intelligentsia stratum are found in all seven fields of civilian employment as well as among the military, pensioners, students and other groups not in regular civilian employment. Furthermore, there would appear to be no close correlation between the level of party "saturation" and the scale of white-collar-intelligentsia representation in the various sections of the workforce. For instance, this stratum is at least as well represented among educational, health and scientific workers as it is in the bureaucracies, yet the latter have a far higher ratio of party members.

These two variables, then, operate to some extent at least as independent determinants of party membership levels. It would seem a reasonable inference, therefore, that, insofar as the incidence of CPSU membership can be taken as a measure of elite status, the Soviet elite is focused on that section of the white-collar-intelligentsia stratum employed in the government and other bureaucracies, while the "lowest" stratum of the Soviet population consists of the non-white-collar section of the agricultural workforce. This inference

416

has considerable importance for general orientation purposes. However, as the examination of major employment categories which follows will show, it is in need of considerable qualification and refinement.

Government Officials

The first step of any revolutionary regime must be to place its members in all or most key positions in the state. After a brief period when certain posts were allocated to Left Socialist Revolutionaries, membership of the Council of People's Commissars, the new revolutionary government, quickly became a monopoly of Bolshevik Party members. Simultaneously, as the party took over power at local levels in the name of the soviets, local party leaders moved into the key jobs in the executive committees of the soviets, and before long bolsheviks constituted an overwhelming majority in these bodies. Data from some 60 percent of local soviets in the second half of 1919 showed that party members and candidates made up 89 percent of the membership of executive committees of guberniya congresses of soviets, 86 percent of the executive committees of uezd congresses of soviets, 93 percent of executive committees of city soviets in guberniya administrative centers and 71 percent of executive committees of town soviets in uezd administrative centers.[4] Subsequently, as the executive committees grew in size and as power increasingly passed to an inner group or presidium, there was some increase in the proportion of nonparty members.[5] At the same time, while precise data is unavailable, the presidia themselves appear to have been virtual

[4] M. Vladimirsky, *Sovety, ispolkomy i s"ezdy sovetov: Vypusk I* (Moscow, 1920), p. 7.

[5] The beginnings of this process were already discernible in 1921. See *ibid., Vypusk II* (Moscow, 1921), p. 15.

417

party preserves from their inception.[6] It was only at the low-est levels of the rural administration that party saturation of the government executive hierarchy remained incomplete. In 1927 nonparty officials still occupied half the chairman-ships of volost executive committees and three-quarters of the village soviet chairmanships.[7] By 1929 a third of the vil-lage Soviet chairmen, 96.3 percent of the chairmen of volost and raion executive committees and 99.7 percent of the chairmen of uezd and okrug executive committees were party members.[8] These figures reveal a remarkably rapid com-munization of volost chairmanships in these two years, co-inciding with the hardening of Stalin's line against the peas-antry and his break with the "Right." Soon after this the ad-ministrative situation in the rural areas was transformed by collectivization and the restructuring of territorial-adminis-trative divisions. The raion executive committee, whose key members were almost entirely party members, now became the basis of rural administration, functioning primarily through the collective and state farms and later also the MTS's, reducing the village soviets to a very subsidiary role.

In 1933 party members accounted for 99.4 percent of the chairmen and deputy chairmen of soviet executive com-mittees at the krai and oblast levels, 99.6 percent at the city level and 98.7 percent at the raion level.[9]

Subsequently official information on the party saturation of particular categories of posts becomes very scarce. One re-source for eking it out is lists of deputies to soviets, some of

[6] For a discussion of party penetration of the soviets and their executive bodies during the 1920's, see Theodor Seibert, *Red Russia* (London, 1932), pp. 89-95.

[7] See *XVs"ezd*, Vol. I, pp. 448-449.

[8] Bubnov, in *BSE* (1st edn.), Vol. II, cols. 541-542.

[9] *Sostav rukovodiashchikh rabotnikov i spetsialistov Soiuza SSR* (Moscow, 1936), p. 283.

which show both the post held by the deputy and whether or not he is a party member. An analysis has been made of thirteen such lists of deputies to oblast, city and city raion soviets elected between 1950 and 1961, and totaling almost 2,500 deputies.[10] Of course there is no reason to assume that the level of party saturation of any particular employment category in the population at large will correspond with that shown by a relatively small sample of soviet deputies. As one might expect, the soviet sample appears to show considerably higher levels than the general population. However, it would seem reasonable to treat the incidence of party membership in the soviet sample as *prima facie* evidence of the *relative* party saturation of particular employment categories, and to treat cases of 100 percent saturation of the soviet sample as *prima facie* evidence that these posts were in general limited to party members. The assumption here is that the choice of soviet deputies does not involve criteria which will seriously distort our sample in these two regards. While such independent evidence as exists tends to confirm this, it nevertheless remains an assumption. This analysis will be referred to as "the deputy sample."

The deputy sample suggests that those key posts in the government executive hierarchy which had already become a party monopoly by the 1920's or early 1930's remained a party monopoly in the 1950's. All 56 ministers and deputy ministers in republic governments and all 159 chairmen and deputy chairmen of oblast, city and raion executive committees in the sample were party members.

[10] The soviets analyzed were: Leningrad oblast (1950 and 1961); Moscow oblast (1959); Alma-Ata and Frunze oblasts (1950); Riga, Baku and Alma-Ata cities (1950); Frunze (1953) and Tallin (1957); Pervomai, Sverdlov and Proletarsky raions of Frunze (1953). Lists taken from Russian-language republic newspapers, *Leningradskaia Pravda* and *Leninskoe Znamia*.

419

So much for key posts. But what of government official-dom as a whole? Although there has been a general tendency for the incidence of party membership to rise, a large pro-portion of more junior government officials have always been nonparty people. Moreover, at least up to the early 1930's, nonparty officials continued to be found at even quite senior levels. In 1924, 86 percent of department chiefs, assistant chiefs and collegium members in central commissariats were party members and 14 percent were nonparty.[11] By 1933 all directorate, department and sector chiefs and their deputies and assistants were in the party, but only 78 percent of the chiefs of other minor divisions of the Council of People's Commissars and Central Executive Committee.[12]

In 1929 it was stated that of all employees in the various levels and grades of the governmental apparatus, one-quarter were party members. In those departments concerned with the administration of industry the proportion was only 14 percent.[13]

Comparative figures are available on the incidence of party membership in the medium and upper grades of the govern-

[11] *XIII S"ezd*, p. 114.
[12] *Sostav rukovodiashchikh rabotnikov i spetsialistov Soiuza SSR*, p. 282.
[13] *XVI konf.*, p. 459. In 1923 communists constituted 5 percent of all officials in VSNKh (the central industrial administration), in-cluding 15 percent of the "responsible officials" (*Izv Ts K*, No. 5, June 1923). By 1924 these proportions had risen to 9 percent and 17 percent respectively and by December 1925 to 14 percent and 29 percent (*Partiinye, professional'nye i kooperativnye organy i gosap-parat* (Moscow, 1926), (p. 46). In April 1927, 20 percent of all VSNKh officials were party members (*XV S"ezd*, Vol. I, p. 446). From then until 1930 there was evidently a further 4 or 5 percent rise. For data on the growth of party membership in other branches of the government service during the 1920's see *Kommunisty v sostave apparata gosuchrezhdenii i obshchestvennykh organizatsii* (Moscow, 1929), pp. 18ff; and *XV S"ezd*, Vol. I, pp. 446-447.

ment service at the republic, krai, oblast and raion levels in 1929 and 1933 (see Table 46).[14] These make a useful distinction between those officials charged with administrative responsibilities and those employed in a specialist or professional capacity or in research. Predictably, party membership was much more common among the former. This also applied in the central government, where 86 percent of the more senior administrative officers were party members, compared with 39 percent of the more senior professional officers.[15]

Table 46 also shows that, despite the increasing party saturation of government officialdom, nonparty officials still abounded up to at least the middle levels. (The very high party percentages shown for the raion executive committees are rather misleading here, since the data referred to only a tiny upper group of raion officials.)

There were big differences in the proportion of party members in different branches of the government service. As might be expected the People's Commissariat for Foreign Affairs showed a high party saturation. In Soviet missions abroad, not only were all department and sector chiefs and their assistants and deputies (i.e. all "line" officials) members of the CPSU, but so too were all but one of the 51 professional specialists. In the Commissariat itself, 76 percent of the medium and senior officials and specialists were party members.[16] By contrast, in the central offices of the People's Commissariat for Agriculture, party saturation of medium

---

[14] SOURCES: Based on data in *Sostav rukovodiashchikh rabotnikov i spetsialistov Soiuza SSR*, pp. 287-288. The data cover 6,225 republic-level officials in 1929 and 7,696 in 1933; 13,877 krai and oblast officials in 1929 and 23,207 in 1933; and 25,043 raion-level officials in 1929 and 7,304 in 1933. The last-named evidently represented a sample of raions only.

[15] *Ibid.*, p. 282.

[16] *Ibid.*, pp. 298-301.

421

TABLE 46: Party Membership of Government Officials, 1929-1933

Level	Senior and medium administrators Percent		Specialists without administrative powers Percent	
	1929	1933	1929	1933
Republic governments	47.8	61.0	19.3	16.1
Krai and oblast executive committees and directorates	48.4	62.6	7.4	14.3
Raion executive committees	62.7	92.9	5.2	15.1

and senior officials was 51 percent, and this fell to 34 percent in oblast agriculture directorates and 17 percent in raion agriculture departments.[17]

While the purges of 1933 to 1938 must have led to some reduction in the party saturation of the government bureaucracy, this reduction was probably far less than the overall 50 percent contraction of the party membership might suggest. Numerically the heaviest expulsions were among rank-and-file workers and especially peasants, and the purge period saw a substantial shift in the class composition of the party in favor of the white-collar workers. Moreover, purged officials were usually replaced by "worker" or "peasant" communists who had been put through training courses, and beginning in 1937 by young graduates of technical schools and institutes newly recruited to the party. At the Eighteenth Congress in 1939 Stalin spoke of the promotion of over half a million "members of the party and people standing close to the party" to leading party and government posts since 1934.[18] By the time of the German invasion party member-

[17] *Ibid.*, p. 252.
[18] *XVIII s"ezd*, p. 30.

ship levels among government officials probably exceeded those in 1933.

Since then there has probably been some further increase, but certainly not proportionate to the overall growth of the party. The period since World War II has seen a vast expansion in the Soviet industrial establishment, a relatively heavy employer of party members. At the same time much effort has been put into expanding party membership on the farms. The large intake of party members under Khrushchev was biased in favor of the humbler employment levels, especially in production units. It is doubtful, therefore, if the increase in the number of party members who were government officials did much more than keep pace with the expansion of the government service over this period. In the process certain additional categories of posts probably became conventionally limited to party members, but it is doubtful if the period has seen any striking extension in the range of party-restricted posts. In 1933, 85 percent of department heads in oblast and krai executive committees and 81 percent of department heads in raion executive committees were party members.[19] In the 1950-1961 soviet deputy sample all 140 department heads of regional and city executive committees were in the party, but only 24 out of 29 (83 percent) of those in raion executive committees. In 1959 there were 550 communists, or somewhat over half the total staff, in the Kiev Economic Council.[20] If this body is roughly equated with a republic industrial ministry, this suggests a substantial, but not radical increase in the level of party saturation since the early 1930's.

Two special categories of officials deserve separate com-

[19] *Sostav rukovodiashchikh rabotnikov i spetsialistov Soiuza SSR*, p. 283.

[20] *Partiinaia rabota v promyshlennosti* (Kiev, 1959), p. 416.

423

ment. First, the police. Complete, or virtually complete, party saturation of the internal security police is usually assumed by Western writers. There appears to be no confirmation of this supposition in Soviet published sources, but it is supported by the testimony of former Soviet citizens with relevant experience. Thus Konstantin Shteppa writes that "all police officials who are connected with functional duties must be party members."[21] So far as the ordinary police (the militia) are concerned, it was stated in 1965 that "the majority of those working in the organs of the militia are communists or komsomol members."[22] The deputy sample included only 20 militia officials, but all of these were CPSU members. A fortiori it would appear that at least a majority of security police officials were in the party. We must reserve judgment, however, on the level of party saturation among the most junior police employees, both in the militia and the security police.

Second, the courts. Though these are constitutionally separate from the executive branches of the government, it will be convenient to consider them here. Not all Soviet judges are in the party, though ever since the 1920's the proportion has been very high. As early as 1923 the chairmen of all guberniya courts were party members, as were 97 percent of the deputy chairmen and 76 percent of all members of guberniya courts.[23] By 1927 complete party saturation had been extended to deputy chairmen of guberniya courts, and by 1931 all but 5 percent of the *members* of

[21] Konstantin Shteppa (W. Godin), "Feliks Dzerzhinski: Creator of the Cheka and Founder of 'Chekism,'" in Simon Wolin and Robert M. Slusser, eds., *The Soviet Secret Police* (London, 1957), p. 65.

[22] *PZh*, No. 20, October 1965, p. 17.

[23] M. V. Kozhevnikov, *Istoriia sovetskogo suda* (Moscow, 1957), p. 187.

the equivalent oblast and krai courts were communists.[24] It would seem safe to assume virtually complete party saturation of the judiciary from the oblast level up since the 1930's. The lowest level of the judiciary are the people's judges, who, in the earliest years of the Soviet regime were predominantly noncommunists. Between January 1922 and January 1925, however, party membership among people's judges rose from 36 percent to 81 percent,[25] and by 1931 it reached 92 percent in the R.S.F.S.R.[26] After a setback during the purges, which reduced the proportion of party members among people's judges to 85 percent,[27] the increase was resumed, and by 1954 only 2.3 percent of all people's judges were nonmembers of the party.[28]

A high rate of party membership is also a feature of the administrative and other nonjudicial personnel of the courts and the *prokuratura* (Public Prosecutor's Department). As early as 1923, 38 percent of court investigators (*narodnye sledovateli*) were party members.[29] In 1933 party membership among the more senior court officials ranged from 100 percent in republic courts to 92 percent in raion courts. Even among court employees with specialist training but lacking administrative responsibilities the proportion was 61 percent.[30] Public prosecutors and their deputies and assistants down to the raion level were virtually all party members.[31]

[24] *Ibid.*, p. 265.
[25] O. S. Ioffe, ed., *40 let sovetskogo prava* (Leningrad, 1957), Vol. I, pp. 587-588.
[26] Kozhevnikov, *op.cit.*, p. 264.
[27] *B*, No. 7, April 1938, p. 33. It is worth noting that as many as 10 percent of all people's judges at this time were members of the komsomol (*ibid.*).
[28] *Vybornost' i podotchëtnost' Narodnykh Sudov* (Moscow, 1957), p. 13.
[29] Kozhevnikov, *op.cit.*, p. 186.
[30] *Sostav rukovodiashchikh rabotnikov i spetsialistov Soiuza SSR*, pp. 308-309.
[31] *Ibid.*, pp. 310-311.

The principal point of access of nonparty people to the work of the courts is as lay assessors, who assist the judges in basic ("people's") courts and number over half a million. Since World War II approximately half of all lay assessors have been party members and half nonparty.[32]

Management

How far does "management" in the U.S.S.R. constitute an economic elite separate from the political elite of the party? A complete answer to this would need to take into account such matters as career patterns and training of managers and party officials, representation of management on party committees and operative relations between management and party officials. This is obviously beyond the scope of the present study, but there is one basic aspect of it which should come within our purview, namely the extent to which Soviet managerial personnel are members of the party at all. Here we will be interested not only in overall percentages, but in the incidence of party membership at *different levels* of the industrial hierarchy.

During NEP Soviet factories were still largely managed by "bourgeois specialists," with the party exercising its functions of supervision and control through the so-called triangle system under which the party secretary and trade union chairman participated along with the factory director in managerial decisions. Meanwhile control through the state was ensured by grouping enterprises in trusts, which made most of the commercial decisions. These arrangements were radically changed in 1927-1928, when enterprises were made

[32] See *Vybornost' i podotchëtnost' Narodnykh Sudov*, p. 17; *40 let sovetskogo prava*, Vol. II, p. 580; and *Entsiklopedicheskii slovar' pravovykh znanii* (*Encyclopedic* Dictionary of Legal Knowledge), (Moscow, 1965), p. 245.

separate financial entities and the "triangle" was replaced by "one-man management" (*edinonachalie*).[33]

Party membership patterns among managerial personnel in the 1920's reflected these developments. In 1924, 75 percent of the chairmen of industrial trusts coming under the all-union government were party members, and a year later the proportion had risen to 93 percent.[34] By contrast the proportion of CPSU members among factory directors was only 29 percent in 1923 and 48 percent in 1924. By 1929, however, 93 percent of all factory directors were communists. In enterprises with under 500 employees the proportion was 91 percent and in those with 500 or more it was now 100 percent.[35]

By the early 1930's it had become very unusual for a factory director not to be a CPSU member, and the incidence of party membership now began to increase rapidly at subordinate management levels. Taking directors and their assistants and deputies as a single group, the proportion of party members among them rose from 29 percent in May 1930 to 70 percent in October 1933.[36] Among workshop and department chiefs and professional staff, party saturation increased from 19 to 26 percent.[37] In the case of junior supervisory personnel, however, no increase occurred. The proportion of foremen (*mastera*) and leading hands (*desiatniki*)

---

[33] See Alexander Baykov, *The Development of the Soviet Economic System*, pp. 114-117.

[34] *Partiinye, professional'nye i kooperativnye organy i gosapparat*, pp. 54-56. For a detailed analysis of managerial personnel in the early years of NEP, see *Komsostav krupnoi promyshlennosti* (Moscow, 1924).

[35] *XVI s"ezd*, p. 79.

[36] *Sostav rukovodiashchikh rabotnikov i spetsialistov Soiuza SSR*, p. 32.

[37] I. A. Kraval', ed., *Kadry spetsialistov v SSSR—ikh formirovanie i rost* (Moscow, 1935), p. 221.

who were party members was 36.5 percent in 1930 and 34.9 percent in 1933.[38]

There is abundant evidence from this period that the incidence of party membership was (1) higher among "line" than among "staff" management, and (2) far higher among those sections of management possessing administrative powers than among specialists employed in a purely professional, nonadministrative capacity. In 1933, 37 percent of workshop chiefs, heads of shifts and other production sectors were party members, compared with 29 percent of the heads of departments and sectors of central factory administrations. Meanwhile among specialists lacking administrative powers, the proportion was 14 percent in the case of those employed in the central factory administrations and 23 percent in the case of those employed in production sectors.[39] Similar contrasts are found among the senior staff of trusts and combines, i.e. the level of industrial administration immediately above the enterprise. In October 1933, 81 percent of trust and combine chiefs and their deputies and assistants were party members, compared with 34 percent of directorate, department and sector chiefs and their deputies and assistants, and 7 percent of senior professional officers lacking administrative powers.[40]

One effect of the growth of party membership among enterprise management in the early 1930's was that the contrasts in party saturation between the enterprise level and

[38] Sostav rukovodiashchikh rabotnikov i spetsialistov Soiuza SSR, p. 32.

[39] Kraval', op.cit., p. 223. In 1929 the proportion of party members among the "middle level" of factory management was 25 percent, and among specialists lacking administrative powers, 12 percent (see XVI s"ezd, p. 79).

[40] Sostav rukovodiashchikh rabotnikov i spetsialistov Soiuza SSR, p. 36.

superior levels of the industrial administration now disappeared. In fact, as may be seen from Table 47,[41] leading

TABLE 47: COMMUNISTS IN THE MANAGERIAL-ADMINISTRATIVE HIERARCHY OF THE PEOPLE'S COMMISSARIAT FOR HEAVY INDUSTRY, OCTOBER 1933

Level	All leading officials and specialists	
	Number employed	Percent of CPSU members
Central offices of Commissariat	573	26.2
Republic offices of Commissariat	388	21.7
Regional offices of Commissariat	1,027	25.7
Chief directorates (glavki)	3,127	23.8
Trusts, combines	16,040	18.9
Local offices and departments	3,248	21.6
Enterprises of all-union jurisdiction	197,960	29.2
Enterprises of republic jurisdiction	6,823	30.2
Enterprises of local jurisdiction	5,459	30.6

Note: At this time approximately two-thirds of all industrial management and specialists in the U.S.S.R. came under the People's Commissariat for Heavy Industry.

officials and specialists at the enterprise level now included a higher percentage of communists than at any superior level of the industrial hierarchy, including the central administration of the commissariat itself.

As in the case of government officials, it is safe to assume that party membership levels among industrial management fell during the middle 1930's, but were substantially or fully restored by the time of the German invasion. There is little evidence, however, that the party leadership sought either

[41] SOURCE: *Ibid.*, p. 40.

then or later to achieve any further substantial increase in the level of party saturation of lower managerial strata, or to render any further categories of post, below the level of enterprise director, a party monopoly.

The resolution of the Eighteenth Party Conference held in February 1941, the only CPSU Conference devoted exclusively to problems of industry, and one which is still treated as a milestone in the development of Soviet industrial policies, included the following passage on the choice of managerial personnel.

It is necessary to boldly promote to leading posts in industrial plants, factories and railroads workers of ability and initiative who are good organizers, especially people possessing engineering qualifications and expert in their particular line.

It is necessary to advance not only party members, but also nonparty bolsheviks, bearing in mind that among nonparty people there are many capable and honest workers, who, despite their not being in the party or possessing much experience, nevertheless often work better and more conscientiously than certain experienced communists.

Party organizations must *be prompt in raising the question of replacing worthless or weak workers. . . . Gasbags and people incapable of real live work must be relieved and posted to lower-level jobs, irrespective of whether they are party members or not.*[42] (Emphasis in original)

This would appear to express the approach to managerial appointments in the postwar and post-Stalin periods as well. While a fairly high party saturation of managerial strata has evidently been maintained and directorships have been restricted to party members, the stress in managerial appoint-

[42] *KPSS v rez*, Vol. II, p. 977.

ment policy has been on technical competence, organizational ability and conscientiousness, and possession of a party card has been accepted neither as a criterion for the possession of these qualities nor a substitute for them.

As to the actual levels of party saturation little statistical information is available since the 1940's. In 1943, when many Soviet industrial plants had been evacuated beyond the Urals, 34 percent of the 354 workshop chiefs and 20 percent of the 1,115 foremen (*mastera*) in the West Siberian city of Tomsk were party members.[43] This compared with national percentages of 37 percent for workshop chiefs and 35 percent for foremen in 1933 (see above, pp. 427-428), the latter percentage comprising both *mastera* and *desiatniki*, a more junior grade of foreman. Of course, party membership levels fell off generally on the home front during the war, and these percentages cannot necessarily be regarded as typical either for the immediate prewar or for the postwar period. Nonetheless, the changed ratios between workshop chiefs and foremen appear significant, and may indicate a continuation of the decline in relative party saturation of minor supervisory personnel which we observed to be under way in 1929-1933.

The vast expansion in Soviet industry since World War II has undoubtedly led to a great increase in the absolute number of party members holding managerial jobs. It may also have involved some advance in the relative weight of managerial personnel within the white-collar segment of the party membership, although there are indications that the tide may have been flowing in the opposite direction by the late 1950's and early 1960's (see p. 338). At the same time,

[43] *Tomskaia gorodskaia partiinaia organizatsiia v gody Velikoi Otechestvennoi voiny 1941-1945 gg.: sbornik dokumentov* (Tomsk, 1962), p. 223.

it seems highly unlikely that there was any substantial rise in the proportion of party members among Soviet management personnel over this period. We have already noted that the percentage of party members among persons with specialist qualifications employed in the Soviet economy, after rising steeply up to World War II, thereafter tended to level out. Of course, many "specialists" do not hold managerial jobs, and not all managerial personnel have specialist training. However, as David Granick pointed out in his interesting comparative study of Soviet and American management, the proportion of Soviet managerial personnel lacking specialist training declined markedly between the 1930's and 1950's, and this was particularly so among factory directors, who are easily the most strongly represented management category in the party.[44] This suggests that the proportion of party members among managerial personnel is unlikely to have increased more rapidly than among the "specialist" group as a whole, and the probabilities are that this proportion has remained fairly stable and is not radically different from what we have noted in the early 1930's.

As for the ratio between party representation among different categories of industrial employees, the 1950-1961 deputy sample suggests that here too the patterns of the early 1930's are still broadly in force, although it provides further indications of a relative decline of the foreman stratum as compared with the intermediate management stratum (see Table 48).[45] All heads of trusts, combines and other units above enterprise level were party members. All but two directors of factories and other enterprise-level units were in the party. Both exceptions were deputies to the Baku City Soviet in 1950; one was a 43 year-old Russian ship's captain

[44] David Granick, *The Red Executive* (London, 1960), p. 62.
[45] SOURCE: see p. 419 on "the deputy sample" and footnote 10.

TABLE 48: PARTY MEMBERSHIP AMONG INDUSTRIAL EMPLOYEES
ELECTED TO CERTAIN SOVIETS IN 1950-1961

Level of employment	Size of sample	Number in party	Percent in party
Directors of plants, factories, trusts, etc.	255	253	99
Subdirectorial management	125	64	51
Specialists lacking administrative powers	69	18	27
Foremen and other junior supervisory posts	194	75	38
Workers	632	111	18

and the other a 50 year-old Azerbaidzhani factory director. The majority of deputy directors and chief engineers were communists, but there were many exceptions. Below this level there was no category of posts which appeared from the sample to have been usually held by party members.

In rural production the commonest managerial figure is the kolkhoz chairman. Though his claim to elite status suffers in comparison with industrial executives from his severe dependence upon MTS (until 1958), government and especially raion party officials, the kolkhoz chairman nevertheless represents for a substantial part of the Soviet rural society a powerful and prestigious establishment figure, and he therefore deserves inclusion in our survey.

Under Stalin very little information was published about party representation among kolkhoz officials. In October 1933 about a half of all kolkhozes contained no communists at all. A large proportion of the others contained only one communist,[46] and he was certainly not always the chair-

[46] B. Abramov, *Organizatorskaia rabota partii po osushchestvleniiu leninskogo kooperativnogo plana* (Moscow, 1956), p. 152.

man. This means that well under half the kolkhoz chairmen at this time were party members, and it may have been as low as a quarter. The proportion undoubtedly fell during the purge period, and is unlikely to have risen significantly above the 1933 level until after World War II. In 1948 about two-fifths of all kolkhoz chairmen were party members.[47] The consolidation of the kolkhozes which began in 1950 radically altered this situation. By July 1953 the proportion of kolkhoz chairmen who were CPSU members had risen to 79.6 percent. It rose further to 90.5 percent in April 1956 and to 93.5 percent in April 1959.[48] Figures are not available for later years, but presumably the rise continued, as the number of kolkhozes was still falling and the average size of kolkhoz party organizations continued to increase (see pp. 331-332).

Thus, whereas in industrial enterprises the chief executive position was virtually limited to communists by the early 1930's, this situation was not achieved in the main type of agricultural enterprise until thirty years later. It is worth noting, moreover, that the "communization" of the post of kolkhoz chairman coincided with organizational changes and educational advances which transformed the typical incumbent of this post from something between bailiff and village

[47] In 1948, 13.8 percent of all kolkhoz communists were farm chairmen (*PZh*, No. 5, March 1948, p. 21). At this time the number of kolkhoz communists probably numbered about two-thirds or three-quarters of a million (see pp. 291-295, 332). Thus about 90,000 to 100,000 of them were farm chairmen, and there were at this time nearly a quarter of a million kolkhozes in the U.S.S.R. Before demobilization the proportion of kolkhoz chairmen who were party members must have been far lower. In the Omsk oblast in January 1945 it was 17 percent. See Sukhinin, *op.cit.*, pp. 227-228.

[48] *Sel'skoe khoziaistvo SSSR: statisticheskii sbornik* (Moscow, 1960), p. 474.

headman to a farm executive with training and powers comparable with those of the director of a medium-scale factory. From what has been said about kolkhoz chairmen it follows that no other categories of kolkhoz personnel warrant consideration as part of a managerial elite before the 1950's. The changes which began in 1950, however, also elevated the status and responsibilities of such kolkhoz officials as deputy chairmen, brigade-leaders, and livestock-sector managers. Simultaneously, just as the "communization" of factory directors was followed in 1930-1933 by a big expansion of party membership at intermediate managerial levels, so the later 1950's saw a similar expansion among corresponding categories of kolkhoz officials. No union-wide figures are available, but in Belorussia in 1958 almost two-thirds of the kolkhoz deputy chairmen and one-third of the livestock-sector managers and brigade-leaders were party members.[49] Average Soviet levels may have been somewhat higher than this, and have almost certainly risen in subsequent years. For data on agronomists, veterinarians and other agricultural specialists employed in the kolkhozes we must turn to Kazakhstan. Here in 1962 about two-fifths of all such employees were party members.[50]

There is no ambiguity as to the status and importance of the chief executives of state farms (*sovkhozy*) and Machine-Tractor Stations. As may be seen from Table 49,[51] state farm executives showed a level of party saturation in the early 1930's comparable with what we found earlier among indus-

[49] See *KPB v bor'be za dal'neishee razvitie narodnogo khoziaistva respubliki v poslevoennye gody*, pp. 239-240.

[50] See *Narodnoe khoziaistvo SSSR v 1961 godu: statisticheskii ezhegodnik*, p. 465, and *Kompartiia Kazakhstana na vtorom etape osvoeniia tseliny*, p. 367.

[51] SOURCE: *Sostav rukovodiashchikh rabotnikov i spetsialistov Soiuza SSR*, p. 258.

TABLE 49: Party Membership among State Farm and MTS
Officials, 1933

Level of employment	Percent members of CPSU State farms	MTS
Directors and deputy directors	70.0	94.4
Chiefs of staff ("nonproduction") sectors	26.8	68.0
Chiefs of production sectors	27.0	72.0
Specialists without administrative powers	11.5	15.1
Minor supervisory personnel	21.6	15.5

trial executives, while in the case of MTS executives the
level was far higher, reflecting the role of the MTS as the
principal instrument of party and state control over the kolkhozes. These enterprises also showed the relatively low party
saturation of the "specialists without administrative powers"
category which has also been observed in industry, but the
markedly higher saturation of "line" as against "staff" executives found in industry was not apparent in the state farms
and MTS's.

Only patchy information is available on party membership
in these units in later years. The 1950-1961 deputy sample
suggested that state farm and MTS directors were invariably
party members, and that party saturation of intermediate
managerial levels remained higher in the MTS's than the
state farms. In 1958 the MTS's were abolished and their
equipment taken over by the farms. Meanwhile the number of
state farms grew rapidly after 1953, and with it their share
of Soviet agricultural production. At the same time the differences in scale, powers and administration which had
existed between state and collective farms were greatly narrowed. While the former probably still retained a somewhat

higher level of party saturation than the latter, state farm and kolkhoz executives were rapidly being assimilated to a single pattern, with levels of party membership comparable with their opposite numbers in industry.

Professionals

In the previous chapter we saw that, although the incidence of party membership rises at each successive level of education, party members are still in a minority even among persons who have completed a higher education (see p. 401). Furthermore, in the case of many better-educated communists, their membership of the party is *prima facie* connected more with their exercise of administrative or managerial functions than with their professional qualifications. What, then, can be said about the connection between party membership and intellectual qualifications and occupations as such? This question is clearly pertinent to the problems of this chapter, since the Soviet "intelligentsia" as a whole, and particularly certain sections of it, enjoy high levels of social prestige, and in some cases very high income. While official data tend to be ill-adapted for making the kind of distinctions and comparisons necessary for our present purposes, certain general conclusions on this question can be established.

First of all, we should note a point which emerges from the deputy sample. Persons in intellectual occupations who do bear large administrative responsibilities, such as directors of schools, higher educational and research establishments, hospitals, libraries and theaters, while they tend to be party members, are frequently not. There is thus a significant contrast here with the chief executives of production enterprises. In the deputy sample, 41 out of 60 heads of higher educational and scientific research establishments (68 percent) and 53 out of 67 school directors (79 percent) were in the party. At the same time, heads of studies in schools were only half as likely as directors to be communists, and ordinary teachers only one-sixth as likely, so their administrative responsibilities were clearly the main factor in the directors' being in the party.

Nicholas De Witt has calculated that the percentage of party members among Soviet professionals, after rising from 4 percent in 1929 to 15 percent in 1939 and to 30 percent in 1947, increased only by a further 1 percent between then and 1959.[52] Table 50[53] compares the number of party members among four major professional groups in 1947 and 1964. It refers not to occupation, but to professional qualifications, and therefore does not distinguish between those working in a purely professional capacity and those occupying executive or administrative posts. The latter would be particularly numerous among the engineers and agricultural specialists, who provide not only the majority of managerial personnel but also large numbers of party and government officials. A significant number of those with teaching qualifications are

[52] De Witt, *Education and Professional Employment in the USSR, op.cit.,* p. 534.

[53] SOURCES: *PZh*, No. 20, October 1947, p. 83; E. I. Bugaev and B. M. Leibzon, *Besedy ob ustave KPSS* (Moscow, 1964), p. 36; *Narodnoe khoziaistvo SSSR v 1963 godu: statisticheskii ezhegodnik*, p. 487; Nicholas De Witt, *Soviet Professional Manpower: Its Education, Training and Supply* (Washington, 1955), p. 243. In calculating the percentage of party membership among agricultural specialists, it has been assumed that the figures given by Bugaev and Leibzon refer only to communists with institute diplomas, and not to those who have graduated from agricultural secondary schools. If the latter were included the party saturation would be reduced to 17 percent. Cf., for instance *Kompartiia Kazakhstana na vtorom etape osvoeniia tseliny*, p. 367, and *Sel'skoe khoziaistvo SSSR: statisticheskii sbornik*, p. 462. For data on professional groups among party members in Gorky oblast in 1957, see *PZh*, No. 18, September 1957, p. 40. For data from Kirgizia, see *SK*, February 26, 1960.

TABLE 50: Party Membership among Major Professional Groups, 1947 and 1964

Profession	Number in party		Percent of party membership		Approximate party saturation Percent	
	1947	1964	1947	1964	1947	1964
Teachers	80,000	700,000	1.3	6.4	16.0	25.0
Doctors	40,000	110,000	0.7	1.0	19.0	22.0
Engineers	148,000	592,000	2.5	5.4	38.0	42.0
Agricultural specialists	24,000	118,000	0.4	1.1	19.0	44.0

probably also in administrative positions. These data show that, despite the small increase in party saturation of the professional strata in the postwar period, these four professional groups between them advanced from 5 percent to 14 percent of the CPSU membership between 1947 and 1964. The explanation, of course, is the great expansion in the professional share of the Soviet workforce over this period. If the calculations of party membership levels among agricultural specialists are correct, the most striking fact emerging from the table is the rapid "communization" of this group between 1947 and 1965. This presumably resulted from the great emphasis on building up party membership on the farms over the period and the stress under Khrushchev on administrative personnel in rural areas possessing agricultural qualifications. It is less clear why teacher-communists increased their numbers so much faster than engineer-communists, but this provides further evidence of a trend to improve the ratio of nonadministrative to administrative personnel among "intelligentsia" members of the party (cf. p. 328). Despite this trend, however, the two categories of professionals most

439

commonly involved in management and administration continued to be represented in the CPSU in far larger proportions than the others.

We have already noted the extremely high party membership levels among Soviet judges and public prosecutors. With other categories of lawyers the proportion was evidently lower. In 1958, 481 of the 1,125 members of the Moscow College of Advocates (43 percent) were communists.[54]

A priori one might expect the journalists to show a higher level of party saturation than any other professional group, in view of the ideological sensitivity of their work, but the information to verify this is lacking. All journalists identified in the deputy sample were editors of newspapers or journals, and these were all communists. With the possible exception of journalists, however, there appears to be no major professional group in the Soviet Union containing a clear majority of party members. In the case of teachers and doctors, communists are outnumbered by noncommunists by three or four to one. Insofar, therefore, as the professional strata enjoy special prestige in the community this must have an independent basis and cannot derive mainly from any tendency to belong to the CPSU.

Creative and performing artists constitute one group whose possession of an independent claim to elite status is beyond doubt. Most important here are the writers, in view of the Russian tradition of literature as the conscience of society. The proportion of communists among members of the Union of Soviet Writers increased from about a third to a little over a half between the formation of the Union in 1934 and its Fourth Congress in 1967. Because of the growth of the Union's membership, however, the number of noncommunists earning their living as writers has actually increased over the

[54] *Sovetskii advokat* (Moscow, 1958), p. 11.

440

period, amounting to nearly 3,000 in 1967.[55] That many leading writers remain outside the party is indicated by the fact that about a quarter of the delegates to both the Third (1959) and Fourth (1967) Congresses were noncommunists.[56]

Less information is available on the other arts. The deputy sample included 60 writers, artists, composers, actors and musicians, of whom 30 were party members. It seems a common belief among Soviet artists that party membership is essential, except in isolated instances, for access to those honors and offices that guarantee a reasonable income, but it is difficult to check such assertions. It might be argued that what matters here is not the statistical incidence of party membership. but whether or not particular artists enjoying exceptional popularity, influence or respect are party members. However, the claim of individual noncommunist artists to a role of independent social or intellectual leadership clearly draws some legitimation from the statistically large contribution that noncommunists have always made to officially approved artistic expression in the U.S.S.R.

Scientists and Scholars

Even more than the creative and performing artists, Soviet scientists and scholars enjoy an assured place in the Soviet hierarchy of prestige and reward. Yet the concerns of science, like those of the arts, overlap at many points with the concerns of the party ideologists, and both scholars and artists have received from the party not only lavish endowment and encouragement but also constant direction and supervision,

[55] *Pervyi vsesoiuznyi s"ezd sovetskikh pisatelei* (Moscow, 1934), p. 663, and *P*, May 24, 1967.

[56] *Tretii s"ezd pisatelei SSSR: 18-23 maia 1959 goda: stenograficheskii otchët* (Moscow, 1959), p. 64, and *Literaturnaia gazeta* (Moscow), May 31, 1967.

producing an endemic and frequently tragic tension between professional integrity and ideological orthodoxy. Meanwhile, the party leader too is a victim of this tension, being pulled one way by his vested interest in achieving good results and the other way by his concern to prevent ideological subversion. The general strategy of the party has been the same in science as in the arts: to strive for higher levels of party membership without, however, restricting opportunities for scientific work to communists; to ensure party organizational control; and to subject theoretical and policy initiatives to scrutiny by officials within the party apparatus itself.[57]

The personnel of Soviet higher educational establishments and research institutions constitute a single social category of *nauchnye rabotniki* (literally "scientific workers"—we will translate it "scholars"), arranged in an integrated hierarchy: assistant, junior scientific associate, senior scientific associate, *dotsent*, professor, corresponding member of the academy, academician. It is with this social category that we are now concerned. They numbered 96,000 in 1939, 145,000 in 1947, 284,000 in 1958 and 566,000 in 1963.[58] In 1963, 2 percent of them held the degree of Doctor of Science (usually rated somewhat higher than the American Ph.D.), and 20 percent held the degree of Candidate of Science (usually rated between the American M.A. or M.Sc. and Ph.D.).

From the beginning the Soviet public was habituated to respect for noncommunist scholars, including perhaps the

[57] For a valuable account of party procedures within the network of institutes coming under the Soviet Academy of Sciences, see Alexander Vucinich, *The Soviet Academy of Sciences* (Stanford, 1956), pp. 36-40.

[58] *Narodnoe khoziaistvo SSSR: statisticheskii sbornik*, p. 233; *Kul'turnoe stroitel'stvo SSSR: statisticheskii sbornik* (Moscow, 1956), p. 248; *Narodnoe khoziaistvo SSSR v 1963 godu: statisticheskii ezhegodnik*, p. 589.

most renowned of all, the psychologist and physiologist Academician Pavlov, who was well known to be a practicing Christian. In 1924 only 6.5 percent of Soviet scholars (including 4.6 percent of the professors) were CPSU members,[59] and the figure was still only 8 percent in 1930.[60] Throughout the 1920's and 1930's, however, extensive recruitment of graduate students to the CPSU and posting of party members to graduate courses was preparing the way for a dramatic expansion of party representation in higher educational and research establishments. This was particularly marked in the social sciences. The percentage of party members among graduate students in member institutions of the Russian Association of Scientific Institutes in the Social Sciences shot up between 1924 and 1929 from 11 percent to 41 percent.[61] Even with the trend away from youthful recruitment to the party, which began in the late 1930's (see p. 457) the party membership rate among graduate students remained high. Table 51[62] shows that in 1939 there were only two fields —art and medicine—where less than a quarter of all graduate students were party members, and in the social sciences and economics the proportion was over a third.

The rapidest phase of "communization" of the Soviet scholarly community probably occurred in the 1930's and early 1940's. There is insufficient data to follow this in detail, but by the early postwar period 37 percent of Soviet scholars were CPSU members, compared with 8 percent in 1930. Subsequently "communization" proceeded more slowly, reaching 40 percent in 1950 and 43 percent in 1955.[63]

[59] K. T. Galkin, *Vysshee obrazovanie i podgotovka nauchnykh kadrov v SSSR* (Moscow, 1958), p. 88.
[60] *XVI S"ezd*, p. 502.
[61] Galkin, *op.cit.*, pp. 104-105.
[62] SOURCE: *Ibid.*, p. 114.
[63] *Kul'turnoe stroitel'stvo SSSR: statisticheskii sbornik*, p. 248.

443

TABLE 51: PARTY MEMBERSHIP AMONG GRADUATE STUDENTS BY
FIELD OF STUDY, 1939

Field of study	Students enrolled for candidate's degree	
	Number	Percent in CPSU
Industry and construction	2,748	29.5
Transport and communications	662	32.3
Agriculture	849	28.9
Social sciences and economics	661	35.1
Education	2,296	25.2
Art	270	8.1
Medicine	1,689	11.8

By the mid-1960's it probably approximated 50 percent.[64]

These are global percentages, and they warrant closer examination. Firstly, it should be appreciated that they refer only to the *professional* staff of scholarly institutions. When nonprofessional staff—technicians, office personnel, cleaners, etc.—are also included, the party membership rate falls sharply. In the research institutions of Moscow in 1958, for instance, it was just over 20 percent.[65]

Secondly, and predictably, it was still the case that "the greatest number of communists is observed among that section of the country's scholars working in the social sciences."[66] In 1947, 17 percent of engineering professors were

[64] Estimate based on the fact that the percentage of party members among doctors and candidates of science reached the same level in 1956 as the percentage among Soviet scholars as a whole in 1955, and the fact that the former reached 51 percent in 1965. For sources, see footnote 72.

[65] A. A. Levsky, in K. I. Suvorov, ed., *Nekotorye voprosy organizatsionno-partiinoi raboty v sovremennykh usloviiakh* (Moscow, 1961), p. 313.

[66] Galkin, *op.cit.*, p. 162.

CPSU members compared with 58 percent of social science and philosophy professors.[67]

Thirdly, there is evidence that party membership rates are, or have been, higher among scholars in research institutes than in higher education establishments. In 1947 the percentages were about 39 and 34 percent respectively.[68] Now one important trend in the Soviet scholarly community is that research institute personnel have increased their numbers far more rapidly than higher educational establishment personnel: between 1947 and 1963 the former grew from two-fifths to three-fifths of all Soviet scholars. Since they tended to have a higher party membership rate than their colleagues in educational establishments this has probably been a factor in the increased party saturation of the scholarly community as a whole.

Finally, there is the question of the incidence of party membership in the upper and lower grades of the profession. We have already noted that in 1924 the proportion of communists among professors was well below the average for all scholars (see p. 443). In his book on the Soviet Academy of Sciences, Alexander Vucinich noted that this difference in party penetration of the upper and lower grades had reached an extreme point in the research institutes coming under the Academy on the eve of World War II. Under 5 percent of the academicians and corresponding members of the Academy were communists, compared with 25 percent of the senior research associates and 50 percent of the junior research associates. Vucinich considered that this gap between party saturation of the upper and lower grades persisted into the

[67] De Witt, *Soviet Professional Manpower: Its Education, Training and Supply*, p. 179.
[68] *Ibid.*, and *Kul'turnoe stroitel'stvo SSSR: statisticheskii sbornik*, p. 248.

postwar period.[69] Furthermore, De Witt has reported that in 1947 only 25 percent of professors were communists, compared with 34 percent of all teachers in higher educational establishments.[70]

It is difficult to decide how much weight to give to the several different possible reasons for this gap. How far is it due to a more permissive attitude towards first-rate scholars, allowing them to avoid the burdens and distractions of party membership which are pressed more insistently on their humbler colleagues? Has it anything to do with a concern among the mediocre to strengthen their position by acquisition of a party card? Or is the main reason simply that the top men tended to be older and so had embarked on their academic careers at times when the pressure on young scholars to join the party was relatively weak?

Be this as it may, there is reason to believe that this gap had been greatly narrowed by the 1960's. Table 52[71] shows party membership rates among three senior categories of Soviet scholars—doctors of science, who may be employed in either teaching or research institutions, and professors and *dotsents*, the two top teaching grades—at the time of their appointment to these positions. It shows that party membership rates in all three categories were *below* the average for all Soviet scholars in 1947 (37 percent), but had passed the average by 1950 (40 percent) and were well above it in 1955 (43 percent). Though further communization of these groups ceased after 1953, it remained above the party membership level for all scholars. Further pertinent facts emerge when the professorial appointees are compared

---

[69] Vucinich, *op.cit.*, p. 38.

[70] De Witt, *Soviet Professional Manpower: Its Education, Training and Supply*, p. 179.

[71] SOURCE: Compiled from data in Galkin, *op.cit.*, pp. 161-162.

TABLE 52: Communists among Senior Scholars Appointed in 1947-1956

Year of award or appointment	Awarded doctor of science		Appointed professor		Appointed *dotsent*	
	Number awarded	Communists Percent	Number appointed	Communists Percent	Number appointed	Communists Percent
1947	621	31.1	650	31.8	2,600	36.0
1948	557	36.8	543	38.5	1,696	51.5
1949	566	41.3	596	41.5	2,089	53.2
1950	492	46.8	499	41.4	1,824	55.0
1951	529	45.5	506	46.5	2,067	58.5
1952	475	51.5	408	50.4	2,029	62.4
1953	569	54.0	399	56.9	2,294	61.9
1954	663	56.0	591	51.5	3,241	61.2
1955	621	54.5	386	58.4	2,224	61.3
1956	539	54.5	423	58.6	2,613	60.0
Total	5,632	47.5	5,001	46.5	22,677	56.0

with the *dotsents*. At the beginning of the period, the former contained a considerably lower percentage of party members than the latter, and the difference widened till it reached a maximum of 14 percent in 1950. Then it began to narrow, especially after the death of Stalin, and by 1956 the party saturation among appointees to both positions was very close. The same tendency is indicated in the figures for party membership among all doctors and candidates of science—43 percent in 1956, 47 percent in 1961 and 51 percent in 1965. Furthermore, the gap between the doctors (the top fiftieth of Soviet scholars) and candidates (the next fifth) had been narrowed to only 2 percent by 1965.[72]

[72] Calculated from data in *PZh*, No. 1, January 1962, p. 48 and No. 10, May 1965, p. 12; *Narodnoe khoziaistvo SSSR: statisticheskii sbornik*, p. 233; *Narodnoe khoziaistvo SSSR v 1961 godu: statisticheskii ezhegodnik*, p. 702; *Narodnoe khoziaistvo SSSR v 1964 godu: statisticheskii ezhegodnik*, p. 699.

So far we have considered only the extent of party saturation of the scholarly community. But what proportion do communist scholars represent of the total party membership? The proportion, though small, has increased strikingly since World War II, as can be seen from Table 53.[73] From less

TABLE 53: SCHOLARS AS PERCENT OF CPSU MEMBERSHIP, 1947-1965

| | | Doctors and candidates of science | |
Year	All scholars	All USSR	Uzbekistan
1947	0.86		
1951			0.26
1955	1.39		0.51
1956		0.53	
1961		0.57	
1964	2.50*		0.52
1965		0.60	

* Based on estimate that 50 percent of all scholars were CPSU members.

than one party member in a hundred, they have grown to one in forty. Taking the scholarly community as a whole, this increase appears to have been most marked in the decade after 1955. Among the doctors and candidates of science, the rapidest increase in their relative weight in the party evidently occurred in the early 1950's.[74]

The CPSU is still far from becoming a mandarinate. Yet

[73] SOURCES: Compiled from sources listed in note 72, and also *KP Uzbekistana v tsifrakh*, pp. 123, 144, 190.

[74] At first sight this appears to conflict with the trends in the incidence of party membership in the upper and lower grades described earlier. The explanation is that the number of doctors and candidates of science in the U.S.S.R. has increased far more slowly over the past decade than has the total number of scholars.

the still small minority of scholars in the party should not be seen in isolation. For in a vague and informal, but nonetheless significant way they link up and legitimate the standing of a number of other specialized elites—the various categories of professionals, artists and "cultural workers." Taken together these groups now constitute the most rapidly expanding segment, both of the Soviet population, and of the CPSU membership.

Some Conclusions

In the mid-1960's about one adult Soviet citizen in twelve was a party member. The representation of different occupations, however, varies widely. While a sufficiently detailed analysis would perhaps enable us to arrange various occupations in a continuum ranging from near zero to 100 percent party saturation, most occupational groups tend to cluster in certain ranges of saturation, on the basis of which we may distinguish three main categories.

1. *Party-restricted occupations.* These include not only full-time party officials, but also members of government executive bodies (councils of ministers, executive committees of soviets), the heads of government departments and directorates from the city level up, and the directors of state-owned enterprises, in none of which the number of nonparty members exceeds 1 percent. Other occupations, which may be called "virtually party-restricted," since noncommunists may range up to perhaps 5 percent, includes judges, army officers (see pp. 341-342), probably the police, and most recently kolkhoz chairmen. With respect to these groups, and particularly the army officers, the qualification needs to be made that their younger members may still be in the komsomol rather than the CPSU itself.

449

2. *High-saturation occupations*, in which the incidence of party membership ranges from about one in two to one in five. The most important groups here are government officials (perhaps one in two), management (one in two or three), minor supervisory personnel (perhaps one in three or four), scholars (one in two), and professionals lacking administrative or managerial responsibilities (one in four or five). Within or between these groups a number of subgroups may be distinguished, showing a fairly wide range of party saturation. Thus among the scholars, social scientists may be at least twice as likely to be party members as are natural and applied scientists. Certain groups of professionals and scholars who do have administrative positions, such as directors of schools and research institutes, are highly party saturated but still not party restricted. The same applies to such management subgroups as deputy directors and chief engineers, and such government officials as heads of raion executive committee departments. Among both government officials and management, "line" posts tend to be considerably more party saturated than "staff" posts.

3. *Low-saturation occupations*. Other occupational groups, possessing neither professional qualifications nor managerial or administrative authority, show levels of party membership which range from a little above the national average of one in twelve to a small fraction of this ratio. In industry and construction party membership ratios in 1965 were one in fifteen for employees classified as workers and one in three for all other employees.[75] Undoubtedly many

[75] This estimate is based on (a) the fact that slightly over half of the some three and a half million communists in industry in 1965 were classified as workers (*PZh*, No. 10, May 1965, p. 14; cf. p. 329); (b) an estimated workforce in industry and construction of 32 million (see *Narodnoe khoziaistvo SSSR v 1964 godu: statisticheskii ezhegodnik*, p. 546); (c) the estimate that workers account for about

of those classified as workers held minor supervisory positions,[76] but there is insufficient information to adjust for this. There are also probably big differences as between various levels of skill and branches of industry, but extremely little information is available about individual trades. There are indications of low party membership rates among miners. In 1956 only one in thirty-three of the coalcutters, drillers and other "leading tradesmen" in the Stalino (now Donetsk) oblast were communists. Among the topmost grade, the combine machinists, the ratio was one in twenty-one.[77] It should be noted that despite the large numerical increase in worker communists in the years after 1956, average party membership levels in industry increased only slightly.[78] The biggest other group of low-saturation occupations is in farming. In 1965 the incidence of party membership among kolkhozniks excluding chairmen, deputy chairmen, specialists, brigade leaders, livestock superintendents and farm mechanics, but including such minor supervisory personnel as team-leaders (*zvenevye*), was about one in twenty-one. On the state farms

85 percent of this workforce and other employees for about 15 percent (derived from analysis of occupation and class figures in *Itogi vsesoiuznoi perepisi naseleniia 1959 goda: SSSR*, pp. 104, 146-149. Supporting data is forthcoming from Belorussia, where 6.7 of the manual workers in industry and 6.2 percent in construction were communists in 1967. See N. Polozov, "V partiiu otbirat' dostoinykh" (Enlist Worthy People in the Party), *Kommunist Belorussii*, No. 1, January 1967, p. 62.

[76] See *Itogi vsesoiuznoi perepisi naseleniia 1959 goda: SSSR*, p. 11.

[77] *PU*, January 23, 1956. For other indications of low party membership in the mining industry, see *P*, February 15, 1956, and October 14, 1958. For a report of low levels in the building industry, see *BR*, January 11, 1958.

[78] Compare figures in *K*, No. 8, May 1962, p. 12; *Narodnoe khoziaistvo SSSR: statisticheskii sbornik*, p. 190; *Narodnoe khoziaistvo SSSR v 1963 godu: statisticheskii ezhegodnik*, p. 475.

the incidence may have been somewhat higher.[79] Farm mechanics (including tractor drivers, combine-harvester operators, etc.) constitute a farm aristocracy with party membership levels intermediate between our "high" and "low" categories. In Kazakh kolkhozes in 1961 one farm mechanic in eight was a party member.[80] On all farms in 1965 the level seems to have been about one in six.[81] Up to the later 1950's livestock workers seem to have been at the opposite extreme. Party membership ratios among kolkhoz livestock workers in three oblasts of the Ukraine in 1955 ranged from one in thirty to one in ninety-five.[82] In the following year in Uzbekistan one in forty of the herdsmen and milkmaids was in the party.[83] Subsequent efforts to build up party representation among livestock workers, at times reaching campaign proportions, have no doubt had some effect. In 1958 one livestock worker in fifteen in Kazakhstan was a communist, but this figure may include such managerial personnel as livestock superintendents.[84]

Rank-and-file members of the armed forces constitute another large low-saturation group (see p. 341), although it must be remembered that most of them are young and many are in the komsomol. The two occupational groups which

[79] Estimate based on party membership figures in *PZh*, No. 10, May 1965, p. 15; on occupation figures in *Narodnoe khoziaistvo SSSR v 1963 godu: statisticheskii ezhegodnik*, pp. 364, 376 and 369; and the data on party membership among managerial and specialist groups reported on p. 178.

[80] See *Kompartiia Kazakhstana na vtorom etape osvoeniia tseliny*, p. 367, and *Narodnoe khoziaistvo SSSR v 1961 godu: statisticheskii ezhegodnik*, p. 468.

[81] See *PZh*, No. 10, May 1965, p. 15 and *Narodnoe khoziaistvo SSSR v 1964 godu: statisticheskii ezhegodnik*, p. 428.

[82] *PZh*, No. 9, May 1955, p. 17.

[83] *PV*, January 28, 1956.

[84] See *Kompartiia Kazakhstana na vtorom etape osvoeniia tseliny*, p. 367, and *Sel'skoe khoziaistvo SSSR: statisticheskii sbornik*, p. 462.

probably stand at the bottom of the party membership ladder are members of kolkhoz households working only on their family plots, and nonemployed housewives, but on these groups we have no membership data at all.

We are now in a position to refine our proposed concept of the CPSU as a "representative elite." The CPSU is certainly an elite in Soviet society, and it certainly consists of representatives of all sections of that society. Yet the majority of its members are drawn from groups which are relatively high in power, income or prestige, and persons in these groups are, on the average, *several times* more likely to be party members than persons who are not. Thus the "elite of the nonelite" is spread very thin. On the other hand, there are only two elites—the armed forces and (presumably) the police—which are close to being fully communized. The elites based on administration, management, the professions, the arts, science and scholarship, while they include statuses which are restricted to party members, all consist from 50 to 80 percent of noncommunists. Though the CPSU links up the various elites of Soviet society, it does so by overlapping with them, not by incorporating them. The political significance of the two exceptions is obvious.

Chapter 15

Driving Belts

SUCH SOVIET organizations as the komsomol, trade unions, soviets, consumer cooperatives, DOSAAF (a spare-time military training association), sporting and cultural societies, however widely they may differ in scale, functions, structure and legal status, have one important feature in common, namely that they are open to participation by the generality of citizens. The generic soviet term is "mass organizations," the primary sense of the word "mass" here being not "large-scale," but "open to the general public,"[1] and more specifically, "not restricted to party members." The most important "mass organizations" are the soviets, the trade unions and the komsomol, and it is mainly these that we will be concerned with in this chapter.

Stalin saw these organizations as "levers" or "driving belts," linking the party with the masses and steering them in pursuit of party objectives. Though soviet writers no longer use these images, they imply the same kind of relationship when they write of these organizations mobilizing the masses under the direction of the party for the achievement of party policies. Such a relationship is, indeed, prescribed in Article 126 of the Soviet Constitution, which states that CPSU members constitute the "guiding necleus" in all voluntary organizations in the U.S.S.R.

Two aspects of the position of these organizations are of immediate interest to us. First, though they are open to par-

[1] For Soviet uses of the noun *massa* and the adjective *massovyi*, see Akademiia Nauk SSSR, Institut Iazykoznaniia, *Slovar' Russkogo Iazyka* (Moscow, 1958), Vol. II, pp. 317, 319.

ticipation by the general public, the minority of citizens who in fact actively participate in them are thereby imbued with a special prestige and authority which mark them off from other people, that is they acquire some of the features of an elite. Indeed those elected to the soviets have sometimes been referred to by a phrase which is also used of the party membership—"the best sons and daughters of the Soviet people." This brings us to the second aspect. It is clear that if these organizations are to serve as links between the party and the population at large, some of their members must be in the party and some not. For the student of Soviet society, it is a matter of some interest to discover the scale and levels of party participation in these organizations, since this will help him to judge whether or not they constitute or include social or political elites with an identity separate from the party membership.

The komsomol (All-Union Leninist Communist Youth League) is the only nonspecialized Soviet organization for young people in their 'teens and twenties (the lower age limit has fluctuated between 14 and 15, while the upper limit has gradually risen and now stands at 28). In the early years of the Soviet regime the komsomol recruited exclusively among working class and poor peasant youth, and embraced only a small, politically active section of the relevant age-groups. Since the party was also recruiting heavily among young people in their late 'teens or early twenties during this period, it is not surprising that there was a considerable overlap of membership. The close identity that existed between the party and the komsomol up to the early 1930's is illustrated by the fact that official reports of "communist" representation in various bodies often showed a single figure for party and komsomol members.[2] Nonetheless, the fact that the

[2] See, for instance, *XV s"ezd*, Vol. i, pp. 445-449.

komsomol was felt to have a separate identity making it a political factor in its own right, was brought out during the mid-1920's, when the Stalin machine was locked in bitter struggle with the supporters of Trotsky for influence and control over the youth of the country (particularly the students), and a directive was issued requiring the proportion of *komsomoltsy* who were party members to be brought up to 25 percent in industrial areas.[3] The enrollment of komsomol members in the party remained high for some years thereafter: it amounted to 35 percent of new candidates in the third quarter of 1926[4] and 18 percent in 1931.[5] In January 1932 approximately one CPSU member in eight was simultaneously a member of the komsomol.[6] Although the komsomol was now "Stalinized" and any danger of an opposition group using it as an organizational base against the party machine was past, efforts were still being made in the early 1930's to build up party representation in the komsomol in those areas where it remained weak.[7]

One paradoxical feature of the komsomol at this period was that, although its members were mainly drawn from the lower social strata, it acted as a channel for white-collar recruitment to the party. This is because komsomol members, consisting as they did of the most loyal, politically conscious, energetic and ambitious youths, tended to be the ones selected for official jobs or study courses, and at this point frequently sought admission to the party. The Central Committee directed its attention to this fact in the late 1920's,

[3] See *SPR*, No. 5, 1926, p. 419.
[4] *Izv Ts K*, No. 1, January 10, 1927, p. 9.
[5] *PS*, Nos. 7-8, April 1932, p. 54.
[6] *Ibid.*, No. 9, May 1932, p. 50. The percentage for urban and rural areas combined was 13.4, but in rural areas taken separately it was only 10.7 percent (*ibid.*, Nos. 11-12, June 1932, p. 47).
[7] See Fainsod, *Smolensk*, p. 420.

when much effort was being devoted to maximizing manual worker recruitment, and the komsomol was identified as one of the "leaks" frustrating these exertions. Following the November 1927 plenum of the Central Committee, which launched the second major campaign for proletarianizing the party membership, komsomol committees were instructed to reduce to a minimum the proportion of white-collar workers among those of their members being transferred to the party.[8] A substantial reduction did occur, but nonetheless between 1928 and 1930 the white-collar worker and intelligentsia category was proportionally about two and a half times more numerous among komsomol members joining the party than among other recruits.[9]

This fact acquired a new significance in the postpurge period, when much stress was placed upon recruiting party members from the komsomol. In June 1937, the Central Committee issued a decision "On Drawing *Komsomoltsy* into the Party," and this was clearly linked with the new emphasis on recruiting the new, Soviet-trained intelligentsia.[10] Meanwhile stress on proletarian background in recruitment to the komsomol was dropped.[11]

At the same time as the party was encouraging the intake of older komsomol members, a tendency was making itself felt to recruit to the CPSU far less energetically among the very young age-groups which had supplied so many of the

[8] See A. Zdziarskii, "Komsomol v roste partii" (The Komsomol in the Growth of the Party) in *God raboty po regulirovaniiu rosta VKP(b)*, (Moscow, 1930), pp. 30-35.

[9] V. Vlasov, "Nedostatki komsomola v ukreplenii riadov partii" (Shortcomings of the Komsomol in Reinforcing the Ranks of the Party), *PS*, No. 21, November 1930, p. 29.

[10] See *ibid.*, No. 6, March 1937, p. 61, and the article "Priëm luchshikh komsomoltsev v partiiu" (Acceptance of the Best *Komsomoltsy* into the Party), *ibid.*, No. 14, July 1937, pp. 42-44.

[11] See Fainsod, *How Russia Is Ruled*, p. 289.

party's recruits during the 1920's. It was probably for this reason that young communists began more and more frequently to leave the komsomol on joining the party, and this was formalized by a party decision of June 1939, which decreed that young party members should be removed from the komsomol records unless they occupied leading komsomol posts (by which was meant all elective positions from group organizers and members of workshop bureaus and primary organization committees up, as well as department chiefs and instructors employed by komsomol committees). The position now was that persons holding komsomol office were allowed to remain in the League beyond the statutory age limit and were at the same time free to join the party, while party members above komsomol age could accept komsomol office and were automatically granted komsomol membership.[12]

This was the first aspect of a new relationship between the party and the komsomol. The second was an enormous growth in the size of the League. In 1926 the komsomol em-

[12] See *PS*, No. 13, July 1939, p. 53. Reprinted in *KPSS o Komsomole i molodëzhi* (Moscow, 1962), p. 230. There are indications that it was some years before the provisions of this decision were fully implemented. Figures are available from Uzbekistan for the years 1931-1954 on the number of persons who were simultaneously members of the party and the komsomol. These fluctuated around 10 to 11 percent of all party members in the early 1930's, fell off during the purges, recovered to 10 percent in 1940, and then declined gradually but still stood at 4.5 percent in January 1946. It is highly doubtful that all or even most of these held komsomol office. Indeed the sharp drop to 2.2 percent of the party membership in the course of 1946 suggests a campaign to enforce the terms of the 1939 decision. In subsequent years the overlap remained at much the same level and stood at 2.1 percent in 1954 (see *KP Uzbekistana v tsifrakh*, pp. 37, 44, 48, 54, 56, 61, 65, 69, 73, 77, 81, 85, 89, 94, 99, 104, 109, 113, 119, 124, 129, 134). In the CPSU as a whole, the proportion of komsomol activists was about 2.5 percent in 1965 (see *PZh*, No. 17, September 1965, p. 51).

braced only 5 percent of the relevant age-groups. By the mid-1930's this had risen to 10 percent, by 1949 to 20 percent and by 1954 to 35 percent. In the towns the majority of young people were now in the komsomol.[13] From being the "politically conscious vanguard" of Soviet youth, just as the party was the politically conscious vanguard of society at large, the komsomol now became an instrument for party control *over* Soviet youth.[14] Komsomol membership as such thereby lost the prestige and authority it had previously possessed, and such attributes were now confined to the inner circles of activists and officeholders of the organization whom we may identify as those chosen as bureau or committee members or as delegates to conferences or congresses at all levels. Our interest therefore switches to the question of party representation among these "inner circles" of the komsomol membership.

All komsomol officials of any importance are party members. In 1949 CPSU membership was made compulsory for gorkom and raikom secretaries of the komsomol. Although the rules were amended in 1954 to permit nonparty appointments to these posts "in exceptional cases," the overwhelming majority of komsomol officials from this level up undoubtedly remained party members.[15] At lower levels, however, party representation falls off sharply. Local figures given for CPSU membership among komsomol primary organization secretaries in 1965 ranged from 25 percent in Moscow[16] to 10 percent in Sakhalin.[17]

[13] Ralph Talcott Fisher, Jr., *Pattern for Soviet Youth: A Study of the Congresses of the Komsomol, 1918-1954* (New York, 1959), pp. 279-280.

[14] For another examination of the party-komsomol relationship, see Allen Kassof, *The Soviet Youth Program: Regimentation and Rebellion* (Cambridge, Mass., 1965), p. 52.

[15] Fisher, *op.cit.*, p. 253.

[16] *K*, No. 3, February 1965, p. 28.

[17] *PZh*, No. 19, October 1965, p. 76.

Further evidence comes from an examination of delegates to komsomol congresses. These constitute a handpicked elite of the organization, which includes not only senior officials, but persons active at all levels and in all fields of komsomol work. Party representation at komsomol congresses reached a maximum of 98 percent in 1924. In subsequent years it fell off somewhat, but was still 91 percent in 1931. A sharper decline began in the mid-1930's. At the Tenth Congress (1936) it was 78 percent, at the Eleventh (1949) 70 percent, at the Twelfth (1954) 67 percent, and at the Thirteenth (1958) and Fourteenth (1962), it was only 59 percent.[18] These trends were no doubt connected with the changes in the political role of the komsomol which we have already discussed. A closer examination of party representation at postwar congresses, however, suggests that this connection was more complex than might appear at first sight.

Komsomol congresses in the 1930's were attended by about 800 delegates. The postwar congresses up to 1958, however, were 50 to 60 percent larger than this, while the 1962 and 1966 congresses were both enormous gatherings of nearly 4,000 delegates. This raises the question whether the percentages cited above of party representation at these congresses were percentages of *comparable* groups. In fact, the groups were not fully comparable, and the way they differed is pertinent to our subject.

Now the 1939 decision limiting joint party and komsomol membership to komsomol officials coincided with the re-staffing of the apparatus of the League following the Ezhov

---

[18] Fisher, *op.cit.*, p. 410 (for data on congresses up to the Twelfth); *XIII s"ezd Vsesoiuznogo Leninskogo Kommunisticheskogo Soiuza Molodëzhi: stenograficheskii otchët* (Moscow, 1959), p. 94; *XIV s"ezd Vsesoiuznogo Leninskogo Kommunisticheskogo Soiuza Molodëzhi: stenograficheskii otchët* (Moscow, 1962), p. 180.

purge. This postpurge generation retained many senior komsomol positions in the postwar period, and the result was that, just as the komsomol was becoming a truly mass youth organization, as an *institution* it came to be increasingly identified with an officialdom of party members nearing middle age. First Secretary N. A. Mikhailov, for instance, was aged 46 when he "graduated" from komsomol work in 1952. At the 1949 congress 47 percent of the delegates were aged over 25, and at the 1954 congress 64 percent.[19] Against this background, the increased size of postwar congresses may be seen as an attempt to counter the current image of the komsomol as an organization dominated by ageing party *apparatchiks*. For this expansion allowed the inclusion of more younger people from outside the hard core of leading officials. At the 1949 and 1954 congresses full-time komsomol officials made up something over 40 percent of the delegates, compared with 65 percent at the last prewar congress.[20] At the 1958 congress the proportion of officials was down to a third.[21] Without this big increase in the size of congresses (which allowed a greater proportion of nonofficials to attend), the average age of congress delegates would have contrasted even more grossly with the average age of the ordinary League member, and this was probably what prompted these changes. However, since nonofficials were less likely to be party members, one side effect of this was a reduction in party representation at the congresses. Indeed, given the changed balance between officials and nonofficials, it might be argued that the surprising thing is that party representation did not fall more sharply than it did. If one assumes that virtually all the

[19] Fisher, *op.cit.*, p. 412.

[20] *Ibid.*, p. 410.

[21] *XIII s"ezd Vsesoiuznogo Leninskogo Kommunisticheskogo Soiuza Molodëzhi: stenograficheskii otchët*, p. 94.

full-time officials were party members, the proportion of party members among the nonofficials seems to have been about the same at the 1949 and 1954 congresses as it had been at the last of the prewar congresses.

We should not assume, however, that the postwar continuation of the trend to greater nonparty attendance at komsomol congresses was completely lacking in significance. For one thing, the leadership was in a position to ensure, if it so wished, that the additional nonofficials among the delegates were so selected as to prevent a reduction in party representation. By failing to do so they identified the komsomol as an organization in which national prestige and standing could be achieved by a large, and growing, number of nonparty members.

Since the death of Stalin, the party-komsomol relationship has been affected by two conflicting trends. On the one hand, greater efforts have been made to counter the "balding apparatchik" image of the League. Many younger (though still not so young!) members were brought into leading positions. The amendment of the komsomol rules to allow nonparty members to be chosen as gorkom or raikom secretaries "in exceptional cases" was probably prompted by the same consideration.[22]

The other trend related to the great expansion of party recruitment during this period, which was heaviest among young adults. More than two and three-quarter million recruits to the party between 1956 and 1964 were komsomol members at the time of joining.[23] Many of these must have continued to hold minor part-time komsomol office and this

[22] Ralph T. Fisher states that it "was intended to facilitate the developing of younger leaders" (op.cit., p. 253).
[23] PZh, No. 1, January 1962, p. 46 and No. 10, May 1965, p. 10.

462

must have increased party representation considerably in the lower reaches of the komsomol apparatus.

These conflicting trends were reflected in the composition of congress delegates. The proportion of delegates aged over 25 fell from 64 percent in 1954 to 48 percent in 1958. The proportion of party members fell far more modestly—from 67 percent to 59 percent.[24] Even more revealing was the composition of the 1962 congress. This comprised more than three times as many delegates as did previous congresses. As a far less select group, one might have expected it to include considerably fewer party members. Instead, the percentage of CPSU members was the same as at the previous congress.[25]

Indeed, by the early 1960's higher party saturation of komsomol officials and activists was being openly pushed by the party apparatus. In 1960, youth work at the Bratsk hydroelectric project, where the komsomol organization was in the hands of a hundred or so young party members, was cited as an example to be emulated.[26] Subsequently local party organizations were rebuked for not seeing that more party members were elected to lower-level komsomol posts.[27] These moves clearly sprang from a heightened concern in the

[24] Fisher, *op.cit.*, pp. 410-412; *XIII S"ezd Vsesoiuznogo Leninskogo Kommunisticheskogo Soiuza Molodëzhi: stenograficheskii otchët*, p. 94. It is not known how many delegates to the 1962 congress were aged over 25, but only a fifth of them were older than 28. See *XIV s"ezd Vsesoiuznogo Leninskogo Kommunisticheskogo Soiuza Molodëzhi: stenograficheskii otchët*, p. 179.

[25] *XIV s"ezd Vsesoiuznogo Leninskogo Kommunisticheskogo Soiuza Molodëzhi: stenograficheskii otchët*, p. 80.

[26] See S. Shchetinin, "Podderzhivat' i razvivat' initsiativu komsomola" (Support and Develop Komsomol Initiative), *PZh*, No. 8, April 1960, p. 25.

[27] *Ibid.*, No. 19, October 1965, p. 76 and *K*, No. 3, February 1965, p. 28.

Soviet leadership for the political "health" of the rising generation, with its distaste for ideology, self-centeredness and frequent infatuation with the West. Brezhnev made this explicit in his report to the Twenty-Third Party Congress in March 1966.

> Certain young people want to steer clear of life's seething mainstream, they are happy to live off the efforts of others, demand much from the state and forget about their obligations to society and to the people. Bourgeois ideologists seek to use such . . . people in their own interests. . . . The whole ideological and political work of the party and the komsomol . . . is a great force heightening the concern of young people for their state, for protecting and defending the great achievements of socialism, and serving as a sharp weapon against the influence of bourgeois ideology and morality.
>
> Party organizations should strengthen their leadership of the komsomol. . . . The party nucleus in komsomol organizations should be reinforced. It cannot be regarded as correct that of the two and a half million communists aged up to 30 only 270,000 are working in the komsomol. Young communists must be drawn more actively into work in komsomol organizations, this being treated as a most important party assignment.[28]

Thus the dominant trend for some years previously, which had involved a partial disengagement of the komsomol elite of officials and activists from its identification with the party, was now being reversed. The first fruits of this reversal may be perceived at the Fifteenth Komsomol Congress in May 1966, which was the first congress since 1924 at which the

[28] *P*, March 30, 1966.

party saturation of delegates showed a slight increase.[29] It remained to be seen, however, how far this would go, given the evident distaste of young communists for komsomol assignments and the sharp reduction in party recruitment after 1965.

Trade Unions

The relationship between party membership and trade union participation is far less complex than that between party membership and komsomol participation. For one thing, people do not "graduate" from the trade unions to the party. Nor is there any question that simply belonging to a Soviet trade union ever imparted prestige or authority. Membership is open, broadly speaking, to all employees in government-run institutions and enterprises; while it is not compulsory to join, the great majority do. Whereas there was a stage when the whole komsomol membership could be regarded as an elite, elite status in the trade unions has always been confined to their inner circles of officeholders and activists. Furthermore, since 1921, when the attempt of the Workers' Opposition to win for the trade unions an autonomous role in the "proletarian dictatorship" was defeated,[30] they have figured quite unambiguously as an *instrument* of the party dictatorship, rather than as a participant in it, as an organization external to and thoroughly subordinate to the party, unlike the komsomol, which, especially up to the 1930's, was more the junior partner of the party, if not its *alter ego.*

Because of the influence of other parties and of intraparty

[29] The increase was slightly over 1 percent as compared with the 1962 Congress (to 60.3 percent), out of an almost identical number of delegates. See *Komsomol'skaia Pravda,* May 19, 1966.

[30] See Isaac Deutscher, *Soviet Trade Unions* (London-New York, 1950), pp. 42-58.

opposition groups within the trade unions, they were the object of particularly energetic organizational penetration by the party apparatus in the early 1920's. A resolution was passed at the Eleventh Congress in 1922 on the "verification and renewal" of trade union officials, which prescribed minimum periods of party membership for union officials and leading committee members from the guberniya level up.[31] Later in the same year the process of "verification and renewal" was extended to subordinate levels, right down to the factory committees. While encouragement was still to be given to suitable nonparty workers to participate in trade union activities, local party officials were instructed to exercise active control over trade union elections, "installing everywhere the most active, dependable and authoritative party members, who should be predominantly workers."[32]

In the next three or four years this policy was evidently pushed so singlemindedly as to threaten that balance between party control and nonparty participation that we noted earlier as an essential feature of the "driving-belt" function. In November 1926 the Fifteenth CPSU Conference was told that the lack of nonparty people in active trade union work threatened the party members who ran the unions with "isolation from the masses." It was resolved to place more nonparty people in union jobs not only at factory level but also in the regional and central offices of unions.[33] This, however, was easier said than done. The trouble was that intensified party recruitment of activists in the factories, particularly after 1927, meant that a worker deemed suitable and willing to hold trade-union office was likely also to be encouraged to join the party, while on the other hand there was the problem of finding suitable responsibilities to entrust to new party re-

[31] *KPSS o profsoiuzakh* (Moscow, 1957), p. 123.
[32] *Ibid.*, p. 129.   [33] *Ibid.*, p. 224.

cruits from the factory floor. Not surprisingly, therefore, we find the Central Committee complaining in May 1928 about the "wholly inadequate" response to the November 1926 decision.[34]

Soon after this, Stalin's break with the "Right" led to a massive purge of trade union officialdom, which had been headed by the "right-wing" leader Tomsky. In 1930, when floods of factory workers were being enrolled in the party, the Sixteenth Congress called for the restocking of union committees with new cadres of workers.[35] The evidence is inadequate to judge, however, whether the final result was a greater or lesser party saturation of the union elite.

In fact beginning at this point, information about party membership among trade union activists and officials, like so many other aspects of the party's composition, becomes very scanty. In 1939, 80 percent of the members of factory trade union committees and 83 percent of those of workshop committees were nonparty.[36] There can be little doubt, however, that the 17 to 20 percent who were CPSU members included the bulk of the factory trade union officers.

Despite the rapid growth of the party in the years after 1939 it is questionable whether there was any considerable increase in the party saturation of factory-level trade union activists during the 1940's and early 1950's, in view of the disproportionate recruitment of white-collar workers during parts of this period, the syphoning-off of worker communists to fill official jobs, particularly during the war, and the post-war industrial expansion which meant spreading the existing communists more thinly. It was probably not until the great increase in worker recruitment under Khrushchev that sig-

[34] *Ibid.*, p. 281.
[35] *KPSS v rez*, Vol. II, pp. 615-616.
[36] *XVIII s"ezd*, p. 158.

nificant changes occurred in the level of party representation at the base of the trade union hierarchy. In 1965 approximately a third of all members of trade union committees and councils, from the factory level up to the Central Council, were communists.[37] Though the incidence no doubt rose steeply as one ascended the hierarchy, factory committee places constituted such a large proportion of all committee and council places that the average party saturation at factory level can have been little below a third. This meant that it was now about half as high again as in 1939 (about 30 percent as against 20 percent).

Little data is available on the incidence of party membership among union officials at different levels. Emily Clark Brown, in her study of local union relationships with party and management, concluded that "top trade union officers can be assumed to be party members, as are many, if not all, of the responsible union officers at the regional level."[38] In fact, high levels of party saturation are probably found among union officials at lower echelons as well, though there is little hard evidence on this. The deputy sample included 34 union officials, from factory committee chairman up, all of whom were party members.

[37] *PZh*, No. 17, September 1965, p. 51. Separate figures for trade union committees at different levels are not available. However, in Belorussia in 1950, 24 percent of the 40,000 members of factory trade union committees were communists, and 63 percent of the members of committees at district and higher levels. See A. M. Mikhailov, in V. M. Sikorskii et al., eds., *Iz istorii bor'by Kompartii Belorussii za uprochenie sovetskoi vlasti i sotsialisticheskoe stroitel'stvo* (From the History of the Struggle of the Belorussian Communist Party for Consolidation of Soviet Power and for Socialist Construction), Minsk, 1959, p. 182. At this time Belorussia was an area of relatively low party membership.

[38] Emily Clark Brown, "The Local Union in Soviet Industry: Its Relations with Members, Party and Management," *Industrial and Labor Relations Review*, Vol. 13, No. 2 (January 1960), 201.

We have noted indications of a heightened concern in the 1960's to maintain or expand party representation among komsomol officials and activists. In 1965 an article appeared in the Central Committee journal *Party Life* suggesting a similar concern with respect to the unions. Stating that "the majority of party organizations recommend for election to leading trade union bodies party members who enjoy the confidence of the masses," the article complained about the defects of trade union work in Turkmenia, where "unfortunately not all party committees and primary party organizations manifest constant concern about union cadres, with the result that in a number of organizations weak or even quite incongruous (*sluchainye*) people have turned up in leading trade union posts." The main point of criticism was that the party saturation of factory and local union committees in Turkmenia had fallen below the levels of the two previous years, and five enterprises were cited where not a single communist had been placed on the union committee. This situation was deemed serious enough to call for discussion by the Presidium of the Turkmen Central Committee.[39] This fact, together with its reporting in the Central Committee journal, suggest that the maintenance of at least the existing levels of party representation in the trade unions was now a matter of considerable concern to the party leadership.

The Soviets

While the soviets have never played any considerable part in policy formation or control over government, and their functions have mainly been those of legitimation and identification and of mobilization under close control both of the party committees and of "their own" and superior govern-

---

[39] N. Nesterov, "Zabotit'sia o profsoiuznykh kadrakh" (Show Concern about Trade Union Cadres), *PZh*, No. 20, October 1965, pp. 56-58.

ment executives, they nonetheless occupy a special place in the system of "driving belts," by virtue of their constitutional status and the fact that, like the party, they are claimed to consist of "the best" people from all walks of life.[40] Since the Civil War, elections to the soviets have been uncontested, with the selection of candidates closely controlled by the party.

Up to 1936 only the city and village soviets were elected directly by the public. Above these levels there were district, province, republic and all-union congresses of soviets, consisting of delegates "elected" at the next level down, and each electing its executive committee. Since 1936 each administrative level has had its soviets, elected by direct vote, the local and regional soviets every two years, and the Supreme Soviets of the U.S.S.R. and the Union Republics every four years.

The changes effected by the 1936 Constitution and the flux of administrative divisions in the 1920's and early 1930's make it difficult to generalize about party membership levels in the soviets prior to World War II. However, a few important facts may be discerned.[41]

Firstly (and predictably) average party saturation increased in successively higher and larger units. Thus in 1921, 42 percent of the delegates to uezd congresses were communists compared with 75 percent of delegates to guberniya

[40] On the composition of the soviets, see T. H. Rigby, "Selection of Leading Personnel in the Soviet State and Communist Party," unpublished Ph.D. thesis, University of London, 1954, Chap. 2.

[41] The comparisons and generalizations about party membership in the soviets up to the early 1930's are based on analysis of figures appearing in the following sources: Vladimirskii, *Sovety, ispolkomy i s"ezdy sovetov, Vypusk I*, and *Vypusk II*; *XIII S"ezd*, p. 116; *XV S"ezd*, Vol. I, pp. 448-449; *Partiinye, professional'nye i kooperativnye organy i gosapparat*, pp. 33, 35; *BSE* (1st edn.), Vol. XI, cols. 541-542; Julian Towster, *Political Power in the USSR: 1917-1947* (New York, 1948), pp. 349-350; Seibert, *op.cit.*, p. 91.

congresses. In 1925 party members made up 6 percent of village soviet deputies and 51 percent of city soviet deputies. There are figures from 1919, 1923 and 1924 which give details separately for cities which were uezd centers and cities which were guberniya centers, and the latter show consistently higher levels of party representation. In 1929, 53 percent of the members of volost and raion executive committees were communists, compared with 68 percent in okrug and uezd executive committees and 75 percent in oblast and krai executive committees.

Secondly, and this is again predictable, party membership levels were higher in the executive committees than in the congresses of soviets. In 1921, for instance, the respective averages were 73 percent and 42 percent at the uezd level and 88 percent and 75 percent at the guberniya level. In 1925, 17 percent of delegates to volost congresses of soviets were party members, compared with 48 percent of members of volost executive committees. However, the All-Union Congress of Soviets and Central Executive Committee presented an exception to this pattern from 1927 on (see Table 54).[42]

Thirdly, once the Civil War was over, there was no general tendency for party membership levels to increase. This contrasted with the steady communization of the chief executive posts in the soviets (see p. 418), and it is particularly striking when one recalls that the incidence of party membership in the Soviet population as a whole increased sixfold between 1924 and 1933. In the city soviets the proportion of party members settled down in the mid-1920's at about a half (it was 51 percent in 1925, 46 percent in 1929, and 50 percent in 1931). In some cases, where very high party saturation was achieved during the Civil War, there was actually a de-

[42] Based on table "Percentage of Non-Party People in the Popular Federal Assemblies," Towster, *op.cit.*, p. 350.

TABLE 54: Party Membership in Congress of Soviets and Central Executive Committee of the U.S.S.R., 1922-1936

Year	Party members Congress of Soviets	Percent C.E.C.
1922	94.1	97.4
1924	90.0	91.0
1925	78.1	84.1
1927	72.7	69.7
1929	72.6	71.8
1931	75.3	
1935	79.0	71.7
1936	72.0	

cline before it settled down at a new point. Up to the early 1920's, for instance, average party membership in guberniya executive committees fluctuated between 80 and 90 percent. Later in the decade, however, the level in the roughly equivalent oblast, krai and autonomous republic executive committees ranged between 70 and 75 percent. Similar changes occurred in the Congress of Soviets and Central Executive Committee of the U.S.S.R. (see Table 54). An important element in such cases of declining party representation was the passing of residual decision-making functions from the executive committees to their presidia (see p. 417), but they cannot be wholly attributed to this, and one must assume that a positive value was placed on achieving at least significant levels of nonparty participation in even the most august of these representative bodies. There was one important exception to this general picture of stable (or even declining) party representation, and this was at the lower levels in rural areas, where party members were initially extremely few. Thus the proportion of CPSU members in village soviets rose from 6 percent in 1925 to 10 percent in 1929 to 15 percent in 1931, and there was a similar expansion at the volost level.

Following the adoption of the 1936 Constitution, elections to the new Supreme Soviet of the U.S.S.R. were held in 1937, to the republic supreme soviets in 1938, and to the local soviets in 1939. Though exact comparison is not possible, the new raion, oblast, krai and republic soviets may be roughly equated with the old executive committees at these levels, and the two houses of the new Supreme Soviet with the corresponding houses of the old Central Executive Committee. The character of the village and city soviets was little changed.

Comparison on this basis reveals remarkably little change in levels of party representation between the early and late 1930's. It was 72 percent in the 1929 and 1935 Central Executive Committees, and 76 percent in the 1937 Supreme Soviet. The various levels of regional and republic executive committees had shown party membership ratios of 60 to 80 percent. Apart from the supreme soviets of the union republics, no average figures for party representation in the soviets appear to have been published for the 1938-1939 elections, but in those soviets where the number of party members has been established, the percentages nearly all fell within this range. Here are the figures:

Union republics: average—72; R.S.F.S.R.—78; Azerbaidzhan—75; Armenia—61; Kazakhstan—80;
Autonomous republics: Adzhar—76; Moldavia—75; Tatar —70; Volga-German—72; Kara-Kalpak—56;
Oblasts: Moscow—71; Leningrad—73; Kiev—71; Alma-Ata—72.

In 1931 an average of 50 percent of all city soviet deputies were party members. Available percentages for 1939 are:

Moscow—48; other towns of Moscow oblast—48; Leningrad—54; other towns of Leningrad oblast—47; Tashkent—58; Baku—50. In 1931 party members averaged 15 percent of village soviet deputies and 44 percent in raion executive committees. The only available 1939 figures for these levels are from the Moscow and Leningrad oblasts, which one would expect to be somewhat higher than the national average. Party members averaged 27 percent of the village soviet deputies in the Moscow oblast and 18 percent in the Leningrad oblast. For raion soviets the figures were 61 percent in the Moscow oblast and 51 percent in the Leningrad oblast.[43]

Since World War II significant changes have occurred in party representation in the soviets, but there has been no single pattern of change found in all levels of soviets. The Supreme Soviet of the U.S.S.R. showed a marked increase in party saturation up to the death of Stalin (apparently connected with a reduction in the number of manual workers and peasants),[44] followed by a continuous decline from 1954 on (see Table 55).[45] By 1966 the percentage of CPSU members in the Supreme Soviet was practically identical with what it had been in 1937, although in the meantime the

[43] SOURCE: for individual republic soviets—*P*, June 1938, passim; for oblast and local soviets—*ibid.*, December 1939, passim; for average of union republic soviets—*Itogi vyborov i sostav deputatov verkhovnykh sovetov soivznykh i avtononomnykh respublik—1967 g.* (*statisticheskii sbornik*) (Results of Elections and Composition of Deputies to the Supreme Soviets of Union and Autonomous Republics—1967: Statistical Compilation), (Moscow, 1967), pp. 84-85.

[44] See T. H. Rigby, "Changing Composition of the Supreme Soviet," *The Political Quarterly*, Vol. xxiv, No. 3 (July-September 1953), 307-316.

[45] SOURCES: *Zasedaniia Verkhovnogo Soveta SSSR: stenograficheskii otchët*, post-election sessions for relevant years; *P*, August 4, 1966.

TABLE 55: Party Membership in the Supreme Soviet of the U.S.S.R., 1937-1966

Year elected	Communists as percent of all deputies	
	Soviet of the union	Soviet of nationalities
1937	81.0	71.0
1946	84.4	77.6
1950	85.5	81.3
1954	79.8	75.9
1958	76.3	75.8
1962	75.2	76.4
1966	74.7	75.7

considerable gap which had existed between party representation in the two houses had now almost disappeared.

In the supreme soviets of the union republics (see Table 56),[46] party representation was significantly higher in 1947 than in the previous elections of 1938, but then began a fairly general and substantial decline, which was arrested (though not significantly reversed), in 1967.

In the local soviets, postwar trends have been more complex. Although oblast soviets seem to have shown little change, party membership levels in soviets at all subordinate echelons rose sharply above prewar levels. The average party membership for all local soviets was slightly over 40 percent in 1947, compared with 31 percent in 1939.[47] The biggest jump took place in the village soviets (which doubled their percentage of party members in Leningrad oblast), and the

[46] SOURCES: Tables 56, 57 and 58 are based on figures appearing in *Pravda, Moskovskii Bol'shevik, Moskovskaia Pravda, Leningradskaia Pravda* and the principal Russian-language newspapers of the union republics, at the time of the relevant elections.

[47] See Towster, *op.cit.*, p. 349.

475

TABLE 56: PARTY REPRESENTATION IN SUPREME SOVIETS OF UNION REPUBLICS, 1947-1967

Republic	Communists as percent of all deputies					
	1947	1951	1955	1959	1963	1967
R.S.F.S.R.	79.1	74.0	70.2	67.4	67.2	67.2
Ukraine	77.8	73.9	74.3	68.3	68.0	68.0
Belorussia	76.8	74.6	75.8	68.3	69.4	69.4
Uzbekistan			78.5	73.2	71.8	72.2
Kazakhstan	77.3	70.0	74.4	68.7	66.2	66.2
Georgia	79.0	78.7		73.9	71.2	71.4
Azerbaidzhan		73.9	73.6	80.0	78.0	77.9
Armenia			69.7	68.0	68.0	67.4
Turkmenia			74.0	67.4	67.4	67.4
Kirgizia			68.1	67.2	67.6	67.3
Tadzhikistan			74.7	72.0	69.3	69.5
Lithuania			74.6	72.7	65.2	66.5
Latvia	71.7	74.5	76.5	77.5	63.6	63.9
Estonia				68.0	64.6	65.1
Moldavia			74.1	65.9	64.1	64.1
Average	76.3	74.5	73.2	70.4	68.3	68.5

Note: Gaps indicate that no data have been located.

next biggest in the rural raion soviets (see Table 57).[48] This reflected the influx of communists into the rural areas consequent on the demobilization of peasants who had been enrolled in the party during the war.

The rise in party representation in the local soviets continued fairly generally for some years after 1947, but began to be reversed in the late 1950's. Of the 13 republics for

[48] The following additional percentages for individual postwar years may be cited: Alma-Ata oblast, 1947—71.8; Tashkent oblast, 1950—74.3; five largest cities of Latvia, 1947—59.6, 61.1, 57.8, 49.3, 61.8; Kishinev city, 1950—60.1; Kiev city, 1947—53.6; Tallin, 1947—64.5; Vilnius, 1947—60.7; Panevezhis, 1947—34.8; average urban raions of Riga, 1947—approximately 55; average urban settlement soviets in Leningrad oblast, 1947—55.0.

TABLE 57: Party Representation in Certain Local Soviets, 1939-1953

Soviet	Communists as percent of all deputies			
	1939	1947-1948	1950	1953
Moscow oblast	71.3		66.9	70.0
Leningrad oblast	73.3	80.0	74.8	
Moscow city	48.2			61.0
Leningrad city	53.9		59.2	
Baku city	50.0	64.4	57.0	60.1
Tashkent city	58.4		64.1	
Tbilisi city		56.9	58.0	59.0
Alma-Ata city		67.4	57.7	
Other Towns in Leningrad oblast	47.0	61.6		
Raion Soviets in Leningrad oblast	51.2	69.1		
Village Soviets in Leningrad oblast	18.4	36.4		

which comparable percentages are available, 12 showed an average increase in 1953 as compared with 1947, and 9 in 1957 as compared with 1953. In local soviets elected in 1965, however, average party representation was lower than in 1957 in 10 out of 15 republics. Comparing 1965 data with those for 1947, there was a decrease in average party saturation in 7 republics and an increase in 8, but all but 2 of the latter constituted, or included, territories newly acquired by the Soviet Union during World War II. If these are excluded, party membership levels in the local soviets appear to have been much the same in 1965 as in 1947, and about 10 percent higher than in the 1930's. In 1967, for the first time in a decade, the majority of republics showed an increased party representation in their local soviets. Though the average increase was small, this evidently reflected a de-

TABLE 58: Party Representation in Local Soviets, by Republics, 1947-1967

Republic	Communists as percent of all deputies									
	1947-1948	1950	1953	1955	1957	1959	1961	1963	1965	1967
R.S.F.S.R.	46.8	52.5		48.9	45.5	44.9	45.6	44.9	45.0	46.1
Ukraine	31.8	34.0	36.9	40.7	42.5	43.8	45.8	46.5	46.3	47.0
Belorussia	26.7	30.4	35.6	40.8	43.3	44.2	43.5	42.6	41.6	43.5
Uzbekistan	47.2	48.2	50.7	53.5	54.7	51.1	40.1	45.7	46.0	46.3
Kazakhstan	52.3	48.1	50.9	52.1	50.0	49.0	49.4	45.4	44.4	44.6
Georgia	40.1	49.4	48.7	48.9	48.1	44.4	43.8	48.1	47.5	47.6
Azerbaidzhan	50.3	49.9	52.6	54.1	54.5	51.6	51.2	51.2	49.9	50.5
Armenia	52.6	54.5	57.4	57.2	59.6	51.9	53.4		47.4	47.5
Turkmenia	48.3	49.4		48.9	47.8	48.1	47.1	43.4	43.4	43.3
Kirgizia	46.8	45.3	47.4	46.6	42.2	45.4	45.7	46.5	45.4	46.5
Tadzhikistan	44.2	46.7	50.0	53.0	56.1	54.0	50.1	46.3	46.1	46.1
Lithuania	11.6	16.4	21.5	29.4	32.1	33.1	36.7	36.9	38.9	42.3
Latvia	18.3	31.2	35.9	39.9	43.0	42.9	41.6	27.8	41.5	43.2
Estonia	22.7	30.2	33.9	34.1	33.7	37.3	38.7	38.5	39.8	38.6
Moldavia	13.4	25.7	32.7	35.6	39.2	38.5	41.9	41.4	41.7	47.7

cision to resume the earlier trend towards higher party saturation of these bodies. Meanwhile, another marked trend operative over the whole postwar period has been the leveling up in party representation in the soviets as between the various republics.

We have noted the correspondence which existed from the inception of the Soviet regime between the hierarchical level of soviets and their party saturation. This correspondence has persisted since World War II, though the differences between hierarchical levels have been narrowed, mainly due to much improved party representation at the lower levels, but also partly to significant reductions at some higher levels. In 1959 and 1967 the average percentage of deputies who were members or candidates of the CPSU was as follows:[49]

[49] *Sostav deputatov Verkhovnykh sovetov soiuznykh, avtonomnykh respublik i mestnykh sovetov deputatov trudiashchikhsia 1959 g.*

	1959	*1967*
Supreme Soviet of the U.S.S.R.	76.1 (1958)	75.2 (1966)
Supreme Soviets of Union Republics	70.4	68.5
Supreme Soviets of Autonomous Republics	68.5	66.7
Krai, oblast and okrug soviets	62.3	58.2
Raion soviets	58.6	54.8
City soviets	52.5	51.9
Urban raion soviets	53.0	52.8
Urban settlement soviets	46.4	45.1
Village soviets	41.0	43.1

The lower percentage of party members in the local soviets appears to reflect functional requirements rather than a shortage of suitable communists, although at earlier periods the latter was the principal limiting factor. Legitimation of political processes is an important function of the soviets at all levels and, because party membership is symbolic of authority, the more authoritative and august the body the higher the level of party membership felt to be appropriate to it. Fostering identification with the regime and the system is a second function of the soviets. This is the main reason why considerable nonparty representation is preserved even at the

(Composition of Deputies of Supreme Soviets of Union and Autonomous Republics and of Local Soviets of Working People's Deputies in 1959), (Moscow, 1959), pp. 7, 17, 35, 41, 47, 53, 59, 65; *Itogi vyborov i sostav deputatov Verkhovnykh sovetov soiuznykh i avtonomnykh respublik—1967: statisticheskii sbornik*, pp. 21, 45; *Itogi vyborov i sostav deputatov mestnykh sovetov deputatov trudiashchikhsia—1967g.: statisticheskii sbornik* (Results of Elections and Composition of Deputies to the Local Soviets of Working People's Deputies—1967: Statistical Compilation), (Moscow, 1967), pp. 12-13.

higher levels. However, the fostering of identification is even more important with respect to various elite groups than to the low status groups that make up the mass of the population. This calls for a heavy representation of such groups, which consist mainly of party members, in the higher level soviets. Finally, while the higher level soviets are practically limited to these symbolic functions, the local soviets also participate significantly in rule-application (day-to-day decision making and administration) and mobilization, and the regime is concerned to harness to these tasks through the soviets considerable numbers of nonparty "activists."

In the previous chapter, while discussing the administrative elite, we pointed out that key members of the executive committees of local soviets appear always to be party members. These executive committees, however, are also of interest as a link between the administrative and "driving-belt" functions of the Soviet mechanism, and it is therefore worth enquiring whether the opportunities for nonparty "activists" to participate in the work of the soviets extend to these inner bodies or whether they can participate only in the capacity of rank-and-file deputies. The data indicate that such opportunities are in fact available to small numbers of nonparty people, though mainly at the lowest level of the soviet hierarchy. In 1967 deputies who were not CPSU members or candidates made up 30 percent of the executive committee members in village soviets, 24 percent in urban settlement soviets, 10 percent in city soviets, 5 percent in raion soviets, and 3 percent in krai, oblast and okrug soviets.[50]

Before we leave the soviets, one further aspect deserves brief mention. Although as a rule only a small minority of the party members elected to the soviets are leading officials, many others tend to be persons enjoying relative prominence

[50] *Ibid.*, pp. 212-213.

in the party, as reflected in their election as delegates to party conferences or even as members of party committees; and the converse also applies. While a systematic exploration of this aspect would take us too far from our central topic, a few illustrations may be worth citing.

Of the 709 delegates to the 1949 party congress in Georgia, 38 were deputies to the Supreme Soviet of the U.S.S.R., 178 deputies to the Supreme Soviets of Georgia and the Abkhaz and Adzhar Autonomous Republics, 381 deputies to oblast, city and raion soviets, and 35 deputies to village and urban settlement soviets—a total of 91 percent of all delegates.[51] The overlap appears to be less at local levels, but still high. Thus of the 600 delegates attending the Tbilisi city party conference in 1951, 193 were deputies to the Tbilisi city soviet and 96 were deputies to the Supreme Soviets of the republic or the U.S.S.R.; if deputies to urban raion soviets in Tbilisi were added, the total would almost certainly exceed 50 percent of all conference delegates.[52] Of the 80 full and 17 candidate members elected to the Tashkent City Committee of the CPSU in July 1948, 55 and 11 respectively (i.e. almost two-thirds) had been elected to the City Soviet in February of that year. Some of these were party officials, others government officials, and others again were persons prominent in various other fields of economic, cultural or administrative activity, while a handful occupied relatively humble posts.[53]

It is difficult on the available data to measure this overlap from the opposite direction, i.e. to establish the percentage of deputies to particular soviets elected to party congresses and

---

[51] *ZV*, January 29, 1949. Cf. *ibid.*, January 21, 1956, *KP*, January 27, 1956, and *BR*, January 27, 1956.

[52] *Ibid.*, January 12, 1951. For similar data on Moscow city conference delegates, see *MP*, April 1, 1951, and September 18, 1952.

[53] *PV*, 1948, passim.

481

committees at various levels. About a quarter of the deputies to republic and oblast soviets, as a rule, would appear to gain election as delegates to the corresponding party congresses or conferences. Undoubtedly many others figure as delegates to conferences or congresses at higher and lower levels, but there seems no way of estimating the percentage. The proportion of city soviet deputies elected to the corresponding party conferences would appear to be smaller, and the proportion elected as party committee members much smaller again.

Some Final Points

Of the many mass organizations existing in the U.S.S.R., only three have been selected for investigation in this chapter. This selection has been prompted by a number of considerations. Most obviously, these organizations constitute by far the most important of the "driving belts" linking the party with the general population and "mobilizing" it in pursuit of the party's goals. A connected factor is that far more information is available about the composition of these than of other mass organizations. Further, although their political importance makes them in some ways untypical, their diversity in other respects renders them moderately suitable as a sample of mass organizations. Finally, the prestige attaching to active membership in these organizations marks them as significant elites in the Soviet community, and therefore as worthy of study alongside the other elites discussed in the previous chapter.

It is not easy to generalize about the driving-belt elites and their relationships with the party membership. Clearly, there is some arbitrariness in our equating elite status with "active membership," and defining this so as to include all deputies to soviets and all komsomol members up to the 1930's, but only the "inner circles" of the trade unions and the post-1930's komsomol. Any attempt at cross-comparison in quantified terms is therefore liable to prove misleading, and we must limit ourselves to certain very broad conclusions.

Firstly, the question posed at the beginning of this chapter as to whether these mass organizations constitute or include elites with an identity separate from the party membership must be answered in a qualified affirmative. The prestige attaching to active membership in these organizations is far from being monopolized by party members. Although their officials down to quite a low level are all communists, the soviets, trade unions and komsomol provide opportunities for many hundreds of thousands of noncommunists to enjoy political status in their local communities, and for a small number to do so on a broader regional or national stage.

Secondly, there has been no simple, general formula governing the levels of party and nonparty representation in the various driving-belt elites. From time to time decisions have been made to correct the balance in one direction or the other, and even those levels where the balance is relatively static show significant fluctuations over time which evidently reflect changes in political circumstances and the evaluations of top leaders.

Thirdly, we have noted a considerable cross-representation between the soviets and the elective bodies (conferences, congresses, committees) within the party itself, especially at upper hierarchical levels. The membership of these party bodies probably overlaps (though to a lesser degree) with the other driving-belt elites as well. This means that considerable numbers of party members are prominently involved both in internal party activities and in one (or more) of the mass organizations. It also means that the interlocking of the party with these organizations is considerably more complex

483

than a study of their full-time officials, overall party membership levels and formal relationships would indicate.

Finally, we must note the large numbers of party members participating in the mass organizations, and consider what this implies. In March 1965 there were over 900,000 communists in the local soviets, 988,000 in elective trade union bodies, 303,000 in elective komsomol bodies, and "many thousands in elective work in other mass organizations of the working people."[54] We have already noted that some quarter million party members serve as people's assessors in the local courts (see p. 426). There are many other citizens' bodies more or less closely associated with the work of local government. Here are some of the most important, showing the numbers of citizens *in the R.S.F.S.R. only* who were involved in 1964.[55]

Street and house committees	920,000
Parents' committees in schools, kindergartens, etc.	1,140,000
Councils of clubs and libraries	455,000
Women's councils	298,000
Pensioners' councils	194,000
Volunteer fire brigades	707,000
Volunteer militia (*druzhinniki*)	3,351,000
Comradely courts	693,000
Shop and restaurant commissions	386,000
Sanitary posts and brigades	571,000

In the 1960's the total number of citizens participating in such bodies throughout the U.S.S.R. numbered over twenty millions. We can only guess at how many of these were CPSU

[54] *PZh*, No. 17, September 1965, p. 51.
[55] L. G. Churchward, "Soviet Local Government Today," *Soviet Studies*, Vol. XVII, No. 4, April 1966, p. 440.

members. It is known that 35 percent of the members of the volunteer militia squads in Belorussia in 1961 were communists (most of the rest komsomol members).[56] A party saturation level of 25 to 50 percent for these many and varied citizens' bodies would probably be realistic. In any case, even if we allow for some party members participating in more than one of them, it is clear that several million communists will be required if they are all to be provided with a substantial "guiding nucleus" of party members.

This is obviously an important consideration for the party in framing its membership policies. It has been a recurrent theme in this book that the party needs members not only to staff key positions at all levels and in all spheres of the life of society, but also to ensure a significant party presence in all work-groups. This latter need has exerted constant pressure for the diversification of the party membership, preventing it from being too closely identified with the bureaucracy. The need for party members to provide a guiding nucleus in the multifarious mass organizations, societies, and citizens' auxiliary bodies obviously works in the same direction. Furthermore, if the role of such organizations is to continue to increase, as current doctrine on the "transition to communism" requires, it will be difficult for the party to pursue restrictive recruitment policies for any prolonged period.

[56] See V. S. Karpik et al., eds., *Sovetskaia obshchestvennost' i ukreplenie pravoporiadka* (Minsk, 1961), p. 54.

485

Chapter 16

Geographical Distribution

DIFFERENCES IN the incidence of CPSU membership as between various regions and types of community constitute perhaps the most important element in the political geography of the U.S.S.R. These differences appear to rest for the main part on inequalities in the representation of different occupational and ethnic groups, which we have discussed in previous chapters.

Town and Village

In tsarist times the bulk of the bolshevik underground was located in a handful of major industrial centers and this pattern does not appear to have been much modified by the mass recruitment of 1917. Of the 177,000 members whom delegates claimed to represent at the Sixth Congress in August 1917, 40,000 were in Petrograd, 15,000 in Moscow, 20,000 in the Urals and 15,000 in the Donbass.[1] As the bolshevik regime established itself, a network of party organizations spread throughout the country, and at the end of the Civil War tens of thousands of young peasants who had become party members while serving in the Red Army were dispersed to their villages. Even then, however, three out of five party members were living in the towns, although the latter contained only one-seventh of the country's population.

This urban emphasis became further accentuated in the ensuing years, due to the withdrawal of many peasants from the party during the early 1920's and the influx of workers during the Lenin enrollment, the effects of which were only

[1] See *VI s"ezd*, pp. 204-206.

partially offset by the relatively high peasant recruitment in
1925-1927. While the number of townsmen in the party increased from 314,000 to 840,000 between the 1922 and
1927 party censuses, the number of villagers increased only
from 201,000 to 307,000.[2] Moreover, a disproportionate
share of the urban communists continued to be concentrated
in the traditional centers of party strength. In 1927, 20 percent of the party were living in the Moscow and Leningrad
guberniyas and a further 25 percent in the other major industrial areas.[3] These patterns became even more entrenched
with the proletarianization drive of the late 1920's.

The growth of the party membership since the 1930's has
been accompanied by vast changes in its geographical distribution. These have reflected not only recruitment policies,
but also the enormous demographic movements in the Soviet
Union which resulted from industrialization and urbanization, mass deportations, the war, and migration to new areas
of industrial and agricultural development, particularly in the
eastern parts of the country.

The main trends in the urban-rural balance of the party
membership are fairly clear, although they are difficult to
quantify with much precision, due to problems of comparing
and interpreting the available information as much as to its
scarcity.[4]

---

[2] Adapted from *Sotsial'nyi i natsional'nyi sostav VKP(b)*, p. 18.

[3] *Ibid.*, p. 20.

[4] In a number of cases where a figure is given for communists
"in the countryside" (*na sele* or *v derevne*) or for rural communists
(*sel'skie kommunisty*), it is not clear whether this figure is limited
to the farming population or also includes administrative, educational,
trading and other personnel living in the villages. There is a similar
difficulty about figures for communists living "in the rural districts"
(*v sel'skikh raionakh*). Some raion administrative centers are classified
as "rural settlements" (*sel'skie poseleniia*) and others as towns or
"settlements of urban type" (*posëlki gorodskogo tipa*), and of those

The collectivization era saw a substantial resurgence of rural party membership, which reached 790,000 in October 1933.[5] Even then, however, the party remained more strongly urban in character than it had been in 1927, let alone in 1922. Moreover, the rural party organizations were harder hit than those in the towns in the 1933-1934 purge, and because of this and of the rapid urbanization of the 1930's, we may assume that they contained a significantly smaller proportion of the party membership at the outbreak of World War II than before the purges.

After the war, the demobilization of peasant communists recruited during their military service brought a sharp improvement in the incidence of party membership in rural areas as compared with the towns. In 1947 there were 1,714,000 rural communists, out of a total party membership of some 6.3 millions.[6] Subsequent years have seen important changes in the deployment of communists in rural areas (see Chapters 8 and 10), but their overall share of the party membership has probably remained fairly constant. Against

---

classified as towns some are administratively subordinate to the raion and some directly to the oblast, krai or republic. Moreover the definitions vary from republic to republic and have also changed over time, while individual raion centers are constantly being reclassified. It is sometimes unclear whether the phrase "in the rural districts" refers only to the villages, whether it includes the raion centers as well or whether it includes some classes of raion center but not others. These difficulties frustrate any attempt to make precise comparisons over time. (See S. A. Kovalëv, "Tipy poselenii—raionnykh tsentrov SSSR" [Types of Settlement Serving as Raion Centers in the U.S.S.R.], in V. V. Pokshishevskii and S. A. Kovalëv, *Geografiia naseleniia SSSR* [Moscow, 1962]).

[5] I. Glazyrin, *Regulirovanie sostava KPSS v period stroitel'stva sotsializma*, p. 89.

[6] "Shiroko razvernut' politicheskuiu rabotu v derevne" (Widen the Scope of Political Work in the Countryside), *B*, No. 6, March 1947, p. 6.

the background of continued urbanization, however, this has meant a continued improvement in the *relative* incidence of party membership in the rural population.

Despite the increase of available data about the composition of the party in the post-Stalin period, there is little direct information about the ratio of townsmen to villagers. In September 1953 Khrushchev stated that the number of communists "in the countryside" (*na sele*) now exceeded a million, but he was almost certainly referring to primary producers only.[7] In February 1954 he stated that there were about three million communists "in the rural districts" (*v sel'skikh raionakh*), the context indicating that this figure applied not only to villagers but also to communists living in small towns subordinate to the raion soviets.[8] Thus neither of these figures is directly comparable with the figures we have quoted for rural membership in 1933 and 1947, which appear to refer to all village-dwellers, *including* local soviet officials, teachers, medical workers, shopkeepers, etc., but excluding inhabitants of small towns in the rural raions. Subsequently considerable information has been forthcoming about the membership of collective and state farm organizations, and about the number of communists engaged in agriculture, but again not about rural communists as such. The

[7] N. S. Khrushchev, *Stroitel'stvo kommunizma v SSSR i razvitie sel'skogo khoziaistva* (Moscow, 1962), Vol. I, p. 72. If this figure had referred to all communists in the villages, it would have implied a reduction in rural membership since 1947 by half a million or so. It is not impossible that there was some reduction in this period, as the overall growth of the party was slow and may not have been sufficient to offset the drift of party members from the villages in pursuit of promotion. However, a reduction on this scale is scarcely feasible. Moreover, other evidence implies that communists working in the farms and MTS's alone numbered over a million in 1953 (see Table 24, p. 332).

[8] *Ibid.*, p. 281.

following considerations, however, provide the basis for a rough estimate:

1. As we have noted, rural party membership was about 1,700,000 in 1947. From then until 1953 the total CPSU membership grew by about one-ninth. If the increase in rural areas was roughly the same as in the towns, rural membership was therefore about 1,900,000 in 1953.

2. We know that the number of party members engaged in agriculture was about 1,190,000 in 1953 and 2,164,000 in 1965 (see Table 24, p. 332). Virtually all of these can be assumed to be village-dwellers.

3. The number of rural communists in 1953 who were not engaged in agriculture may thus be estimated at about 700,000. Assuming that they increased at about the same rate as the rest of the nonagricultural population, they evidently numbered about 1,080,000 in 1965.

4. The total number of rural communists in 1965 was therefore about three and a quarter millions.[9]

If anything, this estimate may be too high, since there are reasons for thinking that the nonfarming rural membership may have grown more slowly than assumed above, especially in 1947-1953. If so, however, the overestimate is most unlikely to exceed 300,000, or 10 percent.

Table 59 summarizes what can be discovered and surmised

[9] The only area for which detailed data on rural party membership are available for the Khrushchev period is Kazakhstan. Unfortunately, however, differences in categorization would prevent us from employing these data as a check on our nationwide estimates, even if it were assumed possible to generalize from a single (and far from average) republic. The most one can say is that the Kazakhstan data do not suggest any gross inaccuracy in our estimate. See *Kompartiia Kazakhstana na vtorom etape osvoeniia tseliny*, p. 366.

TABLE 59: URBAN AND RURAL COMMUNISTS, 1922-1965

Year	Number of communists		Percent of total		Per 10,000 of population	
	Urban	Rural	Urban	Rural	Urban	Rural
1922	314,000	201,000	61	39	155	18
1927	840,000	307,000	73	27	319	26
1933	2,765,000	790,000	78	22	670*	70*
1947	4,586,000	1,714,000	76	24	740*	155*
1965	8,500,000*	3,250,000*	72	28	700*	300*

* Estimates. Party-population ratios for 1933 and 1947 assume population estimates for which the author is indebted to Mr. J. A. Newth.

about the urban-rural distribution of the party membership since the 1920's. Its precision should not be exaggerated. It involves elements of guesswork, and we cannot be certain that the criteria of "urban" and "rural" exactly correspond throughout. Even allowing for a high margin of error, however, some striking and important trends emerge. We see that the proportion of rural members was at its maximum at the end of the Civil War and has never closely approached the same level since. Since the later 1920's the ratio of urban to rural members has been remarkably constant at about three to one. Meanwhile, however, the contrast between the incidence of party membership among townsmen and among villagers has been constantly narrowed from twelve to one in 1927 to under two and a half to one in 1965. Perhaps the most remarkable conclusion to emerge from this table is that the proportion of townsmen who were party members was very little more in 1965 than it had been in 1933. For some years after 1947 there was almost certainly a marked decline in the incidence of party membership among townsmen,

491

and the mass recruitment of 1954-1965 was required to offset it.

In the future, both the practical needs of control and the ideological commitment to "eliminating the differences between town and country" will exert pressures to further narrow the gap between urban and rural membership, and this will be a continuing obstacle to reducing the scale of party recruitment in the villages. Meanwhile, further urbanization will also necessitate substantial recruitment in the towns if the existing level of party membership is to be maintained there. The urban-rural balance thus contains inbuilt pressures making for continued expansion of the party.

Types of Urban Community

What proportion of urban communists live in towns of different sizes and types? Here our information is very fragmentary, but it does permit certain tentative conclusions.

Although the heaviest concentrations of party members are undoubtedly still to be found in the major cities, a substantial proportion has long been located in small towns, especially those serving as raion administrative centers. Towns with a population up to 50,000 normally come under the rural raion authorities,[10] and these towns clearly exercise a strong attraction for communists in the rural raikoms. The tendency for communists to congregate in the raion centers at the expense of the villages was noted long before Khrushchev began his campaign to expand the farm organizations after the death of Stalin. Deploring this tendency in 1948, a

[10] See *Vedomosti Verkhovnogo Soveta RSFSR*, No. 7, 1967, p. 3; D. L. Zlatopol'skii, *Gosudarstvennoe ustroistvo SSSR* (Moscow, 1960), p. 286. A small proportion of raion centers have a population over 50,000, and there are even a few with over 100,000 inhabitants. See S. A. Kovalëv, in V. V. Pokshishevskii and S. A. Kovalëv, *Geografiia naseleniia SSSR*, p. 57.

Central Committee spokesman gave as an example a raion where there were 189 communists in the raion center and only 118 in the villages.[11] While this was probably a "bad" case, there were others which were far "worse."[12] More general data is available from the Ukraine for the same year, 1948. At this time 327,100 communists were located in the rural raions of the Ukraine, or nearly half the party membership of the republic.[13] Of these, some 167,000 were members of farm, MTS or village territorial organizations, and most of the rest, i.e. nearly a quarter of all communists in the Ukraine, must have been located in the raion centers and small towns. We have already noted Khrushchev's statement in 1954 that the rural raions contained about three million of the CPSU's seven million members and candidates. His breakdown of these three millions, although incomplete and presented in terms of employment rather than domicile, is relevant to our present enquiry. He stated that 30 percent of them were working at the raion echelon and 20 percent in industrial undertakings.[14] These two categories thus totaled about one and a half millions, or over a fifth of the party membership. A little earlier we estimated that about 1.9 million of these 3 million party members in the rural districts were village-dwellers. The apparent discrepancy arises from the fact that many raion centers are not classed as "towns."

[11] *PZh*, No. 2, January 1948, p. 53.

[12] In the Lvov oblast in 1951 there was one raion where only 25 out of 300 communists were located in the villages, and another where only 22 out of 216 were so located (see *PU*, February 21, 1951). At the other extreme there was a raion in the Stalingrad oblast where as early as 1948, 666 out of 832 communists were members of farm or MTS organizations (see *PZh*, No. 5 [March], 1948, p. 20).

[13] *PZh*, No. 5, March 1948, p. 11.

[14] N. S. Khrushchev, *Stroitel'stvo kommunizma v SSSR i razvitie sel'skogo khoziaistva*, Vol, I, p. 281.

In 1954 over 50 percent were in fact classed as "rural settlements," although half of these had more than 3,000 inhabitants and some had more than 10,000.[15] If we are correct in our supposition that rural membership was about the same in 1954 as in 1947, about 400,000 "rural" communists in 1954 must in fact have been living in raion centers. In any case, Khrushchev's breakdown of the 1954 CPSU membership suggests the following approximate distribution:

		percent
1.	Towns with over 50,000 inhabitants	56
2.	Smaller towns and raion centers classed as "rural settlements"	22
3.	Other rural settlements	22

On the available data it is difficult to estimate changes in this distribution in subsequent years, although it is probably safe to assume some reduction in the relative weight of small town and raion center communists.[16]

[15] S. A. Kovalëv, in V. V. Pokshishevskii and S. A. Kovalëv, *Geografiia naseleniia SSSR*, pp. 57, 67.

[16] The number of raions in the U.S.S.R. fell from 4,368 to 3,501 between 1954 and 1960 (*ibid.*, p. 67). In 1965 they numbered 2,636 (*PZh*, No. 3, February 1965, p. 6. This undoubtedly brought a reduction in the number of communists working in raion echelon institutions, who formed the largest group of party members in raion centers. Meanwhile the general increase during the Khrushchev era in the proportion of communists working in production enterprises probably benefited the villages and larger towns more than the smaller towns. Nevertheless, if there has been some trend away from the smaller towns, this can scarcely have been a very dramatic one. One raikom secretary regarded as an exemplary rural party organizer revealed in 1961 that 700 communists in his raion were located in the villages and 600 in the towns. Since this ratio is unlikely to have favored the towns more than the national average, it allows for only minor change since 1954. (See Z. N. Glukhov, *Kadry reshaiut uspekh dela* [Moscow, 1961], p. 149.)

If our calculations are correct, something like three-quarters of all urban communists in 1954 were in towns of over 50,000 inhabitants. Since such towns contained only about 60 percent of the urban population,[17] there would appear to be some positive correlation between the size of towns and the occurrence of party membership. This is presumably because the larger towns tend to contain more advanced industry and cultural and administrative facilities, especially those on the higher echelons which are relatively party saturated. That these are in fact the relevant variables cannot, unfortunately, be clearly established on the available evidence, but consideration of a number of particular cases appears to point up their importance.

Let us start with Moscow itself, which is, of course, not only by far the greatest industrial and cultural center of the U.S.S.R., but also the headquarters of the Union and R.S.F.S.R. governments and of innumerable paragovernmental and "mass" organizations. In 1961 Moscow contained about 6 percent of the urban population of the U.S.S.R. as against at least 8 percent of the urban party membership.[18]

After Moscow, Leningrad is not only easily the most populous city in the U.S.S.R., but the most important industrial, educational, scientific and artistic center. On the eve of the October Revolution Leningrad contained nearly a quarter of all Russia's bolsheviks or almost three times as many as Moscow. In subsequent years, and indeed throughout the Stalin period, Leningrad's share of the party membership rapidly declined: it was approximately halved between 1927

---

[17] *Itogi vsesoiuznoi perepisi naseleniia 1959 goda: SSSR*, p. 35. Both the 1939 and 1959 censuses showed 40 percent of the urban population to be located in towns and urban settlements of fewer than 50,000 inhabitants.

[18] *P*, October 29, 1961.

and 1941, and contracted by a further quarter from then until 1957.[19] Even then, however, after all the losses of the wartime blockade and Stalin's postwar purges,[20] Leningrad still held about 4.5 percent of the urban party membership, though it contained only 3.4 percent of the urban population of the U.S.S.R. There were more communists in Leningrad than in twelve out of the fifteen Union Republics.

Many large towns serve as the administrative centers of oblasts, krais or republics, and the little information that is available indicates that these, too, tend to have a relatively high rate of party membership. This may be illustrated by the cases of Riga (a republic capital) and Yaroslavl (an oblast center). The size of delegations to the Seventeenth Congress of the Communist Party of Latvia (in 1960) indicated that some 45 percent of the party membership of the republic were located in Riga.[21] It was stated in 1952 that half the communists in the Yaroslavl oblast were living in the city of Yaroslavl.[22] Yet in the relevant years these cities contained only about one-quarter of the total population and one-half of the urban population of their respective areas (republic, oblast).[23]

Both Riga and Yaroslavl are by far the largest cities in their areas and they are important with respect to *all three* of the variables which have been proposed as relevant to party membership levels, namely administration, industry

[19] See *Sotsial'nyi i natsional'nyi sostav VKP(b)*, p. 20, and *Leningrad: Entsiklopedicheskii spravochnik* (Moscow-Leningrad, 1957), pp. 123, 138.

[20] See Conquest, *Power and Policy in the U.S.S.R.* (London, Macmillan; New York, St. Martin's Press, 1961). Chap. 5.

[21] *S Lat*, February 18, 1960.

[22] *P*, August 26, 1952.

[23] See *Itogi vsesoiuznoi perepisi naseleniia 1959 goda: SSSR*, pp. 20, 24, 30.

and cultural facilities. The same applies to Moscow and Leningrad. Comparison of membership levels in certain other cities, however, enables us partly to dissociate these variables, and therefore to form some impression of the influence they may exert separately.

The three largest towns in Lithuania are Vilnius (the republic capital), Kaunas and Klaipeda. The first two are about equal in size and a little over twice as large as Klaipeda. However, the incidence of party membership in the population of Kaunas and Klaipeda is roughly equal, while in Vilnius it is twice as high.[24] Clearly, it is not size as such that has determined these differences in party membership levels. Nor, evidently, are they due to differences in industrial importance: there is considerable industry in all three cities, but none of them is a major industrial center. What most distinguishes Vilnius from these other cities is its heavy concentration of administrative and cultural institutions, and we must suppose this to be the main reason for its relatively high party membership levels.

Our evidence on the other variable mentioned, namely industrial importance, is more ambiguous. That this may function independently as a membership-generating factor is suggested by the case of Kutaisi, the Georgian city whose significance derives entirely from its role as the chief steel center of the Caucasus. In 1960 the proportion of party members in Kutaisi was about 80 percent as high as in the republic capital of Tbilisi, a far higher ratio than would be expected from the data on provincial cities in other republics.[25] Unfortunately other cases enabling us to isolate the

[24] *S Lit*, September 28, 1961. Based on the size of delegations to the republic party congress.

[25] *ZV*, September 29, 1961; *Itogi vsesoiuznoi perepisi naseleniia 1959 goda: SSSR*, pp. 30-31.

influence of the industrial factor are hard to find. A careful examination of the distribution of party members as between different oblasts of the Ukraine in the late 1950's and early 1960's, however, sheds some further light.

In part the Ukrainian evidence supports the impressions already recorded. The Kiev oblast, containing the republic capital, has easily the greatest number of party members. The sixteen predominantly agricultural oblasts of the Central and Western Ukraine (excluding the Kiev oblast) contain 58 percent of the republic's population but only 44 percent of the CPSU membership. The party is overrepresented in the five heavily industrialized eastern oblasts. The degree of overrepresentation, however, is not as great as one might expect: they contain 32 percent of the republic's population and 36 percent of the party membership. Within this eastern area, moreover, the Kharkov and Dnepropetrovsk oblasts are considerably more party saturated than the Donbass (Donetsk and Lugansk oblasts), though they contain a far larger rural population. More striking still, there are two oblasts outside the industrialized East—Odessa and the Crimea—which also have a higher ratio of party members than the Donbass; while the Lvov oblast (in the West), whose population is only two-fifths urban as compared with five-sixths in the Donbass, has a party membership rate only one-tenth lower than the Donbass.[26]

[26] Based on census data and estimates of party membership derived from representation at party congresses. See *Itogi vsesoiuznoi perepisi naseleniia 1959 goda: SSSR*, p. 24; *PU*, January 20, 1956, February 17, 1960 and September 28, 1961. Incomplete breakdowns of delegates in Credential Commission reports at republic congresses have been supplemented here by a name-count of delegates from Ukrainian oblasts to the Twenty-Second Congress of the CPSU: see *XXII s"ezd*, Vol. III, pp. 363-584. The eight oblasts discussed in the text are listed below, with estimates of the number of communists per 1,000

There are thus a number of features of party membership distribution in the Ukraine which appear anomalous in terms of those factors affecting membership levels which have so far been noted. Examination of these anomalous cases may therefore enable us to refine and possibly extend our catalogue of such factors.

The mediocre party saturation of the Donbass is probably due in the main to relatively low membership levels in the mining industry, other evidence of which has already been noted (see p. 451). The far higher membership levels in the Kharkov and Dnepropetrovsk oblasts are associated with a vast concentration and variety of manufacturing industry as well as numerous scientific and educational establishments. It is also worth comparing these two oblasts. The former is considerably more party saturated, though it contains a larger rural population, suggesting that the city of Kharkov itself has a notably higher ratio of party members than the industrial centers of the Dnepropetrovsk oblast. This may be be due to the greater scale of Kharkov industry, though perhaps no less important is the long history and continued prominence of Kharkov as an administrative and cultural center (it was the capital and main focus of party strength in the Ukraine till the 1930's).

The heavy party membership in the Odessa oblast is probably due to the political and economic importance of Odessa itself (population 667,000 in 1959), as the Soviet Union's principal Black Sea port, as well as to its concentration of

---

of their population (in 1961); the percentage of their population classified as urban in the 1959 census is shown in brackets.

Industrial oblasts	*Others*
Donetsk—36 [86]	Kiev—55 [55]
Lugansk—37 [79]	Crimea—72 [65]
Kharkov—53 [62]	Odessa—47 [47]
Dnepropetrovsk—48 [70]	Lvov—33 [31]

cultural facilities, which have formed one of the main generators of population growth in the city.[27] Similar factors probably also operate in the Lvov oblast, where Lvov (410,000) contains many economic, administrative and cultural facilities serving large areas of the Western Ukraine.

The high party membership levels in the Crimean oblast, however, are not explicable in these terms. Though its population is two-thirds urban, none of the Crimea's cities exceeds 200,000 in population, is important industrially or contains administrative or cultural institutions of more than local significance. Yet this is the most party-saturated oblast in the Ukraine, far more so even than the Kiev oblast itself. Large concentrations of military and naval personnel, in the Sevastopol base and other defense facilities, no doubt provide part of the answer.[28] Yet other areas are also replete with armed forces personnel (this may be an additional factor making for high party membership rates in the Lvov oblast, for instance), and it is hard to believe that the Crimea is sufficiently exceptional in this regard for this to fully account for its remarkable party membership levels.

The only other special feature of the Crimea is its tourist and health resorts, for which the area is best known in the Soviet Union. The indications therefore are that these resorts contain an exceptionally high proportion of party members. We can only speculate, however, as to how many of these are employed in the resorts, how many are communists undergoing convalescence or rest-cures, and how many are retired persons.[29]

[27] See V. V. Pokshishevskii and S. A. Kovalëv, *op.cit.*, p. 107.

[28] See p. 255 for indications that the navy has particularly high membership levels. This may also be a factor in the heavy membership ratios in the Leningrad oblast and Soviet Far East.

[29] The hypothesis that the Crimea's tourist and health resorts provide the key to its high party membership levels naturally prompts us

This comparative analysis of party membership levels in different oblasts of the Ukraine could be matched by similar analyses of areas of the R.S.F.S.R. and the other larger republics. Since, however, the observations permitted by our data are no more than suggestive, lacking statistical force, there seems little point in multiplying examples, though it should at least be added that the non-Ukrainian material does tend to suggest the same observations as the Ukrainian. These observations are as follows: (1) Considerable industrial development is found in nearly all areas with high party membership ratios. (2) The kind of industrial development matters. In particular, the combination of coal mining, metallurgy and heavy engineering (as found in the Donbass) is less conducive to high membership levels than diversified engineering and manufacturing. (3) Where an area shows membership levels notably in excess of what might be expected from the scale of urbanization and industrialization, it is nearly always found to contain a center of major administrative and cultural importance. (4) Though the scale and character of urban development appear to account for most aspects of party membership distribution, other factors sometimes assume overriding importance (e.g. the presence of heavy military concentrations or resort centers). (5) It is noteworthy that the largest concentrations of party members

---

to look for analogies elsewhere. Though it would seem that other factors may suffice to account for the high membership rates in the Odessa oblast, it is worth noting that convalescent and holiday facilities are also a significant employment factor in Odessa (V. V. Pokshishevskii and S. A. Kovalëv, *op.cit.*, pp. 107-108). More indicative, perhaps, is the case of the Krasnodar krai, which has high membership levels relative to its degree of urbanization, and contains the R.S.F.S.R.'s most important tourist and convalescent area in the stretch of Black Sea coast around Sochi (see *P*, January 14, 1958 and November 22, 1962). One is reminded of the high conservative vote in the seaside towns of southern England.

are found in the most comfortable, pleasant and interesting cities and districts in the republic. One is reminded of Khrushchev's problem of getting bureaucrats and scientists to work out of Moscow and the perennial tendency of rural communists to gravitate to the relative comfort of the district center. Perhaps a desire by party members (and their wives) for *la dolce vita* operates as an independent factor affecting CPSU membership distribution.

Regional Distribution

It remains to note some salient facts about the broad regional distribution of the CPSU membership. As can be seen from Table 60[30] and the map on page 504, this departs markedly from the general pattern of population distribution in the U.S.S.R. Between 1939 and 1961 the extremes of regional over- and under-representation contracted considerably. Even then, however, the variation among the 16 major regions ranged from 47 percent above the national average to 31 percent below it.

While representation in most regions moved closer to the national average, there were certain exceptions. The Central Region, no doubt because of Moscow, became even more overrepresented than before. It is noteworthy, however, that even in 1961 it was less party saturated than the Northwestern Region, dominated by Leningrad. By contrast, party representation in Belorussia, the Ukraine and Moldavia sank much further below the U.S.S.R. average after 1939, due to the effects of World War II. In 1961 the Central Region of

[30] SOURCE: Party membership figures are calculated from name-counts of oblast, krai and republic delegations to the Eighteenth (1939) and Twenty-Second (1961) CPSU Congresses. See *XVIII s"ezd*, pp. 694-733 and *XXII s"ezd*, Vol. III, pp. 363-584. Population figures are taken from *Itogi vsesoiuznoi perepisi naseleniia 1959 goda: SSSR*, pp. 20-29.

TABLE 60: GEOGRAPHICAL DISTRIBUTION OF SOVIET POPULATION AND CPSU
MEMBERSHIP, 1939-1961

Region	Percent of Soviet population		Percent of CPSU membership		Percent of CPSU over/under-representation	
	1939	1959	1939	1961	1939	1961
R.S.F.S.R.						
1. Northwestern	6.6	5.5	11.5	8.1	+74.0	+47.0
2. Central	14.9	11.9	20.4	16.8	+37.0	+41.0
3. Volga-Viatka	5.1	3.9	3.3	3.7	−34.0	− 5.0
4. Central Black Earth	6.1	4.2	4.6	3.9	−25.0	− 7.0
5. Volga (Middle and Lower)	7.1	6.0	5.3	7.0	−26.0	+17.0
6. North Caucasus	6.2	5.2	6.2	5.5	0.0	+ 6.0
7. Urals	8.5	8.9	6.4	7.9	−25.0	−11.0
8. West Siberia	4.7	4.9	2.6	4.5	−45.0	− 8.0
9. East Siberia	3.1	3.3	2.7	2.9	−13.0	−12.0
10. Far Eastern	1.5	2.1	2.8	2.8	+87.0	+33.0
Western Republics						
11. Ukraine (incl. Moldavia)	18.2	21.4	18.0	17.0	− 1.0	−21.0
12. Belorussia	3.3	4.1	2.9	2.9	−12.0	−29.0
13. Baltic Republics		2.9		2.1		−28.0
Asian Republics						
14. Transcaucasia	4.7	4.5	6.0	5.3	+28.0	+18.0
15. Kazakhstan	3.6	4.5	2.5	3.9	−31.0	−13.0
16. Central Asia	6.2	6.5	2.6	4.5	−58.0	−31.0

the Russian Republic contained approximately the same
number of communists as the Ukraine and Moldavia, though
it had only half their population. The (Middle and Lower)
Volga Region and the adjacent North Caucasus Region also
showed trends in their party membership ratios which di-
verged from the standard pattern. The former has enjoyed
a higher than average rate of urbanization, but certainly not

503

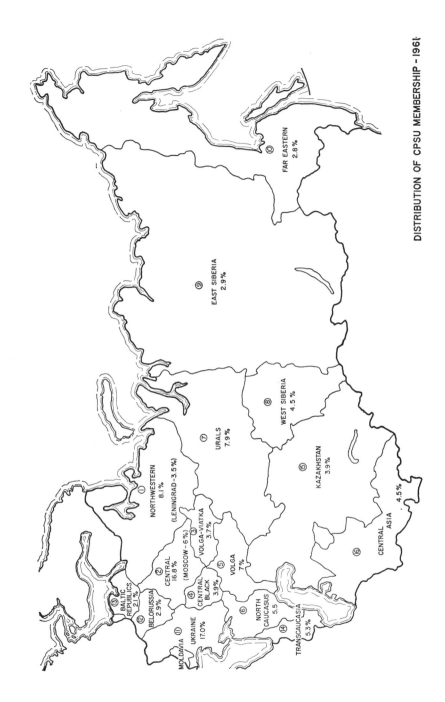

DISTRIBUTION OF CPSU MEMBERSHIP - 1961¹

① NORTHWESTERN
8.1%
(LENINGRAD - 3.5%)

② CENTRAL
16.8%
(MOSCOW - 6%)

③ VOLGA-VIATKA
3.7%

④ CENTRAL
BLACK
3.9%

⑤ VOLGA
7%

⑥ NORTH
CAUCASUS
5.5

⑦ URALS
7.9%

⑧ WEST SIBERIA
4.5%

⑨ EAST SIBERIA
2.9%

⑩ FAR EASTERN
2.8%

⑪ UKRAINE
17.0%

⑫ BALTIC
REPUBLICS
2.1%

⑬ BELORUSSIA
2.9%

⑭ TRANSCAUCASIA
5.3%

⑮ KAZAKHSTAN
3.9%

⑯ CENTRAL
ASIA
4.5%

MOLDAVIA

enough to account for its striking shift from under- to over-saturation. The latter, with its modest trend towards over-saturation, has shown a *lower* than average rate of urbanization. One factor, at least in the former case, may have been the immigration of communists from more westerly areas in the course of World War II, but it is doubtful if this is the full explanation.

The Asian areas of the R.S.F.S.R. deserve special mention. The Urals and Western Siberia are two of the most important industrial regions of the U.S.S.R. and contain a relatively small rural population, yet their party membership levels remain below the national average. As in the Donbass, mining and metallurgy are the key industries in these areas, so we have here further evidence that intensive industrial development of this kind is not particularly conducive to high party membership. It might be added that if there is any validity in the suggestion that the general comfort and pleasantness of an area is an independent factor in its party membership levels, this factor would operate in a strongly negative direction in these regions. The same applies to the East Siberian Region which also has a higher than average ratio of town-dwellers and a lower than average ratio of party members. The Far Eastern Region presents an entirely different picture. In 1939 it contained more party members in relation to population than any other region in the country. This undoubtedly reflected the large concentrations of military, naval and corrective labor camp personnel in the area. By 1961 it had slipped back to the third most party-saturated region, presumably due to the drastic contraction of the corrective labor camp system, but its party membership levels still contrasted sharply with those in the rest of Soviet Asia.

There is not enough information to extend this analysis of the regional distribution of party membership beyond 1961, although something may be learned from the data on the distribution as between republics assembled in Table 61.[31] Before examining these data, certain discrepancies between the 1961 membership figures used in Tables 60 and 61 should first be noted. The former are calculated from the size of delegations to the Twenty-Second CPSU Congress in October 1961 and allot communists in the armed forces to the republics and regions where they were currently serving. Table 61 reproduces membership breakdowns by republic published by the Central Committee, the figures are for January, and armed forces communists appear to be allotted according to their normal domicile.

Between 1961 and 1965 the ratio of party members in the Soviet population increased by 8 per 1,000. While there were significant changes in the relative degree of party saturation as between republics, these changes cannot be reduced to a single pattern: some made for a narrowing of differences between republics, others for a widening of differences. The Ukraine, Belorussia and Estonia, areas of relative undersaturation, showed a higher than average rate of increase, but then so did the relatively oversaturated R.S.F.S.R. Meanwhile Georgia and Armenia, where membership levels were relatively high, as well as Azerbaidzhan and Central Asia, where they were low, all showed a lower than average rate of increase.

The relatively fast party membership increase in the Ukraine and Belorussia in these years is consistent with the rapidly improving representation of Ukrainians and Belorussians which was noted earlier (see p. 379). Comparison of Table 61 with Table 37 (p. 378), however, reveals that party membership levels in the various republics were often

[31] SOURCES: For population figures see *Ezhegodnik BSE*, 1961 and 1965; for party membership figures see *PZh*, No. 1, January 1962, p. 44 and No. 10, May 1965, p. 8.

TABLE 61: INCIDENCE OF PARTY MEMBERSHIP IN POPULATION OF UNION REPUBLICS, 1961-1965

Republics	Population		Party membership		Communists per 1,000 of population	
	Jan. 1961	Jan. 1965	Jan. 1961	Jan. 1965	Jan. 1961	Jan. 1965
U.S.S.R. as a whole	216,000,000	229,100,000	9,275,826	11,758,169	43	51
R.S.F.S.R.	120,000,000	125,800,000	6,257,849	7,766,394	52	62
Ukraine	43,091,000	45,100,000	1,370,997	1,829,638	32	41
Moldavia	3,040,000	3,303,000	59,908	85,379	20	26
Belorussia	8,226,000	8,533,000	225,541	314,279	26	37
Latvia	2,142,000	2,241,000	72,519	95,742	34	43
Lithuania	2,804,000	2,949,000	60,551	86,366	22	29
Estonia	1,221,000	1,273,000	37,848	54,836	31	43
Georgia	4,200,000	4,483,000	216,866	248,375	52	55
Azerbaidzhan	3,973,000	4,518,000	153,221	198,539	38	44
Armenia	1,893,000	2,134,000	85,062	104,305	45	49
Kazakhstan	10,400,000	12,000,000	345,115	450,486	33	36
Uzbekistan	8,665,000	10,130,000	224,519	314,279	26	31
Kirgizia	2,225,000	2,569,000	65,866	84,721	30	33
Tadzhikistan	2,104,000	2,432,000	52,014	67,624	25	28
Turkmenia	1,626,000	1,862,000	47,950	57,206	29	31

in marked contrast to the membership levels of their basic nationalities, and changes in the representation of a given republic and of its basic nationality often differed sharply as well. Logically, there are two distinct factors which may produce such differences: a nationality may have different party membership levels inside "its" republic and beyond its borders, and there may be differences in party membership levels as between the basic and other nationalities of a republic. In particular cases, one can rarely be certain how much weight should be allotted to each of these factors, although population ratios usually give fairly strong indications. Three patterns may be distinguished. Azerbaidzhan and

507

the four Central Asian republics have party membership
levels practically identical with those of their basic nationalities. The inhabitants of the Baltic republics, Moldavia and
the R.S.F.S.R. show higher membership levels than their
basic nationalities. In the case of the R.S.F.S.R. the difference
is relatively small and has developed only since 1961; the
change is probably due in the main to improved recruitment among the previously underrepresented non-Russian
minorities in the republic, though this is conjectural. Differences in the other republics are more marked, especially in
the cases of Latvia and Estonia, and the main reason is almost certainly the far lower party membership levels among
the local nationalities than among resident minority groups,
particularly the Russians (this has been shown to be the case
in Moldavia, see p. 389). The fact that party membership
levels in Latvia, Lithuania, Estonia and Moldavia rose more
rapidly between 1961 and 1965 than did the membership
levels of their basic nationalities shows that party recruitment
among these nationalities worsened rather than improved
relative to overall recruitment in "their" republics during
these years.

In the remaining five republics party membership levels
are lower than those found among their basic nationalities.
In the case of the Kazakhs this appears to reflect their relative overrepresentation in the party organization of "their"
republic (see p. 396). A possible factor here is the youth of
many of the non-Kazakhs who have poured into the republic
since the 1950's. Up to World War II the Ukrainians and
Belorussians were, by contrast, relatively underrepresented in
"their" party organizations, and, while this situation may
since have been moderated, it is unlikely to have been reversed. It would seem, then, that members of these nationalities are more liable to be party members if they live outside
"their" republics than at home. There is little ambiguity in

the data on the Georgians and Armenians. All but 3 to 4 percent of Soviet Georgians live in the Georgian Republic, where, however, they form less than two-thirds of the population. Clearly the minority nationalities in Georgia, of which the largest groups are the Armenians and Russians, have far lower membership levels than the Georgians themselves. By contrast, Armenians form the overwhelming majority of the inhabitants of "their" republic, but this contains only slightly over half of all Soviet Armenians. The fact that in 1965 party membership levels were 12 per 1,000 higher among Soviet Armenians than among the population of the Armenian Republic must therefore mean that Armenians of the *diaspora* joined the party in far higher proportions than Armenians at home.[32]

In conclusion, one further comment may be made on the data on the regional distribution of CPSU membership assembled in Table 60. Beneath the more detailed regional differences that have been discussed, a global regionalization may be discerned. Soviet Asia viewed as a whole, and the six republics forming the western borderlands of the U.S.S.R., both show relatively low party membership levels. By contrast, Russia proper west of the Urals, together with the North Caucasus and Transcaucasia, with 50 percent of the Soviet population, contain 60 percent of the CPSU membership. This area remains, as it was in the 1920's, the "heartland" of the CPSU.

[32] The Georgian and Armenian cases, however, point up the inevitable incompleteness of the deductions that may be drawn from these data. The deductions actually made in these two cases were dictated by the data, but these data leave completely open whether or not the complementary factors were also operating, i.e. whether Georgians outside Georgia were more likely than those inside to be members of the party, and whether Armenian inhabitants of Armenia were more likely to be party members than non-Armenian inhabitants. The deductions made with respect to other republics and nationalities, where the data are more ambiguous, are all the more likely to be incomplete as well as, to a greater or lesser degree, conjectural.

509

Conclusion

Determinants of CPSU Composition

DURING THE half century since the CPSU became the state party of Soviet Russia, it has undergone constant changes of size, social composition and relative representation of various categories of the Soviet population. Some of these changes have followed a consistent course, while others have been subject to interruptions, reversals and fluctuations of pace and direction. These changes have been traced in detail in the preceding pages, and it is our task now to take stock of their determinants, so far as these emerge from a study of official membership policies and of how these policies have operated in practice.

The functions of the CPSU in the Soviet political and social system have undoubtedly been of paramount importance. As a quick summary of our main findings we may say that party membership patterns and policies have been primarily due to the party's role as "the leading and directing force of Soviet society," which gives "guiding directions" having "the force of law" to all social organisms, systematically supervises and coordinates the carrying out of these directions and mobilizes the masses to ensure their success, and assigns members to serve as the "guiding nucleus" of all institutions and associations. The chief consequences of this role have been these:

1. The membership has had to include a substantial body of full-time party officials, which appears to have reached a maximum of perhaps a quarter million in the late Stalin era and is evidently somewhat smaller now.

2. It has meant limiting a wide range of jobs involving

administrative or ideological authority in all spheres of activity to persons who, as CPSU members, are subject to party indoctrination, discipline and responsibility.

3. In addition, it has demanded that all groups inportant for decision making or opinion formation or enjoying high actual or potential prestige should contain a substantial nucleus of party members, who can attune them to the party line and offset any tendency to develop as foci of social leadership alternative to the party. This is a factor in party membership patterns among army officers, scholars and artists. It probably also helps to explain efforts to make party members out of the heroes and natural leaders who emerged on the wartime battlefronts.

4. It has involved providing all governmental bodies and nongovernmental associations with a sufficient party representation to ensure that they function as "driving belts" for the party rather than acting at cross-purposes to it.

5. It has required a leavening of party members in all occupational and residential groups to set an example of party-approved conduct and opinion and to act as the party's eyes, ears and mouthpiece.

These considerations have combined to produce high levels of party saturation (but not always complete incorporation) of all "elite" segments of society, and a scattering of party members through all other social groups.

A more systematic functional analysis, employing the categories developed in the Introduction, reveals a number of important additional aspects. Party membership levels have been highest in those structures concerned with internal order-maintenance (police, judges, procuracy) and with rule and policy making (upper levels of the bureaucracy); very high levels are also probable in specialized communications structures (mass media, publishing houses), but inadequate data are available here. Structures designed for external order-maintenance (armed forces) and rule and policy application (bureaucracy, economic administration and management) have high concentrations of party members in their authority roles, with "line posts" down to a fairly low level effectively reserved for party members, but only moderate party membership levels among their subordinate personnel.

The party itself has served as the structure primarily responsible for the functions of political socialization and recruitment, legitimation and identification, political initiative and initiative-aggregation, and political mobilization. It has sought relatively high levels of representation in those other structures that make a subsidiary contribution to these functions—educational and research establishments (especially in the social sciences), soviets, trade unions, komsomol and other "driving belts." Ideal performance of these functions would require a party membership broadly representative of the social categories (occupational, ethnic, educational, sex, age, etc.) of which the population is composed, but parity of representation has in fact never been approached. The history of the party membership reveals a strong tendency for these functions to act as weaker determinants of party membership patterns than the other political functions mentioned above. They tend to come to the fore in periods of external danger or internal instability marked by leadership splits or rapid structural change (the Civil War, after Lenin's death, collectivization and the first Five Year Plan, World War II, after Stalin's death), promoting diversification and "democratization" of the party membership. In periods of relative security and structural consolidation (following the Civil War, the middle and later 1930's, Stalin's postwar years, and, with qualifications, the period since 1964), these functions have declined in importance relative to the internal

512

order-maintenance and rule- and policy-application functions, promoting a tendency to "elitization" of the party membership.

The official ideology has operated on two levels to influence CPSU membership patterns. On the one hand, it has a functional role as the focus of all legitimation and identification processes, and, as such, operates as an "objective" factor claiming the attention of the leadership in framing membership policies. On the other hand, it operates as a "subjective" factor limiting what membership patterns the leadership can accept as proper or permissible. Though analytically separable, there appears little chance of allotting separate weights to these two aspects in considering the impact of doctrine on particular membership decisions.

Entrenched Leninist concepts envisage the party as intimately linked with, and representative of, the masses, especially the industrial workers, but at the same time as leading them, molding their moods and aspirations rather than being passively molded by them. This implies a membership with "roots" in the masses, but more or less heavily weighted in favor of the "leading," "most active" segments of society. Thus the pressures from the ideology have been broadly congruent with those flowing from the party's political and social functions. Partly, perhaps, because of this, ideology has usually figured as a subsidiary factor, readily yielding rationalizations for policies motivated by quite other considerations. It has nonetheless functioned as a constraint on more extreme policies, hindering moves to "open-door" recruitment and, on the other hand, more than once reinforcing pressures towards "democratization" when the membership has become too heavily identified with high-status groups.

We have seen ample evidence that considerations of power realization, appropriation and deployment may influence party membership policies. Probably for the reasons identified in the Introduction (see p. 44), it has been power considerations at the top rather than at the intermediate or lower levels of the power structure that have been found to be relevant to our topic. In most cases where power issues and party membership issues have become enmeshed, moreover, they have been articulated largely in doctrinal terms, and, at least during the early 1920's, elements of genuine doctrinal commitment have been involved alongside doctrinal manipulation. The principal cases discussed in the text are these: the dispute between the Politburo and the opposition in 1920-1922 over the level of recruitment of workers; Lenin's disagreement with his colleagues over how restrictive current recruitment ought to be; Trotsky vs. the "triumvirate" in 1923-1924 on the issue of concentrating party work in the factories or among the youth; Stalin vs. Zinoviev in 1925 on the relative intake of workers and peasants; and Stalin's subsequent stress on worker rather than peasant recruitment when moving against the "Right."

Direct evidence of the effect of power considerations on subsequent membership policies is hard to find. However, two lines of speculation may be worth recording here to alert us to possibly relevant evidence which may later come to hand. The first is as follows. Andrei Zhdanov was evidently Stalin's most influential adviser on party affairs from about 1939 until his death in August 1948. Apart from the war years, party recruitment was at its most "elitist" during the Zhdanov ascendancy (in effect, that is, in 1939-1941 and 1947-1948). From 1949 to 1953, when Malenkov was Stalin's right-hand man for party matters, membership policies, though still favoring high-status groups, did so far less markedly. Zhdanov and Malenkov are believed to have been at loggerheads between 1946 and 1948, and this may have been one of the issues on which they contended for Stalin's blessing. The second line of speculation, for which only a minor scrap of evidence has been recorded in our account of the period, relates to the radical shift to more active recruitment in 1954. There can be little doubt about Khrushchev's personal commitment to this policy. If, on the other hand, Malenkov was personally identified with the policies of 1949-1953, with their very restricted recruitment, it seems possible that this figured as one of the issues around which Khrushchev and Malenkov conducted their struggle for the position of *primus inter pares* within the ruling oligarchy in 1953-1954.

Control over the party's disciplinary machinery and thereby over expulsions is obviously a significant factor in the internal politics of the Soviet regime. This factor assumed particular importance during the various "purges" and "verifications" of the 1920's and 1930's, which were all more or less openly slanted against the supporters of current or defeated "oppositions" (though this was greatly muted in the case of the 1921 purge). The power implications of large-scale recruitment campaigns may be less apparent. A rapid influx of new members, which may involve the creation and subdivision of thousands of party organizations, generates a strong demand for new party cadres and necessitates the redeployment of existing ones, thus affording the masters of the party apparatus with rich opportunities of "rewarding their friends and punishing their enemies." Mass recruitment campaigns have therefore played a significant part in power contests and in consolidating new power balances in the leadership. This was an important element in the recruitment drives of the mid-1920's, the early 1930's, the late 1930's and almost certainly of the years following 1954 as well.

We would suggest, then, that the history of the CPSU mem-

515

bership since 1917 is largely explicable in such functional terms. This does not mean, of course, that the party leaders have had something like our functional map in mind, and have systematically sought to conform their membership policies to it. Particular functional imperatives, albeit conceptualized or rationalized in terms of Marxist-Leninist categories, have indeed frequently prompted decisions about "regulating" the party membership in one direction or another. At other times these imperatives have been only imperfectly understood and the response of the policy makers has been cruder and more confused. Further, an important part has been played by the voluntary element in party recruitment, which has tended to work in the interests of certain membership functions; in some cases this has been a matter of functional requirements simply coinciding with personal motivation, in others these requirements (e.g. political socialization and recruitment) have been mediated through the personal motives making for self-selection.

At the same time, it will hardly surprise us that a number of things in the history of the CPSU membership remain unaccounted for in such a functional analysis. If the human body manifests some remarkable inadequacies in relation to the functional demands made on it, how much more is this true of human social arrangements, even those most subject to rational calculation and design! Because of the untidy, approximate character of social systems, there is always a good deal left over in a functional analysis, and to the social scientist the special interest of what is left over (extrafunctional and dysfunctional elements) is that it is here he finds the main sources of change and development (like mutations in genetics).

A number of causes may be cited for the extrafunctional and dysfunctional elements observable in the CPSU membership: (a) the leadership has not always been clear as to what "mix" of members it needed; (b) its administrative machinery has often been slow to respond or otherwise inadequate to recruit just the members aimed at; (c) because of the way different variables are combined in society (e.g. ethnic and occupational categories) it has sometimes been impossible to satisfy certain functional needs without sacrificing others; (d) membership policies have had unexpected side effects, both short-term and long-term; and (e) the voluntary element in recruitment has skewed the distribution of several variables in given categories of recruits. These causes have sometimes occurred singly, but more often in combination, and the last mentioned has usually been present in some degree.

Perhaps the most obvious dysfunctional element is that various social categories have been underrepresented to a degree that has seriously impaired the legitimation and identification function of the CPSU membership. Contrasts in the representation of different nationalities, though tending to narrow, still remained sharp fifty years after the Revolution. These were partly due to cause c, but partly also to cause e: different nationalities have not equally *wanted* to join the party. The same two causes evidently account for the grossly unequal representation of men and women (which is dysfunctional mainly because of the doctrinal obstacles to acknowledging a sexual division of labor). The party's political recruitment function inevitably brings with it the endemic problem of "careerism" and, as the case of Ovechkin's blacksmith cited in the Introduction indicates, tends to discourage noncareerist workers who might make good party members. As already noted, a number of functions suffer from the overrepresentation of relatively powerful and privileged groups, which, however, results from

517

other functional demands. The same applies to the overrepresentation of workers compared with peasants, and of townsmen compared with villagers.

We have noted the substantial correspondence between crisis conditions and rapid party expansion on the one hand, and conditions of social and political consolidation and party membership stability or decline on the other, and suggested reasons for this in terms of party membership functions. However, the resultant jerkiness in the party's growth has its costs. With rapid expansion, the number of new members tends to outrun the ability of party organizations to train and indoctrinate them, thereby impairing the functional utility of the membership in important respects and necessitating a drastic (rather than moderate) cutback in recruitment in the ensuing period. Membership stability or decline leads to a more or less rapid dissipation of the party's representation in the humbler social strata, given the membership's political recruitment function and the marked drop-out tendency among nonupwardly mobile workers and peasants admitted during the preceding high-pressure recruitment stage. This in turn tends to provoke an exaggerated recruitment drive among the "masses" when the leadership senses some threat to internal or external security. Thus the party's intake rate tends to a rather unhealthy dialectic. One area where the effects of this dialectic is felt particularly acutely is the armed forces.

One necessary condition of effective government is that leading role incumbents should contrive to realize and appropriate power adequate to their roles and to develop suitable techniques for deploying this power. Thus, while political systems may certainly be compared in terms of their effective institutionalization of the power function, "power struggle" is not *in itself* dysfunctional. It is essential to stress this point, which of course is implicit in our discussion above of the part played by power considerations in the history of the CPSU membership. At the same time, it is a common failing of political systems that leading role incumbents acquire too little or too much power for their needs, and when they acquire too much their quirks of mind and personality, insufficiently disciplined and canalized by other functional imperatives, may then become a dysfunctional element in the system. Party membership policies in 1921-1923 perhaps provide an example of this. It made sense at this time to restrict the party's growth and to sift the existing membership, but the sharp and prolonged contraction of membership, which seems to have been mainly due to Lenin's obsessional concern for the "purity" of his party, probably impaired *all* the political functions of the membership.

Similarly, the contraction of membership in the mid-1930's and the restrictive policies of the early 1950's, evidently due largely to Stalin's hypersuspiciousness and megalomania, seem on balance to have been seriously dysfunctional.

Among the unintended political effects of party membership policies, perhaps the most important to emerge from this study (albeit in hypothetical terms that demand further investigation) is the part played by the age structure of the membership in facilitating or impairing the "circulation of elites." The political recruitment function of the party membership leads to expectations of promotion which evidently figure large in the motivation of many party members. However, the low average age of recruits combined with the alternation of periods of mass recruitment and membership stability or contraction tends to produce recurrent bottlenecks in promotion of a quite acute kind. It is suggested that the pressures built up in the party at such periods are important for understanding the political history of the U.S.S.R. and specifically that they have some relevance to the purges

519

of the 1930's and the purge evidently being initiated by Stalin on the eve of his death. By the same token, the more normal age profile of the party membership emerging in the 1960's should have the political effect of moderating such pressures.

Furthermore, the enormous and multifaceted importance of the party membership in the operation of Soviet politics and government means that the characteristics of the party membership inevitably affect the *style* of its operation. Thus it is essential to keep in mind the predominantly youthful, semiliterate and largely Great Russian composition of the party in the 1920's in studying the political struggles of those years. The contrast in political style between the 1940's and 1960's is also due, in part, to the marked raising of average age and educational levels between the periods.

On the face of it the overall growth rate of the CPSU presents serious difficulties for any attempt to analyze the history of the party membership in functional terms. The political functions of the CPSU membership were much the same in the 1960's as they were in the early 1920's, but meanwhile the membership had multiplied more than twentyfold. Granted, it might be argued that the membership was manifestly inadequate for its functions in the early 1920's, and that Soviet political, administrative and economic institutions did not acquire their present structure until a decade or so later. Even if we make the 1930's our base-point, however, we are faced with a fourfold increase in thirty years, as against a population increase of less than 30 percent. It might be hypothesized that this reflects long-term changes in the political system, with the relatively membership-intensive socialization and mobilization functions increasing their importance at the expense of the internal order-maintenance function. There is probably something to this, at least as far as the post-Stalin period is concerned, but such changes have not been sufficiently radical to account for membership growth of the order observed.

A clue is provided by certain facts that emerged in Chapters 13, 14 and 16. Despite the great expansion of the party over the period and the considerable increase in the percentage of party members who were in professional employment or possessed a higher education, the proportion of *all* Soviet citizens in professional employment or possessing a higher education who are in the party has changed little since World War II. Meanwhile, despite the fact that the proportion of communists in the urban population as a whole has remained much the same since the early 1930's while the proportion in the rural population has quadrupled, the percentage of townsmen in the total CPSU membership has declined only slightly. The explanation of these apparent paradoxes is at the same time the explanation of the party's overall growth rate. In broad terms it is this: the membership-intensive categories of the Soviet population are themselves subject to rapid growth, and the party is therefore obliged to grow proportionately if its level of saturation of these categories, and therewith the functional utility of its membership, are not to be impaired. Furthermore, heavy recruitment among these membership-intensive groups requires a balancing intake from the urban and rural "masses" so as to prevent their share of the total membership from declining too drastically and thereby undermining the legitimation and identification role of the party membership. The party's long-term growth rate is thus in large measure a by-product of the social changes due to industrialization and modernization.

This relationship is worth considering a little more closely. Since the numerical weakness of party organizations clearly contributed to the difficulties encountered by official policies in the countryside, at least up to the 1950's, efforts to in-

521

crease rural membership were inevitable and would have pushed the party's numbers up even without rapid urbanization. The quadrupling of the party saturation of the rural population between 1933 and 1965 accounts for about two and a quarter of the eight and a half million members added to the CPSU in this period. If the ratio between the urban and rural population had remained unchanged it would have added three and a quarter millions. In fact, however, while the rural population fell slightly between 1933 and 1965, the urban population trebled, and this meant an enormous proliferation of new industrial, administrative, cultural and other organizations, all of which required an adequate guiding nucleus of party members. Had it not been for this change in the urban-rural balance, the size of the party in 1965 should have been not eleven and three-quarter millions but only six and a quarter (on the admittedly unrealistic assumption of "other things being equal").

In addition to the transfer of population from village to town, however, changes were taking place in the social composition of both the urban and rural populations, changes which led to large proportional increases of those occupational and educational categories which, for reasons related to the political functions of the party membership, were relatively membership-intensive. Perhaps the best way of summarizing the effects of these changes on the social composition of the party is to consider the census category "persons of mental labor," which includes officials, managerial personnel, professionals and some minor nonmanual groups. According to the 1959 census figures this category numbered 2.6 millions in 1926 and 20.5 millions in 1959. Though official party membership figures allow only rough approximations, it may be estimated that about a fifth of these were in the party in 1926 and a quarter in 1959. This relatively stable saturation level is remarkable when one considers that the percentage of communists in the adult population as a whole increased roughly fivefold in this period. Yet so rapidly has this category of the population growth and so overrepresented has it remained in the party that it accounted for some four and a half million of the seven million members added between 1926 and 1959; or to put it another way, if "persons of mental labor" had remained the same proportion of the working population as in 1926, the party ought to have numbered about four millions in 1959 instead of eight millions. In practice, of course, urbanization and the growth of the "mental labor" category were not separate processes, but largely overlapped, and our attempts to quantify their respective effects on the composition of the party must be qualified in the light of this. Nonetheless, it is clear that these processes together largely account for the high secular growth rate of the party.

This throws fresh light on the alternating periods of mass recruitment and membership stability or contraction. The burgeoning towns and official, managerial and intellectual strata require a constant flow of new communists to keep up their party saturation levels. If recruitment is inadequate, they will attract them from the villages and from manual occupations, thereby causing a rapid lowering of party saturation levels in the latter, which in turn requires a new phase of mass recruitment.

Thus a self-generating element is built into the party membership structure, and as long as the party's functions and the overall tendencies of Soviet society remain unchanged, further substantial growth in the CPSU membership is to be expected. Yet there is a wider aspect to this question. How large can an "advanced detachment" get without merging with the mass of the army? The party's established role in

Soviet society is bound up with the selective quality of its membership, with its being open only to the few and not the many, with the *special* rights and obligations membership confers, with a certain mystique compounded of the remoteness of the party's internal processes from the experience of most ordinary people and the credibility of its claim to be in some sense the continuation of Lenin's chosen band of professional revolutionaries, and with the authority all this permits the communist to assert among "the masses." As joining the party becomes a normal expectation of a larger and larger proportion of young adults, as the point is reached where not just a few but most people have friends or relatives in the party, as familiarity with the party's internal processes thereby spreads, this mystique of the party as an order of men set apart from and above the masses and this social and political authority of the individual party member tend to dissolve. There are many signs that this was already happening by the 1960's, and the new membership policies introduced after the removal of Khrushchev under the slogan "it is better for ten who work not to call themselves party members . . . than for one chatterbox to have the right and opportunity to be a party member" were evidently aimed at refurbishing the mystique and restoring the authority of the party member. Yet, if our analysis is correct, a program of low recruitment and increased expulsion cannot be continued for long without beginning to impair the performance by the party membership of a number of important political functions. Moreover, since sooner or later a new campaign to replenish the party ranks would have to follow, it would again exacerbate all those dysfunctional features associated with the alternation of periods of rapid growth and membership stability or contraction which bade fair to disappear during the Khrushchev period.

524

This, then, was the dilemma facing those responsible for CPSU membership policies fifty years after the October Revolution. It faced them, however, as part of another and greater question, namely, what changes in the way the party exercises its "leading and directing" role are required by the transformation of the Soviet Union into a complex industrialized society? In more and more areas of Soviet life, effective decision making is coming to mean professional decision making, and this is clearly incompatible with detailed supervision and control by party officials or by the "party masses." In some such areas the party has had to learn to confine itself to the tasks of overall policy making, indoctrination and reconciling technically necessary innovations with the official ideology. If, as seems likely, the present trend to marketization in Soviet economic administration is eventually carried much further, the party will have to restrict itself to these tasks in the economy as well, the area of primary preoccupation both of the party's apparatus and its membership to date. This will require radical changes in the ways the party membership participates in various functions of the Soviet political system. The current policy dilemma regarding the party membership thus comes at a time when the party leaders are called upon to rethink fundamentally what they need party members for. If they prove equal to this task this book may turn out to cover not just a convenient number of years, but a definite phase in the history of the CPSU.

Bibliography

This is a list of sources used in the present book, i.e. it does not include items known to exist and believed to be relevant which could not be traced by the author. Also excluded are items referred to only incidentally or for background.

1. PARTY NEWSPAPERS AND JOURNALS

A. DAILY NEWSPAPERS (*dates indicate period used by author*)

Bakinskii rabochii. Baku. Organ of Azerbaidzhan Central Committee and Government and Baku City Committee. 1941-1966 (gaps during war).

Kazakhstanskaia pravda. Alma-Ata. Organ of Kazakh Central Committee. 1945-1966.

Kommunist. Erevan. Organ of Armenian Central Committee. 1946-1966.

Kommunist Tadzhikistana. Dushanbe. Organ of Tadzhik Central Committee. 1946-1966.

Leningradskaia pravda. Leningrad. Organ of Leningrad City and Oblast Committees. 1947-1962.

Leninskoe znamia. Petrozavodsk. Organ of Karelo-Finn Central Committee. 1946-1955.

Leninskoe znamia. Moscow. Organ of Moscow Oblast Committee. 1958-1962.

Moskovskii bol'shevik. Moscow. Organ of Moscow Oblast and City Committees. 1946-1949 (supplanted by *Moskovskaia pravda*).

Moskovskaia pravda. Moscow. Organ of Moscow City and, until 1957, Oblast Committees. 1950-1962.

Pravda. Moscow. Organ of CPSU Central Committee. 1917-1967.

Pravda Ukrainy. Kiev. Organ of Ukrainian Central Committee and Government. 1946-1966.

Pravda vostoka. Tashkent. Organ of Uzbek Central Committee. 1941-1966 (gaps during war).

Sovetskaia Belorussia. Minsk. Organ of Belorussian Central Committee. 1946-1966.

Sovetskaia Estonia. Tallinn. Organ of Estonian Central Committee. 1947-1966.

Sovetskaia Kirgizia. Frunze. Organ of Kirgiz Central Committee. 1943-1966.

Sovetskaia Latvia. Riga. Organ of Latvian Central Committee. 1947-1966.

Sovetskaia Litva. Vilnius. Organ of Lithuanian Central Committee. 1947-1966.

Sovetskaia Moldavia. Kishinev. Organ of Moldavian Central Committee. 1947-1966.

Sovetskaia Rossiia. Moscow. Organ of Central Committee Bureau for R.S.F.S.R. and R.S.F.S.R. Government. 1957-1966.

Sovetskaia Ukraina. Kiev. Organ of Ukrainian Central Committee. 1940-1941.

Turkmenskaia iskra. Ashkhabad. Organ of Turkmen Central Committee. 1946-1948, 1951-1966.

Zaria vostoka. Tbilisi. Organ of Georgian Central Committee and Tbilisi City Committee. 1941-1966 (gaps during war).

B. CENTRAL COMMITTEE JOURNALS (*dates show period of publication*)

Bol'shevik (since 1952 *Kommunist*). 18 (until 1952, 24) issues per year. 1924—

Izvestiia Tsentral'nogo Komiteta Rossiiskoi (from 1924: *Vsesoiuznoi*) *Kommunisticheskoi Partii* [bol'shevikov]. Fortnightly (more frequently in early years). 1919-1929.

Partiinoe stroitel'stvo. Fortnightly. 1930-1946.

Partiinaia zhizn'. Fortnightly. 1946—(not available 1949-1954).

Politicheskoe samoobrazovanie. Monthly.

Voprosy istorii KPSS. Bimonthly until 1962, monthly since 1963. 1957—

C. REPUBLIC PARTY JOURNALS (*dates indicate period used*)

Kommunist Belorussii. Minsk. Monthly. 1959-1966. For part of period Belorussian language version *Kamunist Belarusi* used.

Kommunist Moldavii. Kishinëv. Monthly. 1961-1966.

BIBLIOGRAPHY

Kommunist Sovetskoi Latvii. Riga. Monthly. 1961-1966.
Kommunist Turkmenistana. Ashkhabad. Monthly. 1957-1959.
Kommunist Ukrainy. Kiev. Monthly. 1964-1966.
Partiinaia zhizn' Kazakhstana. Alma-Ata. Monthly. 1964-1966.

2. *OFFICIAL REPORTS, DOCUMENTS AND SPEECHES*

A. STENOGRAPHIC REPORTS OF PARTY CONGRESSES
AND CONFERENCES

Shestoi s"ezd RSDRP (bol'shevikov): protokoly. Moscow,
Gospolitizdat, 1958. (Sixth Congress)
*Sed'maia (aprel'skaia) vserossiiskaia i Petrogradskaia ob-
shchegorodskaia konferentsiia RSDRP (bol'shevikov).
Aprel' 1917 goda: protokoly.* Moscow, Gospolitizdat, 1958.
(Seventh Conference)
*Sed'moi ekstrennyi s"ezd RKP(b) Mart 1918 goda: steno-
graficheskii otchët.* Moscow, Gospolitizdat, 1962. (Seventh
Congress)
Vos'moi s"ezd RKP (b) Mart 1919 goda: protokoly. Moscow,
Gospolitizdat, 1959. (Eighth Congress)
*Vos'maia konferentsiia RKP(b) Dekabr' 1919 goda: proto-
koly.* Moscow, Gospolitizdat, 1961. (Eighth Conference)
Deviatyi s"ezd RKP(b) Mart-Aprel' 1920 goda: protokoly.
Moscow, Gospolitizdat, 1960. (Ninth Congress)
*Desiatyi s"ezd RKP(b) Mart 1921 goda: stenograficheskii
otchët.* Moscow, Gospolitizdat, 1963. (Tenth Congress)
*Odinnadtsatyi s"ezd RKP(b) mart-aprel' 1922 goda: steno-
graficheskii otchët.* Moscow, Gospolitizdat, 1961. (Eleventh
Congress)
*Dvenadtsatyi s"ezd Rossiiskoi Kommunisticheskoi Partii (bol'-
shevikov): stenograficheskii otchët, 17-25 aprelia 1923 g.*
Moscow, "Krasnaia nov'," 1923. (Twelfth Congress)
*Trinadtsatyi s"ezd RKP(b) Mai 1924 goda: stenograficheskii
otchët.* Moscow, Gospolitizdat, 1963. (Thirteenth Congress)
*XIV s"ezd Vsesoiuznoi Kommunisticheskoi Partii (b) 18-31
dekabria 1925 goda: stenograficheskii otchët.* Moscow-Leningrad, Gosizdat, 1926. (Fourteenth Congress)

*Piatnadtsatyi s"ezd VKP(b) Dekabr' 1927 goda: stenografi-
cheskii otchët.* Moscow, Gospolitizdat, 1962. 2 vols. (Fifteenth Congress)

*Shestnadtsataia konferentsiia VKP(b) aprel' 1929 goda: steno-
graficheskii otchët.* Moscow, Gospolitizdat, 1962. (Sixteenth Conference)

*XVI s"ezd Vsesoiuznoi Kommunisticheskoi Partii(b): steno-
graficheskii otchët.* Moscow-Leningrad, Gosizdat, 1930.
(Sixteenth Congress)

*XVII s"ezd Vsesoiuznoi Kommunisticheskoi Partii(b) 26
ianvaria-10 fevralia 1934 g: stenograficheskii otchët.* Moscow, Partizdat, 1934. (Seventeenth Congress)

*XVIII s"ezd Vsesoiuznoi Kommunisticheskoi Partii(b) 10-21
marta 1939 g: stenograficheskii otchët.* Moscow, Gospolitizdat, 1939. (Eighteenth Congress)

*XX s"ezd Kommunisticheskoi Partii Sovetskogo Soiuza 14-25
fevralia 1956 goda: stenograficheskii otchët.* Moscow, Gospolitizdat 1956. 2 vols. (Twentieth Congress)

*XXII s"ezd Kommunisticheskoi Partii Sovetskogo Soiuza
17-31 oktiabria 1961 goda.* Moscow, Gospolitizdat, 1962.
3 vols. (Twenty-Second Congress)

B. OTHER CENTRAL PARTY REPORTS AND DOCUMENTS

*Kommunisticheskaia Partiia Sovetskogo Soiuza: v rezoliutsi-
iakh i resheniiakh s"ezdov, konferentsii i plenumov TsK*
(The Communist Party of the Soviet Union: In Resolutions
and Decisions of Congresses, Conferences and Plenums of
the CC). 7th edn. Vols. 1, 2, 4. (Vol. 4 being a supple-
mentary vol. issued after reprinting of Vols. 1 and 2 as a
three-vol. set.) Moscow, Gospolitizdat, 1953 (Vols. 1 and
2); 1960 (Vol. 4).

*Protokoly Tsentral'nogo Komiteta RSDRP(b). Avgust 1917g.
—fevral' 1918g.* (Protocols of the Central Committee of the
RSDWP(b). August 1917—February 1918). Moscow,
Gospolitizdat, 1958.

Spravochnik partiinogo rabotnika (The Party Worker's Handbook)
No. 5, Moscow, Gosizdat, 1926.

No. 6, Moscow-Leningrad, Gosizdat, 1928. 2 vols.

No. 8, Moscow, Partizdat, 1934.

No. 9, Moscow, Partizdat, 1935

Partiia v bor'be za vosstanovlenie narodnogo khoziaistva (1921-1925). Dokumenty i materialy (The Party in the Struggle for the Restoration of the National Economy [1921-1925]. Documents and Materials). Moscow, Gospolitizdat, 1961.

Kommunisticheskaia Partiia v period Velikoi Otechestvennoi voiny (iiun' 1941 goda—1945 god): dokumenty i materialy (The Communist Party in the Period of the Great Patriotic War [June 1941—1945] : Documents and Materials). Moscow, Gospolitizdat, 1961.

KPSS o Komsomole i molodëzhi (The CPSU on the Komsomol and Youth). Moscow, Molodaia gvardiia, 1962.

Manin, V. N. and Moskovskii, V. P., eds. *KPSS o Vooruzhennykh Silakh Sovetskogo Soiuza: sbornik dokumentov* (The CPSU on the Armed Forces of the Soviet Union: Collection of Documents). Moscow, Gospolitizdat, 1958.

Khrushchev, N. S. *O merakh dal'neishego razvitiia sel'skogo khoziaistva SSSR* (On Measures for the Further Development of Agriculture in the U.S.S.R.). Moscow, Gospolitizdat, 1953.

Malenkov, G. M. *Report to the Nineteenth Party Congress on the Work of the Central Committee of the CPSU (b).* Moscow, Gospolitizdat, 1952.

C. DOCUMENTS OF REGIONAL AND REPUBLIC PARTY ORGANIZATIONS

Barchukov, P. V. *Vosstanovitel'nyi period na Donu (1921-1925gg.): sbornik dokumentov* (The Reconstruction Period on the Don [1921-1925]: Collection of Documents). Rostov, Rostovskoe knizhnoe izdatel'stvo, 1962.

Gogolev, N. A., et al. eds. *Khabarovskaia kraevaia partiinaia organizatsiia v period Velikoi Otechestvennoi voiny (1941-1945 gody): sbornik dokumentov i materialov* (The Khabarovsk Krai Party Organization in the Period of the Great Patriotic War [1941-1945]: Collection of Documents and

Materials). Khabarovsk, Khabarovskoe knizhnoe izdatel'stvo, 1964.

Golikova, Z. A., et al. *Kompartiia Kazakhstana na vtorom etape osvoeniia tseliny: sbornik dokumentov i materialov* (The Communist Party of Kazakhstan in the Second Stage of Reclaiming the Virgin Lands: A Collection of Documents and Materials). Alma-Ata, Kazakhskoe gosudarstvennoe izdatel'stvo, 1963.

Ivanov, G. P., ed. *Dokumenty otvagi i geroizma: Kuban' v Velikoi Otechestvennoi voine 1941-1945gg: sbornik dokumentov i materialov* (Documents of Courage and Heroism: The Kuban in the Great Patriotic War of 1941-1945: Collection of Documents and Materials). Krasnodar, Krasnodarskoe knizhnoe izdatel'stvo, 1965.

Kirovskii obkom KPSS. *Kirovskaia oblastnaia partiinaia organizatsiia v gody Velikoi Otechestvennoi voiny : sbornik dokumentov* (The Kirov Oblast Party Organization in the Years of the Great Patriotic War: Collection of Documents). Kirov, Kirovskoe knizhnoe izdatel'stvo, 1961.

Mochalov, V. G., ed. *Vladimirskaia partiinaia organizatsiia v gody vosstanovleniia narodnogo khoziaistva, 1921-1925 gody: sbornik dokumentov* (The Vladimir Party Organization in the Years of Reconstruction of the Economy, 1921-1925: Collection of Documents). Vladimir, Vladimirskoe knizhnoe izdatel'stvo, 1963.

Naumova, A. T. *Permskaia partiinaia organizatsiia v gody Velikoi Otechestvennoi voiny* (The Perm Party Organization in the Years of the Great Patriotic War). Perm, Permskoe knizhnoe izdatel'stvo, 1960.

Osipov, V., et al. eds. *Saratovskaia partiinaia organizatsiia v gody vosstanovleniia narodnogo khoziaistva: dokumenty i materialy 1921-1925 gg.* (The Saratov Party Organization in the Years of Reconstruction of the National Economy: Documents and Materials for 1921-1925). Saratov, Saratovskoe knizhnoe izdatel'stvo, 1960.

Pol'skaia, A. I., ed. *Astrakhanskaia partiinaia organizatsiia v gody Velikoi Otechestvennoi voiny 1941-45 gg. Sbornik dokumentov i materialov* (The Astrakhan Party Organization in the Years of the Great Patriotic War 1941-45. Collection of Documents and Materials). Astrakhan, "Volga," 1962.

Sairanov, Kh. S., et al. eds. *Rezoliutsii oblastnykh konferentsii Bashkirskoi partiinoi organizatsii i plenumov obkoma KPSS* (Resolutions of Oblast Conferences of the Bashkir Party Organization and of Plenums of the Obkom). UPa, Bashkirskoe knizhnoe izdatel'stvo, 1959.

Sidorov, I. I., et al. eds. *Iaroslavtsy v gody Velikoi Otechestvennoi voiny: sbornik dokumentov* (People of Yaroslavl Oblast in the Years of the Great Patriotic War: Collection of Documents). Yaroslavl, Iaroslavskoe knizhnoe izdatel' stvo, 1960.

The Smolensk Archive. (For details see Fainsod, *Smolensk under Soviet Rule.*)

Sukhinin, E. D., et al. eds. *Omskaia partiinaia organizatsiia v period Velikoi Otechestvennoi voiny 1941-1945 gg.* (The Omsk Party Organization in the Period of the Great Patriotic War). Omsk, Omskoe knizhnoe izdatel'stvo, 1960. 2 vols.

Tomskaia gorodskaia partiinaia organizatsiia v gody Velikoi Otechestvennoi voiny 1941-1945 gg.: sbornik dokumentov (The Tomsk City Party Organization in the Years of the Great Patriotic War 1941-1945: Collection of Documents). Tomsk, Tomskoe knizhnoe isdatel'stvo, 1962.

D. KOMSOMOL AND WRITERS' UNION CONGRESSES

XIII s"ezd Vsesoiuznogo Leninskogo Kommunisticheskogo Soiuza Molodëzhi: 15-18 aprelia, 1958 goda: stenograficheskii otchët (The XIII Congress of the All-Union Leninist Communist League of Youth: April 15-18, 1958: Stenographic Account). Moscow, Molodaia gvardiia, 1959.

XIV s"ezd Vsesoiuznogo Leninskogo Kommunisticheskogo Soiuza Molodëzhi: stenograficheskii otchët (The XIV Congress of the All-Union Leninist Communist League of Youth: Stenographic Account). Moscow, Molodaia gvardiia, 1962.

Pervyi vsesoiuznyi s"ezd sovetskikh pisatelei, 1934: stenograficheskii otchët. (The First All-Union Congress of Soviet Writers: Stenographic Account). Moscow, 1934.

[*Tretii*] *Vsesoiuznyi s"ezd pisatelei* [*SSSR*]: *18-23 maia 1959 goda: stenograficheskii otchët* (The Third Congress of Writers of the U.S.S.R.: May 18-23, 1959: Stenographic Account). Moscow, Sovetskii pisatel', 1959.

3. *STATISTICAL COMPILATIONS*

A. BASIC STATISTICAL SOURCES ON CPSU MEMBERSHIP

Vserossiiskaia perepis' chlenov RKP 1922 goda (All-Russian Census of Members of the RCP in 1922). Moscow, Izdatel'stvo Ts K RKP, 1922-1925.

Partiia v tsifrovom osveshchenii: materialy po statistike lichnogo sostava partii (The Party Shown in Figures: Materials on the Statistics of the Personal Composition of the Party). Moscow-Leningrad, Giz, 1925.

Sotsial'nyi i natsional'nyi sostav VKP(b): Itogi vsesoiuznoi partiinoi perepisi 1927 goda (Social and National Composition of the CPSU [b]: Summing up of the All-Union Party Census of 1927). Moscow-Leningrad, Giz, 1928.

Bubnov, A. S. "Statisticheskie svedeniia o VKP (b)" (Statistical Data on the CPSU [b]), *Bol'shaia sovetskaia entsiklopediia* (Large Soviet Encyclopedia). 1st edn. Vol. XI, cols. 531-542, Moscow, Ogiz, 1930.

"Iz spravki Glavnogo politicheskogo upravleniia Krasnoi armii o roste i sostave armeiskikh partiinykh organizatsii za 1941-1946 gg" (From Report of the Chief Political Directorate of the Red Army on the Growth and Composition of Army Party Organizations for 1941-1946). *V I KPSS*, No. 5 (May), 1965.

"Voprosy chlenstva v VKP(b)" (Questions of Membership in the CPSU [b]). *PZh*, No. 20 (October), 1947.

"KPSS v tsifrakh (1956-1961 gg)" (The CPSU in Figures [1956-1961]). *PZh*, No. 1 (January), 1962.

"KPSS v tsifrakh (1961-1964 gody)" (The CPSU in Figures [1961-1964]). *PZh*, No. 10 (May), 1965.

"Priëm v KPSS i nekotorye izmeneniia v sostave partii za 1966 god" (Admissions to the CPSU and Certain Changes in the Composition of the Party in 1966). *PZh*, No. 7 (April), 1967.

BIBLIOGRAPHY

"KPSS v tsifrakh" (The CPSU in Figures). *PZh*, No. 19 (October). 1967.

B. PARTY MEMBERSHIP IN REPUBLICS

Beisembaev, S. B. and Pakhmurnyi, P. M., eds. *Kommunisticheskaia Partiia Kazakhstana v dokumentakh i tsifrakh* (The Communist Party of Kazakhstan in Documents and Figures). Alma-Ata, Kazakhskoe gosudarstvennoe izdatel'stvo, 1960.

Bezrukova, N. D., comp. *Kommunisticheskaia Partiia Uzbekistana v tsifrakh: sbornik statisticheskikh materialov: 1924-1964 gody* (The Communist Party of Uzbekistan in Figures: A Collection of Statistical Materials, 1924-1964). Tashkent, "Uzbekistan," 1964.

"Kommunisticheskaia Partiia Ukrainy v tsifrakh" (The Communist Party of the Ukraine in Figures). *PZh*, No. 12 (June), 1958.

"Kompartiia Latvii—odin iz boevykh otriadov KPSS—neskol'ko tsifr, faktov, sravnenii" (The Communist Party of Latvia—One of the Militant Detachments of the CPSU—a Few Figures, Facts, and Comparisons). *Kommunist sovetskoi Latvii*, No. 4 (April), 1965.

"Kompartiia Latvii v tsifrakh" (The Communist Party of Latvia in Figures). *Kommunist sovetskoi Latvii*. No. 7 (July), 1962.

"KPB u lichbakh" (The Belorussian CP in Figures). *Kamunist Belarusi*, No. 5 (May), 1962.

Rost i regulirovanie sostava Kommunisticheskoi Partii Kirgizii (1918-1962 gg) (The Growth and Regulation of the Composition of the Communist Party of Kirgizia [1918-1962]). Frunze, Irfon, 1962.

C. PARTY MEMBERS IN NONPARTY ORGANIZATIONS

Itogi vyborov i sostav deputatov mestnykh sovetov deputatov trudiashchikhsia—1967g: statisticheskii sbornik (Results of Elections and Composition of Deputies to the Local Soviets of Working People's Deputies—1967: Statistical Compilation). Moscow. Izdatel'stvo Izvestiia, 1967.

535

*Itogi vyborov i sostav deputatov Verkhovnykh sovetov soiuz-
nykh i avtonomnykh respublik—1967g: statisticheskii sbornik* (Results of Elections and Composition of Deputies to
Supreme Soviets of Union and Autonomous Republics—
1967: Statistical Compilation). Moscow, Izdatel'stvo Izvestiia, 1967.

*Kommunisty v sostave apparata gosuchrezhdenii i obshchest-
vennykh organizatsii: Itogi vsesoiuznoi partiinoi perepisi
1927 goda* (Communists on the Staff of State Departments
and Public Organizations: Data of the All-Union Party
Census of 1927). Moscow, Gosizdat, 1929.

Komsostav krupnoi promyshlennosti (Managerial Personnel
in Large-Scale Industry). Moscow, 1924.

Kraval', I. A., ed. *Kadry spetsialistov v SSSR—ikh formirovanie i rost* (Specialist Cadres in the USSR—their Formation and Growth). Moscow, "Soiuzorguchët," 1935.

*Partiinye, professional'nye i kooperativnye organy i gosap-
parat: K XIV s"ezdu RKP(b)* (Party, Trade Union and
Cooperative Organs and the State Apparatus: [Data] for
the Fourteenth Congress of the CPSU). Moscow-Leningrad,
Gosizdat, 1926.

*Sostav deputatov Verkhovnykh sovetov Soiuznykh, Avto-
nomnykh respublik i Mestnykh sovetov deputatov trudia-
shchikhsia 1959 g.* (Composition of Deputies of Supreme
Soviets of Union and Autonomous Republics and of Local
Soviets of Working People's Deputies in 1959). Moscow,
Izdatel'stvo "Izvestiia," 1959.

*Sostav rukovodiashchikh rabotnikov i spetsialistov Soiuza
SSR* (The Leading Officials and Specialists of the Union of
S.S.R.). Moscow, "Soiuzorguchët," 1936.

Vladimirskii, M. *Sovety, ispolkomy i s"ezdy sovetov: Vypusk
I* (Soviets, Ispolkoms and Congresses of Soviets: Issue I).
Moscow, Gosizdat, 1920.

———. *Sovety, ispolkomy i s"ezdy sovetov: Vypusk II*
(Soviets, Ispolkoms and Congresses of Soviets: Issue II).
Moscow, Gosizdat, 1921.

D. Sources of Population and Employment Statistics

Narodnoe khoziaistvo SSSR: statisticheskii sbornik (The National Economy of the U.S.S.R.: A Statistical Collection). Moscow, Gosstatizdat, 1956.

Narodnoe khoziaistvo SSSR v 1961 godu: statisticheskii ezhegodnik (The National Economy of the U.S.S.R. in 1961: A Statistical Yearbook). Moscow, Gosstatizdat, 1962.

Narodnoe khoziaistvo SSSR v 1963 godu: statisticheskii ezhegodnik (The National Economy of the U.S.S.R. in 1963: A Statistical Yearbook). Moscow, Gosstatizdat, 1965.

Narodnoe khoziaistvo SSSR v 1964 godu: statisticheskii ezhegodnik (The National Economy of the U.S.S.R. in 1964: A Statistical Yearbook). Moscow, Gosstatizdat, 1965.

Kul'turnoe stroitel'stvo SSSR: statisticheskii sbornik (Cultural Construction in the U.S.S.R.: Statistical Collection). Moscow, Gosstatizdat, 1956.

Sel'skoe khoziaistvo SSSR: statisticheskii sbornik (Agriculture in the U.S.S.R.: A Statistical Collection). Moscow, Gosstatizdat, 1960.

Itogi vsesoiuznoi perepisi naseleniia 1959 goda: SSSR (Data of the All-Union Population Census of 1959: U.S.S.R). Moscow, Gosstatizdat, 1960.

Isupov, A. A. *Natsional'nyi sostav naseleniia SSSR* (The National Composition of the Population of the U.S.S.R.) Moscow, "Statistika," 1964.

4. *OTHER SOVIET BOOKS AND ARTICLES*

Abramov, B. *Organizatorskaia rabota partii po osushchestvleniiu leninskogo kooperativnogo plana* (The Organizational Work of the Party for the Achievement of Lenin's Cooperative Plan). Moscow, Gospolitizdat, 1956.

Afanas'ev, I. "Ob ukreplenii pervichnykh partiinykh organizatsii v kolkhozakh" (On the Reinforcement of Primary Party Organizations in the Kolkhozes). *PZh*, Nos. 7-8 (April), 1946.

Aleksandrov, P. "Priëm v nashu partiiu luchshikh liudei nashei rodiny" (Admission to Our Party of the Best People of Our Motherland). *PS*, No. 1 (January), 1938.

Anikeev, V. V. "Svedeniia o bol'shevistskikh organizatsiiakh s marta po dekabr' 1917 goda" (Information on Bolshevik Organizations from March to December 1917). *V I KPSS*, No. 2 (March-April), 1958.

Arutiunian, Iu. V. *Sovetskoe krest'ianstvo v gody Velikoi Otechestvennoi voiny* (The Soviet Peasantry in the Years of the Great Patriotic War). Moscow, Izdatel'stvo Akademii Nauk SSSR, 1963.

Bakhshiev, D. *Partiinoe stroitel'stvo v usloviiakh pobedy sotsializma v SSSR* (The Building of the Party Under the Conditions of the Victory of Socialism in the U.S.S.R.). Moscow, Gospolitizdat, 1954.

Barsukov, N. and Iudin, I. "Rasshirenie sotsial'noi bazy KPSS" (Broadening the Social Base of the CPSU). *Politicheskoe samoobrazovanie*. No. 6 (June), 1965.

Berkhin, T. B. *Voennaia reforma v SSSR (1924-1925)* (Military Reform in the U.S.S.R. [1924-1925]). Moscow, Voenizdat, 1958.

Bol'shevistskie organizatsii Ukrainy (noiabr' 1917-aprel' 1918 gg.) (Bolshevik Organizations of the Ukraine [November 1917-April 1918]). Kiev, Gospolitizdat USSR, 1962.

Bugaev, E. I. and Leibzon, B. M. *Besedy ob ustave KPSS* (Chats about the CPSU Rules). Moscow, Gospolitizdat, 1964.

Buriatskii obkom KPSS—Partiinyi arkhiv i otdel propagandy i agitatsii. *Iz istorii partiinoi organizatsii Buriatii: sbornik statei* (From the History of the Party Organization of Buriatia: A Collection of Articles). Vypusk II. Ulan-Ude, Buriatskoe knizhnoe izdatel'stvo, 1961.

Chivirev, F. "K voprosu o rabote s kommunistami-odinochkami" (On the Question of Work with Isolated Communists). *PS*, No. 14 (July), 1935.

Donskoi, V. M. ed. *Velikaia partiia Lenina (k 60-letiiu II s"ezda RSDRP)* (The Great Party of Lenin [For the 60th anniversary of the II Congress of the RSDWP]). Moscow, Izdatel'stvo VPSh i AON pri TsK, 1963.

Efimov, P. "Sviazi armii i naroda nerazryvny" (The Links of the Army and the People Are Indissoluble). *PZh*, No. 3 (February), 1962.

Egorov, N. "Armiia i formirovanie novogo cheloveka" (The

Army and the Forming of the New Man). *PZh*, No. 9 (May), 1964.

Epishev, A. A. "O vozrastaiushchei roli KPSS v rukovodstve Vooruzhënnymi Silami" (On the Growing Role of the CPSU in the Leadership of the Armed Forces). *V I KPSS*, No. 2 (February), 1963.

Frenkel, A. "O predstoiashchei chistke partii" (On the Forthcoming Purge of the Party). *PS*, Nos. 23-24 (December), 1932.

Fridberg, S. "Iz opyta raboty s partaktivom" (Experience in Working with The Party *Aktiv*). *PS*, No. 10 (May), 1935.

Gaister, A. and Levin, A. "O sostave sel'skikh partorganizatsii" (On the Composition of Rural Party Organizations). *B*, Nos. 9-10 (May), 1929.

Galkin, K. T. *Vysshee obrazovanie i podgotovka nauchnykh kadrov v SSSR* (Tertiary Education and the Training of Scientific Cadres in the U.S.S.R.). Moscow, Sovetskaia nauka, 1958.

"Glavnye uroki proverki partdokumentov" (The Chief Lessons of the Verification of Party Documents). *PS*, No. 2 (January), 1935.

Glazyrin, I. *Regulirovanie sostava KPSS v period stroitel'stva sotsializma* (The Regulation of the Membership of the CPSU in the Period of the Building of Socialism). Moscow, Gospolitizdat, 1957.

Glukhov, Z. N. *Kadry reshaiut uspekh dela* (Cadres Determine Success). Moscow, 1961.

God raboty po regulirovaniiu rosta VKP(b) (A Year's Work on the Regulation of the Growth of the CPSU [b]). Moscow, Gosizdat, 1930.

Iaroslavskii, E. *Za bol'shevistskuiu proverku i chistku riadov partii* (For a Bolshevik Verification and Purge of Party Ranks). Moscow, 1933.

Ioffe, O. S., ed. *40 let sovetskogo prava* (40 Years of Soviet Law). Leningrad, Izdatel'stvo leningradskogo universiteta, 1957. 2 vols.

Iosifov, F. "Partiinaia rabota s kommunistami-odinochkami" (Party Work with Isolated Communists). *PS*, Nos. 1-2 (January), 1935.

Istoriia Velikoi Otechestvennoi voiny Sovetskogo Soiuza: 1941-1945 (History of the Great Patriotic War of the Soviet Union: 1941-1945). Moscow, Voenizdat, 1960-1965. 6 vols.

Ivanov, N. Ia., et al. eds. *Leningrad: kratkii istoricheskii ocherk* (Leningrad: A Brief Historical Sketch). Leningrad, Lenizdat, 1964.

Ivanov, V. M. *Iz istorii bor'by partii protiv "levogo" opportunizma* (From the History of the Party's Struggle Against "Left" Opportunism). Leningrad, Lenizdat, 1965.

Kalinin, M. I. *O kommunisticheskom vospitanii: izbrannye rechi i stat'i* (Selected Speeches and Articles on Communist Training). Moscow, Molodaia gvardiia, 1958.

Karasev, A. V. *Leningradtsy v gody blokady 1941-1943* (Leningraders in the Years of the Blockade, 1941-1943). Moscow, Izdatel'stvo Akademii Nauk SSSR, 1959.

Karpik, V. S., et al. eds. *Sovetskaia obshchestvennost' i ukreplenie pravoporiadka* (The Soviet Public and the Strengthening of Legality). Minsk, Izdatel'stvo Akademii Nauk Belorusskoi SSR, 1961.

Kasimov, E. "Regulirovaniu rosta riadov KPSS—neoslabnoe vnimanie" (Unflagging Attention to Regulating the Growth of the Ranks of the CPSU). *Kommunist Turkmenii*, No. 9 (September), 1958.

Khanazarov, K. Kh. *Sblizhenie natsii i natsional'nye iazyki v SSSR* (The Drawing-Together of Nations and National Languages in the U.S.S.R.). Tashkent, Izdatel'stvo Akademii Nauk Uzbekskoi SSR, 1963.

Khatasevich, M. "O sostave i rabote partiacheiki na sele" (On the Composition and Work of the Party Cell in the Countryside). *B*, Nos. 3-4 (February), 1925.

Khrushchev, N. S. *Stroitel'stvo kommunizma v SSSR i razvitie sel'skogo khoziaistva* (The Building of Communism in the U.S.S.R. and the Development of Agriculture). Moscow, Gospolitizdat, 1962-1964. 8 vols.

Kiselëv, A. D., et al. *Ideologicheskaia rabota KPSS na fronte (1941-1945 gg.)* (Ideological Work of the CPSU at the Front—1941-1945). Moscow, Voenizdat, 1960.

Kiselëv, T. "40 let Kommunisticheskoi partii Belorussii"

(Forty Years of the Communist Party of Belorussia). *PZh*, No. 23 (December), 1958.

Kniazev, S. P., et al. *Na zashchite Nevskoi tverdyni* (In Defense of the Neva Redout). Leningrad, Lenizdat, 1965.

Komkov, G. D. *Ideino-politicheskaia rabota KPSS v 1941-1945 gg.* (Ideological-Political Work of the CPSU in 1941-1945). Moscow, Nauka, 1965.

Konovalov, V. A. *Murmanskaia partiinaia organizatsiia v period oborony Zapoliar'ia"* (The Murmansk Party Organization in the Period of the Defense of the Polar Area). *V I KPSS*, No. 6 (June), 1966.

Kozhevnikov, M. V. *Istoriia sovetskogo suda* (History of the Soviet Law Court). Moscow, Gosiurizdat, 1957.

Krainiukov, K. V., et al. *Partiino-politicheskaia rabota v sovetskikh vooruzhennykh silakh v gody Velikoi Otechestvennoi voiny 1941-1945* (Party-Political Work in the Soviet Armed Forces in the Years of the Great Patriotic War, 1941-1945). Moscow, Voenizdat, 1963.

Kukushkin, S. *Moskovskie bol'sheviki v gody pervoi mirovoi voiny i fevral'skoi revoliutsii* (The Moscow Bolsheviks in the Years of the First World War and of the February Revolution). Moscow, 1963.

Kultyshev, S. S. "Rost riadov partii v 1945-1950 godakh" (Growth of the Party's Ranks 1945-1950). *V I KPSS*, No. 2 (March-April), 1958.

Kurbatova, P. I. *Smolenskaia partiinaia organizatsiia v gody Velikoi Otechestvennoi voiny* (The Smolensk Party Organization in the Years of the Great Patriotic War). Smolensk, Smolenskoe knizhnoe izdatel'stvo, 1958.

Lenin, V. I. *Polnoe sobranie sochinenii* (Complete Collected Works). 5th edn. 55 vols. Moscow, Gospolitizdat, 1958-1965.

Leningrad: *Entsiklopedicheskii spravochnik* (Leningrad: An Encyclopedic Handbook). Moscow-Leningrad, Izdatel'stvo Bol'shaia sovetskaia entsiklopediia, 1957.

"Leninskie normy partiinoi zhizni" (Leninist Norms of Party Life). *K*, No. 14 (September), 1965.

Levitin, S., comp. *Kommunisticheskaia partiia v period*

Velikoi Otechestvennoi voiny (*iiun' 1941 goda—1945 god*): *sbornik konsul'tatsii* (The Communist Party in the Period of the Great Patriotic War [June 1941 to 1945]: Collection of Consultations). Moscow, Moskovskii rabochii, 1960.

Lukoshko, V. S. *Sblizhenie sotsialisticheskikh natsii v period razvernutogo stroitel'stva kommunizma* (The Drawing Together of Socialist Nations in the Period of Large-Scale Building of Communism). Moscow, Izdatel'stvo VPSh i AON pri TsK KPSS, 1963.

Malenkov, G. "Vovlechenie rabochikh v Partiiu" (Drawing Workers into the Party). *B*, Nos. 21-22 (November), 1926.

Marianskii, I. "Ostrye voprosy raboty kolkhoznoi iacheiki" (Difficult Questions in the Work of the Kolkhoz Cell). *PS*, No. 10 (May), 1932.

Markov, S. F. "Ukreplenie sel'skikh partiinykh organizatsii v period podgotovki massovogo kolkhoznogo dvizheniia" (Strengthening of Rural Party Organizations in the Period of Preparing the Mass Kolkhoz Movement). *V I KPSS*, No. 3 (May-June), 1962.

Maslov, I. *KPSS v bor'be za ukreplenie edinstva svoikh riadov i osushchestvlenie politiki sotsialisticheskoi industrializatsii strany* (*1925-1927 gg.*) (The CPSU in the Struggle for Strengthening Unity of Its Ranks and for Achieving the Policy of Socialist Industrialization of the Country [1925-1927]). Moscow, Gospolitizdat, 1955.

Mil'chakov, A. "Rost partii i zadachi perestroiki partiinoi raboty" (Growth of the Party and Tasks of Reconstructing Party Work). *PS*, No. 13 (July), 1931.

Mitrofanova, A. V. *Rabochii klass Sovetskogo Soiuza v pervyi period Velikoi Otechestvennoi voiny* (The Working Class of the Soviet Union in the First Period of the Great Patriotic War). Moscow, Izdatel'stvo Akademii Nauk SSSR, 1960.

Murashev, A. A. *V leninskuiu partiiu* (Into the Party of Lenin). Moscow, Gospolitizdat, 1960.

Musaev, A. M. "Iz opyta raboty partiinykh organizatsii Severnogo Kavkaza po rasstanovke kommunistov v sel'sko-khoziaistvennom proizvodstve (1953-1958 gg.)" (From the Experience of the Work of Party Organizations of the

North Caucasus in the Assignment of Communists in Agricultural Production, 1953-1958). *V I KPSS*, No. 6 (June), 1967.

Nekrasov, K. V. *Bor'ba kommunisticheskoi partii za edinstvo svoikh riadov v period mezhdu XV i XVI s"ezdami VKP(b)* (Struggle of the Communist Party for the Unity of Its Ranks in the Period between the 15th and 16th Congresses of the CPSU). Vologda, Vologodskoe knizhnoe izdatel'stvo, 1959.

Nesterov, N. "Zabotit'sia o profsoiuznykh kadrakh" (Show Concern about Trade Union Cadres). *PZh*, No. 20 (October), 1965.

Neznanov, S. V., ed. *Partiia—organizator kolkhoznogo stroia* (The Party—Organizer of the Kolkhoz System). Moscow, Gospolitizdat, 1958.

"O kurse priëma novykh chlenov v VKP(b)" (On Progress in Admitting New Members into the CPSU). *PS*, No. 15 (August), 1938.

"O rabote politotdelov MTS, o kolkhoznoi iacheike, i o vzaimootnosheniiakh politotdelov i raikomov" (On the Work of the Politotdels of MTS's, on the Kolkhoz Cell, and on the Interrelationships of Politotdels and Raikoms). *PS*, No. 12 (June), 1933.

Ocherki istorii Kommunisticheskoi Partii Moldavii (Essays on the History of the Communist Party of Moldavia). Kishinev, Partiinoe Izdatel'stvo TsK KP Moldavii, 1964.

Omel'ianenko, *Kommunisty Donbassa v Velikoi Otechestvennoi voine* (Communists of the Donbass in the Great Patriotic War). Stalino, Stalinskoe oblastnoe knizhnoe izdatel'stvo, 1959.

Osipov, G. V. *Sotsiologiia v SSSR* (Sociology in the U.S.S.R.). Moscow, 1955, 2 vols.

Ostapenko, F. P., ed. *Voprosy istorii KPSS perioda Velikoi Otechestvennoi voiny* (Problems of the History of the CPSU in the Period of the Great Patriotic War). Kiev, Izdatel'stvo Kievskogo universiteta, 1961.

Partiinaia rabota v promyshlennosti (Party Work in Industry). Kiev, Gospolitizdat USSR, 1959.

Pavlovskii, E. N., ed. *Geografiia naseleniia v SSSR: osnovnye problemy* (Geography of the Population of the U.S.S.R.: Basic Problems). Leningrad, "Nauka," 1964.

"Perestroika partiinoi raboty" (Reconstruction of Party Work). *PS*, Nos. 11-12 (June), 1930.

Peskarev, G. "Dinamika rosta i problema regulirovaniia sostava partii" (Dynamics of Growth and the Problem of Regulating the Composition of the Party). *PS*, No. 17 (September), 1931.

Petrov, Iu. P. *KPSS—rukovoditel' i vospitatel' Krasnoi armii (1918-1920 gg.)* (The CPSU—Leader and Educator of the Red Army, 1918-1920). Moscow, Voenizdat, 1961.

———. *Partiinoe stroitel'stvo v Sovetskoi armii i flote (1918-1961)* (Party-Building in the Soviet Army and Navy, 1918-1961). Moscow, Voenizdat, 1964.

Pisarev, I. Yu. *Narodonaselenie SSSR* (The Population of the U.S.S.R.). Moscow, Sotsekgiz, 1962.

"Po-bol'shevistski raspoznavat' i razoblachat' vragov sotsializma" (Identify and Unmask in Bolshevik Fashion the Enemies of Socialism). *PS*, No. 2 (January), 1937.

Pod'iachikh, P. A. *Naselenie SSSR* (The Population of the USSR). Moscow, Gospolitizdat, 1961.

Pokshishevskii, V. V. and Kovalëv, S. A. *Geografiia naseleniia SSSR* (The Geography of the Population of the U.S.S.R.). Moscow, Geografizdat, 1962.

Polozov, N. "V partiiu otbirat' dostoinykh" (Enlist Worthy People in the Party). *Kommunist Belorussii*, No. 1 (January), 1967.

Ponomarev, B. N., et al. *Istoriia Kommunisticheskoi Partii Sovetskogo Soiuza* (History of the Communist Party of the Soviet Union). Moscow, Gospolitizdat, 1959.

Postyshev, P. "Tekushchie zadachi marksistsko-leninskogo vospitaniia" (Current Tasks of Marxist-Leninist Training). *PS*, Nos. 15-16 (August), 1931.

"Priëm luchshikh komsomol'tsev v partiiu" (Acceptance of the Best Komsomolites into the Party). *PS*, No. 14 (July), 1937.

"Protiv kampaneishchiny v priëme sochuvstvuiushchikh" (Against Campaign Methods of Recruiting Sympathizers). *PS*, No. 22 (November), 1934.

544

"Proverka partdokumentov—serëznoe ispytanie partiinykh kadrov" (The Verification of Party Documents Is a Serious Test of the Party's Cadres). *PS*, No. 15 (August), 1935.

Prusinov, I. P. "Povyshenie vliianiia partii v Vooruzhënnykh Silakh" (Increasing the Party's Influence in the Armed Forces). *V I KPSS*. No. 2 (February), 1965.

Radzhabov, S. A. and Nikolaev, Iu. A., ed. *Istoriia Tadzhikskogo naroda* (A History of the Tadzhik People). 3 vols. Moscow, Nauka, 1964-1965.

Rafikov, E. A. "Ukreplenie partiinykh organizatsii Krasnoi Armii v pervyi period Velikoi Otechestvennoi voiny" (Strengthening of Party Organizations in the Red Army in the First Period of the Great Patriotic War). *V I KPSS*, No. 3 (March), 1964.

Rashin, A. G. *Naselenie Rossii za 100 let* (The Population of Russia over 100 years). Moscow, Gosstatizdat, 1956.

Rizel', F. "Rost partii za dva goda" (Growth of the Party over Two Years). *PS*, No. 10 (May), 1930.

Rumiantsev, I. "Povtornaia proverka partdokumentov" (A Repeated Verification of Party Documents). *PS*, No. 17 (September), 1935.

Serdiuk, Z. "Priëm v partiiu v kievskoi partorganizatsii" (Admission into the Party in the Kiev Organization). *PS*, No. 22 (November), 1938.

"Ser'ëzno, vdumchivo otbirat' v partiiu" (Show Thought and Seriousness in Recruitment to the Party). *PZh*, No. 16 (August), 1964.

Shamberg, M. "Nekotorye voprosy vnutripartiinoi raboty" (Some Questions of Intra-Party Work). *PS*, No. 4 (February), 1946.

————. "Protiv volokity v priëme novykh chlenov v VKP(b)" (Against Red Tape in Admitting New Members into the CPSU). *PS*, No. 7 (April), 1938.

Shchetinin, S. "Podderzhivat' i razvivat' initsiativu komsomola" (Support and Develop Komsomol Initiative). *PZh*, No. 8 (April), 1960.

Sherstiuk, F. E. "Ukreplenie rabochego iadra v period industrializatsii" (Strengthening of the Worker Nucleus in

545

the Period of Industrialization). *V I KPSS*, No. 5 (September-October), 1960.

Shliapin, I. M., et al. *Kommunisticheskaia partiia v period Velikoi Otechestvennoi voiny* (The Communist Party in the Period of the Great Patriotic War). Moscow, Voenizdat, 1958.

Sikorskii, V. M., et al. eds. *Iz istorii bor'by Kompartii Belorussii za uprochenie sovetskoi vlasti i sotsialisticheskoe stroitel'stvo* (From the History of the Struggle of the Belorussian Communist Party for the Consolidation of Soviet Power and for Socialist Construction). Minsk, Izdatel'stvo Belgosuniversiteta, 1959.

Sikorskii, V. M., et al. eds. *KPB v bor'be za dal'neishee razvitie narodnogo khoziaistva respubliki v poslevoennye gody* (CPB in the Struggle for the Further Development of the Economy of the Republic in the Postwar Years). Minsk, Izdatel'stvo vysshego, srednego spetsial'nogo i professional'nogo obrazovaniia BSSR, 1961.

Smitten, E. "O regulirovanii rosta partii" (On Regulation of the Party's Growth). *PS*, No. 12 (June), 1926.

Sorokin, V. "Priëm novykh chlenov v VKP(b)" (Enrollment of New Members in the CPSU). *PS*, No. 9 (May), 1941.

Spirin, L. M. "Partiinye i komsomol'skie mobilizatsii v Krasnuiu Armiiu v gody Velikoi Otechestvennoi voiny" (Party and Komsomol Mobilizations for the Red Army during the Great Patriotic War), *V I KPSS*. No. 3 (March), 1963.

Stalin, J. V. *Problems of Leninism*. Moscow, Foreign Languages Publishing House, 1945.

Stavitskii, I. V. "Ukreplenie armeiskikh partiinykh organizatsii v gody Velikoi Otechestvennoi voiny" (Strengthening of Army Party Organizations in the Years of the Great Patriotic War). *Voprosy Istorii*, No. 5 (May), 1958.

Stepin, S. M. *Natsional'nyi vopros v programme KPSS* (The National Question in the Program of the CPSU). Minsk, Izdatel'stvo Ministerstva vysshego, srednego spetsial'nogo i professional'nogo obrazovaniia BSSR, 1963.

Suvorov, K. I., ed. *Nekotorye voprosy organizatsionno-partiinoi raboty v sovremennykh usloviiakh* (Some Problems of Organizational-Party Work under Contemporary Conditions). Moscow, Izdatel'stvo VPSh i AON pri TsK KPSS, 1961.

Suvorov, K. I., et al. *Partiia i massy* (The Party and the Masses). Moscow, "Mysl'," 1966.

Sverdlov, Ia. M. *Izbrannye proizvedeniia* (Selected Works). Moscow, Gospolitizdat, 1959-1960. 3 vols.

Tandit, L. "Bol'shevistskoe vospitanie molodykh kommunistov" (The Bolshevik Training of Young Communists). *B* Nos. 10-11 (October-November), 1938.

Telpukhovskii, V. S. *Kommunisticheskaia partiia v period Velikoi Otechestvennoi voiny* (The Communist Party in the Period of the Great Patriotic War). Moscow, "Moskovskii rabochii," 1960.

————. "Kommunisticheskaia partiia—vdokhnovitel' i organizator pobedy sovetskogo naroda v Velikoi Otechestvennoi voine" (The Communist Party—the Inspirer and Organizer of Victory in the Great Patriotic War). *V I KPSS*, No. 2 (March-April), 1958.

————. *Velikaia Otechestvennaia voina* (The Great Patriotic War. 1941-1945. Brief Outline). Moscow, Gospolitizdat, 1959.

Timofeevskii, A. A., et al. eds. *V. I. Lenin i stroitel'stvo partii v pervye gody sovetskoi vlasti* (V. I. Lenin and the Building of the Party in the First Years of Soviet Power). Moscow, "Mysl'," 1965.

Tiurin, D. I. *Chlenstvo v KPSS: rabota partiinykh organizatsii po priëmu v partiiu i vospitaniiu molodykh Kommunistov* (Membership in the CPSU: Work of Party Organizations in Admitting Young Communists to the Party and Training Them). Moscow, "Mysl'," 1966.

Trapeznikov, S. P. *Kommunisticheskaia partiia v period nastupleniia sotsializma po vsemu frontu. Pobeda kolkhoznogo stroia v derevne (1929-1932 gg.)* (The Communist Party in the Period of the Advance of Socialism on All Fronts. The Victory of the Kolkhoz System in the Countryside, 1929-1932). Moscow, Izdatel'stvo VPSh i AON pri TsK KPSS, 1961.

Tulepbaev, B. A. *Kompartiia Uzbekistana v bor'be za krutoi pod"ëm sel'skogo khoziaistva 1953-1958 gg.* (The Communist Party of Uzbekistan in the Struggle for a Sharp

Improvement in Agriculture). Tashkent, Gosizdat Uzbekskoi SSR, 1959.

Ukraintsev, V. V. *KPSS—Organizator revoliutsionnogo preobrazovaniia vysshei shkoly* (CPSU—the Organizer of the Revolutionary Transformation of Higher Schooling). Moscow, Vysshaia Shkola, 1963.

Vaganov, F. M. "O regulirovanii sostava partii v 1928-29 gg." (On Regulation of the Party Membership in 1928-29). *V I KPSS*, No. 6 (June), 1964.

Vasil'ev, A. F. "Partorganizatsii Iuzhnogo Urala vo glave perestroiki promyshlennosti na voennyi lad" (The Party Organizations of the Southern Urals at the Head of the Reorganization of Industry onto a War Footing). *V I KPSS*, No. 1 (January-February), 1960.

Vasil'ev, Iu. *Tiumenskie kommunisty v Velikoi Otechestvennoi voine* (Tiumen Communists in the Great Patriotic War). Tiumen, Tiumenskoe knizhnoe izdatel'stvo, 1962.

Vlasov, V. "Nedostatki komsomola v ukreplenii riadov partii" (Shortcomings of the Komsomol in Reinforcing the Ranks of the Party). *PS*, No. 21 (November), 1930.

————. "Protiv samoteka—za ukreplenie proletarskogo iadra" (Against Letting Things Slide—for a Strengthening of the Proletarian Nucleus). *PS*, No. 17 (September), 1930.

Voprosy organizatsionnogo stroitel'stva bol'shevistskoi partii (Problems of Organizational Structure of the Bolshevik Party). Moscow, "Moskovskii bol'shevik," 1945.

"Voprosy priëma novykh chlenov v VKP(b)" (Problems of Admission of New Members into the CPSU). *PS*, Nos. 19-20 (October), 1938.

Voropaev, D. A. and Iovlev, A. M. *Bor'ba KPSS za sozdanie voennykh kadrov* (Struggle of the CPSU for the Creation of Military Cadres). 2nd edn. Moscow, Voenizdat, 1960.

Zasorin, V. "Priëmom v partiiu nado rukovodit' " (Admissions into the Party Must be Guided). *PZh*, No. 8 (April), 1963.

Zlatopol'skii, D. L. *Gosudarstvennoe ustroistvo SSSR* (The State System of the U.S.S.R.). Moscow, Gosiurizdat, 1960.

5. NON-SOVIET BOOKS AND ARTICLES

Almond, Gabriel A. and Coleman, James S., eds., *The Politics of the Developing Areas.* Princeton, Princeton University Press, 1960.

[*The*]*Anti-Stalin Campaign and International Communism.* New York, Columbia University Press, 1956.

Armstrong, John A. *The Soviet Bureaucratic Elite: A Case Study of the Ukrainian Apparatus.* New York, Frederick A. Praeger, 1959.

————. *The Politics of Totalitarianism.* New York, Random House, 1961.

————. ed., *Soviet Partisans in World War II.* Madison, University of Wisconsin Press, 1964.

Aspaturian, Vernon V. "The Soviet Union" in Roy C. Macridis and Robert C. Ward, *Modern Political Systems: Europe.* Englewood Cliffs, N.J., Prentice Hall, 1963.

Avtorkhanov, A. "Politicheskie itogi XX s"ezda KPSS i perspektivy kollektivnogo rukovodstva" (Political Results of the Twentieth CPSU Congress and the Perspectives for Collective Leadership). *Vestnik Instituta po izucheniiu SSSR,* No. 2, 1956.

————. *The Communist Party Apparatus.* Chicago, Henry Regnery Co., 1966.

Baron, Salo W. *The Russian Jew under Tsars and Soviets.* New York, Macmillan, 1964.

Bernstein, T. P. "Leadership and Mass Mobilization in the Soviet and Chinese Collectivization Campaigns of 1929-1930 and 1955-56: a Comparison," *China Quarterly,* No. 31 (July-September), 1967.

Brown, Emily Clark. "The Local Union in Soviet Industry: Its Relations with Members, Party and Management," *Industrial and Labor Relations Review,* Vol. 13, No. 2 (January), 1960.

Brzezinski, Zbigniew K. *The Permanent Purge.* Cambridge, Mass., Harvard University Press, 1956.

Carr, E. H. *A History of Soviet Russia.* 7 vols. published, others forthcoming. London, Macmillan, 1950—

Churchward, L. G. "Soviet Local Government Today," *Soviet Studies,* Vol. XVII, No. 4 (April), 1966.

Cleary, J. W. "Politics and Administration in Kazakhstan

1955-1964." Unpublished Ph.D. thesis, Australian National University, 1967.

Daniels, Robert V. *Conscience of the Revolution: Communist Opposition in Soviet Russia.* Cambridge, Mass., Harvard University Press, 1960.

De Witt, Nicholas. *Education and Professional Employment in the USSR.* Washington, D.C., National Science Foundation, 1961.

——. *Soviet Professional Manpower: Its Education, Training and Supply.* Washington, D.C., National Science Foundation, 1955.

Deutscher, Isaac. *Soviet Trade Unions.* London-New York, Royal Institute of International Affairs, 1950.

——. *Stalin: A Political Biography.* New York-London, Oxford University Press, 1949.

——. *The Prophet Unarmed.* London, Oxford University Press, 1959.

Duverger, Maurice. *Political Parties: Their Organization and Activities in the Modern State.* Trans. Barbara and Robert North. London, Methuen, 1954; New York, Wiley, 1954.

Erickson, John. *The Soviet High Command 1918-1941.* London, Macmillan, 1962.

Fainsod, Merle. *How Russia Is Ruled.* Rev. edn. Cambridge, Mass., Harvard University Press, 1963.

——. *Smolensk under Soviet Rule.* Cambridge, Mass., Harvard University Press, 1958; London, Macmillan, 1958.

Fisher, Ralph Talcott, Jr. *Pattern for Soviet Youth: A Study of the Congresses of the Komsomol, 1918-1954.* New York, Columbia University Press, 1959.

Galay, Nikolai. "The Soviet Armed Forces and the Twenty-Second Party Congress." *Bulletin* (Institute for the Study of the USSR), Vol. IX, No. 1 (January), 1962.

Granick, David. *Management of the Industrial Firm in the USSR: A Study in Soviet Economic Planning.* New York, Columbia University Press, 1954.

——. *The Red Executive.* London, Macmillan, 1960; Garden City, N.Y., Doubleday, 1962.

Hanchett, Walter S. "Some Observations on Membership Figures of the Communist Party of the Soviet Union." *American Political Science Review*, Vol. 52 (December), 1958.

Hodnett, Grey. "What's in a Nation?" *Problems of Communism*, Vol. xiv, No. 5 (September-October), 1967.

Kassof, Allen. *The Soviet Youth Program: Regimentation and Rebellion*. Cambridge, Mass., Harvard University Press, 1965.

Kolarz, Walter. *Russia and Her Colonies*. London, George Philip, 1952.

Kruzhin, Pëtr. "The Periodical Press." *Bulletin* (Institute for the Study of the USSR), Vol. XII, No. 11 (November), 1965.

Lewin, M. *Russian Peasants and Soviet Power: A Study of Collectivization*. London, Allen and Unwin, 1968.

Lorimer, Frank. *The Population of the Soviet Union: History and Prospects*. Geneva, League of Nations, 1946.

Meyer, Alfred G. *The Soviet Political System: An Interpretation*. New York, Random House, 1965.

[Nicolaevsky, Boris I.]. *Letter of an Old Bolshevik*. New York, Rand School Press, 1937. Also available in *Power and the Soviet Elite*, ed. Janet D. Zagoria, London, Pall Mall Press, 1966; New York, Frederick A. Praeger, 1966.

Pipes, Richard. *The Formation of the Soviet Union*. Cambridge, Mass., Harvard University Press, 1954.

Rigby, T. H. "Changing Composition of the Supreme Soviet," *The Political Quarterly*, Vol. xxiv, No. 3 (July-September), 1953.

―――. "The Selection of Leading Personnel in the Soviet State and Communist Party." Unpublished Ph.D. thesis, University of London, 1954.

―――. "Social Composition of Recruitment and Distribution of CPSU Membership," *American Slavic and East European Review*, No. 3, 1957.

Schapiro, Leonard. *The Communist Party of the Soviet Union*. New York, Random House, 1960.

―――. *The Origin of the Communist Autocracy: Political Opposition in the Soviet State: 1st Phase, 1917-1922*. London, London School of Economics and Political Science and G. Bell and Sons, 1955.

————. "The Party's New Rules," *Problems of Communism*, Vol. IX, No. 1 (January-February), 1962.

Seibert, Theodor. *Red Russia*. London, George Allen and Unwin, 1932.

Shvarts, S. M. *Antisemitizm v Sovetskom Soiuze* (Antisemitism in the Soviet Union). New York, Chekhov Publishing House, 1952.

Towster, Julian. *Political Power in the USSR: 1917-1947*. New York, Oxford University Press, 1948.

Trotsky, Leon. *The New Course (and the Struggle for the New Course with a New Introduction by Max Shachtman)*. Ann Arbor, University of Michigan Press, 1965.

Vucinich, Alexander. *The Soviet Academy of Sciences*. Stanford, Stanford University Press, 1956. (Hoover Institute Studies, Series E, Institutions, No. 3.)

Wolin, Simon and Slusser, Robert M., eds. *The Soviet Secret Police*. New York, Frederick A. Praeger, 1957; London, Methuen, 1957.

Index

571

ployment of party members, 228-30; (1933-41), membership in kolkhozes, 235; (1936), expulsions, 209; (1948-50), membership figures, 280; (1948-53), employment of party members, 287; (1952-54), 284; (1952-56), 298, 299; (1954-55), 159; (1949-58), 305; (1956), party membership among livestock workers, 452; employment of farm Communists, 336; party membership among scholars, 440; party membership among students, 345-46; age structure of membership, 355-57; ethnic composition of population, 369, 381, 395; ethnic composition of party membership, 369, 372, 381, 395; illiteracy in party, 404-06

Uzbeks, party membership among: (1961-65), 378; (1965-67), 377; in Uzbek S.S.R., 369, 381, 395; in Kazakh S.S.R., 382

vanguard role of party: Lenin's concept, 4-5, 43; Lenin enrollment provides necessary cadres, 118; party as educational vanguard, 403; role threatened by continued expansion, 523-25

Vilnius, party membership in, 497

"virtual representation," by party members, 38

Vitebsk (1933), faults in party records, 206

Vucinich, Alexander, 445

"war Communism," 89

Western oblast: (1935), rural party membership, 233, 234; (1935), expulsions, 207

white-collar workers: among 1917 recruits, 66; (1921-23), hold on to membership, 106-08; (1920's-1930's), and recruiting komsomol members to party, 456-57; (1956-65), party membership among, 337-39; (1961), justification for recruitment, 303-04; (1961-65), in industrial party organizations, 330; definitions, 67, 159-63; and intelligentsia, 67; and employment groups, 416; expansion as built in factor in party growth, 522-23. See also intelligentsia, recruitment policy, social position

withdrawals from party, voluntary: in Civil War, 77; (1920), 84; in early 1920's, 105-08; (1923-24), 134; (1924-27), 157-58; (1930-32), 195; (1933-35), 204-05; (1958-64), 311-12

women: (1920's), special recruitment efforts, 139, 156; World War II recruitment, 270; as housewives in party, 344; in line posts, 359; literacy among, 403. See also sex structure of party

"workers' control," and bureaucratization, 59

"workers' democracy": (early 1920's), 92; and worker-oriented recruitment, 138

"Workers' Opposition," 90-91; and worker-oriented recruitment, 93-94; influence in factories destroyed, 119; (1929-30), purge, 179; alleged recruitment policy, 194; and trade unions, 465

STUDIES OF THE RUSSIAN INSTITUTE

PUBLISHED BY COLUMBIA UNIVERSITY PRESS

THAD PAUL ALTON, *Polish Postwar Economy*

JOHN A. ARMSTRONG, *Ukrainian Nationalism*

ABRAM BERGSON, *Soviet National Income and Product in 1937*

EDWARD J. BROWN, *The Proletarian Episode in Russian Literature, 1928-1932*

HARVEY L. DYCK, *Weimar Germany and Soviet Russia, 1926-1933: A Study in Diplomatic Instability*

RALPH TALCOTT FISHER, JR., *Pattern for Soviet Youth: A Study of the Congresses of the Komsomol, 1918-1954*

MAURICE FRIEDBERG, *Russian Classics in Soviet Jackets*

ELLIOT R. GOODMAN, *The Soviet Design for a World State*

DAVID GRANICK, *Management of the Industrial Firm in the USSR: A Study in Soviet Economic Planning*

THOMAS TAYLOR HAMMOND, *Lenin on Trade Unions and Revolution, 1893-1917*

JOHN N. HAZARD, *Settling Disputes in Soviet Society: The Formative Years of Legal Institutions*

DAVID JORAVSKY, *Soviet Marxism and Natural Science, 1917-1932*

DAVID MARSHALL LANG, *The Last Years of the Georgian Monarchy, 1658-1832*

GEORGE S. N. LUCKYJ, *Literary Politics in the Soviet Ukraine, 1917-1934*

HERBERT MARCUSE, *Soviet Marxism: A Critical Analysis*

KERMIT E. MC KENZIE, *Comintern and World Revolution, 1928-1943: The Shaping of Doctrine*

CHARLES B. MC LANE, *Soviet Policy and the Chinese Communists, 1931-1946*

JAMES WILLIAM MORLEY, *The Japanese Thrust into Siberia, 1918*

ALEXANDER G. PARK, *Bolshevism in Turkestan, 1917-1927*

MICHAEL BORO PETROVICH, *The Emergence of Russian Panslavism, 1856-1870*

OLIVER H. RADKEY, *The Agrarian Foes of Bolshevism: Promise and Default of the Russian Socialist Revolutionaries, February to October, 1917*

OLIVER H. RADKEY, *The Sickle Under the Hammer: The Russian Socialist Revolutionaries in the Early Months of Soviet Rule*

ALFRED J. RIEBER, *Stalin and the French Communist Party, 1941-1947*

ALFRED ERICH SENN, *The Emergence of Modern Lithuania*

ERNEST J. SIMMONS, editor, *Through the Glass of Soviet Literature: Views of Russian Society*

THEODORE K. VON LAUE, *Sergei Witte and the Industrialization of Russia*

ALLEN S. WHITING, *Soviet Policies in China, 1917-1924*

PUBLISHED BY TEACHERS COLLEGE PRESS

HAROLD J. NOAH, *Financing Soviet Schools*

PUBLISHED BY PRINCETON UNIVERSITY PRESS

PAUL AVRICH, *The Russian Anarchists*

LOREN R. GRAHAM, *The Soviet Academy of Sciences and the Communist Party, 1927-1932*

ROBERT A. MAGUIRE, *Red Virgin Soil: Soviet Literature in the 1920's*

JOHN M. THOMPSON, *Russia, Bolshevism, and the Versailles Peace*